GOETHE

AND

THE GREEKS

GOETHE
&
THE GREEKS

BY

HUMPHRY TREVELYAN

FOREWORD
BY
HUGH LLOYD-JONES

CAMBRIDGE UNIVERSITY PRESS

CAMBRIDGE

LONDON   NEW YORK   NEW ROCHELLE

MELBOURNE   SYDNEY

Published by the Press Syndicate of the University of Cambridge
The Pitt Building, Trumpington Street, Cambridge CB2 1RP
32 East 57th Street, New York, NY 10022, USA
296 Beaconsfield Parade, Middle Park, Melbourne 3206, Australia

First published 1941
Reissued and first paperback edition 1981

Library of Congress catalogue card number: 81—3908

British Library Cataloguing in Publication Data
Trevelyan, Humphry
Goethe and the Greeks.
1. Goethe, Johann Wolfgang von—Criticism and interpretation
2. Civilization, Greek
I. Title
830'.6   PT2216.G/

ISBN 0 521 24137 5 hard covers
ISBN 0 521 28471 6 paperback

Transferred to digital printing 2004

Um Mitternacht ging ich, nicht eben gerne,
Klein, kleiner Knabe, jenen Kirchhof hin
Zu Vaters Haus, des Pfarrers; Stern um Sterne,
Sie leuchteten doch alle gar zu schön;
    Um Mitternacht.

Wenn ich dann ferner in des Lebens Weite
Zur Liebsten musste, musste, weil sie zog,
Gestirn und Nordschein über mir im Streite,
Ich gehend, kommend, Seligkeiten sog;
    Um Mitternacht.

Bis dann zuletzt des vollen Mondes Helle
So klar und deutlich mir ins Finstere drang,
Auch der Gedanke willig, sinnig, schnelle
Sich ums Vergangne wie ums Künftige schlang;
    Um Mitternacht.

FOREWORD

HUGH LLOYD-JONES

Goethe's relationship to the Greeks is a very wellworn subject, particularly in Germany. German classical scholars have written much about it, some of it excellent; Rudolf Pfeiffer and Karl Reinhardt[1] come to mind. But others have lapsed into sentimental adulation, which has stimulated an adverse reaction. Humphry Trevelyan's book gives a full account of the facts, and discusses them with calm and sober intelligence; it continues to be indispensable. In 1949, eight years after its publication, Ernst Grumach brought out the two splendid volumes of his *Goethe und die Antike*,[2] in which Goethe's writings and recorded utterances about each ancient author and each topic relating to the study of antiquity are arranged under the appropriate headings.

In 1807 a new classical periodical, the *Museum der Altertumswissenschaft*, was dedicated to "Goethe, dem Kenner und Darsteller des *griechischen Geistes*".[3] The person responsible for the dedication was Friedrich August Wolf, the leading Greek scholar of the time, and the view of Goethe's Hellenism which it implies was widely held throughout the nineteenth century and has never been without defenders. But even during Goethe's own lifetime it did not go unopposed. In 1817 the Romantic poet Ludwig Tieck wrote that Goethe's reverence for antiquity was "an empty superstition for a lifeless phantom

[1] The relevant literature is enormous; I have been content to cite in the notes some studies by classical scholars which have appeared since Trevelyan's book first appeared in 1941 which supplement it in a useful way. In particular I would name the articles on Goethe by Karl Reinhardt included in *Tradition und Geist*, Göttingen, 1960, and cited below; Rudolf Pfeiffer, "Goethe und der griechische Geist", *Deutsche Vierteljahrsschrift für Literaturwissenschaft und Geistesgeschichte* 12 (1934), 283f.=*Ausgewählte Schriften*, Munich, 1960, 235f.; Albin Lesky, "Goethe der Hellene", *Almanach der Universität Innsbruck*, 1949=*Jahrbuch des Goethe-Vereins* 67 (1963), 39f. = *Gesammelte Schriften*, Bern, 1966, 629f.; Wolfgang Schadewaldt, *Nachwort* to *GA* (n.2 below) II 971f., reprinted in *Goethestudien*, Zurich, 1963.

[2] Ernst Grumach, *Goethe und die Antike* (2 vols.), Berlin, 1949: this is subsequently referred to as *GA*.

[3] *GA* II 946.

with no substance",[1] and that opinion was shared by many of his contemporaries. In 1888, the last year of his activity, Nietzsche wrote that "Goethe did not understand the Greeks":[2] this pronouncement, seemingly based on a crude equation of Goethe's attitude with that of Winckelmann, has found many echoes since. In 1935 Miss E. M. Butler, afterwards Schroeder Professor of German at Cambridge, argued in a book called *The Tyranny of Greece over Germany* that the admiration felt for Greek cultures by German writers, from Lessing to George, was an unmitigated disaster. This work seems to have been written in a fit of emotional disturbance caused by the National Socialists' coming to power; but it has interest as an extreme example of a widespread tendency.

Goethe's relationship to Greek art and literature is a matter of considerable importance, not only for the understanding of his own life and works, but for the history of European culture. Whatever we may feel about the nature of his Hellenism, we can hardly deny that he, more than any other individual, was responsible for the immense energy devoted to classical studies by Germany during the nineteenth century. At different times he took great pains in order to obtain the kind of acquaintance with Greek art and literature that his purposes required, and considering the number and the nature of his preoccupations, the knowledge of it which he ended by possessing must be thought very considerable. He had a high regard for scholarship; he employed a good scholar, Friedrich Wilhelm Riemer, as his indispensable assistant; and he made effective use of his friendship with scholars of the highest rank, like Friedrich August Wolf and Gottfried Hermann. But we must be on our guard against the tendency of professors to claim him as one of themselves. His interest in antiquity was above all practical, designed to serve his own purposes; in this respect, as in every other, the needs of the immediate moment, what the Greeks called *kairos*, counted for much in his life.[3] There was always

---

[1] 18.12.1817, to K. W. F. Solger.

[2] In the section of *Götzen-Dämmerung* called "Was ich den Alten verdanke", s.4 (in *Kritische Gesamtausgabe*, ed. G. Colli and M. Montinari, VI 3, Berlin and New York, 1969, 153). See Erich Heller, "Nietzsche and Goethe", in *The Disinherited Mind*, London, 1952, 3rd edn 1971, 91f.

[3] See Schadewaldt, *op. cit.* (n.1, p. vii), ad init.

an ambiguity in his feelings about scholarship, and he remained in the best sense of the words an amateur, a dilettante. At the start of his career, classical studies were less highly regarded than at any time since the Renaissance. The wars of religion had inflicted severe damage upon them, as upon other branches of culture; the seventeenth century, despite notable achievements, had been on the whole a period of decline. It was then that the leading spirits of the French Enlightenment decided that they could now dispense with the aid of the ancient classics, which had helped their forebears to emerge from medieval darkness, but which had now been left behind in the advance towards illumination.

No country had suffered more from the wars of religion than Germany; and there the standing of classical studies sank particularly low. Early in the eighteenth century, prevailing trends were hostile to antiquity. Rationalists agreed with the French that it was out of date; pietists disapproved of it because it had been unchristian. Greek studies were particularly backward; since the Renaissance, despite certain notable exceptions, most people had seen the Greeks through Roman spectacles. Of course many people had some acquaintance with classical mythology, usually derived from such compilations as the moralising and euhemerising handbook of Goethe's great-uncle, Johann Michael von Loën. Also, the French faction that had defended antiquity in the Battle of the Books had a not uninfluential German representative in Johann Christoph Gottsched, the disciple of Boileau; but the only literary products of this tendency were the facile Anacreontics of such writers as Gleim and Götz and the rococo Hellenism of the early Wieland.

However, signs of a new tendency could be discerned. J. M. Gesner in Göttingen and J. F. Christ in Leipzig put new life into classical teaching in their respective universities. The influence of Fénelon's *Télémaque*, using a Homeric subject to inculcate the newly fashionable virtues of simplicity and sincerity, could be seen in Germany. In a treatise published in 1740 the Swiss writer Johann Jacob Breitinger defended Homer against the strictures of Charles Perrault. Klopstock and Lessing both derived inspiration from the ancients; Lessing's studies of ancient drama combined with his own plays to loosen the hold of

French dramatic theorising. In 1755, when Goethe was six, Winckelmann[1] brought out his *Gedanken über die Nachahmung der Griechen in der Malerei und Bildhauerkunst*; eight years later came his great history of ancient art. The public was beginning to tire of the baroque and the rococo, and Winckelmann's *Gedanken* met with an immediate success.

The boy Goethe picked up ancient mythology rapidly, both from books and from puppet-shows with titles like *Die Tragödie der rasenden Erzzauberin Medea*; he learned Latin well enough to delight in Ovid's *Metamorphoses*, and made a start in Greek. But among the various languages with which he played about, Greek was the one he knew least well; in the novel consisting of letters from six or seven brothers and sisters supposed to be written from different places and in different languages which he wrote when he was twelve or thirteen,[2] Greek is used only in an occasional postscript added by the brother who writes Latin. It is a great deal more significant that at this age he read all of Racine and most of Corneille. After his illness in 1764, his study of philosophy in the condensed version of J. J. Brucker's history of the subject gave him a general acquaintance with the views of the principal Greek thinkers: and by the use of similar compendia he tried to obtain a notion of the main outlines of Greek history. This made him aware of the deficiency of his linguistic knowledge; and when the time came for him to attend the university, he wished to study classical philology at Göttingen. In 1763 Christian Gottlob Heyne had taken up an appointment there, and no man living would have been better capable of giving Goethe the kind of training that he felt he needed. But Goethe's father insisted that he go to Leipzig to study law.

There were at Leipzig several people who could have helped Goethe greatly, if he had made a serious effort to pursue his Greek studies. But in what on the face of it seem the somewhat desultory intellectual activities of this period in his life Greek had little part; the disappointment of an encounter with some modern Greeks who proved unable to give him the assistance he had hoped for may have discouraged him. But one experi-

---

[1] Cf. Rudolf Pfeiffer, *History of Classical Scholarship* II, Oxford, 1976, 167f.

[2] Goethe's own dating is corrected by Hanna Fischer-Lamberg, *Der junge Goethe* I, Berlin, 1963, 451.

ence of this time proved important in this connection. The school of art directed by Adam Friedrich Oeser, who had taught Winckelmann, contained a few casts of Greek statues, and Oeser drew Goethe's attention to the casts of ancient gems contained in the Daktyliothek of Philipp Daniel Lippert, which offered one of the few means of getting some notion of ancient art then readily available. Goethe was at all times deeply sensible to visual impressions; small objects of art were scarcely less fascinating to him than large ones, and he took special pleasure in the study of gems and coins. Oeser also introduced him to the works of Winckelmann. The great history of art, which had appeared in 1763, he did not read until he was in Rome in 1786; but he read at Leipzig, probably in 1766, Lessing's *Laokoon*, Winckelmann's essay on the imitation of the Greeks in painting and sculpture, and the two essays published to supplement that work during the following year. The effect of this may not have been immediate, for in 1768 he visited Dresden without seeing the collection of antiquities; but in 1769, after his return home from Leipzig, he made an expedition to Mannheim to see the Elector's collection of casts, and a letter written at the time shows that the experience made a deep impression.

Trevelyan has rightly pointed out that what impressed Goethe at this time was not Winckelmann's aesthetic theory but his picture of the Greeks as a people devoted to physical and intellectual beauty and free from the constraints imposed by a society such as that which Goethe himself lived in. It was now that he formed the opinion which he never had occasion to revise, that the Greeks had been the people who, beyond all others, had lived in accordance with Nature. Winckelmann's celebrated notion that the essence of Greek art lay in "noble simplicity and quiet greatness" did not at this time appeal to him. One of the casts that he had seen in Mannheim was of the Laocoon group, and Goethe took a lively interest in the celebrated controversy which it occasioned. Winckelmann had praised the sculptors for making Laocoon merely moan in his agony, and not scream as he does according to Virgil; Lessing had defended Virgil, pointing out that plastic art had different principles from literary art, and that Greek writers had been as ready as Virgil to represent the vocal expression of physical agony. Sculptors, on the other hand, Lessing thought, moderated that expression in order that their statues should be beautiful. The young Goethe was greatly struck by Lessing's treatise; but he refused to accept this theory. The Greeks, whose art was based so firmly upon Nature, could not have watered down the expression of strong emotion so as to give beauty to their statues; and Goethe suggested that Laocoon does not scream only because he cannot do so, the attitude in which he is portrayed rendering it impossible. Whatever may be thought about this ingenious solution of the problem, it is remarkable that even at the age of twenty Goethe asserted his conception of the Greeks as living and creating in accordance with Nature in such a characteristic fashion.

The encounter with Herder in Strasburg during the winter of 1770/1, so decisive in many ways, brought about a marked change in his attitude towards the Greeks. Herder's assertion of the rights of natural feeling against the intellectualism of the Enlightenment implied that the poetry of unsophisticated ages, epic, folksongs and ballads, scorned by the sophisticated admirers of Voltaire, in fact possessed a special value. The Goethe of the *Sturm und Drang* period admired Ossian; he admired Shakespeare far more; but a yet more important author in his eyes was Homer, upon whom he flung himself with altogether fresh enthusiasm. Wood's essay on Homer's original genius, which fell into his hands at this time, confirmed him in the impression that Homer above all other poets wrote in accordance with the dictates of Nature. Using the Latin version by Samuel Clarke that was reprinted in Ernesti's edition, he worked hard to understand the Greek, laying the foundations of what was to become a close acquaintance with the poems. In a letter of 1771,[1] he claims to be able to read Homer almost without the aid of a translation; Homer was probably the only Greek author with whom he attained this degree of familiarity.

At this time Goethe also read a little Plato and Xenophon, and formed the design of writing a play about the death of Socrates; but this, like so many of his projects, came to nothing. He also read Anacreon, Theocritus and Pindar, who all figure in his *Wanderers Sturmlied*, where he contrasts the two former

[1] 6 (?), 1771, to J. D. Salzmann (*GA* I 118).

with the latter; but he can have had little notion of the real
character of any of these authors. "Anacreon" at that time
meant not the real lyric and elegiac poet of the sixth century
B.C., but the Anacreontic poems of later ages, from the Hellenistic to the Byzantine, which had naturally been dear to the age
of the rococo. I am inclined to question Trevelyan's view that
Goethe will have found Theocritus relatively easy; at any rate,
neither the praise of him in *Wanderers Sturmlied* nor any sub-
sequent mention of him by Goethe suggests a very close
acquaintance. Like most readers of the seventeenth and
eighteenth centuries, Goethe thought of Pindar as a rude giant
with no respect for rules: that derives from the account of
Pindar given by Horace in the second ode of the fourth book,
not from the real author, then most imperfectly understood,
even by scholars. The short lines in which *Wanderers Sturmlied*
is written derive from the short lines in which it was customary
to print the text of Pindar before Boeckh worked out the
correct division of the periods in his edition of 1811/1821; and
the passage about Pindar might have been written without
knowledge of Pindar's actual work. In 1772 Goethe worked
hard at Pindar, doubtless using a translation. He made a translation of the fifth Olympian ode,[1] ironically enough a poem
whose Pindaric authorship has been questioned since ancient
times and is rejected by most modern scholars; his ignorance of
the principle of metrical responsion between strophe and antistrophe does not prevent it from being a fine piece of work,
since Goethe followed the words of the original, which are not
irregular or "dithyrambic" in the modern sense.

How much acquaintance with Greek tragedy lies behind the
reference to it in the address on Shakespeare's birthday given
by Goethe in 1771 is not easy to determine. But definite
evidence of his knowledge of at least one tragedy is contained
in the delightful short satire "Götter, Helden und Wieland" of
1773. Its marked resemblance to a dialogue of Lucian may be
due to indirect influence; but it is worth remembering that
Lucian had been the favourite author of Rektor Albrecht who

[1] *GA* I 227–8. On "Goethes Pindar-Erlebnis", see O. Regenbogen,
Griechische Gegenwart, Munich, 1942 = *Kleine Schriften*, Munich, 1961, 520f.;
F. Zucker, "Die Bedeutung Pindars für Goethes Leben und Dichtung",
Das Altertum I (ed. J. Irmscher, Berlin, 1955), 171f.

taught Goethe Hebrew when he was a boy.[1] In this work Goethe ridicules what he thought the unsympathetic and patronising treatment of the Greeks in Wieland's *Alceste* and in the letters relating to it which Wieland had published in the *Teutscher Merkur*. The rococo habit of using Greece to provide a trivial kind of décor is amusingly made fun of; but even more interestingly Goethe protests against an attitude to the legend which is still common among readers. For Wieland, as for many moderns, Admetus' acceptance of his wife's sacrifice of her life in order to save his appeared intolerable. To Goethe it seemed perfectly natural; and though Euripides' attitude is doubtful in that he certainly allows the rightness of Admetus' conduct to seem questionable in the scene in which he reproaches his parents for not having been willing to make the sacrifice, there can be little doubt that the inventors of the original legend saw the matter as Goethe did.[2] Goethe would have had little sympathy with modern attempts to show by invoking a supposed irony or other unconvincing devices that Admetus is being blamed for an attitude which to him seemed natural; and we find here a signal instance of his natural sympathy with Greek modes of thought, even when they are surprising or shocking to Christian or humanitarian sentiment.

Goethe makes a colossal Hercules of boundless vital energy ridicule Wieland for having represented him as "ein wohl-gestalteter Mann mittlerer Grösse"; and his Hercules is typical of the figures from Greek mythology whom he uses as symbols during his period of *Sturm und Drang*. Prometheus stands for the creative power of the arts, Ganymede for inspiration, Dionysus, under the name of Bromius, for the universal vitalising power; Apollo, Mercury and Minerva also figure in the poetry of his "Titanic" phase, interspersed with such figures from German and other mythology as served his purpose. Goethe was still far removed from the classicism of his later life, in which Greek influences, as well as Greek images, were

[1] See Paul Friedländer, "Aristophanes in Deutschland", *Die Antike* 8 (1932), 236 = *Studien zur antiken Literatur und Kunst*, Berlin, 1969, 537, who seems to me slightly to exaggerate Aristophanic influence on the work. On Rektor Albrecht, see *GA* I 314–15. For Lucian's influence on Wieland, see Christopher Robinson, *Lucian and his Influence in Europe*, London, 1979, 157f.

[2] See Kurt von Fritz, *Antike und Abendland* 5 (1956), 53f. = *Antike und moderne Tragödie*, Berlin, 1962, 295f.

effective; at this time such Germanic characters as Götz von Berlichingen, the buffoon Hanswurst and Dr Faustus, originally a popular sixteenth-century caricature of a Renaissance human-ist, might equally well lend themselves to his requirements.

In a letter to Herder of 1772[1] Goethe quoted from Pindar's eighth Nemean ode the saying that one should be content not to miss the mark in any of one's actions, but should have strength to master one's powerful longings. These words well describe the use he made of the Greeks during his first Weimar period, between his move to that place in 1775 and his depar-ture to Italy in 1786. In his mind they stood for the self-discipline that could help him to shake off the strains that had troubled him during his period of *Sturm und Drang*. In the *Triumph der Empfindsamkeit*, written during the winter of 1777/8, Goethe ridiculed the sentimental affectation of the age, which his own *Werther* could hardly have been denied to have encouraged; the facile invocation of the Greeks which often accompanied this tendency does not escape his mockery. Into this satire Goethe "criminally" (*freventlich*), as he put it, worked a poem of great power and beauty, his *Proserpina*. Trevelyan must be right in saying that the upper world for which Proser-pina longs must stand for Goethe's ideal conception of Greece as a place whose inhabitants lived according to Nature, enjoy-ing the repose and self-control which during this phase of his career meant so much to him. These qualities, fostered by the influence of Charlotte von Stein, are all-important in his *Iphigenie*, the prose version of which was begun in February of 1779. How much Greek tragedy he had read when he com-posed it is disputed. Scholars have claimed to find allusions to many Greek plays, and he may have known some or all of these from the *Théatre des Grecs* of the Abbé Brumoy (1730) or from the *Das tragische Theater der Griechen* of J. J. Steinbrüchel (1763). But the only two whose influence can be demonstrated are the *Iphigenia in Tauris* of Euripides and the *Philoctetes* of Sophocles; the depiction of Iphigenia's dilemma owes some-thing to that of the dilemma of Neoptolemus. It is worth noting that on 23 March 1780 Goethe read aloud the *Helena* of Euripides to the Grand Duchess Anna Amalia: Musgrave's edition of the year before may have come into his hands. This

[1] 10(?).7.1772 (*GA* I 226–7).

play is in several ways akin to the *Iphigenia in Tauris*;[1] both describe the escape of a heroine from captivity in a barbarian country, productive of anxiety but ending happily, and both create a magical atmosphere and finish in peace and reconciliation. Although in later life Goethe spoke unkindly of the *Helena*, I cannot help wondering whether he knew it when he wrote his *Iphigenie*; it surely had some influence on the Helen episode of Faust. Still, though *Iphigenie* has a Greek subject and derived inspiration from Greek models, it is far further from the world of Greek tragedy than some of Goethe's later works; it is more like French tragedy, except that the interior life of the characters receives more attention. These characters, with what Trevelyan calls "their gentle nobility and unselfishness, their perfect consideration for each others' feelings" breathe the atmosphere of the world of Charlotte von Stein, whose influence was at that time doing so much to tame and restrain the passionate young poet of the period of *Sturm und Drang*. Her letters to Goethe, which she later recovered and destroyed, were all in French.

A work that in some respects comes closer to the Greek world than *Iphigenie* is the prose drama *Elpenor*, begun in 1781, when Goethe's interest in Greek tragedy had been stimulated by the presence in Weimar of the Swiss translator J. C. Tobler, and taken in hand again and finally abandoned two years later. The plot is Goethe's own invention, but it is like the plot of a Greek tragedy; Goethe was acquainted with the Roman mythographer Hyginus, and one wonders if he knew the summary of the plot of Euripides' *Cresphontes* which it contains.[2] The work has a Greek setting, and the characters, with their passionate hates and loves, are liker to those of a Greek tragedy than the characters of *Iphigenie*; but this play also was to end in peace and reconciliation. Trevelyan believes that the real reason for Goethe's failure to finish it lay in the inconsistency which this involved; the morality of the gentle *Iphigenie* of the first Weimar period and that of the bitterly revengeful Greek Electra were not easily to be reconciled.

Goethe had other Greek authors also in hand during the first

---

[1] On the resemblances, see Cesare Questa, *Il ratto dal serraglio*, Bologna, 1979, 14f.

[2] Hygini Fabulae, ed. H. I. Rose, 2nd edn 1963, cxxxvii (pp. 100f.).

Weimar period. During 1777–8 he read some Aristophanes, and even adapted the *Birds* for the purpose of a modern satire. But nothing in his writings suggests an intimate relationship with this author, over whom he once even fell asleep; Aristophanes is firmly rooted in his own time and place, and presents difficulties which the aids available to Goethe could hardly have enabled him to overcome.[1] It is strange to find him studying the Orphic hymns, which praise various gods and personified abstractions in high-flown poetic language. We now know them to date from about the end of the second century A.D., and to contain much Stoic matter;[2] but before the nineteenth century they were held to be a product of early Greek religion. Part of their content derives ultimately from Plato; it has been remarked that the wonderful poem *Urworte: Orphisch* (1820), which expresses so much of Goethe's view of life and to which I will return later, is Platonic rather than Orphic. Herder and Tobler interested Goethe in the epigrams of the Greek Anthology, and this stimulated him to compose epigrams of his own in elegiac metre; the same period saw the beginning of his experiments with the German accentual hexameter. Meanwhile he was building up his collection of casts, and was thinking much of Greek art, and particularly sculpture; the writings of the German painter Raphael Mengs served as a surrogate for those of Winckelmann. The Mignon of *Wilhelm Meisters Lehrjahre*, on which Goethe was now working, longs, like Proserpina, for the South; the wish to obtain a direct acquaintance with Greek art must have been among the many factors which impelled Goethe to take off for Italy in 1786. But when he arrived there, Greek art was only one of the things that contributed to the deep satisfaction which the expedition caused him.

Goethe had little time for the relics of the Middle Ages; at Assisi he ignored St Francis, having eyes only for a temple of Minerva that is not especially remarkable. He was impressed

[1] See Wilhelm Süss, *Aristophanes und die Nachwelt*, Leipzig, 1911, 116f. I prefer his brief treatment to the lengthier discussion of Friedländer, *op. cit.* (n.1, p. xiv), 537f.

[2] See R. Keydell, Pauly-Wissowas *Real Encyclopädie der cl. Altertumswissenschaft* XVIII, Stuttgart, 1942, 1321f.: the best edition of the hymns is by W. Quandt, 2nd edn, Berlin, 1955.

by certain Roman relics, such as the amphitheatre at Verona, the Colosseum and the Pantheon, but finally came away with the impression that Roman art was largely derivative, and had not much to offer him. But about the art of the Renaissance he felt very differently; on his first visit to Rome he was overwhelmed by the Sistine Chapel, and he was deeply impressed by the art of Raphael, in which he recognised, not without reason, an affinity with the Greeks. Always markedly responsive to the beauties of Nature, he was enraptured by the Italian countryside, and he was fascinated by the warmth and openness of Italian life. The South of Italy in particular delighted him, and he felt that it preserved much of the character it had had in ancient times, when it was permeated by Greek influences.

In those days Greek art, even in Italy, was far more difficult to study than it is now. Many of the works which are now most admired had not then been discovered; for example, the remains of the shrine of Zeus at Olympia, the Parthenon, the temple of Aphaea in Aegina and that of Apollo at Bassae. Many of the works which were then most admired are now known to be of far later date than was then supposed, or even to be Roman copies of lost originals. But Goethe showed an astonishing capacity to make the most of what was then available.

At the very beginning of his stay, he saw in the Maffei Museum in Verona Greek reliefs that were later the subject of wonderful descriptions in the account of his Italian journey that he published in 1816.[1] In the Veneto Palladio's work aroused his admiration, and served him as an example of the creative imitation of ancient models by a man of genius. In Padua he acquired a copy of Winckelmann's history of ancient art, which he had not read before; now it served him as an indispensable guide in all his study of the subject. Winckelmann had performed the essential task of distinguishing the four main periods of Greek art, the archaic, down to Phidias, the grand or lofty period, when Phidias, Polyclitus, Scopas and Myron were at work, the beautiful period, from Praxiteles to

[1] See G. Rodenwaldt, "Goethes Besuch im Museum Maffeianum zu Verona", 102 (*Winckelmannsprogramm der archäologischen Gesellschaft in Berlin*, 1962).

Lysippus and Apelles, and the later period of imitation. Rome contained only two works believed to date from Winckelmann's archaic period, to which Goethe believed that he could add a third, the Minerva Giustiniani.[1] Goethe also felt special admiration for the Apollo Belvedere and the Laocoon group;[2] the former is probably of the fourth century B.C., but the latter seems to be dated by a new discovery in the first century A.D. None the less, enough was available to give Goethe the general impression of Greek art which he needed, and to supply his imagination with a powerful stimulus. He observed that the representation of the gods by Greek artists seems to conform to certain closely defined types, and since he believed that the gods stood for the fundamental forces which create and sustain the universe, he felt this fact to be specially significant. His preoccupation with the idea of Nature and the need to follow it in life and art had led him to embrace a kind of Platonism peculiar to himself. Just as while in Sicily he was occupied with the notion of the *Urpflanze*, the original form of vegetation, so during his last stay in Rome he was occupied with that of the *Urmensch*, the essence common to all humanity. The Greeks, he believed, had obtained an insight into that essence, and the types that represented the major gods gave expression to the different qualities that belonged to it. From studying these Goethe believed he had deduced the norm which was the common denominator of all the variations, and so attained a knowledge of the rules which the artists had followed in producing them. For some years after his return from Italy he worked with the assistance of his friend, the expert on art Heinrich Meyer, to confirm the truth of what he called his principle by the systematic examination of many works of art. Whether or not it had any basis in fact, Trevelyan is right to say that for Goethe it "had all the power and depth of a religious revelation", and for many years it had a most potent effect on its discoverer.

Goethe's journey to Naples and Sicily gave him the chance to make the acquaintance of some remarkable specimens of Greek architecture of the classical period. Nothing in his

[1] See *GA* II 536f. and Max Wegner, *Goethes Anschauung der antiken Kunst*, Berlin, 1944, 48f.

[2] See *GA* II 529f. and 547f. and Wegner, *op. cit.*, 57f. and 69f.

travels is more remarkable than his account of his visit, in March of 1787, to the fifth-century temples at Paestum.[1] The "squat, tapering column-masses, pressed close against one another" seemed to him at first "oppressive, even terrifying". "Yet I quickly pulled myself together," he goes on, "remembered the history of art, thought of the age which found such a style fitting, called to mind the austere school of sculpture, and in less than an hour I found myself at home." I am not sure that Trevelyan is right to infer from the strictly factual character of Goethe's description of the fifth-century temple at Segesta that he was not greatly impressed by it; his account of the temples at Agrigento, where the so-called temple of Concord certainly aroused his admiration, is equally precise and unemotional. When he was leaving for Sicily, the Prince of Waldeck asked if on his return he would care to accompany him to Greece. Greece would certainly have been uncomfortable, and Goethe might not have been able to see many monuments of ancient art; yet when we think of some of the descriptions of it written by travellers of this period, we must regret that he declined the invitation.

In Karlsbad, just before his departure for Italy, he had *Iphigenie* in hand, reading the *Electra* of Sophocles with its problems in his mind. During his progress through Verona and the Veneto and his first stay in Rome he was occupied in translating it from prose into verse, at the same time studying Euripides, who he wrote helped him to understand that love of rhetoric and argument which was even stronger in the Greeks than in the Italians. His alterations, particularly the complete rewriting of the fourth act which he carried out in Venice, were designed to make the play more like a Greek tragedy, and laid greater stress on the dark history of the House of Atreus. While in Bologna he conceived the plan of another drama, *Iphigenia at Delphi*, which was designed to present a direct clash between the Iphigenia-morality and the Electra-morality. Iphigenia and Orestes, returning from Tauris, reach Delphi at the same time as Electra, who has gone there to dedicate the axe with which so much blood has been shed in the House of Atreus. Electra,

[1] For the relevant extracts from the *Italienische Reise*, see *GA* 1 454f. (Paestum), 455f. (Agrigento), 459f. (Segesta); cf. Wegner, *op. cit.* 9f., 10f. and 13f.

believing that Iphigenia has sacrificed her brother but not knowing her to be her sister, is about to kill her with the axe when by a fortunate chance she discovers her identity. None of this play was ever written; Goethe was distracted by the excitements of arriving in Rome. By the time he was ready to return to writing poetry, the moment for the new Iphigenia was past; for he had acquired too much sympathy with the Electra-morality to be capable of executing a work in which the Iphigenia-morality was designed to triumph.

In 1786 Goethe came to know the young poet, novelist and scholar Karl Philipp Moritz,[1] known to English readers for his entertaining account of his travels in their country, who after an unhappy life had made a name with his autobiographical novel *Anton Reiser*, and had now taken refuge in Italy after an unhappy love-affair. Goethe took greatly to Moritz, and when he broke an arm, visited him daily and cared for him like a brother. Moritz helped him with the metrical problems posed by *Iphigenie*; his manner of sketching began to show Moritz' influence. After Goethe's return from Sicily the two men earnestly discussed together the questions treated in Moritz' book *Götterlehre, oder mythologische Dichtungen der Alten*, which was published in 1791.[2] The greater part of the book consists of a clearly and elegantly written guide to Greek mythology; but the first thirty or so pages contain a general account of Greek religion that is of great interest. For Moritz the Greek gods stood for the forces that control the universe; Platonism with its world of eternal and immutable ideas was simply the old religion in a new form. The gods maintain order in the universe, treating men as beings of secondary importance, and punishing severely any offence against their honour. Men represent the gods as exalted beings, whose form expresses human qualities at their highest level; but since they are part of Nature, their essential attribute is not goodness, but power. We are assured by Christian Gottfried Körner[3] that Goethe played

[1] See now Mark Boulby, *Karl Philipp Moritz: at the Fringe of Genius*, Toronto, 1980.

[2] The *Götterlehre* was reprinted in 1948 by Moritz Schauenburg, Lahr (Schwarzwald); there is an English translation (Oxford, 1832), from the fifth German edition, entitled *The Mythology of the Greeks and Romans*.

[3] See O. Gruppe, *Geschichte der klassischen Mythologie und Religionsgeschichte*, Munich, 1921, 106.

a considerable part in the working out of these opinions, and there is little doubt that they were shared by him. Before the end of his first stay in Rome, he had adopted this attitude to Greek religion, and before he left for Naples on 21 February 1787 he had lost all sympathy with the Iphigenia-morality of his first Weimar period. Moritz omits to point out that the early Greek gods are moral to this extent, that Zeus in his capacity as the protector of oaths, suppliants and strangers was held to regard men's crimes against each other as an offence against his privileges which he was bound in the long run to punish. But so far as it goes the view of ancient religion taken by Goethe and Moritz is correct and its working out at this particular moment in history is an event of great significance.

Goethe's new attitude to the Greek gods was reflected in the plan for a *Nausikaa*, which he conceived while in Palermo. The subject which he chose has an obvious relation to his own life; again and again he deserted, in obedience to his daimon, as he would put it, a woman whom he had loved and who loved him. At this time he was in process of breaking away from the most important woman in his career, Charlotte von Stein, and Trevelyan must be right in finding in the tragic nature of the plot, which was to culminate in Nausicaa's suicide, a reflection of Goethe's new awareness of the sombre side of the Greek attitude to life. Only 175 lines were written, for the luxuriant vegetation of the gardens of Palermo fatally distracted him in the direction of the search for the *Urpflanze*; they excite the keenest disappointment at his failure to finish the work. One magical couplet wonderfully conveys the beauty of the Sicilian sky:

> Ein weisser Glanz ruht über Land und Meer,
> Und duftend schwebt der Aether ohne Wolken.

Although the "model" of the *Römische Elegien*, so far as they have one, is the Roman elegists, and particularly Propertius, they are highly expressive of the change in Goethe's outlook that reflects his new attitude to Greece. Whether or not Faustina stands for a real person, Goethe's attitude to physical love had certainly undergone a modification during his stay in Italy; and that its effects were not merely temporary is shown by his action in 1788 in installing Christiane Vulpius as his mistress.

Concubines, says an ancient Athenian orator, we have for the sake of our bodily health, unlike wives, whom we have for the procreation of children and hetairai, whom we have for pleasure; I think Goethe would have agreed with him. His new paganism is also reflected in the *Venezianische Epigramme*, which contain his most uninhibitedly erotic verses and also his bitterest polemics.

The years between 1790 and 1793 were an unproductive period for Goethe; perhaps his absorption in the French Revolution was connected with a need for rest after the immense intellectual exertions of the preceding period. His interest in Greek things declines correspondingly; but in 1793 we find him studying Homer and then Plato, and working carefully through the collection of ancient gems lent him by Princess Gallitzin. He distracted himself from world affairs, as he put it, by composing the four thousand hexameters of *Reineke Fuchs*, a work which is free of Homeric allusions but in which Schiller rightly recognised an Homeric tone. In 1794 Goethe's Homeric studies were stimulated by the presence in Weimar of Johann Heinrich Voss, the author of the standard German translation of the two epics, and this time saw the composition of several fine pieces of translation of passages of Homer by Goethe himself. In August 1794 he again visited the cast gallery in Dresden, and with Meyer's aid continued his investigation of the ideal canons adopted by the Greek sculptors.

The utilisation of Greek art and literature played a vital part in the immensely fruitful interchanges between Goethe and Schiller which began during the summer of 1794. The famous letter written by Schiller to Goethe on 23 August of that year shows complete awareness of the central importance to Goethe of his conception of Nature and her laws, and of the use he made of the Greek world in order to gain an insight into their working. Having been born in the north of Europe, where he was not surrounded by an ideal Nature or an idealising art, Goethe had had to correct the world that had been forced upon his imagination in accordance with the pattern which his creative spirit had made for itself; this "could be accomplished only with the aid of guiding principles", and these had been supplied by the study of Greek art and literature. In the essay *Über Anmut und Würde* which he had published in June 1793,

Schiller had argued that man should seek balance between duty and inclination, spirit and matter, *Sittlichkeit* and *Sinnlichkeit*; he should not suppress his sensual instincts, or the higher morality that resided in the harmony between the two principles could never be achieved. This point of view coincided remarkably with that which Goethe had arrived at during his Italian sojourn. In this work and in the later essay *Über naive und sentimentale Dichtung*, Schiller adopts the same view of the Greeks as a people living close to Nature and in accordance with her laws to which Goethe had for so long subscribed. Whether or not one agrees with Schiller in regarding Goethe as a "naive" poet, one who depicts Nature directly instead of reflecting on the difference between the world and the ideal, that is certainly the kind of poet Goethe wished to be.

The aesthetic theory which the two men worked out during their collaboration strongly insisted that a work of art should express in a clear and necessary way the essential determinants (*Bestimmungen*) of its subject; it must not lose itself in details which are not related or are only loosely related to those determinants. From this basic principle the two men deduced the specific character of the various literary genres, taking their departure from a careful examination of Aristotle's *Poetics*.[1] They had no objection to the mixing of genres, which Goethe obviously practised; *Wilhelm Meister* is and is not an epic work, *Reineke Fuchs* too has epic elements, *Hermann und Dorothea* has epic features but is in general an idyll. Schiller saw that the genres predominating in the literature of his own time were those of elegy, idyll and satire, which taken together apply to most of Goethe's poetry. But they used the classification in terms of genre to bring out the nature of the essential determinants in each particular case. Their aesthetic theorising was designed to help literature to deal with the crisis of their own time. Imaginative writers were faced with the problem of the separation between the private and the public spheres, between social production and private acquisition, between man as citizen and man as individual. Hellenism supplied a suitable

[1] See *GA* II 771f.; cf. Max Kommerell, *Lessing und Aristoteles*, Frankfurt a.M. 1940, 258–62.

ideal, since its productions revealed, in the words of Lukács,[1] a unity between "the palpable and realistic expression of the particular and the clear grasp of the essential". What Goethe and Schiller produced was not an aestheticism remote from actual life, nor a mere trifling with forms, but a serious attempt to save literature from a decline into the accurate observation of innumerable petty details. How great the danger was we can see by glancing at the literature of the nineteenth century, but still more easily by thinking of the writings of our own contemporaries.

But when Lukács describes the crisis of the time in purely political and economic terms, it seems to me that he fails to do full justice to the two poets' purposes in a way that illustrates the characteristic weakness of Marxian theorising about literature. In his view they were trying to enable bourgeois literature to cope with the situation created by the French Revolution; they wished to obtain for Germany without revolution the results which the revolution had obtained for France. Their firm insistence on the ideal of Greek antiquity demanded of the rising bourgeoisie a degree of self-assurance and determination which in the long run it proved unable to live up to. But Goethe and Schiller did not see their problem as one created by politics or economics. They did see that writers of their time were faced with a crisis created by the decay of Christian belief; they felt that the collapse of Christianity left the educated man without a religion. Goethe often spoke and wrote of Christianity with violent distaste; at other times he treated it with a mixture of affection and contempt. Yet he was very far from being irreligious; he laid the strongest stress on the importance of what he called *Glaube*.[2] By that he did not mean belief in any creed; his real religion is seen in his belief in the essential excellence of Nature. That as he realised is closer to the religion of the ancient Greeks than it is to Christianity; the essential attribute of their gods was not moral goodness, but power. The Greeks, he wrote, describe terrible things, we describe terribly; "only men able to exist for themselves alone", he

[1] G. Lukács, *Goethe and his Age*, tr. R. Anchor, London, 1968 (original edition, 1947).

[2] The point is well brought out by Heller, *op. cit.* (n.2, p. viii), 96f.

thought, could confront such divinities as the Zeus and the Athena who were portrayed by Phidias.

In 1795 Friedrich August Wolf published his famous *Prolegomena ad Homerum*, in which he contended that the Homeric epics had no essential unity, but had been put together out of miscellaneous lays as late as the sixth century B.C. There had been no Homer, only a succession of Homeridae, "sons of Homer": the Homeric poems were in a sense a joint production of the Greek people. Goethe's immediate reaction[1] was hostile; he would not part readily with his belief in the individual genius of the greatest of all poets. But after thinking the matter over carefully and discussing it with Wolf himself in May 1795, he changed his mind. Indeed, he found the theory well suited to his purposes; for though he could scarcely hope to rival Homer, if there was really no Homer, but only a plurality of Homeridae, surely he too might become one of them.[2]

The idyll *Alexis und Dora*, written in 1796, is a love story set in a scene of unspoiled Nature: it was a rehearsal for a far more ambitious work. Goethe began *Hermann und Dorothea* on 11 September 1796, and completed six of its nine books during the following nine days; he astonished Schiller by turning out 150 hexameters a day. The poem deals with a subject from contemporary life, and has been called an idyll rather than an epic; it has something in common with the epyllia, "little epics" written by Hellenistic poets. But it is a creative imitation of Homer in the best sense of the term: Homer supplies one of the elements combined in order to create a new and original masterpiece. There are few Homeric reminiscences; what is Homeric is not only the directness and "naiveté" of the description of the world and the movement of the action, but the firm concentration on the essentials of the plot and the close relation of each of the details to the purpose of the whole.

An interesting problem is posed by the poem on the unbinding of Prometheus which Goethe planned as early as April 1795, and of which twenty-three lines written in 1797 are all that we have. We know nothing of the plot; but Goethe's attitude to Greek religion suggests that it was very different from that of Shelley's poem on the same subject, in which Prometheus overcomes Zeus and takes over the government of the universe. As

[1] See *GA* I 144f.   [2] See the verses on Wolf at *GA* I 146.

in the case of the lost *Prometheus Unbound* of Aeschylus, it is likelier that any concessions which Zeus may have made to Prometheus did not greatly affect the workings of a power which firmly kept men in a subordinate position and did not feel itself bound by the morality they had evolved. The fragments of this work consist mainly of two choral passages; but there are also two lines of dialogue, not in ordinary German iambic pentameters, but in the remarkable imitation of the Greek iambic trimeter which Goethe used for part of the Helen episode of *Faust* and Schiller for the Montgomery scene of *Die Jungfrau von Orleans*. Karl Reinhardt[1] has shown that Goethe derived this metre from the translation of Aeschylus' *Agamemnon* by Wilhelm von Humboldt, which was not published until 1816, but an early draft of part of which was in Goethe's hands in 1797, a year when he was much occupied with Aeschylus. The rather stiff trimeters of the inventor of the metre altogether lack the marvellous ease and lightness with which Goethe was able to write in it.

Goethe now turned to a highly ambitious work upon an Homeric subject, nothing less than a continuation of the *Iliad*. He prepared himself for the writing of the *Achilleis* by a sustained course of Greek literature—Homer, tragedy, Aristophanes, minor works attributed to Homer, Herodotus, Thucydides, Plutarch; the opening lines of his poem deliberately continue the closing lines of the *Iliad* as Voss translates them. He made a careful study of every ancient treatment of the story of Achilles, and spared no effort to make the outward form of the work as Homeric as was possible. Yet if it has an affinity with any Greek poetry, it is with tragedy rather than with epic; and Goethe knew just as well as Schiller did that the whole plan of the work was unhomeric. The notion of an Achilles who is suffering from the very modern disease of weariness of life—*Weltschmerz*—is far from Homer; so is the romantic passion for Polyxena. Karl Reinhardt[2] has shown in detail how closely the

---

[1] See his "Sprachliches zu Schillers Jungfrau", *Akzente* 2 (1955), 206f. = *Tradition und Geist*, Göttingen, 1960, 366f.

[2] "Tod und Held in Goethes Achilleis", *Beiträge zur geistigen Überlieferung*, Godesberg, 1947, 224f. = *Von Werken und Formen*, Godesberg, 1948, 31f. = *Tradition und Geist*, Göttingen, 1960, 283f.; cf. O. Regenbogen, *op. cit.* (n.1, p. xiii): *Kl. Schr.* 495f.

Achilleis is related to Goethe's personal life and how typical it is of its own period; Goethe became increasingly aware of this. Like Schiller he was coming more and more to realise that his own time was so different from that of the ancient Greeks that his dream of being able to write as they had written was impossible. He finally abandoned the *Achilleis* before coming to the end of the first book, and with Schiller's encouragement decided to recreate Greece while at the same moment lamenting that Greece could not be recreated. So he came back to *Faust*, leaving the six hundred and fifty lines of the *Achilleis* as a fragment of tantalising beauty.

Faust had been begun and planned in its main outlines as early as 1775; in Rome Goethe had altered the plan and had written at least some sections of the first part. In June 1797 he resumed work on it; even as late as 1800, the Helen episode was to be on the lines of a Greek tragedy, with a chorus that sang of Helen's ancestry. September of that year saw the composition of the Helen fragment, 265 lines long. Goethe told Schiller that for a time he was tempted to separate this work from *Faust* and to complete his *Helen* as an independent tragedy; and though he decided against this course of action, he felt so much out of sympathy with the modern world that was to play its part in the romantic section of the work that he seems not to have completed the Helen episode before 1825. It was originally intended to give expression to the delight in action and creation that Goethe had attained to as a result of his Italian experience. This could not be conveyed without the tragic sense of the impossibility of permanently possessing such delight, and for the moment Goethe thought that this would have been too painful.

From September 1800, when he was working on his Helen episode, the tide of Goethe's Hellenism, to all appearances, was receding. He ceased to work intensively at Greek literature; his occupation with Greek art became desultory. True, his productions in the Weimar theatre, for some of which masks were employed, reflected his preoccupation with the notion that Greek drama is concerned with types rather than individuals; and in his play *Die Natürliche Tochter*, produced in 1803, and set in contemporary France, all the characters except the heroine are denoted only by their titles or the names of their professions; but that is not an especially Hellenic feature. The essay on Winckelmann, published in 1805, marks in a sense his farewell to the active pursuit of creative imitation of Greek poetry; modern man, Goethe wrote, was too far separated from Nature by his social conditions and the state of his religion to be capable of attaining that balanced coordination of all faculties which had marked the Greeks during their greatest period. Their "unverwüstliche Gesundheit" depended on a pagan outlook which was fundamentally opposed to the Christian view of life; it is clear that this had more importance in Goethe's eyes than the contemporary political or economic situation.

The last period of his life, from about 1805, is often referred to as his period of *Weltliteratur*, a term which owes its currency to him. He never relaxed his opposition to German romanticism, to which he applied one of his strongest terms of condemnation, the word "unhealthy"; but he was not unkind to romantics in other countries, and he could now take a sympathetic interest in the Christian mysticism of Zacharias Werner, lend a sympathetic ear to the plea of Sulpiz Boisserée that he should support the movement for the completion of Cologne Cathedral, and make a protracted study of Near-Eastern poetry at the time of the *West-Östlicher Divan* and of Chinese poetry at that of the *Chinesisch-Deutsche Jahres- und Tageszeiten*.

At the same time, Trevelyan is right to say that "Greece remained to the end his foremost, in a sense his only, love"; he was now making use of other cultures with the aid of the methods he had learned by his study of the Greeks. In 1817 the sculptures from Aegina in Munich and the frieze from Bassae and the Elgin Marbles in London all became accessible at almost the same time. At first Goethe thought of travelling to England to inspect the Elgin Marbles; in the end he contented himself with ordering a cast of a horse's head from the east pediment, and later ordering a painter to make lifesize drawings of the entire frieze, which he exhibited in his house in Weimar. The following year he finished off and published his essays on Myron's famous sculpture of a cow and on the pictures described by Philostratus. In the former,[1] he argues that the cow is that shown on the coins of Dyrrhachium, and warns against

[1] *GA* II 515.

accepting the claim of the many Greek epigrams on the subject
that its main merit was its naturalism; the latter[1] was originally
meant as an introduction to a volume of etchings representing
the pictures described by the sophist of the third century A.D.
He followed with close interest the controversies excited by the
interpretation of mythology and the ambitious theory of symbolism put forward by the Heidelberg professor Friedrich
Creuzer, sharing the healthy scepticism of the great Leipzig
Hellenist Gottfried Hermann.   The attempt of Creuzer to
derive all Indo-Germanic mythologies from a single source
provoked the amusing verses cited by Trevelyan on pp. 267–8.

Until almost the end of his life, Homer was seldom far from
his thoughts.   In 1820/1 he revised and finally published the
digest of the *Iliad* he had made for his own use in 1798,[2] and so
had occasion to reread Wolf's *Prolegomena*.   His admiration for
the author's learning and acuteness remained unaltered, but he
found that even as his understanding followed Wolf's arguments, a strong conviction of the essential unity of both poems
came over his mind.   Six years later this change of opinion
found expression in verse (see p. 269).[3]

The tragedians, particularly Euripides,[4] also occupied Goethe
during this period, partly because of the stimulus afforded by
his friendship with Gottfried Hermann, whose gifts of books
and articles sometimes provoked interesting reactions. Hermann's study of the tragic tetralogy of 1819 led Goethe to
bring out four years later a brief essay[5] in which he insisted that
there was nothing unsuitable in a poet's intercalating lighter
entertainment amid serious matter, exemplifying this from the
satyr-play which combined with three tragedies to make a
tetralogy; the Euripidean satyr-play *The Cyclops* is the subject
of one of his unfinished essays.[6]   In 1821 Hermann sent him his
paper on the fragments of Euripides' lost tragedy *Phaethon* which
had been discovered in a palimpsest found among manuscripts
that had belonged to Clairmont College, a Jesuit institution
near Paris.   The myth of Phaethon, the mortal offspring of the

---

[1] *GA* II 882f.   [2] *GA* I 174f.   [3] *GA* I 172f.

[4] See in general Uwe Petersen, *Goethe und Euripides: Untersuchungen zur
Euripides-Rezeption in der Goethezeit*, Heidelberg, 1974.

[5] *GA* I 249f.; cf. Petersen, *op. cit.*, 167f.

[6] *GA* I 299.

Sungod, who insists on being allowed to drive his father's chariot and after a brilliant beginning comes to grief, had fascinated Goethe ever since he had read it as a boy in Ovid's *Metamorphoses*; he already owned several copies of works of art that represented it. Hermann's present stimulated Goethe into writing a German reconstruction of the play, incorporating a translation of the verses of the original that survived in the palimpsest and in quotations, and based upon a serious scholarly investigation, as the accompanying notes clearly show.[1] Goethe had the assistance of two trained Greek scholars in Karl Göttling, who supplied him with a literal prose translation of the fragments, and Friedrich Wilhelm Riemer, his usual helper in such matters; but he himself was clearly the director of the enterprise. The scholarly part of it was conducted with much tact and skill, as even a reader equipped with the excellent modern edition of James Diggle,[2] incorporating the new fragment published from a Berlin papyrus in 1907, is well placed to see; and the translation of the actual fragments is one of the finest modern renderings of any Greek poetry, so that one keenly regrets that Goethe did not know the wonderful chorus starting with a description of the nightingale's song at dawn which is contained in the Berlin papyrus.

Goethe also devoted an interesting essay to the speech of Dio Chrysostom which contrasts the treatment of the legend of Philoctetes by each of the three great tragedians;[3] and he made a masterly version of that part of the final scene of Euripides' *Bacchae*[4] in which Cadmus awakens his daughter Agaue to a realisation of the fearful act she has committed under the influence of Dionysiac intoxication. During the last year of his life he was gratified by Hermann's dedication to him of his edition of the *Iphigenia in Aulis*; he read not only that play but the *Ion*, and in a letter to Göttling[5] defended Euripides against the low estimate of him made popular by A. W. Schlegel in his famous lectures on the Greek tragedians. As Euripides' greatest work Goethe singled out the *Bacchae*. "Kann man die Macht der Gottheit vortrefflicher und die Verblendung der Menschen geistreicher darstellen", he wrote, "als es hier geschehen ist?"

---

[1] *GA* 1 276f.; cf. 292f.
[2] J. Diggle, *Euripides, Phaethon*, Cambridge, 1970.
[3] *GA* 1 251f. [4] *GA* 1 288f. [5] *GA* 1 297–8.

He remarked that it is interesting to compare this ancient depiction of a suffering god with Christian descriptions of the agony of Christ, and indeed the twelfth-century author of the *Christus Patiens* used extracts from the *Bacchae* to construct a cento which described that subject.[1]

Goethe in his talks with Eckermann made remarks about Sophocles that are of much interest:[2] he was far from sharing Hegel's opinion that Creon in the *Antigone* represents the point of view of the state, and therefore has some degree of reason on his side. In 1831 he heartily enjoyed Paul-Louis Courier's new translation of Longus' *Daphnis and Chloe*, a work of which he had entertained a high opinion since reading Amyot's version in 1807.[3] Goethe retained enough of the eighteenth-century admiration for a simple life in proximity to Nature to find this author's somewhat artificial naiveté appealing.

Goethe's preoccupation with the Greeks reached its climax and found its summing-up in the final version of the episode of Helen and in the *Klassische Walpurgis-Nacht*[4] written in order to lead up to it in 1825. The whole business of the conjuring-up of Helen to amuse the frivolous Emperor and his courtiers is introduced almost casually, and the suggestion is treated deprecatingly by Mephistopheles. Then comes the moving and perplexing episode of the descent to the mysterious deities called the Mothers, held by Mephistopheles to be necessary before the conjuration can be managed. Goethe told Eckermann that he had learned of the existence of the Mothers from a puzzling reference in Plutarch's life of Marcellus (ch. 20);[5] nothing is known of them from any other source, but for Goethe they are mysterious female spirits of Nature and life. As Trevelyan says, one must be cautious about the exact significance of the episode; but it serves to emphasise the danger

---

[1] For recent discussion and bibliography, see Innocenza Giudice Rizzo, *Siculorum Gymnasium* 29 (1977), 1f.

[2] *GA* I, 261f.

[3] *GA* I 316f.

[4] See Karl Reinhardt, "Die klassische Walpurgisnacht; Entstehung und Bedeutung", *Antike und Abendland* 1 (1945), 133f. = *Von Werken und Formen*, Godesberg, 1948, 348f. = *Tradition und Geist*, Göttingen, 1960, 309f.; cf. Paul Friedländer, "Mythen und Landschaft im zweiten Teil des Faust", 1953 = *Studien zur antiken Literatur und Kunst*, Berlin, 1969, 572f.

[5] *GA* II 858–9.

and difficulty of the enterprise of evoking Helen, and it suggests
an awareness of the dark and mysterious side of Greek religion
not easily explained by the popular and superficial view of
Goethe's Hellenism.

Goethe never quite forgot the rococo Greece of his early
years, which he had come to view with an amused indulgence;
and it makes a last appearance in the *Klassische Walpurgis-
Nacht*, where the strange monsters, horrors and supernatural
beings of various kinds that proliferate in Greek mythology
parade for our amusement. At the same time they help to
strengthen our impression of the uncanny and irrational elements in Greek religion, and to remind us of the important
truth that the whole calling-up of Helen is not a matter-of-fact
episode, but part of a magical phantasmagoria. After the
monsters, the appearance of the wise centaur Chiron and other
more exalted figures bring us nearer to heroic Greece.

Now comes the Helen episode,[1] revised and expanded from
the Helen fragment of 1800. Helen has been sent on ahead from
Troy by Menelaus, and has reached Sparta. She is presented as
a dignified and noble figure; the strictly Greek form of trimeter that Goethe had taken over from Humboldt is here used
with an uncanny skill. The metamorphosis of Mephistopheles
into the sinister Phorkyas conveys yet one more reminder that
Goethe was not unalive to the grotesque elements in Greek
belief. When Faust presents himself to offer Helen a refuge
from the danger that seems to menace her, he speaks in rhyming
couplets; Helen, noticing the difference between these and her
own trimeters, asks Faust to teach her this new trick, and he
does so by setting up lines for her to finish with an obvious
rhyme. In the most natural way in the world, Goethe has
presented a successful takeover bid in terms of metre. Faust
transports Helen to his castle, and for a time their life is unhampered by the sinister elemental forces which surround her;
then with the loss of their son Euphorion, a figure reminiscent
of Phaethon, and with Helen's disappearance, leaving nothing
but her robe, these elements close in once more, and the episode
ends with a Dionysiac orgy like that described by Aeschylus in

[1] See Karl Reinhardt's lecture "Goethe and Antiquity: the Helen Episode
of Goethe's Faust", *Goethe and the Modern Age*, Chicago, 1950, 38f. =
Tradition und Geist, Göttingen, 1960, 274f. (in English).

a wonderful fragment from his lost trilogy about Orpheus (fr. 71 Mette).

To grasp the significance of the Helen episode, we must remember that it is magical; Helen vanishes, and only her robe is left. Goethe was aware that he could not revive the conditions in which the Greeks had lived and worked; his creative imitation of their art could only help him to bring off a dazzling but momentary feat of illusion. None the less, Faust will continue his struggle towards higher forms of existence, profoundly affected by the experience he has undergone.

Trevelyan observes that Goethe used his study of the Greeks to obtain the grasp of southern European culture which he needed in order to correct the bias given to him by his northern origin; he used them, one may add, to strike a balance between the Titanism of this period of *Sturm und Drang* and the resigned attitude of his first Weimar period. He was able to do so effectively because his notion of the Greeks was closely linked with the conception of humanity which formed part of the idea of Nature, highly characteristic of the eighteenth century but at the same time peculiar to Goethe himself, which was central to his whole way of thinking. Still more important than his search for the original plant, the original colour, the original phenomenon was his search for the original man; and he found the original man, the qualities in virtue of which a man is human, to be exemplified in the Greeks.

Such an attitude, Trevelyan writes, would be impossible nowadays, for the value of civilisations outside Europe is now well known even to Europeans, and indeed it became known to Goethe himself during the final phase of his career. Many modern critics would add that the intensive study of ancient civilisation which has been carried out since Goethe's time has shown that he idealised the Greeks to an unreasonable degree. There were undoubtedly naive classicisers who excessively idealised the Greeks and their society: Rousseau's belief in the essential goodness of human nature and Herder's belief in the essential excellence of the cultures of individual peoples led directly to such an attitude. Winckelmann might without grave injustice be accused of having idealised the Greeks, and the tendency was widespread till well into the nineteenth century. One such idealiser was Marx. "The Greeks were natural children," he wrote, "the attraction Greek art has for us does not stand in contradiction to the undeveloped stage of society on which it grew. It is, rather, its result; it is inextricably bound up, rather, with the fact that the immature social conditions under which it arose, and under which alone it could arise, can never return."[1] Once the dictatorship of the proletariat has been established, the state will wither away, and mankind will return to the beautiful simplicity of its historic childhood; the naiveté of this opinion must be connected with the sentimental view of the Greeks which its author shared with many of his contemporaries.

But on close examination Goethe's attitude to the Greeks proves to reveal a high degree of realism. In theory, he told Riemer in 1813,[2] the Greeks strongly believed in freedom; but the freedom which each believed in was his own, for inside each Greek there was a tyrant who needed only the opportunity to emerge, and true despotism arose from the desire for freedom. He warned people against allowing their admiration for Greek art and science to lead them to regard the actions of the Greeks and their behaviour to others as exemplary,[3] and he remarked that the claims of society upon the individual had been far more imperious in ancient Greece than they were in his own time.[4] His writings show no trace of the belief, common among naive classicisers, that the ancient Greeks were more moral in the modern humanitarian sense than the men of his own time. Writing to Fritz von Stein from Rome in 1787, he expressed the fear that with the victory of humanitarianism the world would become one large hospital in which some human beings would nurse others.[5]

Goethe was concerned to fill the gap left by the collapse of Christianity, to which he greatly preferred the religion of the Greeks. In that religion the gods stood for the forces which

[1] See my *Blood for the Ghosts*, London, 1981.
[2] *GA* I 63.
[3] *GA* I 62.
[4] 18.11.1806, to Riemer (*GA* I 63).
[5] 8.6.1787, cited by Schadewaldt, *op. cit.* (n.1, p. vii), 1045. "Nicht als paradiesisches Unschuldsvolk eines Menschenfrühlings, nicht als ein Volk schönen Jünglingen sondern als fest in der Wirklichkeit stehende tüchtige und gesunde Männer sieht Goethe die Griechen": Richard Harder, *Die Antike* 9 (1933), 30=*Kleine Schriften*, Munich, 1960, 460.

control the universe; as Thales put it, everything was full of gods, for the gods corresponded with that Nature in which Goethe so passionately believed. Greek religion put man and his claims in the place which the operations of Nature in the world assigns him, a place in which he is wholly subordinated to the immortal gods. But from Homer's time on the Greeks believed in a kind of kinship between gods and men; Goethe nowhere, so far as I know, quotes the opening of Pindar's sixth Nemean ode, "The race of gods and the race of men are one", but it expresses one of his most cherished beliefs. The highest element in man seemed to him divine, and the more a man felt himself to be a man, the more like he was to the immortal gods. Following Rudolf Pfeiffer,[1] we may take the poem of 1820, *Urworte: Orphisch*, as a guide to his world outlook. Men and gods alike are subject to the rule of necessity; the gods are immortal, but human fate is bounded by death. Each man has his individual nature, his daimon; Goethe would have agreed with Heraclitus that character is a man's daimon. Man's life is subject to the operations of *Tyche*, not blind chance, but a factor which the gods control; it remains inscrutable to man himself. Man is also subject to the urges comprehended under the name of *Eros*, not merely love—though like the Greeks Goethe thought of Love as a dangerous and terrifying force—but all deep longings and ambitions. A man's judgement might be taken from him by *Ate*, delusion or infatuation, a kind of godsent madness; that danger he must resist by cultivating *Sophrosyne*, not so much "moderation" as safe thinking, discretion, resignation to the limits imposed upon humanity dictated by saving common sense. *Sophrosyne* was closely linked with what he called "die göttliche Scheu"; that has been equated with *Aidos*, reverence or respect, but it is even closer to what Plato in the Laws calls "divine fear", *theios phobos*.[2] This quality is linked with the capacity to wonder or admire, *to thaumazein*, in a wonderful passage of Goethe's *Farbenlehre*.

The outcome of man's efforts was decided by *Ananke*, necessity of compulsion, but what gave him strength to bear

---

[1] *Op. cit.* (n.1, p. vii), 242f.

[2] *Laws* 671 D; see the first chapter of Edgar Wind's *Art and Anarchy*, London, 1963, 3f. with n.4 on p. 106; the important article there cited will be found in *The Eloquence of Symbols*, Oxford, 1981, pp. 1f.

up against that knowledge was *Elpis*, Hope. So far Goethe's outlook seems virtually identical with the religious outlook of the early Greeks; but when we come to *Elpis*, we find an important difference between the two. For the Greeks Hope is an ambiguous concept; sometimes it is the chief consolation given to mortals for all the limitations imposed by their condition, but at other times it is a dangerous delusion. Goethe's conception of Hope was closely linked with his belief in a basic affinity between Man and Nature, his belief in the essential goodness of the universe. For all its peculiarity, his idea of Nature was typical of the age in which he lived; in the last resort, the eighteenth-century idea of a benevolent Nature, held as it might be by deists and atheists, was nothing but the residue of the faith in a benevolent God implanted by long centuries of Christianity. The Greeks were a good deal less confident of the interest taken by the gods in man. Their attitude to life was a tragic attitude; the *Iliad* is in one sense of the word a tragedy, and it was from the *Iliad* that the great tragedians got their inspiration. It has often been observed that Goethe drew back when he approached the neighbourhood of tragedy.[1] Iphigenia is not really capable of slaughtering her brother; Faust strikes a bargain with the devil, but we know from the start that for all his remorse over poor Gretchen he is never going to have to pay the devil's bill. Just as much as Rousseau, with whose rejection of the doctrine of original sin he surely sympathised, Goethe shrank from believing in the finality of evil; with that qualification, he had more sympathy with Christianity than is immediately apparent, as the end of *Faust*, for all its ironies, clearly shows. Soon after the end of the last world war, Karl Jaspers remarked that in their present situation Germans were turning to Shakespeare, to the Bible, to Aeschylus rather than to Goethe.[2] Goethe himself once said

[1] See in particular Erich Heller, *op. cit.* (n.2, p. viii), "Goethe and the avoidance of Tragedy", pp. 37f. and George Steiner, *The death of Tragedy*, London, 1961, 166f. "So sind denn seine Dramen, einschliesslich des *Faust*, des *Egmont*, des *Tasso*, auch alle keine Tragödien, obwohl diese Werke in gewisser Weise zeigen, dass Goethe fähig gewesen wäre, Tragödien zu schreiben, wenn er sich dazu hätte bringen können": K. von Fritz, *Antike und Modern Tragödie*, Berlin, 1962, 472, n.47.

[2] K. Jaspers, *Unsere Zukunft und Goethe*, Zurich, 1948, 22, cited by Heller, *op. cit.* (n.2, p. viii), 41.

that he thought he had achieved something as a poet, but that
compared with Aeschylus or Sophocles he was nothing; he was
not given to indulgence in false modesty, and it is likely that he
believed what he was saying. If these poets have access to a
dimension in which Goethe never moves, it is because their
religion gave them a tragic vision of the world which Goethe
lacked; his attitude, like that of the early Greeks in so many
ways, differs from theirs in this vital particular.

For Goethe self-perfection and self-cultivation, *Bildung* and
Kultur, ranked as the highest human activities. Carelessly interpreted, that might give the impression that he was dedicated
to an idle and selfish form of aestheticism; and before the end
of the nineteenth century his name had often been invoked by
believers in such doctrines. Nothing could be more unjust than
this; Goethe believed that the aim of self-perfection was to
acquire excellence, *arete*, *virtus*, *virtù*, which was displayed in
action. For him piety was only a means to an end; the goal of
human effort was not peace in paradise but effective work.[1]
"Des echten Mannes Feier ist die Tat"; both Wilhelm Meister
and Faust are and become *praktikoi*, men of action. In particular, the artist must act; by action he imposes a law upon the
formless succession of experiences, so that they acquire a shape
that gives them permanence; thus man can exercise a creative
power which is akin to the divine creative power visible in
Nature. "If I can go on working to the very end", Goethe said
to Eckermann when he was eighty, "Nature is obliged to
assign to me another form of being when my present form of
being is no longer able to contain my spirit."[2] A Greek would
have smiled grimly at these words, which to him would have
seemed arrant hybris; how can any man oblige Nature, or the
gods, to grant him anything? Goethe would have recognised
that the remark issued from the German, not the Greek, side of
his nature; yet it illustrates the place occupied by Hope, *Elpis*,
in an attitude to life which for all the strength of the Germanic
element in the creator of *Faust* must be acknowledged to have
strong affinities with Greek thinking.

---

[1] See Pfeiffer, *op. cit.* (n.1, p. vii), 248f.
[2] 4.2.1829; see Walter Kaufmann, "Goethe's faith and Faust's redemp-
tion", in *From Shakespeare to Existentialism*, Boston, 1959, 61f.

CONTENTS

A. BACKGROUND

Importance of environment in the formation of Goethe's ideas, p. 1. Ignorance of Greece in sixteenth and seventeenth-century Germany, p. 2. Revival and spread of classical learning; J. M. Gesner, p. 3. Ignorance of Greece among the contemporaries of Goethe's father, p. 5. Spirit of hostility to Greece, and the "Querelle des anciens et des modernes", p. 6. "Anacreontic" poetry: the false revival, p. 10; the true revival: Breitinger and *Télémaque*, p. 11. Winckelmann's *Gedanken*, p. 13. Position in Frankfurt in Goethe's childhood, p. 14.

B. CHILDHOOD (1749–1765)

The Herr Rat's attitude to ancient culture, p. 16. Wolfgang's classical education, p. 16. French reinterpretation of the Greek, p. 20. First interest in Greek philosophy, p. 23. Goethe's efforts to improve his knowledge of Greek literature, p. 24. Conflict with the Herr Rat over the choice of university studies, p. 27.

C. LEIPZIG TO HERDER (1765–1770)

No evidence of Greek reading at Leipzig, p. 29. First acquaintance with Greek art, p. 34. Visit to the Mannheim galleries (1769), p. 37. Goethe's attitude to mythology in Leipzig, p. 40. Winckelmann's influence on Goethe's conception of the Greeks, p. 42. Lessing's *Laokoon*, p. 45. Goethe's views on the essence of Greek art, p. 46. Wieland's influence, p. 48.

A. KNOWLEDGE

Effect of Herder's friendship, p. 50. The language mastered, p. 51. Greek authors read: Pindar, p. 52; Greek tragedy, p. 57; Orphic hymns, p. 63; Homer, p. 64. Contacts with Greek art, p. 65.

B. IDEAS

The new picture of the Greeks; contrast with Rococo Hellenism, p. 68. Greek qualities as seen by Goethe, p. 70. The Greeks as forerunners in his own problems, moral and aesthetic, p. 77. The Greeks not an absolute ideal, p. 83.

Greece in relation to Goethe's moral conflict; *Proserpina*, p. 84. Greece an ideal; new relationship established in *Iphigenie*, p. 90. How far is *Iphigenie* an imitation of Greek tragedy? p. 96. Fundamental difference on the moral plane, p. 99. Greek studies after *Iphigenie*, p. 104. Return to the problem of Greek tragedy; *Elpenor*, p. 106. Orphic hymns and the *Naturaufsatz*, p. 113. Greek Anthology, p. 114. Longing for Italy; Mignon, p. 119.

A. TOWARDS ROME

Flight to Italy: causes and objectives, p. 121. Composition in the style of the ancients; Palladio, p. 125. *Iphigenie* reworked, p. 131. *Iphigenie auf Delphos*; the problem of Greek tragedy nearly solved, p. 135.

B. ROME

General survey, p. 138. Greek sculpture studied with Winckelmann's help, p. 140. The Greek gods; K. P. Moritz's *Götterlehre*; Victory of "Electra-morality", p. 143.

C. NAPLES AND SICILY

Search for the essence of the southern existence, p. 148. Pompeii and Paestum, p. 151. Sicily: difficulty and importance of the decision to go, p. 153. Palermo; journey through the interior, p. 156. Success of the journey; "*Urlandschaft*" and "*Urmensch*" linked by Homer, p. 159. *Nausikaa*, p. 163. Other effects of the Sicilian journey: Doric architecture; Greek tragedy, p. 167.

D. ROME AGAIN

Probing the mystery of the human form, p. 169. The Greek Gods as "ideal characters", p. 173.

A. BACK IN WEIMAR

Goethe's effort to recapture the natural life of the Greeks in Weimar, p. 179. *Römische Elegien*; Homeric style; principle of "reminiscences", p. 182. *Tasso's* style in contrast, p. 186. Sterile period, 1790–1793, p. 187. *Reinecke Fuchs*, p. 188. Renewed study of Homer, p. 189.

CONTENTS   xli

B. SCHILLER

C. CRISIS AND FAILURE

D. HELENA

PREFACE

Goethe-scholars and Goethe-lovers in Germany and England have not ceased for the past hundred years to comment on and re-define Goethe's relations with the Greek tradition. Only four years ago one of the finest of these commentaries appeared: Walther Rehm's *Griechentum und Goethezeit*. But still there is no book that gives a coherent chronological account of the stages by which Goethe gained knowledge and understanding of Greece. The facts upon which a student must base his appreciation of Goethe's attitude to Greece lie scattered in innumerable books and periodicals, many of them out of print and no longer easy of access. My chief purpose has been to give a clear account of the facts, and especially to establish with all reasonable certainty the extent of Goethe's knowledge of Greek things at every stage of his development. In the first three chapters, which deal with the growth of Goethe's knowledge and the development of his ideas, I have therefore recorded every piece of evidence which suggests an interest in Greece. It seemed to me unnecessary to continue this method in the last three chapters, from the Italian Journey to Goethe's death. By that time his knowledge of Greece was essentially complete; and as, during the height of his Hellenism, almost every activity of his life had some contact with Greece, it seemed better to select those facts and utterances which throw light on his conception of the nature and value of the Greek heritage. In the last chapter especially I have given a much condensed account of his Greek interests, and have discussed at length only those questions which seemed to be of particular importance.

Quotations from German are given in English in the text, except in the case of passages in verse, when it seemed better to keep the metrical form in the text, and give an English translation in a footnote. In a book of this kind it would perhaps have been best to have given the original German in a footnote for every prose passage quoted in English in the text. But this would have made the apparatus altogether too cumbersome; and in many cases, where the German could be translated without the loss of any shade of meaning, it would have been unnecessary. I have therefore used my discretion, and have given the original German only where I felt that the translation was inadequate, or in certain cases where the passage quoted was of such cardinal importance, that it appeared to be indispensable to let the reader see the German words. In every case the page reference is given, so that the reader who wishes to assure himself of the German text can do so without much trouble. Some German terms, for which there is no concise equivalent in English, such as *Urmensch* and *naiv*, have been left in German in the text, and their exact meaning has been made clear either in the text or in a footnote.

I have to thank in particular my uncle, Robert Trevelyan, for his help on matters where my knowledge of Greek literature was inadequate, especially in questions relating to antique and modern metres; and for his painstaking scrutiny of my manuscript. I owe also a special debt to Mr A. H. J. Knight, of Trinity College, Cambridge, for his encouragement and advice in connexion with this book.

H. T.

1940

BIBLIOGRAPHY

ARNDT, WILHELM. *Introduction to his edition of "Die Vögel"*, Leipzig, 1886.

BAPP, C. *Aus Goethes griechischer Gedankenwelt.* Leipzig, 1921.

BAUMECKER. *Winckelmann in seinen Dresdener Schriften.* Berlin, 1933.

BAUMGART, HERMANN. *Goethes lyrische Dichtung.* Heidelberg, 1931.

BERNAYS, MICHAEL. *Vorrede* to *Goethes Briefe an F. A. Wolf.* Berlin, 1868.

BETTEX, ALBERT. *Der Kampf um das klassische Weimar.* 1935.

BEUTLER, E. *Vom griechischen Epigramme im achzehnten Jahrhundert.* 1909.

BRESSEM, M. *Der metrische Aufbau des Faust II.* Berlin, 1921.

BRONNER, F. *Goethes Römische Elegien und ihre Quellen*, in *Neue Jahrbücher für Philologie*, 1893.

BÜNEMANN, H. *Elias Schlegel und Wieland als Bearbeiter antiker Tragödien.* Leipzig, 1928.

BURSIAN, CONRAD. *Geschichte der klassischen Philologie in Deutschland.* Munich and Leipzig, 1883.

BUTLER, E. M. *The Tyranny of Greece over Germany.* Cambridge, 1935.

CASTLE, EDUARD. *In Goethes Geist.* Vienna, 1926.

DALMEYDA, GEORGES. *Un fragment de tragédie antique de Goethe.* 1898.

DÜNTZER, H. *Zur Goetheforschung.* 1891.

DÜNTZER, H. *Die drei ältesten Bearbeitungen von Goethes Iphigenie.* 1854.

ELINGER, GEORG. *Alceste in der modernen Literatur.* Halle, 1885.

FAHRNER, RUDOLF. *Karl Philipp Moritz Götterlehre.* Marburg, 1932.

FAIRLEY, BARKER. *Goethe as Revealed in his Poetry.* 1932.

FINSLER, GEORG. *Homer in der Neuzeit.* Berlin, 1912.

FITTBOGEN, GOTTFRIED. *Die sprachliche und metrische Form der Hymnen Goethes.* Halle, 1909.

FRIES, A. *Goethes Achilleis.* Berlin, 1901.

GLASER, RUDOLF. *Goethes Vater.* Leipzig, 1929.

GREVERUS, J. P. *Würdigung der Iphigenie auf Tauris.* Oldenburg, 1841.

GUNDOLF, FRIEDRICH. *Goethe.* Berlin, 1930.

HARNACK, OTTO. *Essais und Studien.* 1899.

HEHN, VICTOR. *Goethes Hermann und Dorothea.* Stuttgart, 1893.

HERING. *Einfluss des klassischen Altertums auf den Bildungsgang des jungen Goethe.* Frankfurt-am-Main, 1902.

xlv

HEUSLER, ANDREAS. *Deutscher und antiker Vers.* Strassburg, 1917.
JUSTI, CARL. *Winckelmann und seine Zeitgenossen.* Leipzig, 1898.
KELLER. *Goethe's Estimate of the Greek and Latin Writers.* Wisconsin, 1916.
KEUDELL, ELISE VON. *Goethe als Benutzer der Weimarer Bibliothek.* Weimar, 1931.
KÖNIG. *Goethes Belesenheit.* Unpublished. (By courtesy of Prof. Schreiber of Yale University.)
KORFF, H. A. *Geist der Goethezeit.* Leipzig, 1923.
LÜCKE. *Goethe und Homer.* Nordhausen, 1884.
LÜCKEN, GOTTFRIED VON. *Goethe und der Laokoon. Natalicium.* Heidelberg, 1930.
MAASS, ERNST. *Goethe und die Antike.* Leipzig, 1912.
MEISSINGER, C. A. *Helena.* 1935.
MENTZEL, E. *Wolfgang und Cornelia Goethes Lehrer.* Leipzig, 1909.
MENTZEL, E. *Der junge Goethe und das Frankfurter Theater.* 1899.
MENZEL, A. *Goethe und die griechische Philosophie.* Vienna, 1932.
MONTGOMERY, MARSHALL. *Friederich Hölderlin and the German Neo-Hellenic Movement.* Oxford, 1923.
MORRIS, MAX. *Der junge Goethe.*
MORRIS, MAX. *Goethes und Herders Anteil an dem Jahrgang 1772 der Frankfurter Gelehrten Anzeigen.* Revised edition, 1915.
MORRIS, MAX. *Goethestudien.*
MORSCH, H. *Goethe und die griechischen Bühnendichter.* Berlin, 1888.
MÜLLER, EMIL. *Antike Reminiszenzen in Goethes Iphigenie.* Zittau, 1888.
NEWALD, RICHARD. *Goethe und die Antike.* Freiburg, Schweiz, 1932.
OLBRICH, CARL. *Nachahmung der klassischen Sprachen in Goethes Wortstellung und Wortgebrauch.* Leipzig, 1891.
PAULSEN, FRIEDRICH. *Geschichte des gelehrten Unterrichts auf den deutschen Schulen und Universitäten.* Leipzig, 1885.
REHM, WALTHER. *Griechentum und Goethezeit.* 1935.
RIGAULT. *Histoire de la querelle des anciens et des modernes.* Paris, 1856.
SAUER, MINOR. *Studien zur Goethephilologie.* Vienna, 1880.
SCHERER. *Goethe-Aufsätze.*
SCHOENE, H. *Antike Vorteile und barbarische Avantagen.* Berlin, 1934.
SCHREYER, H. *Goethe und Homer.* Naumburg, 1884.
STECKNER, HANS. *Der epische Stil von Hermann und Dorothea.* Leipzig, 1927.
STEINER, RUDOLF. *Goethes Faust als Bild seiner esoterischen Anschauung.* Berlin, 1902.
STEJSKAL, KARL. *Goethe und Homer.* Vienna, 1881.
STREHLKE, FR. *Ueber Goethes Elpenor und Achilleis.* Marienburg, 1870.

SUDHEIMER, H. *Der Geniebegriff des jungen Goethe.* Berlin, 1935.

SZANTO, EMIL. *Zur Helena in Faust. Ausgewählte Abhandlungen.* Tübingen, 1906.

TREVELYAN, HUMPHRY. *The Popular Background to Goethe's Hellenism.* 1934. (See the bibliography there for the sources of Chapter I, Section A.)

VALENTIN, VEIT. *Die klassische Walpurgisnacht.* 1901.

VOELCKER, H. *Die Stadt Goethes.* Frankfurt-am-Main, 1932.

VOGEL, JULIUS. *Aus Goethes Römischen Tagen.* Leipzig, 1905.

VOLBEHR, THEODOR. *Goethe und die bildende Kunst.* Leipzig, 1895.

VOLKMANN, R. *Geschichte und Kritik der Wolfschen Prolegomena.* Leipzig, 1874.

WICKHOFF. *Der zeitliche Wandel in Goethes Verhältnis zur Antike, dargelegt am Faust.* Vienna, 1898.

WILAMOWITZ-MOELLENDORFF. *Reden und Vorträge.* 1913.

WILAMOWITZ-MOELLENDORFF. *Euripides Herakles.* Berlin, 1889.

WILAMOWITZ-MOELLENDORFF. *Pindaros.*

ABBREVIATIONS

(employed throughout in the footnotes)

WA. = Weimar (Sophien) Ausgabe of Goethe's works.

JA. = Jubiläums-Ausgabe of Goethe's works.

D. und W. = *Dichtung und Wahrheit.*

G–J. = *Goethe-Jahrbuch.*

Jrb. der G–G. = *Jahrbuch der Goethe-Gesellschaft.*

Schr. der G–G. = *Schriften der Goethe-Gesellschaft.*

Gräf = Hans Gerhard Gräf, *Goethe über seine Dichtungen.*

Eckermann = *Eckermanns Gespräche mit Goethe.*

Bied. = Freiherr v. Biedermann, *Goethes Gespräche.*

Jonas = *Schillers Briefe.* Edited by Fritz Jonas.

Page references to the Weimar Ausgabe are given, for example, thus:

WA. 21, p. 32 = Weimar Ausgabe, Abteilung I (literary works), volume 21, p. 32.

WA. IV, 13, p. 256 = Weimar Ausgabe, Abteilung IV (letters), volume 13, page 256.

CHAPTER I

CHILDHOOD AND YOUTH

A. BACKGROUND

THE opinions and actions of a man in middle life are the outcome primarily of his character, that "geprägte Form, die lebend sich entwickelt"; but they are determined also by the material on which his character has to work—by his environment. The influence of environment begins at birth, before the human individual is conscious of itself; and throughout life it works for the most part unconsciously. At a certain age we begin to realise that we have been influenced by this or that experience, by this or that writer or work of art; but far more profoundly and inescapably our minds are moulded by the things we scarcely notice, by the colour of the sky, by the outlook from our window, by the pattern of the wallpaper, by the talk of our parents and their friends at tea or after dinner. All such things should be taken into account, when an attempt is made to follow from within the development of one of the great minds of the past; but of course this cannot be, for of all historical phenomena such "atmospheres" are the least enduring and the hardest to reconstruct.

A modern reader of Goethe will find especial difficulty in understanding Goethe's attitude to the Greeks, if he knows nothing of the background of knowledge and ignorance, of understanding and fallacy, about Greek things, against which Goethe's earliest impressions were formed. A picture of this background, however incomplete it must of necessity be, will do something to explain the workings of Goethe's mind, which may at times seem strange to us. In the matter of knowledge and appreciation of Greek civilisation no greater difference can be conceived of, than that between the background in Goethe's childhood and the background against which the present generation of cultured Englishmen formed its ideas. Our fathers, if not we ourselves, were taught at school little else but the literature and history of the ancient world; Goethe's father and his contemporaries could not read Greek and knew nothing about Greece and little enough about Rome. The

I

labouring archaeologist and the science of photography have
made every schoolboy familiar with hundreds of the greatest
works of art of ancient Greece, which were unknown in
Goethe's youth. Not least important: Goethe grew up in an
age when the meaning and value of Greece was being re-
discovered, so that enthusiasm was outrunning knowledge.
With us, on the other hand, classicism has had its day; modernism
and utility combine to put knowledge of Greece and Rome
back in its place among the other special sciences; while the
astonishing achievements of archaeology in every field make it
easy for us to look on Greece as just another prehistoric civilisation.

In the sixteenth century Germany had had her renaissance of
classical knowledge and ideals along with the rest of Europe.
New schools and universities had sprung up to spread the
evangel. But in the next century a reaction set in. Its nature
is best illustrated by these words of one Comenius, a leader
among educationalists of the day: "If we would really have
Christian schools, we must get rid of the pagan teachers. You
say: 'Not all are foul; Cicero, Virgil, Horace and others are
respectable and worthy.' I reply: These too are blind pagans,
who entice the mind of the reader from the true God to gods
and goddesses. God has said to his people: Think not of strange
gods and let not their name pass your lips."[1] In spite of the
hostility of organised Christianity, the teaching of Latin literature continued in the schools, but without inspiration. Greek
was taught only as far as was necessary for reading the New
Testament in the original.

At the end of the seventeenth century and the beginning of
the eighteenth new forces joined the attack on the Old Humanism. The Pietists brought new energy to the Christian hatred
of ancient culture, while the Rationalists under Thomasius
despised all the achievements of antiquity on two excellent
grounds: that they were useless and that they were out of date.
Francke, the Pietist, and Thomasius, though leaders of radically
opposed schools of thought, worked together at the newly
founded university of Halle (1696) to keep the "foul pagans"
from polluting the minds or wasting the time of the young

[1] Comenius, *Opera didactica*, 1657.

men. In commenting on the educational policy of the Old Humanism, Thomasius wrote: "Melanchthon certainly deserves praise for introducing the Greek language. But he did not act wisely in occupying the youth with the folly of the Greek orators and poets, and with the useless philosophy of Aristotle. Why did he not have the New Testament or the Septuagint expounded in Greek lessons instead of Euripides, Sophocles, Homer, Aristotle, etc.? I should think the Book of Wisdom, of Judith or Maccabees would be as good or better than that fool Homer and the other pagan poets and orators."[1]

The older universities, such as Leipzig, Wittenberg, or Tübingen, continued more in the tradition of the Old Humanism. But the method of teaching prevented the student from getting any idea of the beauty and greatness of the ancient cultures. It was all dry grammar and endless practice in stilted rhetorical exercises. At Leipzig in 1733 there were no lectures on Greek authors, and Reiske, an eminent Greek scholar of the coming generation, finding no one to help him in his Greek reading, gave it up and took to Arabic.[2]

This was the state of affairs in the schools and universities during the years when Goethe's father and his contemporaries were being educated. If they were lucky they may have read some Virgil, Horace or Caesar, but probably in such a way that they had no desire ever to open those authors again. Of ancient Greece, either of its history or of its literature, they knew nothing.

The revival in classical learning started about twenty years before Goethe was born, but it was slow in gathering way. J. M. Gesner was the founder of the New Humanism. Appointed as Rektor to the Thomasschule in Leipzig in 1730, and then as Professor of Eloquence in Göttingen in 1734, he set all his energies to the building up of a new tradition of classical teaching. With sure instinct he realised that his chief obstacles lay in the prejudice against the "foul pagans", which Christian teachers of Francke's type had fostered, and in the lifeless teaching methods of the Old Humanism. In the recom-

[1] Quoted from Paulsen, *Geschichte des Gelehrten Unterrichts*, p. 360.
[2] Paulsen, *op. cit.* p. 414.

mendations which he drew up for the Brunswick schools in 1737 he urged that the teacher be particular to give the young people a good opinion of the ancients in general and of the pleasure and use of being well read in them. "He should say to them that most of the ancient writers were the most excellent people of their time. Whoever therefore reads and understands their writings, enjoys the society of the greatest men and the noblest souls who have ever been, and thus imbibes beautiful thoughts and words of weight, as always happens in conversation." Classical teaching was to be an easy and delightful conversation with the great men of old. For this purpose new methods of reading the ancient authors must be introduced. They must be read quickly through, so that the pupil enjoys and understands what he is reading. The teacher must draw attention not to the grammar or small points of style, but to the general meaning of the work, to its form and to the means employed by the author to make his thought clear or to adorn it.[1] The practical obstacles to a widespread realisation of this ideal were enormous. There were no teachers; there were no suitable texts. With wonderful pertinacity Gesner stuck to his purpose. Before he died in 1760, the New Humanism had spread far from Göttingen and was accepted as the basis of teaching in many schools and universities.

The movement received help from sources independent of Gesner. J. F. Christ, Professor of Poetry at Leipzig from 1734 to 1756, combined considerable knowledge of ancient art with real taste and a broad view of the value of spiritual culture. His lectures on Antiquities, though not well attended, inspired some of the best minds of the coming generation, among them Lessing.[2] Klopstock too, at Schulpforta from 1739 to 1745, derived the most genuine inspiration from the classical teaching which he received. True love of the ancients lurked still in odd corners of the land. Nevertheless the New Humanism had not spread far enough nor gathered sufficient force by 1750 to have any effect on the minds of the men and women among whom Goethe grew up. Some Greek was taught at the Frankfurt Gymnasium during the 'thirties and 'forties of the eighteenth

---

[1] Preface to Gesner's edition of Livy, 1743.
[2] Schmidt, *Life of Lessing*, p. 44.

century,[1] but there is no evidence to show that any Greek works were read other than the New Testament. Greek art must have been almost unknown among the older generation in Goethe's childhood. There were practically no antique statues in Germany, none at all of the best period of Greek art. Those at Dresden were stowed away in a lean-to, so that even Winckelmann could make little of them.[2] Doubtless there were some casts of ancient works, as in Oeser's academy at Leipzig; but the formation of the famous collection of casts at Mannheim during the late 'sixties was an epoch-making event for the knowledge of ancient art in Germany. Until 1769, when the Mannheim collection was completed by the addition of casts newly made in Italy,[3] there was nowhere in Germany where a student could get a comprehensive view of ancient art. Some, Goethe's father among them, had travelled to Rome and seen the Laocoön and the Apollo with their own eyes; but such fortunate ones were few.

Before the publication of Winckelmann's *Geschichte der Kunst des Altertums* in 1763, there was no book which gave a proper account of the development of ancient art. The two books on antiquities most commonly used, Montfaucon's *L'antiquité expliquée* (first edition 1719) and Caylus's *Recueils d'antiquité* (1752–1767), both had serious shortcomings. Montfaucon was not interested in the ancient works of art for their aesthetic value, but only in so far as they threw light on the mythology and mode of life of the ancients. He made no distinction between Greek, Roman and Etruscan work. Caylus valued ancient art as art,[4] and was the first to distinguish Greek art from Roman, Etruscan and Egyptian; but he discussed and reproduced only those works which he himself possessed, for the most part statuettes, busts and gems, so that the reader got no information about the masterpieces of ancient art.[5]

---

[1] Cf. H. Voelcker, *Die Stadt Goethes*, 1932, and E. Mentzel, *Wolfgang und Cornelia Goethes Lehrer*, p. 211.

[2] Justi, *Winckelmann und seine Zeitgenossen*, Zweite Auflage, Leipzig, 1898, I, p. 274, and Winckelmann, *Werke*, II, p. 405.

[3] *G-J.* xxvii, p. 150 fol., and Goethe's letter to Langer, 30 Nov. 1769: see p. 38 below.

[4] Avertissement to vol. I.

[5] For Goethe's retrospective opinion of Caylus see his letter to Hirt, 9 June 1809.

Even the study of ancient cameos and intaglios, so popular a pastime during Goethe's youth, was not easy for his father's generation. Before the publication of Lippert's *Daktyliothek* in the 1750's the amateur had to depend on engraved reproductions, often "improved" in rococo style,[1] or on the laborious and expensive method of collecting plaster or wax impressions.

In the first half of the eighteenth century a certain knowledge of ancient mythology was still necessary in cultured society. During the years just before Goethe's birth, the literary gentlemen, who still used the old names to adorn their verses, did not demand a very high standard of knowledge from their readers. Hagedorn in his *Oden und Lieder* (1747) thought it advisable to explain in footnotes anything more abstruse than a direct reference to one of the gods; he was afraid, for instance, that his readers would not know whose mother Thetis was. During Goethe's childhood the general public became much better versed in the old myths, so that Wieland in his *Komische Erzählungen* (1765) could adopt a highly allusive style, which assumed in the reader a fair knowledge of such myths as Actaeon, Endymion, Danaë, and indeed most of Zeus's affairs.

The handbooks from which the elder generation derived its knowledge of mythology dated for the most part from the previous century or even earlier. The most popular were Pomey's *Pantheum Mythicum* (1659), Hyginus's *Fables*, first published in the sixteenth century, and Hederich's *Lexicon Mythologicum* (1724). In 1753 a new and very full handbook appeared. It was published as the sixth volume of a *Neue Sammlung der Merkwürdigsten Reisegeschichten*, which a "company of learned persons" in Frankfurt brought out. The handbook was compiled by Goethe's uncle Loën, the same whose translation of the *Iliad* filled the eight-year-old boy with such delighted awe.[2] It does not seem that Loën's work was much known outside Frankfurt. Its treatment of the myths was that of the age that was passing. A book on mythology, published only two years before Winckelmann's *Gedanken*, had to be written with a broader view than Loën could assume, if it was to attract the coming generation.

The tone of Loën's commentary on the myths is curious.

[1] Justi, *op. cit.* I, p. 338.   [2] See below, p. 17.

He succeeds in destroying every claim to value of any kind which might be made for them, so that his readers must have wondered why he ever went to the labour of relating and publishing a collection of such pointless and unedifying tales. The two prongs of the moral pitchfork, with which he tosses the gods and heroes into limbo, are named rationalisation and slander. With the former he makes out Prometheus to be a Caucasian astronomer, who wore himself out by his nightly watchings (hence the story of the eagle devouring his liver); Icarus, sailing with Daedalus in the first sail-boat (hence the tale of the wings), tried to jump ashore too soon and was drowned. Every flower of the poetic imagination in Greek fable and poetry is ruthlessly mown down in Loën's rationalising zeal. The most offensive to Loën's common sense is the Shield of Achilles. For how could all those scenes be depicted on a shield of reasonable dimensions? A certain ingenious M. Boivin had indeed worked it all out in inches, and demonstrated that everything could be fitted in. But Loën remains sceptical. Anyhow, how can Homer know what the lawsuit is about? It is all irrational and preposterous.

Rationalistic blindness of this sort was to be expected from a man of Loën's kind at that time and in that place. The astonishing aspect of his work is the malicious delight which he takes in blackening the characters of the ancient gods and heroes, and so in throwing discredit on the whole Greek nation. Having related all Jupiter's amatory exploits in detail, he sums up: "Such a lover was exceedingly well suited to be the most exalted god of a licentious people." The usual version of the story of the Atreid family, full of violence and cruelty as it is, is not gruesome enough for Loën. He adds to it such details as that Thyestes seduced his brother Atreus's wife, that Atreus later married Thyestes's daughter (his own niece), who however was also raped by her own father, and had a son Aegisthus, who later killed Atreus, his mother's husband. Other heroes, Achilles in particular, fare little better.

Throughout the book there runs a strain of open hostility to the Greeks. How did this curious attitude arise? Was it a bee that buzzed only in Loën's bonnet? or was it common to his generation and country? There is no evidence that Loën was an original thinker, but plenty that he was, in this hostility to the Greeks, repeating ideas that were the common stock of his contemporaries' thought. All the fashionable tendencies in the first half of the eighteenth century combined to make men despise and oppose the Greek tradition in culture. We have already seen how in a general way Pietism and Rationalism worked to eliminate Greek influence from German education; their effect was no less potent in later life. Specific hostility to the ancients was fostered by influences that came to Germany from France. Many of the slanderous charges which Loën makes against the Greek heroes can be traced directly to Bayle's Dictionary, the importance of which as a moulder of thought in Germany as in France cannot be overestimated. To discredit the Greeks was apparently one cardinal point in Bayle's scheme of propaganda. He was glad to repeat and enlarge on any unsavoury story (Achilles's lasciviousness was a favourite theme),[1] however badly authenticated or little known. Yet when it suited his purpose Bayle would take almost excessive precautions in weighing and comparing sources.

In France, for seventy years before Loën's handbook of mythology was published, the problem of the authority and excellence of the ancient writers and artists had been exercising men's minds so vigorously, that the controversy between the partisans of antiquity and modernism had become famous as the "Querelle des anciens et des modernes". In Germany there had been no open quarrel; but men like Loën knew the writings of the protagonists on both sides (Loën mentions the Abbé Terrasson and Boivin), and, as Montgomery says,[2] every educated German in the eighteenth century must have been led back to the *Querelle* by a dozen different paths. In France the moderns had on the whole the better of the battle; at least the many found it easier to follow their arguments than those of the defenders of Greece and Rome.[3] In Germany sentiment was probably even more decidedly modernist, since ignorance of the ancient literatures was more complete there than in France.[4]

---

[1] See article on Achilles, Notes L, O, P.
[2] *Friederich Hölderlin and the German Neo-Hellenic Movement*, p. 115.
[3] For a full account of the *Querelle* see Rigault, *Histoire de la querelle des anciens et des modernes*, Paris, 1856.
[4] Cf. Rigault, *op. cit.* p. 207.

The moderns were rationalists, and they believed in the steady progress of the human race from crude beginnings to ultimate perfection. Their rationalism made them incapable of appreciating poetry. Fontenelle, La Motte and Terrasson, three champions of modernism, all asserted on different occasions that poetry had no function which could not be performed equally well by prose.[1] Perrault, another modern stalwart, made fun of Homer's similes for their irrelevant detail, and called them "comparaisons à longue queue". La Motte took practical steps to remove this blemish from the Father of Poetry, and succeeded so well that his improved translation of the *Iliad* consisted of twelve books instead of twenty-four. He was most proud of having improved the Shield of Achilles. In a society where such an attitude to poetry was customary, no true appreciation of the Greek spirit was possible.

The doctrine of continual progress might have been expected to produce a certain modesty in those who held it, when they considered the long road that still lay before man and the short road that he had already travelled; but the men and women of Versailles and Paris had an inkling that the human race, at least in their part of the world, was not very far from its goal, and that for practical purposes their way of living and their standards of taste could be taken as perfection. In Homer's day, then, humanity was in its barbarous adolescence. "Les mœurs d'Homère semblent ridicules par rapport à celles du temps où nous sommes," wrote Perrault;[2] "comme de voir des héros qui font eux-mêmes leur cuisine, et des princesses qui vont laver la lessive." Kings and nobles who could lose their tempers with each other in public were no fit subject for poetry. Achilles and Agamemnon were, alas! not *honnêtes hommes*. The Versailles code of taste was applied to Homer also in such matters as the use of *mots bas*. Perrault rebuked him for having used "ass" and "swineherd".

The writings of the moderns were known in Germany, and their opinions probably found wide acceptance. Yet the views of Boileau, champion of the ancients in France, also commanded great respect even in Goethe's student days, and their influence

[1] Fontenelle in *Réflexions sur la poétique*; La Motte in *Observations sur l'ode de la Faye*; Terrasson in *Dissertation sur l'iliade*.
[2] *Parallèles des anciens et des modernes*, p. 47.

had been reinforced in the middle of the century by the efforts
of Boileau's disciple Gottsched. Nevertheless, a revival of love
for Greek poetry could not come through Boileau and Gottsched. Boileau knew the ancient writers well and admired
them passionately. But he was a child of his age. He could
not judge the Greeks by their own standards,[1] and was forced
at times to attempt a lame reconciliation between Homer's
practice and the conventions of Versailles. His defence of
Homer's use of *mots bas*[2] shows this weakness most clearly.
By his vigorous recommendation of the ancients as models of
form, Boileau was able to maintain them in a position of distant
reverence; but he did not help any enquiring spirit to understand the real nature of their excellence. Gottsched's influence
was even more sterile. He repeated Boileau's recommendations to formal imitation, but his words lacked conviction, for
he was largely ignorant of the works he commended,[3] and did
not appreciate even those he knew. He was a rationalist
through and through, and repeated with approval all Terrasson's
criticisms of the Shield of Achilles.

All that Gottsched's influence could accomplish was to encourage the Gleims and Götzes to imitation of the Anacreontic
form in the German language. German literature may have
benefited from these technical exercises in lightness and flexi-
bility; but the Anacreontic of the 1740's and 1750's did nothing
to help the deeper understanding of Greek poetry. It made
popular an utterly false picture of Greek life, according to
which the Greeks spent their days, and especially their nights,
reclining flower-wreathed around the convivial board, in endless flirtation with easy-kissing girls. This view of the Greeks,
which made of them the idealisation of rococo manners, found
fullest expression in Wieland's *Agathon*[4] (1766) and *die Grazien*
(1769).

The real revival could only come when men could again
appreciate the irrational basis of poetry and art. The first critic
of German race to show such appreciation was Breitinger, the

---

[1] Lanson, *Histoire de la littérature française*, p. 599.
[2] In the *Réflexions critiques sur Longin*. Réflexion IX.
[3] Cf. his *Critische Dichtkunst*, Part II, ch. 10.
[4] See especially the scene in Hippias's garden, Book V, ch. 3.

Swiss. In his *Critische Abhandlung von der Natur, den Absichten und dem Gebrauch der Gleichnisse*, published at Zürich in 1740, he defended Homer against Perrault's attack on the "long-tailed similes", and his reasons show that he knew what poetry is. As an example of a simile which is beautiful because of its irrelevance, he quotes Homer's comparison of the Trojan camp-fires to stars shining on a windless night over the mountains and glades, "and the shepherd joyeth in his heart";[1] and exclaims with naïve delight: "This simile changes the earth at a stroke into a starry heaven." The defeat of rationalistic standards of criticism was announced in these words of Breitinger. It was only a question of time before Herder should come and give the quietus to the Cartesian hydra.

About 1740, also, a book began to have great influence in Germany, which was to prepare the way for the emancipation of the Homeric heroes from the narrow bands of the Versailles code of manners. This book was Fénelon's *Télémaque*. It had been published in 1699, but the world was then not ready to hear its message of a morality based on simplicity of heart. Montgomery assesses its influence as beginning in Germany about 1730 and reaching its peak between 1750 and 1780.[2] To us the picture of the Homeric world which Fénelon gives, seems in many respects curiously un-Homeric. The author's moral-didactic object is very clear throughout, and the standard of conduct recommended is in many ways that of Versailles. But this was precisely the secret of *Télémaque's* success as mediator between Homer and the eighteenth century.[3] It accustomed the public to think of the heroes as being *honnêtes hommes* and not at all such monsters of barbarism as the moderns made them out to be. When once the prejudice which the moderns had spread abroad had been removed, it was easy for the coming generation to look at the Greek heroes objectively and admire them for their true qualities.

In some ways Fénelon preferred Homer's manners to those of his own day. Sixty years before Werther, in his *Lettre à l'Académie* (1714), he wrote that "le bon homme" Eumaeus touched him more than the heroes of contemporary literature, and asked whether Nausicaa did not spend her time more

---

[1] *Iliad*, VIII, 554 fol.   [2] *Op. cit.* pp. 132, 143.
[3] Montgomery, *op. cit.* pp. 132, 135.

profitably washing her brothers' shirts, than the ladies of the day with their cards and their intrigues. It was this simple sincerity in Homeric manners which made him choose Homer's world as the setting of his pedagogic novel. He condemned the fierceness and unbridled passion of the heroes of the *Iliad*, but he could not help admiring them as splendid products of the poet's mind. Achilles was sent on earth as a scourge of God, to punish men for their crimes; but of his death Fénelon wrote with tender sadness: "Les parques ont accourci le fil de ses jours; il a été comme une fleur à peine éclose que le tranchant de la charrue coupe, et qui tombe avant la fin du jour où l'on l'avait vu naître."[1] Such words did what could be done to counteract Bayle's foolish slanders.

Quickly now, in the late 'forties and early 'fifties of the eighteenth century, hostility of the general public towards the Greeks was breaking down, and changing into admiration and a longing to know more. Lessing's early critical writings contain remarkably little reference to Greek literature. One significant passage occurs in the *Critische Nachrichten auf das Jahr 1751*, in which he accuses the Cartesians of having destroyed poetry by their rationalism, and points out that it is absurd to judge Homer as though he were a proposition in Euclid.[2] Apart from that Lessing planned in his *Beiträge zur Historie und Aufnahme des Theaters* (1750) to translate and comment on dramatic works of all ancient and modern literature, and especially of the Attic tragedy.[3] It is probable that at that date his commendation of Sophocles and Euripides would have been on Gottschedian lines though sincere enough. Anyhow, the plan was never realised. For fifteen years after Breitinger's *Abhandlung*, no work was published which gives us evidence of the change in public opinion towards the Greeks. *Télémaque* was at work during this period, and the critical writings of Batteaux were helping to restore the Greeks to favour.[4] Then in 1755 Winckelmann's *Gedanken über die Nachahmung der Griechen in der Malerei und Bildhauerkunst* appeared, and were

[1] *Télémaque*, Book 14; *Œuvres*, 1820, xx, p. 398.
[2] Lessing, *Werke*, iv, p. 52.
[3] *Ibid.* p. 217.
[4] Montgomery, *op. cit.* pp. 152–7. Especially Batteaux's *Principes de la littérature* (1747–1750).

received by the educated public with enthusiastic approval.[1]
Gottsched and the other leaders of the older generation might
dub Winckelmann a dreamer; the rising generation felt that
he had given them the lead for which they had been waiting.
In the *Gedanken* there is no breath of compromise with the
standards of Versailles or with any of the prevailing moral or
aesthetic fashions. In life and in art the Greeks and the Greeks
alone are Winckelmann's inspiration. In their minds and in
their bodies the Greeks were "the most perfect creations of
Nature", for "in Greece, where man could devote himself to
joy and delight from youth up, and where the bourgeois respectability of to-day never interfered with the freedom of
manners, natural beauty could show itself undisguised, to the
great advantage of the artists".[2] Out of this perfect existence
had grown Greek art, which was for Winckelmann not merely
a better representation of Nature than modern art, but the
absolute ideal, to approach which should be the sole striving
of every artist. "Those who know and imitate Greek works
find in these masterpieces not only Nature at its best, but something more than Nature, namely certain ideal beauties formed
from pictures created only in the mind of the artist."[3] "Hence
the study of Nature must at any rate be a longer and more
toilsome road to the knowledge of perfect beauty, than the
study of the antique."[4] Upon this assumption of the ideal
perfection of Greek art Winckelmann based his challenging ex-
hortation: "The only way for us to be great, ay, if it may be,
inimitable, is the imitation of the ancients."[5] The *Gedanken*
gave the lie direct to the moderns and all the detractors of the
Greeks from Comenius to Loën. Yet the essay was greeted with

[1] Justi, *op. cit.* I, pp. 351, 389 fol.; and Baumecker, *Winckelmann in seinen
Dresdener Schriften*, Berlin, 1933.
[2] *Werke*, I, p. 13: "In Griechenland aber, wo man sich der Lust und
Freude von Jugend auf weihete, wo ein gewisser heutiger bürgerlicher
Wohlstand der Freiheit der Sitten niemals Eintrag getan, da zeigte sich die
schöne Natur unverhüllet zum grossen Unterricht der Künstler."
[3] *Ibid.* p. 8: "Die Kenner und Nachahmer der griechischen Werke
finden in ihren Meisterstücken nicht allein die schönste Natur, sondern noch
mehr als Natur, das ist, gewisse idealische Schönheiten derselben, die von
Bildern bloss im Verstande entworfen, gemacht sind." Cf. p. 16.
[4] *Ibid.* p. 20.
[5] *Ibid.* p. 7: "Der einzige Weg für uns gross, ja, wenn es möglich ist,
unnachahmlich zu werden, ist die Nachahmung der Alten."

delight by the general public; Winckelmann became famous overnight; and the cultured *élite* of Germany eagerly awaited his next pronouncements from Rome. The long night of hostility and ignorance was over. With the decay of rationalism and the spread of classical knowledge the time had come when men would again seek inspiration and guidance from the achievements and example of the Greeks.

In Goethe's boyhood enthusiasm for the Greeks was commoner than a sound knowledge of their literature and art. We may safely assume that, before he went to Leipzig, Goethe came in contact with no one who knew as much about Greece as a sixth-form boy on the classical side in any English public school to-day. Still less can intelligent conversation on classical subjects have been customary among his father's circle in Frankfurt. But even in Frankfurt, in spite of the presence of men like Loën, there were probably some who sniffed the fresh breeze from the Aegean; and from them the boy Goethe may have learned the fashion of the new enthusiasm. But he would have sought the Greeks in any case, for there was something in his nature which drew him to them.[1] This affinity was part of his "geprägte Form". The world in which he grew up, his environment, was ignorant of the Greeks but ready to believe the best of them. Whatever picture of the Greeks his innate sympathy with them might paint for him, the world would influence it little, either by malicious distortion or by cramping knowledge. Goethe was born at exactly the right moment for the development of an ideal, not an historical, view of the Greeks. Born twenty years before, he would have had to fight against the modernist prejudice, and in the heat of battle his glance would have lacked the serenity which in fact carried it so deep into the nature of the Hellenic tradition. Born twenty, even ten years later, he would, with his opportunities, have known so much about the Greeks that he could hardly have seen in them ideal creatures raised above the accidents of time and space.

[1] Cf. *Wilhelm Meister*, Book I, ch. 7, WA. 21, p. 32.

B. CHILDHOOD (1749-1765)

In Goethe's earliest years Germany was awakening again to the meaning of the Greek tradition in Western culture. When Goethe was six, Gesner had been teaching at Göttingen for twenty-one years; Breitinger's *Abhandlung über die Gleichnisse* was fifteen years in print; *Télémaque*, in German or French, was coming to the height of its popularity; and Winckelmann published his *Gedanken*.

In the family on the Hirschgraben there was no tradition of interest in Greek things. The father's library contained, as Goethe says in *Dichtung und Wahrheit*, the Dutch editions of the Latin authors, books about Roman antiquities and lexicons of many languages.[1] Johann Kaspar had probably learnt some Greek at the Coburg Gymnasium,[2] and perhaps had a smattering still at his command. But his education had fallen in the lean years,[3] and it had left with him no love of Greek literature. On the other hand he had no hostility to the Greeks or to antiquity in general. Goethe was started on the Greek language in his ninth year and at ten or eleven he knew the Greek and Latin mythology as well as any modern boy of the same age. Among the father's pictures were scenes from Ovid painted by the elder Tischbein.[4] One of the chief objectives of Johann Kaspar's journey to Italy in 1740 had been to see the remnants of ancient culture. To stand before Virgil's tomb on the hill of Posilipo moved him, he said, more than to be in the presence of martyr's bones. Yet the Laocoön, the Apollo and the other works of Greek art in Rome drew from him little comment.[5] The Herr Rat disliked rhymeless verse in German poetry,[6] but

[1] When this library was sold at the Herr Rat's death in 1782, it had amongst its 1670 volumes Erasmus's Latin translation of Euripides's *Hecuba* and *Iphigenia in Aulis*; a complete Xenophon; the *Batrachomyomachia*, Greek and Latin, 1518, and a Greek-Latin Lexicon, 1652. See *Jahrbuch des freien deutschen Hochstifts*, 1927, pp. 363–82.

[2] *Goethes Vater*, by Rudolf Glaser, Leipzig, 1929, p. 10.

[3] He entered the Gymnasium in 1725.

[4] Hering, *Einfluss des klassischen Altertums auf den Bildungsgang des jungen Goethe*, Frankfurt-am-Main, 1902.

[5] Glaser, *op. cit.* pp. 18, 88, 105, who quotes from the father's diary.

[6] WA. 26, p. 122.

it does not follow that he rejected ancient poetry owing to the
lack of rhyme. Again, though he would not allow Goethe to
study the ancients under Heyne at Göttingen, he showed
thereby only indifference to classical studies, as an unessential,
though perhaps pleasant, ornament to life, not hostility to them
as to something bad in itself. He had above all, not so deep
down below the cold exterior, that glowing picture, tinged
ever more golden as the years passed with the sense of
its goneness, with distance and with inarticulate longing—the
picture of Italy. Italy is indeed not Greece, Rome was never
Athens. We know this well enough. Yet even to our senses
there is a kinship, a quality in both that sets them apart from
our sad transalpine world. Rome and Greece were never
clearly separate in Goethe's feelings, however well his intellect
came in time to realise their difference; and it is not fanciful
to see in the stories of Italy that the father told his son[1] the
earliest stimulant of Goethe's never-stilled longing for the
ancient civilisations and therewith of his tendency to view the
Greeks ideally not historically.

Wolfgang's first impressions of Greece came to him in the
ancient myths, that lived on vigorously enough, though often
in strange forms, in eighteenth-century Germany. He may
have met them first in the puppet shows of the day. Up till
the middle of the 1750's there were frequent puppet shows in
Frankfurt, and among the titles preserved we find *Die Tragödie
von der rasenden Erzzauberin Medea, Prinzessin aus Kolchis, mit
dem Hanswurst*[2]. Italian troupes gave operas full of gods and
goddesses,[3] but these performances too seem to have ceased
after 1755. In that year and the next the Cur-Bayrisch court
players gave, amongst other things, *Pyrrhus und Andromache*,
Oedipus after Voltaire, J. E. Schlegel's *Orest und Pylades*, and
a *Telemachos*. In 1757 the famous Ackermann troupe gave
Voltaire's *Mérope* and Racine's *Iphigénie*.[4] Goethe must have
been at some, if not all, of these performances. Already in his
sixth and seventh years the names, the deeds and passions of
that heroic race, dead three thousand years, were taking

[1] WA. 26, pp. 17, 47.
[2] *Der junge Goethe und das Frankfurter Theater*, by E. Mentzel, in Festschrift
zu Goethes 150. Geburtstagsfeier, 1899, p. 113.
[3] *Ibid.* p. 133.   [4] *Ibid.* p. 136.

possession of his imagination, were entering into a mind that would one day be great enough to compass their greatness and give them room to live again.

These earliest visual impressions began to be supplemented, around Goethe's eighth birthday, by reading. Ovid's *Metamorphoses*,[1] Boysen's *Acerra*,[2] Pomey and Loën's seventh volume[3] enlarged his knowledge of mythology until it was as complete as it had any need to be. Homer's world he learned first through Loën's translation of the *Iliad* and the German verse translation of *Télémaque*.[4]

Beside mythology Wolfgang's knowledge of ancient history and literature remained slight indeed during these years before the French occupation of Frankfurt (January 1759). In the *Labores Juveniles*, one of Goethe's exercise-books preserved by good fortune and now in the Frankfurt Stadtbibliothek, there are references (in exercises dated March 1758) to Greek and Roman history—to Alexander, Xerxes and the relations of the

[1] At some time during 1756 Goethe started to learn Latin. From November onward he had systematic instruction in Latin from J. G. Scherbius (E. Mentzel, *Goethes Lehrer*, p. 124). By the summer of 1757 he was writing a structurally complex Latin with a wide vocabulary (*Labores Juveniles*, MM. I, p. 34). From then on he could have read Ovid or Virgil or any translation of a Greek text.

[2] WA. 26, p. 50.   [3] See above, p. 6.

[4] WA. 26, pp. 50 and 61. The exact dating of events mentioned in *Dichtung und Wahrheit* must often be a matter of guesswork. Goethe relates events which happened at quite different times, as though they fell together or in close succession. I place the first knowledge of mythology through reading (WA. 26, pp. 49 and 50) not before the summer or autumn of 1757, chiefly for this reason: that as already stated, Goethe could not read Latin easily until well on in 1757. Ovid, Pomey, etc. would till then be closed to him. If he went on to Virgil after finishing the *Iliad*, as recounted in *D. und W.* (WA. 26, p. 62), we must place the discovery of Homer too not before the summer of 1757. Mentzel (*Goethes Lehrer*, p. 109) puts it even in 1758. Against all this is the fact that Goethe relates his first acquaintance with Ovid, Pomey and Loën's translation of the *Iliad* as taking place before the outbreak of the Seven Years' War (Sept. 1756). Pfarrer Starck moreover, at whose house he found the *Iliad* and Loën's mythology, was one of the anti-Frederician party in Frankfurt, and it is possible that the hero-worshipping child gave up visiting his house after the war had been in progress some little time, in which case we might put the discovery of Homer at latest in the winter 1756–1757. None of this, however, seems to me to outweigh the reasons given above, and the inherent unlikelihood of a boy of six, however precocious, being able to read Ovid and Latin textbooks of mythology.

late Macedonian empire to Rome.[1] Perhaps something of
Horace was read with the help of Drollinger's translation.[2]
Before Whitsun 1758[3] falls a Latin exercise which takes us
back to that bigoted saying of Comenius, and to Gesner's
struggle against Christian anti-Hellenism.[4] It is to the effect
that Horace and Cicero, though heathens, were more virtuous
than many Christians, as, too, none was greater than Damon in
friendship, Alexander in generosity, Aristides in justice, Diogenes in self-denial, Socrates in patience, Vespasian in good-
comradeship, and Apelles and Demosthenes in industry.[5]
Nothing in the *Labores Juveniles* indicates a methodical study
of the history or the literature of the ancient world. These
chance references and names suggest rather random glimpses
into a world of great deeds, great virtues and great wickedness,
an historical world not much different from that of the mythology in which the boy was daily finding more splendid food
for his imagination. It did not matter yet that these vivid impressions were often false. He might see the Homeric heroes
in Louis XIV baroque-classical theatre-rig or on horseback in
some classico-medieval style of armament.[6] The fact of importance was that his head was full already of Greek gods and
Greek heroes, and that Hellas was for him at least as rich a
mine of phantasy as ancient Israel.[7]

Goethe tells in *Dichtung und Wahrheit* something of his studies
and accomplishments in the Greek language during his childhood. At much the same point as his first acquaintance with
Ovid and the mythological textbooks he mentions the un-
inspiring effect of Cornelius Nepos and the New Testament
in the private classes which he took with neighbours' children.[8]
This meagre report (which may anyhow refer to a stage of
instruction of three or four years later) is supplemented by the

[1] MM. 1, pp. 39–55.
[2] *Ibid.* p. 23 and VI, p. 3 (Damasippus) and MM. I, p. 28.
[3] See WA. 38, p. 201.   [4] See above, pp. 2 and 3.
[5] MM. I, p. 60.
[6] WA. 26, pp. 61 and 92 (in *Der neue Paris*), and see the illustrations in
H. Bünemann's *Elias Schlegel und Wieland als Bearbeiter Antiker Tragödien*,
Leipzig, 1928.
[7] *Wilhelm Meisters Theatralische Sendung*, WA. 51, p. 27.
[8] WA. 26, p. 48.

exercises preserved in the *Labores Juveniles*. The first use by Goethe of Greek script occurs in a Latin exercise of March 1757,[1] where he writes the word Μάρμαρος. It is hardly possible, however, that he was already learning Greek at this date. Fifteen months later he wrote the words καὶ πρὸς τὸν λόγον σοῦ, again in a Latin exercise.[2] The first Greek sentences date from August 1758. His "*Felicitationes matutinae singulis diebus per totum Augustum 1758 excogitatae et patri carissimo apprecatae*"[2] are thirty-one sentences (four in Greek) of good wishes to his father. In the Greek he did not venture far from land: ἀγαθὴ καὶ καλὴ ἡ ἥμερα ἡ (for ᾖ. Iotas subscript are rare throughout the Greek exercises in the *Labores Juveniles*) and χαῖρε καὶ ευτυχωσ εχε are the most ambitious efforts.[3] Nevertheless it is delightful, and pathetic too, to see the eager child inventing ways of his own to have fun with the strange new language, in spite of all the unimaginative methods of his teacher. The "*Novae Salutationes matutinae*", that follow immediately in Morris, show a considerable advance in grammar and vocabulary, though they are not free of mistakes. Ἐυχομαι, ἵνα διάγη ἀυτην ἡμεραν ἐν ελπίδα καὶ δυνάμει τοῦ πνεύματος ἀγίου is a typical example. These sentences are undated, but may be placed in the autumn or early winter of 1758.

The Greek translations from German, begun in January 1759,[4] provide the fullest material for judging Goethe's proficiency in Greek at this early period. The passages set are all religious or biblical in subject, syntactically simple, but demanding a fairly large vocabulary. Here is a typical sentence in Goethe's Greek: τοῦ δὲ χριστοῦ εἰσελθόντος ἐκ τῶν μαδιτῶν (= μαθητῶν) δύο ἀπέστειλεν ἵνα πορευομενοι, ἐν τῇ κώμη δεδομενην ὄνον καὶ πῶλον λύοντες αὐτῶ ἀγώσι τοῦτο καὶ οἱ μαθιταὶ εποίησαι.

The wrongly used genitive absolute at the beginning may serve as proof of what Goethe says himself in *Dichtung und Wahrheit*,[5] that he learned by ear rather than by grammatical rules.

---

[1] MM. I, p. 12.   [2] *Ibid.* p. 60.

[3] I reproduce the Greek exactly as Goethe wrote it with all grammar and spelling mistakes.

[4] MM. I, pp. 65-71.   [5] WA. 26, p. 46.

On New Year's Day, 1759, Frankfurt was occupied by the French, and at the end of April the French theatre was opened. There is little direct evidence of the performance of plays with mythological subjects. Mentzel[1] gives only *Le Mercur galant*, 26 May 1759, and Goethe says that the great tragedians were seldom given.[2] But a certain modernised misuse of the old myths was popular. "Half mythological, half allegorical pieces in Piron's style", Goethe calls them. "The golden winglets of a gay Mercury, the thunderbolt of Jove in disguise, a gallant Danae or however a fair one visited by gods might be called, when it was not actually a shepherdess or huntress to whom they condescended."[3] These were the oft-repeated motives. Perhaps because they represented a new way of using the old tales that were ringing in his head, young Wolfgang was much attracted by them and set to work to concoct a piece of his own,[4] full of princes and princesses, gods and goddesses, among whom Mercury stood out in his mind with an almost corporeal vividness. The French theatre certainly distorted his conception of the Greeks, at a time when he was first coming to be conscious of them as a distinct influence in the culture of the modern world; but it may have done good as well as harm by showing him that the old myths were not dead but could be made as new and as entertaining as any subject drawn from contemporary life.

Though he may have seen few of the French classical tragedies on the stage, he read all of Racine's and most of Corneille's works during his twelfth year.[5] At the same time he plunged into the tangled problem of the Three Unities, reading in particular Corneille's *Discours des trois unités*, and presumably also the *Discours de la tragédie*. Goethe's attitude to the Unities as rules of composition, at this time or at any other, is of no consequence to our present enquiry; but in those days the Unities were inseparably bound up with the question of the authority of the ancients in the theory and practice of playwriting. The Unities were derived from Aristotle's *Poetics*, and Aristotle had based his theories on the whole corpus of the Attic tragedy. Thus through the un-

---

[1] *Goethe und das Frankfurter Theater*, p. 143.   [2] WA. 26, p. 142.
[3] *Ibid.* p. 167.
[4] Probably in 1760; see *Ibid.* p. 352.   [5] *Ibid.* pp. 171–352.

believable reverence in which Aristotle's opinions were held, the Attic tragedy became, in theory at least, the canon for all dramatic composition. "The ancients", by which on exact definition only the Greek tragedians could be meant, hovered above the world of drama like deities, ready to annihilate with thunderbolts anyone who transgressed the laws they had seen fit to establish. Like all the more formidable deities, they were little known to the majority of their worshippers. Probably Goethe became aware of the ancients in this capacity through his interest in the French theatre, in particular after having himself been laid low by canonic thunderbolts from the mouth of his friend Derones.[1] His study of Corneille's theoretical writings can only have confused him strangely. For though the Attic tragedians are referred to in a general way with the reverence due to divine beings, in particular questions of practice Corneille is always ready to uphold his own methods as better than theirs. He boasts of inventing rules that are contrary to ancient usage,[2] he strongly condemns Euripides's use of the *deus ex machina*, disapproves of dividing the acts by choruses and of giving no stage directions, and is full of contempt for the frequent violations of *vraisemblance* in Euripides and Aeschylus.[3] Even Aristotle's taste can be improved on.[4] Yet with all this the unspoken assumption is that the ancient tragedians and Aristotle represent a norm or absolute standard, which must always be kept in mind, although particular changes in both theory and practice are allowable. Corneille's attitude is perhaps not so irrational; later in his life Goethe might have made an eloquent defence of it. But at the age of twelve he saw nothing but the contradictions.[5] To set the ancients up as canons clearly led to difficulties; but that might not be the fault of the ancients. It is probable that his study of Corneille first aroused in him the desire to discover "ces grands génies de l'antiquité" for himself, a desire which became ever

[1] WA. 26, p. 169.
[2] *Discours des trois unités*, Corneille Œuvres, ed. Marty-Laveaux, 1862, I, p. 101.
[3] *Ibid.* pp. 106, 107, 110, 112.
[4] *Ibid.* p. 67, in *Discours de la tragédie*. For this conflict between theory and practice in the French classical drama see Bünemann, *op. cit.* pp. 7, 8, 13, 20.   [5] WA. 26, p. 170.

more insistent during the following years, but which was to wait long for its fulfilment.

In 1762 the Ackermann troupe was again in Frankfurt and played Racine's *Iphigénie*, Crébillon's *Atreus und Thyest* and Elias Schlegel's *Orest und Pylades*.[1] Goethe was now well acquainted with the style of French adaptations of the Greek myths. Yet when the French tragedy inspired him to imitation, it was a biblical subject, not a Greek, that he chose in the story of Belshazzar's feast. It can hardly be that he avoided the Greek subjects owing to some half-conscious realisation that the French classical tragedy was very far from being a true reproduction of the Greek models it pretended to admire. He probably assumed, with most of his contemporaries, that Aristotle's rules contained the essence of Greek tragedy and that Corneille and his followers had recreated the Attic theatre.[2] Goethe could not compare Corneille and Elias Schlegel with the Greeks, for he had never read a Greek tragedy. His eyes cannot have been opened on this subject until, as a student at Leipzig, he read Lessing's *Hamburgische Dramaturgie*.[3]

It is hard to tell how Goethe's studies of the Greek language progressed during the years of French occupation (1759–February 1763). Instruction in the New Testament was apparently continued with some regularity: after church on Sundays passages from the Gospels or Epistles were translated and expounded.[4] New Testament Greek presented by now no difficulties, but there is no indication that any classical author was attempted. The first delight in the new language (Wolfgang was a quick pupil)[5] was allowed by his teachers to die out; no new fuel, only the "repetitious"[6] religious instruction, was given to the flickering flame; the glorious store of Greek literature, that could with proper guidance have led

---

[1] E. Mentzel, *Goethe und das Frankfurter Theater*, pp. 145, 147.
[2] Bünemann, *op. cit.* p. 13.
[3] Lessing, *Werke*, IX, pp. 377 foll. *Hamburgische Dramaturgie*, 46. Stück, also pp. 385, 389, 391, and X, pp. 98, 105, 130 and elsewhere. Lessing had in the *Literaturbriefe* already pointed out Corneille's failure to imitate the ancients (17. Br. III, p. 43), but it is unlikely that Goethe read them before he went to Leipzig (see *G-J.* I, p. 19).
[4] WA. 26, p. 197.   [5] Mentzel, *Goethes Lehrer*, p. 129.
[6] "Trivial gewordene."

him on from stage to stage to high accomplishment, was left unused. As before in the earliest beginnings, so now the boy invented his own ways of making the language a living thing.[1] He composed a novel in letters as from six or seven brothers and sisters living scattered in different parts of the world. Each wrote in the language of his country of residence. One brother, a theological student, wrote in Latin and added from time to time a Greek postscript.[2] This is clear enough evidence that Greek was the Cinderella of the many languages that jostled each other in young Wolfgang's head. Through Dr Albrecht, from whom he learnt Hebrew, he may have come in contact with Lucian's works;[3] this is apparently the only chance he could have had to read a Greek more nearly Attic than the dialect of the New Testament.

The spring of 1764 brought a flood of new impressions to the fourteen-year-old boy—visual in the festivities of Joseph II's coronation, emotional in the joys of a first love-affair and the turmoils of its unhappy end. As the storm passed, Goethe found himself deep in philosophical discussions with the young man who had been set to guide the shaken spirit back to health.[4] To provide himself with facts from which to argue, he flung himself into the history of philosophy. The earliest teachers of all, those philosophers, poets and moralists in one, appealed to him most strongly; the names of Orpheus and Hesiod stood high in reverence along with Job and Solomon. But as soon as philosophy cut loose from poetry and religion and became a science apart, the boy, foreshadowing truly the instincts of the man, was at a loss and sought in vain for meaning. Only Socrates of the Greek philosophers before Zeno struck any spark in him, and he not for his doctrines but for his Christlike life and noble end.[5] Aristotle and Plato he passed

---

[1] WA. 53, p. 382: "Romane in mehreren Sprachen, statt der Exercitien."
[2] WA. 26, p. 197. The date of the *Roman in mehreren Sprachen* is accepted as being 1760 (see Gräf, *Epos*, I, p. 281).
[3] *Ibid.* p. 199.
[4] For the account which follows, of Goethe's study of Greek philosophy, see WA. 27, pp. 11, 12, 382.
[5] In Klopstock's *Messias*, Gesang VII, pp. 394–437, Socrates appears in a dream to Portia and acknowledges Christ as a greater and higher spirit than himself. Goethe had known the *Messias* since 1758.

by unmoved, to fasten then with admiration on the Stoic rule of life (not on its metaphysic). He read Epictetus with some determination despite the friend's remonstrances. This disapproval was doubled when Goethe turned with even greater concentration and energy to Plotinus and Neo-Platonism. He struggled with the *Enneads* in the Greek (a hard task even for a good Greek scholar), got help from a Latin translation, thought he understood, doubted, struggled on and finally gave up.

The textbook that Goethe used for his study of the history of philosophy was, he tells us, "der kleine Brucker", the one-volume adaptation of the great *Historia Philosophiae* by J. J. Brucker.[1] Brucker traces the origins of philosophy from the earliest myths. With an understanding unusual for his day he saw that the myths were parables, in which the earliest teachers had clothed their moral and philosophical wisdom. This idea, that foreshadowed Herder's inspiring teaching of the late 'sixties and 'seventies, was too advanced for Goethe at this early age. At least he could not yet realise what were its implications for the modern poet who wished to use the Greek mythological figures; for many years to come he used the myths merely as ornament, not as they had originally been used, and as he used them later himself, as symbols.

In his account of these philosophical studies in *Dichtung und Wahrheit* Goethe speaks of "the poetry of Orpheus and Hesiod" in a way that suggests he had read something of them at the time. This is intrinsically unlikely, and a glance at Brucker shows the assumption to be unnecessary. Goethe could have learned quite enough from Brucker to make him feel familiar with the nature, content and even form of the works attributed to these poets. Brucker devotes four pages to Orpheus, of which two give an account of his theology and cosmogony. A list of the works included under his name is given. He is said to have introduced from Egypt into Greece "eruditionem, initiationes, theologiam, poesin, melodias" and "excellentissima canendi peritia rudem turbam cicurasse".[2] This exactly corresponds with young Goethe's conception of him as given in *Dichtung und Wahrheit*. Hesiod is less fully

---

[1] Leipzig, 1742–1744. The shortened version is called: *Institutiones Historiae Philosophicae usui academicae juventutis adornatae*, 1747.

[2] *Institutiones Historiae Philosophicae*, p. 85.

treated than Orpheus, but details of his poetry and his ideas are given, and his *Works and Days* are spoken of with admiration. A study of the rest of Brucker's volume provides a useful commentary on Goethe's description of his own opinion of the different philosophies. Socrates's character is described with enthusiasm: "...et laboris patientissimus, supra fidem frugalis, paucisque contentus, religiosus, temperans, prudens, verbo vir: qualis posset esse optimus et felicissimus." A curious discussion of his "genius" ends with the unrationalistic conclusion: "Hoc negari non posse videtur, habuisse Socratem facultatem quandam praesentientem et divinantem praeternaturalem, quocunque demum ex fonte ea provenerit." A short account of his trial and death and a list of his disciples are given. Both Plato and Aristotle receive extensive treatment, but both are sharply criticised for the obscurity of their method of exposition. In the controversies with the friend Goethe evidently based his dislike of Plato and Aristotle on what he had read in Brucker. He did not know Plato the delightful scene-painter and witty dialoguist, nor Plato the poet of myths and parables.

So far Goethe had followed Brucker in each case, or rather Brucker had supplied the boy with just the material he wanted for the support of his instinctive likes and dislikes. Over the Stoics and Plotinus, however, young poet and old historian disagree. Brucker disapproves of the Stoics and warns his readers not to be led by splendid words and promises to believe in a philosophy "impiam in ipso sinu et detestabilem". Plotinus, the founder of the Neo-Platonic philosophy, is thought worthy of only two pages, and his doctrine is dismissed in the following sentence: "facile autem obscuritate Plotinus vincit omnes".

Perhaps in the autumn and winter of 1764, perhaps in the summer of 1765, shortly before his departure for Leipzig, Goethe made an effort to gain a general view of ancient literature, as with Brucker's help he had of ancient philosophy.[1] In

---

[1] WA. 27, pp. 38, 39, 382. Again there is an insoluble vagueness in the time-scheme of *D. und W.*, complicated by the existence of two versions of the same passage. In the text, as published, the study of the history of ancient literature is separated altogether from the study of philosophy, and

this subject, however, no such short cut to a superficial learning existed. His Greek, which had perhaps been slipping away from him in the last two years, was too weak to permit a direct attack on the Greek authors. His Latin was good and he read much in it, perhaps even some translations of Greek works.[1] But his aim seems rather to have been to get a general view of ancient literature at second hand, from some textbook of the type of Brucker, and at the same time to make some plan of campaign for improving his knowledge of the ancient languages and then attacking these heights of knowledge and beauty, before which his technical equipment seemed so hopelessly inadequate. He read Gesner's *Isagoge* and Morhof's *Polyhistor*.[2] The latter work conveys little information (Goethe may at most have learnt from it such small facts as that Orpheus introduced mystical teaching and magical practices from Egypt); it concerns itself with the various methods of acquiring and spreading knowledge. Many chapters are devoted to the best ways of running a library. The part that attracted Goethe's attention begins with the ninth chapter of the second part. A description is given of the education of a boy in the ancient languages and literatures. Progress made, authors read in each year, and the best means of stimulating interest are noted. Homer is recommended to be read immediately after the New Testament and Aesop. At the age of fourteen the pupil should have read: the *Iliad* twice, the *Aeneid*, Terence, the *Metamorphoses*, Sallust, one comedy of Plautus and two of Aristophanes and three books of Livy. Goethe was fifteen when he read Morhof and had read no work of Greek literature except the *Iliad* in a bad German translation. We can hardly doubt

is placed just before the departure for Leipzig (Sept. 1765). In a later reworking (WA. 27, p. 382) the same passage follows immediately on the account of the study of Plotinus and leads up to the sentence: "So kam das Frühjahr 1765 heran." The best thing is to compromise and suppose these studies began in the winter of 1764-1765 and continued to the summer of 1765.

[1] WA. 27, p. 39. Most of the Greek authors were to be had in Latin translations by the great scholars of the sixteenth century. There is no means of telling which of these Goethe may have read. We may assume he read Xenophon's *Cyropedeia*, as source for his *Belsazar* (see MM. VI, p. 19).

[2] WA. 27, p. 39.

that he reflected bitterly on the wasted years and determined to make amends without delay—if he could only find out how.[1]

The summer of 1765 was passing. In a few weeks Goethe would be leaving Frankfurt to study for three years at a university. Which was it to be, and what should he study there? His father had decided: he should study law. For this various universities would do equally well; the simplest thing was to send the boy to Leipzig, his own old university. But Wolfgang had other ideas. A legal career did not attract him. He had decided to devote himself to languages, the Classics and history. He would thus fit himself for an academic post, and, while making teaching his life's work, would be able to follow his poetic bent with more success because of a thorough knowledge of antiquity.[2] The most important point in his plan, and at the same time the most difficult to achieve, was the thorough mastery of "die Altertümer". He knew by now that he must have expert help and guidance for this, and he had made up his mind it should be the best that could be got in Germany. He would go to Göttingen, where the classical school founded by J. M. Gesner was yearly winning new distinction under Heyne's energetic and broad-minded direction.[3] But if Wolfgang had made up his mind, so had the Herr Rat: the boy was to study law and he was to go to Leipzig. Open revolt was out of the question and would not have helped. Goethe was forced once more to see the Ithaca of his desire sink below the horizon. But with a determination worthy of Odysseus he did not give up hope because the winds were contrary. To Leipzig he must go, there was no help for it; and he must say that he would study law. But once there, once out of the Earthshaker's view, he could pursue his goal almost as well as

[1] In the chapter, "De Curriculo Academico", Morhof writes: "Primum quidem Graecae Latinaeque linguae diligentior cultura, sine quibus muta ac elinguis pene est omnis doctrina." This corresponds to *D. und W.*, WA. 27, p. 39, lines 10–16, almost literally.

[2] WA. 27, pp. 41–2.

[3] Heyne had been at Göttingen only two years in 1765, and it is unlikely that his personal fame should already have been so great as Goethe makes out in *D. und W.* But there is no reason to doubt that the classical school at Göttingen was already famous throughout Germany.

at Göttingen.[1] There were classical scholars at Leipzig, too; he had heard already of Ernesti and Morus.[2]

So in the beginning of October 1765 he arrived in Leipzig fully determined, as soon as lectures began, to throw himself into the study of ancient literature and history.[3] Unfortunately he confided his intentions to Professor Böhme, his unofficial tutor. A fatal step. The professor was horrified to find the sixteen-year-old boy setting out so shamelessly to deceive his father. He disapproved anyhow of vaguely humanistic studies that had no practical end in view. Gently but with cogent arguments he crushed Wolfgang's hopes and schemes. The professor's earnest and attractive wife finished the good work. Goethe agreed to make law his principal study. For the longed-for knowledge of the ancient cultures he must get on as before with what chance and blind groping might bring in his way.

This silent conflict between Goethe and his father, ending in the victory of authority, was one of the major events of Goethe's life. By tying him to a course of study into which he could not put all his energies, it confirmed the tendency to which his previous education had exposed him—that of dividing his time between a number of ploys and interests, so that he was receptive to all and proficient in none. From our point of view it is most important to consider its effect upon his attitude to Greek civilisation later in life. If he had been permitted to go to Göttingen and to study there as he chose, he could have obtained as thorough a knowledge of Greek literature, art and history as could then be had in Germany. This would have made him more proof against the ideas of his great contemporaries, Winckelmann, Lessing and Herder. He would have had a store of sure knowledge by which to test their theories. His view of the Greeks would have been more historical. They would have been to him men of flesh and blood, whose ideas and ways were the outcome of the time and place in which they lived and had no absolute value for other

---

[1] There is no other source but *D. und W.* for the account of this conflict between father and son. It would no doubt have been dangerous for Goethe to allude to his secret resolve in letters to Cornelia, and no one else was in his confidence. See, however, letter to Cornelia, 12 Oct. 1765 (WA. IV, I, p. 11, lines 7–12).

[2] WA. 27, p. 43.   [3] *Ibid.* p. 50.

times and places. They would have been to him less the eternal ideal of humanity, and therefore less of an inspiration to his poetry and thought. Familiarity would have bred not indeed contempt, but a cool detachment. Had he known the Greeks better, they might have lost half their power over him.

C. LEIPZIG TO HERDER (1765–1770)

Very soon after his arrival in Leipzig, at almost the same time as his decisive interview with Böhme, a wonderful opportunity of bettering his Greek seemed to present itself to Goethe. He met some Greeks at the Fair in the autumn of 1765 and tried to learn Greek from them. But he was soon bewildered to find that the language they spoke had little resemblance to the Greek he knew, particularly in the pronunciation. The attempt to scan ancient Greek verse in accordance with modern Greek accent brought him to despair.[1] This was the first time he had ever tried to read Greek poetry in the Greek. Malicious fate, that he should make the attempt in circumstances that could lead only to confusion and discouragement!

With this second set-back all Goethe's determination to master the Classics seems to have disappeared. He knew the futility of trying to struggle along by himself; he had set all his hopes on being able to take a properly directed course of classical studies; when that plan came to nothing, he decided to make a virtue of necessity, to put the ancients out of his head and to give himself up to the multifarious interests and attractions of the new life. If he had still been determined to learn Greek and study Greek literature, he could have done it well enough. There were three or four men in Leipzig with one or other of whom he could have taken private lessons and acquired a thorough mastery of the Greek language and from that a good knowledge of Greek literature.[2] He actually dined

[1] WA. 27, p. 379.
[2] J. F. Fischer, Ausserordentlicher Professor since 1762, editor of four dialogues of Plato, a fine Greek scholar; F. W. Reiz, Privatdozent 1766, a pure linguist, used to help pupils out of hours; the great scholar and humanist J. J. Reiske, neglected by the university, since 1758 Rektor of the Nikolaischule; S. F. N. Morus, Professor of Greek and Latin, but a theologian rather than a classic (Conrad Bursian, *Geschichte der klassischen Philologie in Deutschland*, 1883, pp. 417–19).

at the same table with Morus for the first winter of his time in Leipzig and "asked him questions about antiquity",[1] but made no use of this acquaintance to begin a methodical study. For the rest of his time at the university he seems to have read no Greek, and we can only assume that his knowledge of the language grew less rather than more. Even that eloquent passage in Winckelmann, in which the Greek language is acclaimed for its sonority and power as the language of the gods, did not rouse him to read his Homer in the Greek.[2]

There are few references to Greek literature in his letters of this period, and of these only one needs attention. In a letter to his sister Cornelia, in August 1767, he tells her he will call his new collection of poems "Annette" after his girl "en dépit de grecs qui avoit donné les noms des neuf muses aux livres d'Hérodote, et de Platon qui nomma ses dialogues de l'immortalité de l'âme Phaedon, qui étoit son ami et n'avoit beaucoup plus de part à ces dialogues, qu'Annette n'a à mes poésies".[3] It was the practice in Goethe's day and before to print Herodotus with each of the nine books named after a muse; Wesseling's folio edition of 1763, with Latin translation beside the Greek, carried these book-headings. Yet Goethe could have learnt of this practice without ever having had Herodotus in his hand (the original attribution of the names to the books is told by Lucian); that he read much of Herodotus at this time is at any rate highly unlikely.

The reference to Plato deserves some consideration. The first thing that attracts attention is that Goethe speaks of "dialogues" in the plural.[4] This seems to show that his knowledge of the *Phaedo* was more from half-remembered hearsay than from first-hand acquaintance. Yet he seems to have known that Phaedo is merely the narrator of the dialogue and plays little part in the discussion. It is not out of the question that

---

[1] WA. 27, p. 65.
[2] Winckelmann, *Werke*, I, pp. 136-7, in the *Erläuterung der Gedanken über die Nachahmung der griechischen Werke*. See also in Lessing's *Laokoon*, XIII, vol. IX, pp. 88, 89.
[3] WA. IV, I, p. 97.
[4] He first wrote "son" but crossed it out and wrote "ses", evidently before he had written any of the rest of the sentence (*Ibid.* p. 272).

he read some or all of the *Phaedo* at this time, though the translation by Köhler, which he later used, was not yet available. Perhaps the question of the ancient conception of Death, which Lessing's *Laokoon* had raised and which captured Goethe's imagination at this time, led him to read this dialogue. Perhaps —but most probably he was trying to impress the idolising sister with chance scraps of knowledge that he had picked up in lectures or at Oeser's or Breitkopf's or at any of the salons in the university city, where a superficial knowledge of Greek literature was common enough.

Apart from this reference there is nothing, in letters, in *Dichtung und Wahrheit*, or in any other source, that can be interpreted as evidence of any reading of Greek authors by Goethe, either in Greek or in translation, during his three years at Leipzig. This is not positive evidence that he read none. As negative evidence the absence of any mention of a thing in the letters alone or in *Dichtung und Wahrheit* alone is not conclusive. For instance, Goethe never refers to Winckelmann in the letters from Leipzig that have come down to us, and in *Dichtung und Wahrheit* he does not mention reading Shakespeare at Leipzig. But we know from *Dichtung und Wahrheit* that he read Winckelmann, and from the letters that he read Shakespeare. When, however, neither the letters nor *Dichtung und Wahrheit* mention Greek reading, when nothing in his poetry suggests a direct knowledge of Greek literature, the negative evidence is as conclusive as it can be.[1]

He studied Gottsched's *Kritische Dichtkunst* while he was at Leipzig,[2] and may have got from it a little information about Greek literature. But this was at best only the old gleaning of withered facts, that he had been at already before he came to Leipzig. The truth is that knowledge of Greek literature was for him at this time chiefly a means to an end. It was to provide him with a "Massstab des Urteils"—a critical yardstick—by which to judge his own poetical works and those of others.[3]

---

[1] Strack's assertion (*Kommentar zu den "Neuen Liedern"*, 1893) that Goethe was acquainted with the Greek Anthology in Leipzig is effectively disposed of by E. Beutler (*Vom griechischen Epigramme im achzehnten Jahrhundert*, 1909, pp. 68–70).

[2] WA. 27, p. 77.

[3] *Ibid.* pp. 64, 42, 77, 80, and *Tag- und Jahreshefte*, WA. 35, p. 3.

It would have been foolish to spend much time and energy on acquiring the means, when the end could be reached as well in other ways. He had as yet no idea what magical effects the reading and knowing of Greek poetry would have produced in his own creative work, not as a dead yardstick, but as an active force.

So long as his knowledge was derived from indirect sources, many fruitful ideas with which he came in contact must have failed to penetrate fully to his understanding. Especially must this have been so with those parts of Lessing's *Hamburgische Dramaturgie* that deal with the Greek tragedy. Lessing is chiefly concerned to show that Greek tragedy and Shakespeare are real tragedy according to Aristotle's definition, while the so-called tragedies of Corneille and Racine and their followers are not tragedies at all. For Sophocles, Euripides and Shakespeare move us emotionally, they purge us with pity and fear, whereas the French pieces do not. Their interest is merely intellectual.[1] This idea is in itself simple enough to grasp, but, since he knew no Greek tragedies,[2] Goethe must still have been in the dark as to the means which the Greeks employed to produce the effects that Lessing admired so much. The fact that he did know something of Shakespeare at first hand may have made him wonder the more. For if those strange pieces could be regarded as conforming to Aristotle's "rules", how strange might not the Greek pieces also be? One thing alone was clear: the French tragedies were nothing to go by. With a true instinct he went behind Lessing to seek enlightenment in Aristotle's *Poetics* (probably in Curtius's Latin translation);[3] but until he could go further back still and read the plays that Aristotle and Lessing were discussing, their conclusions would remain for him words without meaning.

As, sick and dispirited, he was about to leave Leipzig,[4] the old regrets at wasted opportunities revived. He realised that

---

[1] *Werke*, IX, pp. 385–93, 46th–49th Stück, and X, pp. 127 foll., 81st Stück. These appeared in January and April 1768.

[2] By the beginning of 1769 he must have had a fair idea of the content of the *Philoctetes*, for both Lessing in the *Laokoon* and Herder in the first *Kritisches Wäldchen* discussed the play scene by scene.

[3] Letter to Schiller, 6 May 1797 (WA. IV, 12, p. 117).

[4] In Sept. 1768.

the ancients were still only "far, blue hills, clear in mass and outline", but unknown in detail, just as they had been three years before, when he had come to Leipzig with the firm determination to penetrate those hills and know them. In a moment of new resolve he got from his friend Langer a number of Greek authors in exchange for basketfuls of German writers and critics, and promised himself he would turn his convalescence to profitable use by reading them.[1] Yet there is no sign that he did so during the months that followed. Alchemy and cabalism were his study, Nostradamus and Paracelsus his companions; the bodily brightness of the Homeric heroes and the intellectual light of Socratic dialectic were alike far from him in those dark days.[2] Not until the first months of his residence in Strassburg, where he went in April 1770 to continue his legal studies, did he turn his thoughts again to the Greek poets and thinkers. He then read the *Phaedo* and compared it carefully, point by point, with Moses Mendelsohn's adaptation of the same dialogue.[3] Goethe was at this time strongly under the influence of Christian Pietism.[4] He was attracted to the dialogue no doubt by the remarkably Christian attitude to the relation of soul and body which Socrates shows in the early part of the discussion. This study of the *Phaedo* had no connexion with his Socrates drama of eighteen months later. His interest in Socrates was by then quite a different one.

During his first summer in Strassburg the Greek books that he had got from Langer stood imposingly enough on his shelves but were never used.[5] He was still playing with the

[1] WA. 27, p. 191.
[2] In a letter to Langer, 9 Nov. 1768, he speaks of going with him to Göttingen at Easter, perhaps as before to get a thorough grounding in the Classics from Heyne. Again nothing came of the idea. (*Goethes Briefe an E. T. Langer*, p. 10, P. Zimmermann, Wolfenbüttel, 1922.)
[3] *Ephemerides*, WA. 37, pp. 102 foll. The exact dating is uncertain. I place it in June or July of 1770. See WA. 38, p. 226. Other suggestions of an interest in Socrates in the summer of 1770 occur in letters to Trapp, 28 July (WA. IV, I, p. 240): "Nichts weiss ich!", and to Hetzler, jun., 24 Aug. (*Ibid.* p. 244): the use of the word "Mathesin" in its platonic sense. For his study of the *Phaedo* he used the translation by Koehler, Lübeck, 1769 (see WA. 37, p. 104).
[4] See especially letters to Limprecht, 13 April 1770, and to Fräulein Klettenberg, 26 Aug. 1770 (WA. IV, I, pp. 232, 245).
[5] WA. 27, p. 311.

problem of how to begin and finding many reasons for not beginning. In a letter to a young friend (July 1770),[1] who had asked him how he should go about acquiring a knowledge of ancient literature, he mentions Müller's *Einleitung in die klassischen Schriftsteller*,[2] but rejects it as too detailed. There are others but none that he can recommend. The best thing to do is to read the author and afterwards the *Einleitung*. Time and application are needed, for which reason a young man is always at a disadvantage beside an older. Müller's *Einleitung* dealt only with Latin authors, but Goethe continues: "It is just the same with Homer. The English edition with Clarke's translation is dear,[3] the Leipzig pirate edition is said to have many misprints; I cannot judge about that." Does this mean that he had already started reading Homer in the Greek with the help of Clarke's Latin translation? He must at least have been thinking about it and discussing ways and means. But the whole paragraph sounds disheartened, as though accomplishment were still far behind desire. During those summer months in Alsace Goethe was still waiting for the touch that was to wake his sleeping genius and start it on its great career. He was still bound by the feeling of frustration that his illness had left. But his liberators, Herder and Frederike, were at hand. With his genius once freed, there would be no more frustration. Homer and Theocritus, Plato and Pindar would be wrestled with in turn and mastered, as recreation from the intenser labour of production.

The Leipzig years, though barren of any advance in Goethe's knowledge of Greek literature, brought him his first acquaintance with ancient plastic art. Before the end of his three years in Leipzig he was reproducing in his poems traits from what he had seen, and was probably consciously engaged with the problem: What is the essence of Greek art? What was the inviolable law for a Greek artist?

---

[1] WA. IV, 1, p. 239. Even if these letters to Trapp and Hetzler are to fictitious correspondents (see *Ibid.* p. 278), their value as autobiographical evidence is undiminished.

[2] G. E. Müller, *Historisch kritische Einleitung zu nötiger Kenntnis und nützlichem Gebrauch der alten lateinischen Schriftsteller*, 1747–1751.

[3] *Ilias et Odyssea*, gr. et lat., ed. Sam. Clarke, London, 1729–1732.

It was Oeser, the friend and teacher of Winckelmann, endowed with little talent as a painter but with much insight into the nature of beauty, who first encouraged the young student to read what there was to read and see what was to be seen. Already by the Christmas of 1765, Goethe was a regular pupil in his academy[1] and was soon a favourite with the old man and with his family. From him he heard of Caylus's work,[2] and may, within the limits of its usefulness, have learnt something from it. At the academy there were casts of Laocoön (only the central figure) and a faun with cymbals,[3] but nothing else. The faun, the first Greek statue he had ever seen, impressed itself so deeply on his inward eye, that still in his eightieth year he could recall perfectly how it looked and how it stood in Oeser's studio.[4] Oeser also drew his attention to Lippert's *Daktyliothek*.[5] It was this famous collection of casts of ancient gems which enabled Goethe to get his first view of a large body of antique works of art. The majority of the gems were of course of Roman workmanship (or even modern imitations).[6] They gave him, to our ideas, an over-refined, mannered picture of ancient art, but, as he says in *Dichtung und Wahrheit*, he learnt through them to value the ancients' power of happy invention, of apt composition and of tasteful treatment.[7] He may, as Morris suggests,[8] have tried to reproduce some figures and motifs from these gems in his poems, particularly Amor in the *Hochzeitslied* of October 1767. He may from this have gone on to study the question of dates and styles when he undertook to rearrange a collection of gem impressions belonging to the Breitkopf family.[9] The Breitkopfs also possessed "representations of antiquity" in engravings. Were these reproductions of ancient sculpture? If they were they may have given Goethe his first sight of the then most famous statues

[1] Letter to Cornelia, 12 Dec. 1765 (WA. IV, I, p. 30).
[2] WA. 27, p. 160, and see above, p. 5.   [3] WA. 28, p. 87.
[4] WA. 32, p. 324.
[5] See above, p. 6, and WA. 27, pp. 161, 387.
[6] See Justi, *op. cit.* I, p. 342.
[7] WA. 27, p. 161.   [8] MM. VI, p. 70.
[9] WA. 27, p. 179. The Breitkopfs moved house in the autumn of 1766. Goethe's work with the gem impressions may therefore fall any time after this. By position in *D. und W.* it comes after the trip to Dresden in March 1768.

of antiquity—the Apollo Belvedere, the Niobe group, the Farnese Hercules and so on—about which he had heard much talk, without ever having had the chance to see them even in reproduction.

Oeser it was, too, who led him to read Winckelmann's works.[1] Important as this reading was for the development of his ideas, it added little to his knowledge of Greek art. It is almost certain that he read only the three short essays that Winckelmann wrote before he left Dresden.[2] These are rich in ideas rather than in information. The great *Geschichte der Kunst des Altertums*, which gave an historical account based on all the ancient works of art then extant, of the growth, flowering and decay of Greek and Roman art, was probably left unread by Goethe, who preferred at this time to be inspired rather than instructed.[3] Even if he did attempt it, he must quickly have seen that he could learn nothing from it. Not until, twenty years later, he too was living in Rome, surrounded by the statues of which Winckelmann was writing, could he begin to learn from the *Geschichte der Kunst des Altertums*. He even neglected the one opportunity that came to him at Leipzig to see original works of antique sculpture. Three vestals, as they were then held to be, and an Agrippina, which had been brought from Herculaneum, together with some antique reliefs, were to be seen at Dresden, miserably housed and lighted indeed, but still reckoned by Winckelmann to be the most valuable collection of antiques then in Germany.[4] In March 1768 Goethe spent several days in Dresden with the express purpose, so he says in *Dichtung und Wahrheit*, of getting visual material (*Anschauung*) for the ideas with which his head was filled from the reading of Lessing's *Laokoon*. Yet he "declined" to see these antiques, though Winckelmann commended them in the *Gedanken* as "equal to Greek works of the first rank",[5] and spent all his time in the picture-gallery, where

---

[1] WA. 27, p. 161.
[2] *Gedanken über die Nachahmung der Griechischen Werke in der Malerei und Bildhauerkunst*, published in the spring of 1755; *Sendschreiben über die Gedanken* and *Erläuterung der Gedanken*, both written in the summer of the same year and published 1756.   [3] WA. 27, p. 183.
[4] *Werke*, II, p. 405, and Justi, *op. cit.* I, p. 274.
[5] I, p. 27.

he gave his best attention to the Dutch painters.[1] Perhaps he was suffering from another wave of discouragement at the hopelessness of trying to know the Greeks in a land where knowledge of them was so bitter hard to win, and so had decided to find food for his ideas where the supply was plentiful. The sight of four ancient statues and a pair of bas-reliefs would have been an isolated experience more likely to disturb than to help the difficult business of ordering his thoughts. Moreover, he was familiar with the Laocoön figure from the cast of it in Oeser's studio and would have had innumerable opportunities to compare what Winckelmann and Lessing said of it with the work itself. It is probable he went to Dresden to test, and if possible to confirm, ideas of his own about the nature of art as a whole. The problem of the nature of Greek art was not yet of great importance to him.

Back once more in Frankfurt he had no opportunity to add to the small beginnings that his acquaintance with Greek art had made in Leipzig. But he did not cease to ponder the aesthetic questions raised by Winckelmann and Lessing.[2] The fact, however, that he had seen hardly any of the works of these Greek artists, who were continually called to give evidence by both sides, made it hard for him to come to any conclusion. Now, as he sat in Frankfurt, there came to him reports of a collection of casts, many of which had been newly made in Rome, more complete than anything of its kind in Germany, commodiously housed, and so lighted and arranged that every statue could be studied to the best advantage; and all this at Mannheim, within fifty miles of him.[3] In the last days of October 1769 he made an expedition to Mannheim with the purpose, amongst other things, of studying the casts in the Electoral collection. "Entre bien de jolies choses que j'y ai rencontré," he wrote to Langer,[4] "entre bien de magnifiques qui frappent les yeux, rien n'a pu tant attirer tout mon

---

[1] WA. 27, p. 174.

[2] He read Lessing's *Briefe antiquarischen Inhalts*, which deals in part with questions raised by the *Laokoonstreit*, during the winter of 1768–1769 (see letter to Oeser, 14 Feb. 1769, WA. IV, 1, p. 205, and MM. VI, p. 59).

[3] For these and following details of the Mannheimer Antikensaal see J. A. Beringer's article, *G-J.* XXVIII, p. 150–8.

[4] *Goethes Briefe an E. T. Langer.* This letter 30 Nov. 1769.

être que la grouppe de Laocoon, nouvellement moulée sur l'original de Rome. J'en ai été extasié, pour oublier presque toutes les autres statues qui ont été moulées avec elle et qui sont dans la même salle. J'ai fait des remarques sur le Laocoon qui donnent bien de lumière à cette fameuse dispute, dont les combatants sont de bien grands hommes."

If Goethe had any eyes at all for the other statues besides Laocoön and his sons, he must have gone home with as clear a picture of what Greek sculpture was, as was possessed by any young German of his day, for the collection contained casts of twenty of the most famous antique statues,[1] all in fact that were then regarded as of outstanding beauty and importance. There were, it is true, few works of the great period of Greek art among them, hardly any indeed that are not now recognised as being Greco-Roman work. But still from that day on he had in his mind's eye a picture of Greek art, different from that he had gained in Leipzig from Lippert's *Daktyliothek*, and, with all its limitations, more typical.[2]

[1] Beringer gives the following list: Apollo Belvedere, Dying Gladiator, Laocoön group, Castor und Pollux, Farnese Hercules, Farnese Flora, Borghese Gladiator, the Apoxyomenos, Borghese Hermaphrodite, Venus de Medici, Boy with Thorn, the Wrestlers, the Belvedere Torso, the Faun with Cymbals, the Ildefonso Faun, Antinous, a Dying Niobid, Idolino, Amor und Psyche, and heads of: Homer, Niobe, Alexander and Niobe's daughter.

[2] One question of great interest has been raised by the publication of the letter to Langer, quoted above. Before its publication it was assumed that the visit to the Mannheim collection, which Goethe describes in *D. und W.* as taking place on the return journey from Strassburg to Frankfurt—that is in Aug. 1771—was the first visit. It is now clear that this is not so. But the thought cannot help arising: Perhaps the visit of Oct. 1769 was the *only* visit. Perhaps Goethe, writing forty years later, had forgotten the date and circumstances of his visit and laid it in 1771, naturally assuming that he had made it on the way either to or from Strassburg. As evidence of a visit in Aug. 1771, there is the large role played by Apollo—"Pythos tötend"—in *Wandrers Sturmlied* (early spring, 1772), and one sentence in a letter to Herder of late summer or autumn 1771: "Apollo vom Belvedere, warum zeigst du dich uns in deiner Nacktheit..." (WA. IV, I, p. 264, and MM. II, p. 117). There is unfortunately doubt as to the date of this letter. Morris refers it to "Frankfurt, etwa Oct. 1771", in which case it would support the visit of 1771. But the Weimar Ausgabe heads it "Strassburg, Sommer 1771". If this dating is correct, Goethe must, as he was writing, have been thinking back to what he saw in Mannheim in 1769; and there is then no reference to a visit to Mannheim in the letters of the late summer or autumn 1771.

During the winter following his visit to Mannheim he was concerned to put his ideas about Laocoön into essay form. To enlarge his visual knowledge for this work he studied at least one book of reproductions of ancient art, Barbault's *Les plus beaux monumens de Rome ancienne* (1761).[1] The engravings throughout the work are miserably bad, and no attempt is made at critical explanation of the plates, not even to distinguish the Greek works from those of Roman or Etruscan origin. Goethe cannot have been helped by this work either to greater knowledge of Greek art or to a truer conception of it.

Still he felt how little he knew beside what he would like to know. In April of 1770 he wrote to Langer from Strassburg, described the great tapestries woven from cartoons by Raphael, and fell thereby into violent longing for Italy. "To Italy, Langer! To Italy! But not this year; I have not the knowledge that I need; I have still much to make up. Paris shall be my school, Rome my university."[2] He was thinking here of his ignorance both of Greek sculpture and of Renaissance painting.

There were Roman remains in Strassburg and the neighbourhood. The bas-reliefs at Niederbrunn especially aroused his enthusiasm.[3] But in these he was only seeing in the original what such works as Barbault had already shown him in reproduction. Though he might feel himself in their presence "laved by the spirit of antiquity",[4] it was a far cry from them

Moreover, in this letter to Langer, 30 Nov. 1769, Goethe mentions having written to Oeser after the visit to Mannheim in Oct., to tell him of his discoveries on the subject of the Laocoön dispute. This letter to Oeser is mentioned also in *D. und W.*, but of course as having been written after the visit in 1771. It is not likely that Goethe wrote twice to Oeser on this subject, not likely that he would write at all in 1771, when he had ceased to be under the influence of Oeser's aesthetic ideas. If Goethe never visited Mannheim in 1771, but only in 1769, the description in *D. und W.* of the conflict between classical and Gothic art, which the visit aroused in him is *Dichtung* and not *Wahrheit* (WA. 28, p. 87). This is not impossible, especially as it was a conflict that was much in the air at the time Goethe was writing his memoirs (1812). N.B. In one *Schema* to *D. und W.* Book 7 (WA. 27, p. 388) Goethe put down "Mannheimer Sammlung" immediately after "Dresdener Gallerie". This provides evidence neither for nor against a visit in 1771, except in so far as it shows how little Goethe cared about holding to an exact chronological succession in *D. und W.*   [1] WA. 37, p. 90.

[2] *Goethes Briefe an E. T. Langer*, p. 27.   [3] WA. 27, p. 339.

[4] "Umspülte mich der Geist des Altertums."

to genuine Greek art. They could help him little on the long road that was to lead him at last to an understanding of Greek art as profound as it was original.

This much then Goethe had read or had heard of Greek literature, this much he had seen of Greek art, before he met Herder in September 1770. How did this knowledge affect the development of his thought and of his poetical production? What was his attitude towards the Greek tradition, and what picture of the Greeks did he have in his mind, during his three years in Leipzig and the two that followed?

The strongest impression of the ancient world that he took with him to Leipzig was of the myths. The bright figures of gods and heroes continued to people his mind at the university, but they won for him no deeper significance than they had had when, at the age of ten, he filled his *Schäferspiel* with Danaës and Mercuries. Rather they ceased with familiarity to fill him with the strange wonder that they had at first aroused, and became conventional figures, trite personifications whose sole use was to display the young poet's learning and to give a false pictorial quality to verses that would have been better left unadorned. When he had been only a few months at the university, in January 1766, he composed an ode on the occasion of his uncle Textor's wedding and fitted it out with gods and goddesses on the most splendid scale,[1] because, as he says in *Dichtung und Wahrheit*, he could make nothing of the theme by itself. He was partly aware of the absurdity of this way of using mythology and with half his mind was parodying the style, as he wrote. But he was pleased enough with the result; it won serious approval from the family, and he showed it to Professor Clodius, who had already corrected some of his poems. According to Goethe's account in *Dichtung und Wahrheit*[2] Clodius "declared the use and abuse of such mythological figures to be a false, pedantical, old-fashioned habit", and went unsparingly to work with the red ink. Goethe's eyes were fully opened, he discarded the whole mythological Pantheon and from that time on allowed only Amor and Luna to appear in his shorter poems.[3] This account is in some ways hard to reconcile with a closer knowledge of

[1] WA. 27, p. 137.   [2] *Ibid.* p. 138.
[3] *Ibid.* p. 139.

the facts. In the first place Clodius was not opposed to this way of using mythological figures in poetry,[1] and in the second Goethe continued to use the myths just as he had done before. In the *Ode an Herrn Professor Zachariae* (May 1767) and *An Venus* (May 1768) Apollo, Venus, Mercury, Bacchus and the Harpies are used in the old way to give a note of pompous learning—or at best a touch of colour—to otherwise trivial verses. Here indeed the note of parody is unmistakable. It was a foolish game, this praying to gods in whom no one believed, but he could play it as neatly or as pompously as another. He found it amusing, too, to talk of the "Stymphaliden"[2] and wonder how many of his friends would know what he meant. As for the ballad of *Pygmalion*,[3] here is no sign of a desire to breathe new life into the old figures. The miraculous coming-to-life of the statue, which is the kernel of the old story, is rationalised away, and the whole is made to point the moral that a wise man knows how to accommodate himself better than with a wife. This is not revitalising the old myths, but helping to weaken and kill them by using the mythological names as labels in situations where they do not belong. It was a treatment of them that was popular at the time.

When however he was not showing off in his poetry, when he was speaking to a friend from the bitter earnestness of his heart, Goethe could turn to the Greek myths and use them to symbolise his own feelings. His vain love for Käthchen and the sweet, torturing imaginings it aroused, he likened to the torments of Tantalus.[4] These were the first instinctive beginnings of that creative use of the myths, that he later learnt from Herder to practise as an indispensable means of giving poetic expression to the conceptions of his genius.

Despite the fact that at Leipzig his knowledge of Greek literature advanced not at all, that his knowledge of Greek art made only a halting start and that his understanding of the myths

---

[1] See Carl Alt's excellent essay, *G-J.* xxi, pp. 268 foll. He cites Clodius's poem *Das ländliche Fest* (*Neue Vermischte Schriften*, Vierter Teil, p. 235) and *Triumph des flüchtigen Amors* (Versuche, pp. 577–640).

[2] WA. 37, p. 36.

[3] Date: before July 1768, but not before 1767 (MM. vi, p. 36).

[4] Letters to Langer, 8 Sept. 1768, p. 8. See also H. Sudheimer, *Der Genie-begriff des jungen Goethe*, Berlin, 1935, p. 38.

remained superficial, it was at Leipzig that his relation to the Greeks took an important step forward. He became conscious of the complex of problems that centre round the question: What were the Greeks? He had wondered perhaps before Leipzig why the Greeks were generally regarded with such veneration, and had itched to read these canonical books for himself. But until he read Winckelmann's *Gedanken* and then Lessing's *Laokoon* (both probably in the year 1766) he was not brought face to face with the question: What was the essential nature of the Greeks? What was the essence of their art? And what is their importance to us?

The importance at that time of Winckelmann's name and writings to any German who interested himself in the Greeks cannot be exaggerated. Goethe, as Oeser's pupil, was brought into a peculiarly close relationship with the man and his ideas. He tells in *Dichtung und Wahrheit* of the reverence with which he pored over the *Gedanken* and Winckelmann's other early essays,[1] struggling to make sense even of the most enigmatical passages; of the jubilant expectation with which Winckelmann's arrival in Leipzig was awaited in the summer of 1768, and of the crushing dismay that befell their small circle when, instead of the revered master, the news arrived of his tragic and horrible death.[2]

There can be no doubt that Winckelmann's writings, particularly the *Gedanken über die Nachahmung der Griechen*, made a deep impression on Goethe's mind in Leipzig. The capital importance of the Greek element in ancient culture, the correspondingly subordinate and imitative role played by Rome, was here for the first time made clear beyond all chance of doubting.[3] In them, too, he found a different picture of the Greeks from that given by the French classical tragedy, till then his only source for visual impressions. He was shown now the Greece of the palaestra—of beautiful bodies and of the sun, where the mind of the philosopher and the eye of the

[1] WA. 27, pp. 161, 182.

[2] Winckelmann was stabbed to death in Trieste on 8 June 1768, by an Italian named Arcangeli, who coveted some gold medals that Winckelmann had shown him. For a vital description of Winckelmann's last weeks and fateful end see Miss Butler's account in *The Tyranny of Greece over Germany*, Cambridge, 1935, pp. 40–3.

[3] *Werke*, I, pp. 6, 7, and G. Baumecker, *op. cit.* pp. 36, 37.

artist were alike trained on the aspect of beauty: a land where a kindly climate brought all nature to its most perfect development and led on the hearts of men to a natural joyfulness; where beauty was held in esteem above all else, and where no bourgeois respectability hemmed the free and natural outlet of all youthful joys.[1] This picture he got from Winckelmann as a student in Leipzig, and it remained with him throughout his life;[2] later reading and observations, the influence of Lessing and Herder, only developed and added to the picture, they did not change it.

A picture, then, he got from Winckelmann, a living picture with the power in it of growth; but he got nothing else. The central doctrine of the *Gedanken*, the imitation of Greek art in preference to nature, left him unmoved. He continued to draw from Nature, to copy landscapes when he etched, and to prefer naturalistic to ideal art.[3] In August 1767 he tried, at his father's suggestion, to study a book on the proportions of the body,[4] but found it useless. This is the only evidence of any artistic interest in the human body, let alone in the human body as idealised by the Greeks. Had he become in any sense a disciple of Winckelmann he would have tried to apply the master's teaching to his own poetical productions. He would have given up everything to study Greek literature and to reproduce what he found there in his own poems.[5] But, as we have seen, he read no Greek while he was at Leipzig. Nor did he try to carry out Winckelmann's recommendations for the allegorical use of mythology.[6] We have already seen how he used mythological figures in his poetry. He had none of Winckelmann's reverence for them.

[1] Winckelmann, *Werke*, I, pp. 9–15, 134, 138, 172.

[2] Its first visible manifestation is in a letter to Friederike Oeser, 13 Feb. 1769 (WA. IV, I, p. 198): "Unter Deutschlands Eichen wurden keine Nymphen geboren wie unter den Myrten im Tempe." It has here rather an Arcadian-rococo flavour, but the idea of the "glücklichere Natur" of the Greeks is clearly present.

[3] WA. 27, pp. 171, 175, 188. Volbehr, *Goethe und die bildende Kunst*, Leipzig, 1895, p. 85. Eduard Castle, *In Goethes Geist*, Vienna, 1926, realises the limits of Winckelmann's influence on Goethe in Leipzig.

[4] Letter to Cornelia (WA. IV, I, p. 99).

[5] The fact that Goethe wrote "dithyrambs" in his winter in Leipzig (WA. IV, I, p. 33) need not arouse excitement. Gottsched in his *Kritische Dichtkunst*, p. 83, defines a dithyramb as a "satyrisches Gedicht"!

[6] Winckelmann, *Werke*, I, pp. 58, 59, 170, 190, 201.

Winckelmann had defined the essence of Greek art as being "a noble simplicity and a quiet greatness in attitude as in expression".[1] No matter what bodily and mental sufferings might be portrayed, Greek sculpture showed always "a great and restrained soul".[2] So Laocoön, though every muscle of his body shows the agony he suffers, does not allow this agony to express itself unrestrained (*mit Wut*) either in his face or in his attitude. He moans (*ein beklemmtes Seufzen*), he does not scream. Like Sophocles's Philoctetes he bears his sufferings stoically. Only an artist who could himself endure suffering so heroically, could conceive and execute such a work of art. The ancient artists named the immoderate expression of suffering *parenthyrsus* and regarded it as a serious fault.[3] Winckelmann saw the same noble simplicity and quiet greatness in the Greek works of literature of the best period—"the works of Socrates's school".[4]

This famous conception of the Greeks was no better able to strike root in young Goethe's mind than had been Winckelmann's exhortations to imitate the antique. He may have accepted in principle Oeser's and Winckelmann's doctrine that the highest ideal of beauty was simplicity and repose, but he felt he could not follow this rule, and resigned himself to the conclusion that no young man can be a master.[5] Even this partial acceptance seems to have come first in Frankfurt, during the months of brooding after his illness. In the letters from Leipzig there is no reference to Winckelmann or to his aesthetic ideas. The poems written in Leipzig show no attempt to paint noble simplicity or quiet greatness. They are for the most part the erotic day-dreams of a youth of eighteen, recounted with a slippery, Rococo grace. Where the emotions are stirred below the surface, there is no attempt to keep them from finding their

---

[1] *Werke*, I, pp. 31–3: "Eine edle Einfalt und eine stille Grösse, so wohl in der Stellung als im Ausdrucke."

[2] "Eine grosse und gesetzte Seele."   [3] *Ibid.* p. 33.

[4] *Ibid.* p. 35. What did Winckelmann mean by "Socrates's school"? Did he mean to include Sophocles under this heading? Goethe probably did not break his head over the question and we will not either.

[5] Letter to Oeser, 9 Nov. 1768 (WA. IV, I, p. 178), and to Reich, 20 Feb. 1770 (*Ibid.* p. 229), and *Ephemerides*, WA. 37, p. 101. Volbehr (*op. cit.* p. 75) points out that Oeser's ideal of beauty is mentioned in the same breath with Shakespeare and Wieland.

natural expression: the girl in danger bursts into a storm of sobs and flings her arms round her lover's neck.[1] Goethe might still have accepted Winckelmann's definition of the nature of Greek art and have got from it an impression of the Greeks in which a certain cold stoicism would have outweighed their joyfulness, had not Lessing's *Laokoon* appeared (1766) and saved him.[2] Lessing took exception to the criticism of Virgil implied by Winckelmann in the *Gedanken*. Winckelmann had praised the artists of the Laocoön group, because they had represented Laocoön merely moaning, not screaming terribly as he does in Virgil's account in the *Aeneid*.[3] Lessing defended Virgil on the ground that the plastic arts and poetry are governed by different principles. Poetry does not appeal primarily to the visual sense but to the mind and feelings. It is therefore no fault in poetry to describe things which, if presented to the eye in sculpture or painting, would be ugly and revolting.[4] In their literature the Greeks showed no restraint in giving expression to physical and mental agony. Sophocles's Philoctetes fills the stage and the best part of an act with his cries and groans. Hercules too cries out in his death agony, and the Homeric heroes when they are wounded. We moderns think it indecent to cry and weep. Not so the Greeks! They felt deeply and were not ashamed to give free expression to their feelings.[5] Why then does Laocoön in the group not cry aloud in his agony? Because the Greek artists knew that plastic art has laws of its own, the first of which is: only what is beautiful shall be represented. Rage and despair disfigured none of their works. Violent passions were toned down in their expression until all ugliness was banished from the form.[6]

Lessing's *Laokoon* had the profoundest effect upon Goethe.[7] He saw now clearly the difference in kind between poetical and plastic creation. He was freed from any obligation he

[1] WA. 37, p. 30.
[2] Perhaps, too, Behrisch's whimsical mockery helped to keep him sceptical. The friend assured him he had learnt to express himself clearly and incisively from the greatest contemporary writers, who had pointed out to us, "wie man eine ruhige Ruhe ruhen und wie die Stille im Stillen immer stiller werden könnte": WA. 27, p. 46.
[3] *Aeneid*, II, 222.   [4] Lessing, *Werke*, IX, pp. 6 foll., 22 foll.
[5] *Ibid.* pp. 8, 9.   [6] *Ibid.* pp. 11, 14, 16, 17.
[7] WA. 22, 27, p. 64.

might have felt to follow Winckelmann's rule of stoical self-restraint in his poetry. At the same time the picture of the Greeks that he had from Winckelmann was filled out in an important point. These beautiful, wise, happy creatures, with their free and natural customs, were shown now to have possessed deep feelings too and to have had as healthy and natural an attitude to the expression of them as to everything else in life.[1] Healthy and natural too was their attitude towards death. To them he was no dreadful skeleton but a beautiful boy, the brother of sleep.[2]

But was Lessing any more right than Winckelmann in his definition of the fundamental principle of Greek art? Was it compatible with the healthy directness of their nature that the Greeks should have watered down the expression of strong emotion simply in order that their statues might be "beautiful"? It seems that Goethe asked himself these questions, perhaps not immediately on reading the *Laokoon*, but certainly after the visit to Mannheim in 1769, and answered both with a decided "No". His instinct, and by the beginning of 1769 his settled principle, was to demand from art simply truth to Nature;[3] the Dutch painters were his favourites; he was far less at home with a more ideal art such as the Italian.[4] What delight to find, as in Mannheim he stood for the first time before the whole Laocoön group, that here too the artist had followed only one law, that of truth to Nature! For Laocoön does not scream,

[1] In a letter to Oeser, 14 Feb. 1769 (WA. IV, 1, p. 205), Goethe appears to be on Lessing's side against Herder on the question of Philoctetes's cries. In the first *Kritisches Wäldchen* (*Werke*, III, pp. 13 foll.) Herder maintained with Winckelmann, and against Lessing, that Philoctetes struggles heroically to suppress his cries.

[2] This idea was emphasised by Lessing already in a note to the *Laokoon* (IX, p. 76), so that Goethe was familiar with it before the appearance of *Wie die Alten den Tod gebildet* (1769). Death as the brother of Sleep was not unknown in Christian thought before Lessing. The final Chorale of Bach's cantata No. 56 begins "Komm, o Tod, du Schlafes Bruder".

[3] Letter to Friederike Oeser, 13 Feb. 1769 (WA. IV, 1, p. 198): "Was an einem Gemälde am unerträglichsten ist, ist Unwahrheit", and in the same letter (p. 199): "O, meine Freundin, das Licht ist die Wahrheit....Die Nacht ist die Unwahrheit. Und was ist Schönheit? Sie ist nicht Licht und nicht Nacht. Dämmerung...ein Mittelding. In ihrem Reiche liegt ein Scheideweg so zweideutig, so schielend, ein Hercules unter den Philosophen könnte sich vergreifen."

[4] WA. 27, pp. 163, 174.

because he cannot scream. The snake, biting suddenly in a highly sensitive part of the body, has caused a spasm of the abdomen and an attitude of the whole body, which make any loud cry physically impossible. Goethe wrote at once to Oeser to tell him of this grand and simple solution of the whole controversy, and then set to work to put his ideas into essay form.[1]

He spent the winter of 1769–1770 on this work. In February of the new year he jotted down some remarks on Lessing's view of Greek art,[2] the meaning of which is in some places hard to disentangle, but which show clearly that he did not agree with Lessing that beauty was the highest law for the ancient artists. Lessing had written in *Laokoon*: "Rage and despair disfigured none of their [the Greeks'] works. I am prepared to assert that they never represented a Fury" (in statues or reliefs). He had been attacked for this assertion by his great antagonist, Klotz, and by others, and had defended himself, with perhaps more skill than conviction, in the *Briefe antiquarischen Inhalts*.[3] Goethe now joined with Lessing's attackers and, commenting on the note to the offending statement, maintained that the figures cited by Lessing did show rage and despair on their faces in the highest degree. "The ancients," he continues in this passage in *Ephemerides*, "as I have tried to show elsewhere [presumably in the Laocoön essay], avoided not so much what was ugly as what was false",[4] and concludes: "This is to me

---

[1] *Goethes Briefe an E. T. Langer*, letter of 30 Nov. 1769. Both the letter to Oeser and the essay are lost, but there is every reason to suppose that Goethe's solution of the Laocoön-problem was essentially as I have described it. He says in *D. und W.* that it was so (WA. 28, p. 86), and he gave the same explanation of Laocoön's attitude in his essay of 1797, which (so he wrote to Schiller, 5 July 1797) he based on an essay, written "many years before" and since lost, the main purport of which however he well remembered (cf. *Jrb. der G-G.* x, p. 59). The fragment of a Laocoön essay (WA. 48, p. 235) has been shown by v. Lücken (*Natalicium*, Heidelberg, 1931, p. 88) to date from the years 1773 or 1774.

[2] In *Ephemerides* (WA. 37, pp. 88, 90). Morris supposes them to have been merely copied out of some other work, so far unidentified (MM. VI, p. 145). His chief reason for thinking so—that no essay of Goethe's on this subject of this date is known—has ceased to be valid since the publication of the letter to Langer of 30 Nov. 1769.

[3] *Werke*, x, pp. 246 foll., in the 6th and 8th letter.

[4] "Die Alten, wie ich anderswo zu beweisen versucht habe, scheuten nicht so sehr das Hässliche als das Falsche."

another proof that the excellence of the ancients is to be sought in something other than the creation of beauty."[1]

The Greeks then did not, as Winckelmann had believed, suppress their emotions from a superhuman heroism, nor keep a coolly unmoved spirit no matter to what suffering and terror their senses were exposed. They were too great and simple for that. Neither did they, as Lessing would have it, shrink back from the last consequence of their deep knowledge of suffering, and refuse to express it in their art. They were too great for that also. How could anyone who had read those dreadful myths with a poet's sense, Medea, the house of Tantalus, the Theban cycle, the deaths of Hercules and Laocoön, doubt that the Greeks had known the terror and cruelty of life, as few races have known them? And if they had known them, would they refuse to give form to their knowledge? Goethe may not have formulated the problem to himself quite so consciously as this, but it is clear that he was already aware of three things: that the Greeks knew suffering, that sincerity was the first law of their art, and that they therefore were not afraid to represent the most terrible suffering in sculpture as well as in poetry.

To relieve this dark and tragic side of his picture of the Greeks, Goethe was glad to borrow some traits from Wieland's *Musarion* and *Agathon*. There was nothing irrational in allowing the Greeks to have been at once great experts in the portrayal of suffering and the first exponents of Wieland's "Grazienphilosophie." For, as Goethe explained to Friederike Oeser,[2] "elegance and high tragedy are generically different", and all was well so long as one did not try to include them in the same work of art. To what extent the young Goethe saw in *Musarion* (which he read in slip-proof in July of his last summer at Leipzig) "the antique new and living" before him,[3] cannot be accurately decided. He was strongly opposed to regarding Wieland's works in Greek costume as being primarily portrayals

[1] "Es ist mir das wieder ein Beweis dass man die Fürtrefflichkeit der Alten in etwas Anders als der Bildung der Schönheit zu suchen hat."
[2] Letter of 13 Feb. 1769 (WA. IV, I, p. 199): "Grazie und das hohe Pathos sind heterogen."
[3] WA. 27, p. 91.

of ancient Greek life and customs.[1] He knew that their chief aim was to reflect and satirise contemporary manners. Nevertheless there is much in the character and appearance of Musarion that corresponded with the conception of the Greeks that Goethe had from Winckelmann—the bodily beauty, more perfect than the common run with us, the healthy freedom of outlook on matters of morality, the healthy avoidance of unnatural extremes. All this was now made more visual, more vitally plastic by Wieland's consummate art, and over it all was shed that inexpressible grace,[2] that was for Wieland at this time, and in part too for Goethe,[3] the highest aesthetic-moral quality attainable by mortals. There can be hardly any doubt that this feminine, Rococo ideal of Greek beauty, so different from Winckelmann's vision of the youths in the palaestra, had its effect on Goethe's picture of the Greeks. If he read that seductive work of Wieland's, *die Grazien*, which appeared in 1769, he was encouraged to believe that all this ethereal sex-appeal was of the essence of Greek art. There is no evidence that he did so,[4] and we may hope that he did not.

But it would not have mattered. Wieland's influence was about to be blasted. Dallying Musarions and gauzy Graces were to flee before a row of mighty figures that rose on the horizon of his mind. Socrates the fighter for truth, Hercules the great liver, Prometheus the giver of life, were at hand; and behind them in the dark places the great sufferers, Tantalus, Ixion and many more.

[1] Letter to Reich, 30 Feb. 1770 (WA. IV, I, p. 230).
[2] *Musarion*, lines 145-58, 609, 687-90, 1135-40.
[3] His contempt, on returning from Leipzig, for the young ladies of Frankfurt, who might be more beautiful than those of Leipzig, but had none of "cette grace...cette douceur infinie, qui enchante plus que la beauté même", is pure Wielandism.
[4] He mentions reading *Idris* in Nov. 1768, and *Diogenes* as it appeared in Feb. 1770 (WA. IV, I, pp. 180, 227), but *die Grazien* is not mentioned.

CHAPTER II

FROM HERDER TO WEIMAR
(SEPT. 1770–NOV. 1775)

"Die Riesengestalten der markigen Fabelwelt."

A. KNOWLEDGE

EARLY in September 1770 Johann Gottfried Herder came to Strassburg and stayed until April of the following spring. He was five years older than Goethe, and had already made himself a name in Germany as a powerful critic and an original thinker. Goethe called on him as soon as he heard of his presence in the town, and continued to visit him throughout the winter until shortly before Herder left. The relationship that grew up between them, finely and vividly described in *Dichtung und Wahrheit,* was one of the most fruitful for Goethe of all the many that enriched his long life. Herder's influence in fact during the winter of 1770–1771 was of decisive importance in the development of Goethe's genius. Herder was the champion of those new ideas which were spreading to Germany from France and England. With Rousseau and Blackwell he rejected the overlordship of the intellect and hailed feeling as the primary guide and judge. In poetry or art only that was great which was true to nature or sprang from the depths of instinctive consciousness. A folk-song, a Scotch ballad were greater in their artless truth than all the tragedies of Voltaire; and Homer was supreme because he sang the life that he saw around him, and used only the inspiration of his genius to give his song artistic form. "Truth, feeling, Nature"—with these words of power Herder blew away all the cobwebs of theory, the definitions, critical yardsticks, and other intellectual nostrums that held Goethe's genius in bondage. The effect upon his attitude to Greek culture was profound and varied in its results. Not least important of these was his determination to conquer the language at last and to read his Homer and Plato in the Greek. Only thus, so his master taught,[1] could one get a true and fruitful knowledge of these mighty works of genius; and Herder left no doubt that they must be known. The fire of admiration with which he spoke of the Greeks as

[1] Herder's *Werke,* I, p. 177.

the true livers of life, who felt intensely and lived and sang as they felt, made it for Goethe a holy duty to conquer the difficulties that had baffled him since he was a boy. Yet all this stirring of new ideas, that Herder flung into the ready ground of Goethe's mind, might not have sufficed to lift him over these difficulties, had not a fresh love-affair let loose from its deepest springs the full energy of his mighty spirit.[1]

"A short recipe for the study of Greek!" he wrote. "If you have a Homer, good, if not, buy Ernesti's edition, since it has Clarke's literal translation alongside. Then get Schaufelberg's *Clavis Homerica* and a pack of plain cards. When you have this all collected, begin to read the *Iliad*, take no notice of accents but read with the flow and tune of the hexameter just as it rings in your heart. If you understand, good. If you don't, look at the translation; read the translation and the original, and the original and the translation some twenty thirty verses, till you get some light on the construction, which in Homer is nothing but a series of pictures. Then take your Key, where you will find the words analysed line by line; then write the present and the nominative on your cards, put them in your pocket-book, and learn them at home or out of doors, as one might pray whose heart was wholly set on God. And so always one thirty verses after the other, and when you've worked through two, three books so, I promise you'll stand fresh and free before your Homer and will understand him without translation, Schaufelberg, or cards. Probatum est!"[2] Thus did

[1] Goethe's acquaintance with Friederike Brion began in Oct. 1770, one month after Herder's arrival in Strassburg.

[2] Letter to Sophie La Roche, 20 Nov. 1774 (WA. IV, 2, p. 205). It is clear that Goethe is describing the method he employed in Strassburg four years before. "Hier ein kurzes Rezipe für den werten Baron v. Hohenfelds griechisches Studium! 'So Du einen Homer hast ist's gut, hast Du keinen kaufe Dir den Ernestischen, da die Clärckische wörtliche Uebersetzung beigefügt ist; sodann verschaffe Dir Schaufelbergs Clavem Homericam und ein Spiel weisse Karten. Hast Du dies beisammen so fang an zu lesen die Ilias, achte nicht auf Accente, sondern lies wie die Melodie des Hexameters dahinfliesst und es Dir schön klinge in der Seele. Verstehst Du's, so ist alles getan. So Du's aber nicht verstehst, sieh die Uebersetzung an, lies die Uebersetzung, und das Original, und das Original und die Uebersetzung, etwa ein zwanzig dreissig Verse, bis Dir ein Licht aufgeht über Construction die in Homer reinste Bilderstellung ist. Sodann ergreife deinen Clavem, wo Du wirst Zeile vor Zeile die Worte analysiert finden, das Praesens und den Nominativum, schreibe sodann auf die Karten, steck sie in Dein Souvenir,

he conquer at last, carried on over all obstacles by a genius that turned even grammar and vocabulary lists into a prayer to the Author of life. By the summer of 1771 he stood almost "frisch und frank" before his Homer.[1] In little inns by the sweeping waters of the Rhine, with only a lantern on the table before them, Lerse and he read Homer and Ossian. "Then Goethe would often fall into an ecstasy, would speak words of prophecy, and Lerse feared his reason would snap."[2] It was against this background of storm and lightning flash that the figures of the great Greeks now began to walk in the spaces of his mind.

In August he left Strassburg and was in Frankfurt then for most of the time, until the following May 1772. He read on in Homer, but still found it best, at least when translating extempore to Cornelia, as he loved to do for hours together, to use the Latin translation by Clarke. Nevertheless the swing of the Greek was in his mind, for his German version fell by itself into metrical turns and endings.[3]

He was not slow to use the newly won power to explore further into Greek literature. In Plato and Xenophon he sought material for his drama of the life and death of Socrates.[4] Whether he read at all without a crib cannot be said. Quotations in letters of Greek words and passages prove at least that he had the Greek text before him.[5] Of Plato he certainly read

und lerne dran zu Hause und auf dem Feld, wie einer beten möcht, dem das Herz ganz nach Gott hing. Und so immer ein dreissig Verse nach dem andern, und hast Du zwei drei Bücher so durchgearbeitet, versprech ich Dir, stehst Du frisch und frank vor Deinem Homer, und verstehst ihn ohne Uebersetzung, Schaufelberg und Karten.' Probatum est!"

[1] Letter to Salzmann, June 1771 (WA. IV, 2, p. 258). The final successful attack on the language seems to have been made during his stay in Sesenheim in June 1771. Yet from Herder's letter to Merk (MM. II, p. 100) it seems likely that he had managed to read some Homer before Herder left Strassburg in April. Herder speaks as though he had himself watched the result of this reading on Goethe's imagination.

[2] MM. II, p. 104: "Da geriet Goethe oft in hohe Verzückung, sprach Worte der Prophezeiung und machte Lerse Besorgnisse, er werde überschnappen."

[3] WA. 28, p. 168.

[4] Letters to Herder, New Year, 1772 (WA. IV, 2, p. 11 and MM. VI, p. 183) and July 1772 (WA. IV, 2, p. 16).

[5] ἐξουσία, in letter to Herder (Ibid. p. 11) and to Röderer 21 Sept. 1771 (MM. II, p. 108), and the closing passage of the Apology in the same letter to Herder.

the *Apology*; perhaps also the *Gorgias*[1] and the *Protagoras*;[2] from the *Phaedrus* might come the simile of the charioteer in the letter to Herder, July 1772; from the *Symposium* the allusion in another letter[3] to Alcibiades's relationship to Socrates. Of Xenophon he read of course the *Memorabilia*. During the same winter he turned also to the Greek poets, first to the Anacreontics and Theocritus, then in the early spring of 1772 to Pindar.[4] His reading of Theocritus must have started in October 1771, for in the *Rede zum Shakespeares Tag* he told his listeners how Homer, Sophocles and Theocritus had taught him to feel what greatness was among the Greeks.[5] He probably used Reiske's newly published edition (1765) with Latin verse translation.[6] He may have needed little help in reading the Greek, for Theocritus is not hard when once the peculiarities of the Doric dialect have been mastered.

By March 1772, the date of the composition of *Wandrers Sturmlied*, his interest had deserted Theocritus and was all centred on Pindar,[7] whom he read intensively through the spring and summer of 1772.[8] It is not improbable that he used

[1] MM. vi, p. 180, but König (*Goethes Belesenheit*, p. 327) assumes only knowledge of the New Testament.

[2] *Faust*: "Spottgeburt von Dreck und Feuer"; compare *Protagoras*, ch. 30: ἐκ γῆς καὶ πυρὸς μίξαντες (König, *op. cit.* p. 574).

[3] Letter to Herder, late 1771 (WA. iv, 2, p. 12).

[4] Letter to Herder, July 1772 (*Ibid.* p. 16): "Seit ich nichts von Euch gehört habe, sind die Griechen mein einzig Studium. Zuerst schränkt ich mich auf den Homer ein, dann um den Socrates forsch ich in Xenophon und Plato. Da gingen mir die Augen über meine Unwürdigkeit erst auf, geriet an Theokrit und Anacreon, zuletzt zog mich was an Pindarn, wo ich noch hänge." [5] WA. 37, p. 131.

[6] There were already three German translations of Theocritus; one in hexameters by Lieberkühn, Berlin, 1757; one by F. G. S. Schwabe, Jena, 1769; and one published in Halberstadt, 1771. The last was reviewed by Herder in the *Frankfurter Gelehrte Anzeigen*, Jan. 1771, and so was presumably known to Goethe.

[7] König (*Goethes Belesenheit*) assumes that the reference in Götz to "die Antistrophe von eurem Gesang" proves reading of Pindar. As the phrase occurs in the first version of Götz (*Geschichte Gottfriedens von Berlichingen*, WA. 39, p. 72), which was finished by the New Year of 1772, this would put the reading of Pindar back into the autumn of 1771. I prefer to assume that Goethe was familiar with the term "antistrophe" from some other source, probably his talks with Herder in the previous winter.

[8] Letter to Herder, July 1772, quoted above, and Kestner's letter to Hemming (MM. ii, p. 314). The letter to Herder shows acquaintance with *Olympians*, *Pythians* and *Nemeans* (MM. vi, p. 237).

a text which had no Latin version attached.[1] If this is so, it was an astonishing achievement. A year before he had stood helpless before any Greek but that of the New Testament. Now, as a result of his own efforts unaided, he could follow Pindar wherever the old Greek's sudden fancy might sweep him. The method he used to master Greek during this short year was in keeping with everything else that he did. He learnt more by intuition than by grammar; he felt himself into understanding his Homer or his Pindar. Up to a point this method served him well. But his knowledge of Greek, having no solid foundation, never advanced further than he had been able to carry it in this first rush. He became, as time went on, more familiar with Homer, so that during most of his life he could read him without a crib. But with other authors he was never happy unless he had a translation at hand.

More serious than the mistranslation of an occasional sentence in Pindar was his complete misconception of the nature of the Theban's poetry. Here he erred with his age, which loved to see in Pindar a poet who poured out his song in a divine ecstasy without forethought or rules. Herder, it is true, was well aware of the conscious artist in Pindar.[2] But he seems to have assumed that in the lost dithyrambs Pindar allowed himself a wilder style. This genre, he believed, had in the earliest times sprung from the orgiastic celebrations of the god of wine, and even at a later date the poet "followed no other plan than what the imagination painted...and the dance demanded". The speech of these dithyrambs was novel, bold, irregular. It was the poet's right to coin new words, since the language was still poor. "So too the metre had no rules, just as their dance

---

[1] For the written translation of the fifth Olympian ode, that he made in 1773, he used Heyne's edition with its Latin version (see *Euphorion*, xvi, p. 543). This edition was not yet published in 1772. Goethe must therefore have used some other for his reading in that year. The edition by Stephanus with Latin translation was commonly used in Germany. But if Goethe owned and used Stephanus in 1772, why did he use Heyne a year later? It was not like him to be troubled about having the most modernly exact readings or notes. If however he had struggled in 1772 with a plain Greek text, he would have been glad to get Heyne's edition as soon as it appeared. From his quotations from Pindar in the letter to Herder of July 1772, it is clear he sometimes only half understood what he was reading (MM. vi, p. 237), which is hardly possible if he had a Latin version.

[2] *Werke*, iii, p. 348.

and the tones of their speech had none; but for that very reason it was the more polymetric, sonorous and varied."[1] Herder must have talked to Goethe of Pindar during the winter at Strassburg, but either he did not explain his attitude fully, or Goethe did not grasp all that was said to him.[2] For it is plain from *Wandrers Sturmlied* that Pindar was for Goethe the god-intoxicated dithyrambist, despiser of rules and all conventional checks on the stream of inspiration. Not indeed that *Wandrers Sturmlied* should be taken as an imitation of Pindar. Conscious imitation was contrary to all Goethe's principles at this time. But Pindar's example appeared to him to justify the abandonment of all rules of form. Like the old dithyrambist he sang without plan, just as the imagination poured forth its glowing images.[3] At times intensity of feeling made articulate expression almost impossible ("Weh! Weh! Innre Wärme, Seelenwärme, Mittelpunkt!"). There was no set metre, only a rhythm, which is indeed for its very freedom "the more polymetric, sonorous and varied". New-coined words are frequent—"Feuerflügeln", "Blumenfüssen", "Flutschlamm" in four lines—and grammatically impossible constructions also abound—"Dich, dich strömt mein Lied", "Glühte deine Seel Gefahren, Pindar, Mut". How little this has in common with Pindar's highly formalised lyric has often been pointed out,[4] never with more clearness and force than by Wilamowitz-Moellendorf. "Goethe tried to make himself a picture of the form of this lyric, but he was hardly likely to succeed. In the harsh word-order, that breaks every grammatical rule, he imagined himself to be following Pindar, perhaps also in the rhythms. In fact no greater contrast could exist than that between the lawless style of this unschooled revolutionary and Pindar's rigid technique."[5]

Later in the summer of 1772 he came to see that Pindar's greatness consisted in something more than a passive surrender

---

[1] *Fragmente*, 2. Sammlung; *Werke*, I, pp. 307 foll.

[2] See Minor Sauer, *Studien zur Goethephilologie*, Vienna, 1880, pp. 98 foll. Goethe did not read the *Fragmente* until July 1772 (WA. IV, 2, p. 17).

[3] WA. 28, p. 119.

[4] See *Zeitschrift für den deutschen Unterricht*, 1905, p. 530; also Paul Reiff, *Mod. Lang. Notes*, XVIII, pp. 169 foll.; and Gottfried Fittbogen, *Die sprachliche und metrische Form der Hymnen Goethes*, Halle, 1909, pp. 19, 20.

[5] *Pindarus*, Introduction, p. 5.

to the divine breath.[1] But his translation of the fifth Olympian, made in the summer of 1773, shows that he had not grasped the elementary fact about Pindar's metrical scheme—that strophe and antistrophe correspond with each other exactly line by line and syllable by syllable. Even Herder never realised this. His translation of the first Olympian, made in 1796, at a time when he always imitated the form of the original as closely as possible,[2] is just as much free-verse as Goethe's attempt on the fifth Olympian.

On 14 October 1771, after his return to Frankfurt from Strassburg, Goethe helped to celebrate Shakespeare's name day in company with other admirers of "der grosse Brite". Addresses were delivered, amongst them one by Goethe. Shakespeare, he explained, had freed him from the bondage of the Unities, from the French tyranny of formal perfection, and he had now declared war on all who still tried to bind mankind in these fetters. As though anticipating the objection that the Unities were invented not by the French but by the great Greeks, he continued: "The Greek theatre, that the French took as their model, was in its internal and external nature so constructed that it would be easier for a marquis to imitate Alcibiades than for Corneille to follow Sophocles. Originally an intermezzo in the cult of the god, then solemnly national, the tragedy presented to the people certain single great actions of their forefathers with the pure simplicity of perfection, and stirred whole, great emotions in their souls, for it was itself whole and great. And in what souls! Greek souls! I cannot make clear what that means, but I feel it, and appeal, for brevity, to Homer and Sophocles and Theocritus, who have taught me to feel it."[3]

---

[1] Letter to Herder, July 1772 (WA. IV, 2, p. 16). Interpretation of ἐπικρατεῖν δύνασθαι. See below, p. 76.

[2] *Werke*, XXVI, p. 188, and *Einleitung*, pp. viii–xi.

[3] WA. 37, p. 131: "Das griechische Theater, das die Franzosen zum Muster nahmen, war, nach innrer und äusserer Beschaffenheit, so, dass eher ein Marquis den Alcibiades nachahmen könnte, als es Corneillen dem Sophokles zu folgen möglich war.

"Erst Intermezzo des Gottesdiensts, dann feierlich politisch, zeigte das Trauerspiel einzelne grosse Handlungen der Väter, dem Volk, mit der reinen Einfalt der Vollkommenheit, erregte ganze, grosse Empfindungen in den Seelen, denn es war selbst ganz und gross.

The last sentence, already cited as proof that Goethe was
reading Theocritus in the autumn of 1771, should be equally
conclusive that he knew Sophocles[1] from more than hearsay.
The preceding paragraph, with its confident definition of the
nature of Greek tragedy, should leave no doubt that he had
read at least a representative selection from the works of all
three great Attic dramatists. Yet it is hard to see when he could
have done so. It cannot have been before June 1771. He was
then still learning Greek from Homer.[2] After September 1771,
the whole period until July 1772 is covered by the sentence in
the letter to Herder of July 1772: "Since I last heard from
you...."[3] It is the period to which his account of reading
Plato, Theocritus and Pindar refers. In this account he makes
no mention of any Greek tragedian. The only possibility is
that he read some between June and September 1771. There is
certainly no proof that he did not; but the only evidence that
he did so is this passage in the Rede zum Shakespeares Tag. In
my opinion it is not necessary to conclude from it that Goethe
already had first-hand knowledge of the Athenian tragedy.
We have seen that he could have obtained a fair idea of the
content and nature of the Philoctetes from Lessing's Laokoon and
Herder's first Wäldchen. Since reading those works he had
spent the fruitful winter months with Herder in Strassburg.
It is reasonable to imagine Goethe asking for more explanation
of the nature of Greek tragedy, and Herder pouring out those
ideas which we find in his writings of the years immediately
before and after his stay in Strassburg. When Goethe spoke
with such confidence and familiarity of Sophocles and the
Greek theatre, I believe he had no other picture in his mind
than what he had got from his reading of Lessing and his talks
with Herder. It may be objected that he would never have
pretended to a knowledge of Sophocles which he did not
possess. Certainly not, if it be supposed that vanity was his

"Und in was für Seelen!
"Griechischen! Ich kann mich nicht erklären was das heisst, aber ich
fühl's, und berufe mich der Kürze halber auf Homer und Sophokles und
Theokrit, die haben's mich fühlen gelehrt."
[1] See Keller, Goethe's Estimate of the Greek and Latin Writers, Wisconsin,
1916; and E. Maass, Goethe und die Antike, p. 346.
[2] Letter to Salzmann (WA. IV, 2, p. 258).
[3] See above, p. 53.

object in doing so. When he spoke on Shakespeare's day, however, he was crusading against the Unities; and in that war all was fair that might lend weight to his cause. It was necessary to quote the Greek theatre against the French. How feeble his argument would appear if he admitted that he knew nothing of Aeschylus and Sophocles but what Herder had told him!

Let us examine what Goethe says about the Greek theatre in the *Rede zum Shakespeares Tag*, and compare it with Herder's utterances of this period. Goethe argues that it is irrelevant to cite the Greek theatre against the English in support of the French, for the Greek theatre and the French have nothing in common. The Greek theatre, originating as music and dance in honour of the god, came, in time, to choose out single deeds of the heroic forefathers of the race and to enact each one of these simply and in its entirety, by which means they moved the onlookers with deep and simple emotions. What Goethe packed into two pregnant sentences, and what is here paraphrased, is to be found fully developed in Herder's essay on Shakespeare in *Von Deutscher Art und Kunst* (1773). Herder explains that the simplicity of the action in a Greek tragedy and the Unities of time and place are the result of the origin of Greek tragedy, which grew up out of "the impromptu of the dithyramb, of the miming dance, of the chorus".[1] They were not "rules" applied consciously from without to a material which would otherwise ramble formlessly. The stories of the heroic age were so simple that the poet found difficulty rather in giving them diversity than in holding the action within a set form. The single, short, solemn action took place in a temple or palace or on the market-place. Unities of time and place were there of themselves. In the French theatre there is none of all this. It is a mere doll-like imitation of the Greek, in which the purpose of the Greek theatre—to stir the emotions—is lost entirely. Goethe's explanation of the fact that Shakespearean and Greek drama, though so different in form, are both essentially drama, is also to be found in Herder's essay on Shakespeare.[2] There can be no doubt that Goethe's *Rede zum Shakespeares Tag* is a concentration of the talks that he had with Herder in Strassburg on the subject of the drama in

[1] *Werke,* v, pp. 210 foll.   [2] *Ibid.* p. 226.

its three national forms. The conclusions as to the nature of the Greek drama, that are given in the *Rede* in three short paragraphs, were then doubtless illuminated by examples from Herder's close knowledge of all the extant Greek tragedies, until Goethe felt that he knew the Greek theatre, although he had read not a word of it. No doubt knowledge so acquired from Herder did have some value. But it must have been a confused picture that he had of the Athenian drama, in which neither the plays nor even the three dramatists stood out clearly one from another. It was the sort of knowledge that served well enough for generalisations such as that in the review of Sulzer's adaptation of *Cymbeline*,[1] that Sophocles's pieces show us "nur Tat"—only action. But it did not yet amount to an individual view of Greek tragedy based on personal study of the plays.

Götter, *Helden und Wieland* (September 1773) contains the first indisputable evidence that Goethe had read a Greek drama. The shade of Euripides gives a short paraphrase of passages from his own *Alcestis*—the Prologue, and the scene between Apollo and Death and one strophe from the following chorus: then, fairly closely, Hercules's resolve to wrestle with Death and save Alcestis.[2] Wilamowitz believed that Goethe used only Brumoy's French translation and did not have the Greek text before him.[3] It is in fact curious that Goethe always speaks of the "goddess of Death" although he must have known, however weak his grammar, that θάνατος is masculine, and therefore god not goddess. Brumoy translates θάνατος by "déesse", but is careful to point out that the Greek word would suggest a male deity. The difficulty may perhaps be

---

[1] In the *Frankfurter Gelehrte Anzeigen*, 15 Sept. 1772 (WA. 37, pp. 225–7). One of the hardest problems of *Goethephilologie* is to decide which reviews in *F.G.A.* are by Goethe. Most of the great Goethe-scholars from Biedermann to Max Morris have studied the problem and announced their conclusions. But there is no general agreement except for some half-dozen reviews where the evidence is indisputable. In the present study I shall follow the conclusions contained in Max Morris's *Goethes und Herders Anteil an dem Jahrgang 1772 der Frankfurter Gelehrten Anzeigen* in the revised edition of 1915, and shall show reverent consideration of the opinions expressed in the Weimar Ausgabe.

[2] WA. 38, pp. 29, 30; Euripides, *Alcestis*, Prologue and 25–6, 74–7, 123 foll., 842–55.

[3] Wilamowitz-Moellendorf, *Euripides Herakles*, Berlin, 1889, p. 234 and note.

explained thus: later in the play (lines 964–84) the chorus sings
to the goddess Ananké—Fate or Necessity—who has Admetus
in her grip. It seems that Goethe blended the two figures of
Death and Fate into one goddess. However that may be there
can be no doubt, as Morsch has proved,[1] that Goethe used the
Greek text as well as Brumoy's translation.

The Greek of the tragedies still caused him difficulty. He
was dependent on help from translations; but all the existing
translations had serious limitations.[2] There were indeed Latin
versions printed alongside the Greek text in all the standard
editions of the tragedians, but these editions, which dated from
the sixteenth or early seventeenth century, were rare in
Germany. There is no sign that Goethe used any of them.
Instead he used Pierre Brumoy's *Théâtre des Grecs*, a work, with
all its shortcomings, of immense value in a dark age.[3] Brumoy
treated all of the Greek tragedies and the comedies of Aristophanes, but he translated only six of the tragedies in full,[4] the
rest are related in detail with occasional passages in direct
translation. Besides Brumoy, which was well known in
Germany, a German translation of Sophocles and Euripides
had recently appeared and had attracted some attention in the
literary world. This was J. J. Steinbrüchel's *Das tragische
Theater der Griechen* (1763). The translations were in prose
and, to judge from Herder's comments in the *Fragmente*,[5]
prosaic enough. Goethe must have known of this work. It
is impossible to say whether he used it.

In these conditions it is not to be expected that Goethe read
many Greek tragedies. It has been suggested that he read the
Hercules Furens at the same time as the *Alcestis* in order to get
material for his picture of Hercules in *Götter, Helden und
Wieland*. There is no evidence that he did so and certain con-
siderations make it highly unlikely that he knew even the
story that Euripides was treating. For the figure of Hercules
in Euripides's play corresponds to Goethe's Hercules in only

---

[1] H. Morsch, *Goethe und die griechischen Bühnendichter*, Berlin, 1888, p. 5,
and König, *Goethes Belesenheit*, pp. 439, 448.

[2] See Morsch, *op. cit.* p. 4 and Wilamowitz-Moellendorf, *Euripides
Herakles*, p. 234.

[3] Bünemann, *op. cit.* pp. 21–2.

[4] Of Sophocles: *Oedipus Rex, Electra* and *Philoctetes*; of Euripides: the two
Iphigeneias and the *Alcestis*.   [5] *Werke*, I, p. 291; also II, p. 42.

one thing—in his superhuman strength.[1] There is no trace in him of the jovial boon companion, who drinks and makes love with the commonest, when he is not bound on some great-hearted toil. That Hercules Goethe took from the *Alcestis*.[2] In the *Hercules Furens* the son of Zeus is a figure of the most pitiless tragedy, a great man, who has toiled all his life to conquer one scourge of mankind after another, but who, because of the very greatness of his spirit, is open to attacks from the direst of all scourges of the gods—madness. Admittedly Goethe could not have used any of these tragic traits for the jovial character of his farce. But, had he read the *Hercules Furens*, he must have seized on the figure of Hercules as the most perfect symbol of the tragedy of genius. The danger, the horror of being a *Genie*, were clear to him from the summer of 1772 onwards. He called it sometimes the "curse of Cain",[3] but the figure of the madness-stricken Hercules would have given him a far better symbol for this unspeakable terror. The fact that he never referred to Hercules as a tragic figure[4] is sufficient proof that he had not read the *Hercules Furens*.

There is more to be said for the supposition that Goethe read Aeschylus's *Prometheus Vinctus*. The evidence from a comparison of the texts of Aeschylus's play and Goethe's is inconclusive. There are certain thoughts and phrases in Goethe's work which are reminiscent of phrases in the *Prometheus Vinctus*,[5] but the resemblances are not so close as to prove that Goethe had Aeschylus's words in mind. In both plays the scene between Prometheus and Hermes (Mercury in Goethe's text) takes a similar course.[6] The myth, as Goethe used it, is

---

[1] *Hercules Furens*, 566–72.

[2] Perhaps also from Lucian's *Dialogues in Hades*, XIII (Elinger, *Alceste in der modernen Literatur*, Halle, 1885, p. 39).

[3] WA. IV, 2, p. 92. See also Bied. I, p. 71. See also Sudheimer, *op. cit.* pp. 47–9, 176, 177.   [4] Cf. WA. 37, p. 151: *Von deutscher Baukunst*.

[5] WA. 39, p. 196, lines 40, 41 = Aesch. *P.V.* 1053; p. 197, lines 1, 2 = *P.V.* 518; p. 197, line 47 = *P.V.* 983; p. 201, lines 150–3 = *P.V.* 966–7, and see Morsch, *op. cit.* p. 9.

[6] The greater part of this scene (with the name "Mercury" instead of "Hermes") is translated in Sulzer's *Allgemeine Theorie der schönen Künste* in the article on Aeschylus. It may fairly be assumed (see Rehm, *Griechentum und Goethezeit*, p. 73) that Goethe had read this article and knew this much of the *Prometheus Vinctus* before he started his own play.

different in a score of ways from the form which Aeschylus followed. Most significant of all, the tone of the two completed acts of Goethe's play is utterly different from that of the *Prometheus Vinctus*. The bright, youthful, loving creator of mankind has nothing in common with Aeschylus's dark sufferer. He symbolises primarily the creative power of the artist, sufficient to itself, needing no help from the gods, but not defiant nor hostile to them.[1] For this use of the myth Goethe needed only to follow the well-established tradition of the eighteenth century, which had come down from antiquity through Shaftesbury, Young, Herder and Wieland.[2] The tragic side of the myth was not usually stressed, although of course in such works as Pomey and Hyginus all parts of the story were given. In the Prometheus ode,[3] written some months after the first two acts, there blows a more Aeschylean wind. Prometheus not merely refuses all co-operation with the gods, as equal to equal; his words are full of contempt and hatred. "I know nothing more pitiful under the sun than you gods." It is the voice of the Titan who despises these upstart rulers and can afford to wait till their little day of power is over.[4] Perhaps Goethe read Aeschylus's play during the winter of 1773–1774, hoping, it may be, to gain inspiration for his own play, which had come to a standstill. The remarkable change of tone in the ode suggests the working of some such external influence. Yet even this conclusion can be no more than conjecture.

On 8 June 1774, Goethe wrote to Gottlob Schönborn, describing to him Herder's latest essay, the *Aelteste Urkunde des Menschengeschlechts*. "He has descended", he wrote, "into the depths of his feeling, has stirred up from there all the holy might of simple Nature and now brings it up and sends it over the wide earth in half-conscious, summer-lightning-lit, sometimes morning-friendly-smiling, Orphic song."[5] Such a ring-

[1] See also *Von deutscher Baukunst*, WA. 37, p. 151.
[2] Sudheimer, *op. cit.* pp. 288, 289; and cf. JA. xv, p. 335.
[3] "Bedecke deinen Himmel, Zeus", WA. 39, p. 213.
[4] Aesch. *P.V.* 956–9.
[5] WA. IV, 2, p. 173: "Er ist in die Tiefen seiner Empfindung hinabgestiegen, hat drinne all die hohe heilige Kraft der simpeln Natur aufgewühlt und führt sie nun in dämmerndem, wetterleuchtendem hier und da morgenfreundlichlächelndem Orphischem Gesang von Anfang herauf über die weite Welt."

ing battery of adjectives as attributes of Orphic poetry would hardly have been justified unless he had read some of the Orphic hymns. Again, in a letter to Herder of 1 April 1775,[1] Goethe writes of Orpheus as though he had a right to an opinion about the nature of the mythical Greek poet's writings and teachings. What evidence is there that Goethe had read any of the Orphic hymns?

In 1765 was published a new edition of the *Argonautica* and the hymns by J. M. Gesner, with Latin translation appended. This edition was reviewed by Herder in the *Königsberger Gelehrte und Politische Zeitungen* in 1765.[2] Herder was well acquainted with the hymns long before he and Goethe met at Strassburg.[3] Nothing more likely than that Orpheus too found a place in their discussions (Goethe we know had been drawn to him even as a boy); it is possible that they may have read some of the hymns together, though it must be remembered that at that time Goethe's Greek was in the very first stages of its revival. The world as "the living cloak of the Godhead" is, according to Menzel,[4] an Orphic conception; and there is a passage in the review of Sulzer's *die Schönen Kunste* in the *Frankfurter Gelehrte Anzeigen* which is strongly reminiscent in thought and in style of the Orphic Hymn to Nature.[5] The resemblance is strong enough to suggest the conclusion that Goethe had read at least this hymn before the end of 1772. It is true that in the passages quoted above from letters to Schönborn and Herder, which are the only references to Orpheus for this period, Goethe says nothing about Orpheus that he could not have taken from Herder's *Aelteste Urkunde*, where Orpheus is very fully discussed. It is evident indeed that his comparison of Herder's essay with an Orphic hymn was suggested by what he had read in the essay, not by recent reading of Orpheus. Nevertheless the tone of these two references, together with the passages in *Faust* and the *Sulzerrezension*, justify the assertion that Goethe probably knew something of

---

[1] WA. IV, 2, p. 252.   [2] *Werke*, I, p. 77.
[3] See especially *Werke*, XXXII, pp. 109 foll.
[4] A. Menzel, *Goethe und die griechische Philosophie*, p. 20. Quotation from *Faust*, line 509: "der Gottheit lebendiges Kleid".
[5] WA. 37, p. 210, lines 10–15. For Goethe's authorship see MM. VI, p. 215; *Goethes und Herders Anteil*, p. 155 and WA. 38, p. 316.

the Orphic hymns at first hand. There is nothing unlikely in this assumption. Both Goethe and Herder felt an affinity with the half-articulate mysticism of these curious relics of primitive wisdom.[1] Even if Goethe had read none in the Greek, he certainly knew the nature of the Orphic wisdom with fair accuracy. It is important to realise that the Orphic hymns, which are regarded nowadays at most as a curious backwater of Greek literature, formed for Goethe a trait of some importance in his picture of the Greeks.

While with spasmodic enthusiasm Goethe was devouring Pindar, dipping into Euripides or Orpheus or Aeschylus, Homer was always with him. In Wetzlar on his walks, first with the cumbersome Ernesti edition, then in the pocket Wetstein;[2] in Frankfurt, where the sight of the river-craft lying by the quays under the moon sent him home to read of Odysseus to the adoring friends;[3] fresh from sleep, in the morning ritual—a passage from the *Iliad* to clear the head and stimulate heart and mind[4]—he deepened his loving acquaintance with Homer. Already in the late summer of 1772 the two poems were clear and whole in his mind, so that he could write in the *Frankfurter Gelehrte Anzeigen* with confidence of their form, their composition and poetical qualities;[5] and to Lavater two years later he could relate the whole story of the *Iliad*, as they set out together down Main and Rhein.[6] In the winter following he extended his interest in Homer to a study of the blind singer's features and analysed them for Lavater's great work on Physiognomy.[7] No wonder that in Zürich in the next summer he should have talked of Homer to Bodmer,[8] the translator of both *Iliad* and *Odyssey* and the staunch friend

---

[1] It is doubtful whether Goethe realised that the Orphic hymns, as they exist to-day, date from the fourth century A.D., and have even less connexion with Orpheus than Christian hymns of to-day have with Christ. Heyne, in his introduction to Hermann's *Handbuch der Mythologie*, 1790 (vol. II), wrote that the Orphic hymns were not old, but that the ideas were in part derived from old Orphic mysteries.

[2] Amsterdam, 1707, with Latin version. Cf. WA. 19, p. 78 and Kestner's letter to Hemming (MM. II, p. 314).

[3] WA. IV, 2, p. 61: letter to Kestner, Jan. 1773.

[4] *Künstlers Morgenlied*, WA. 2, pp. 178–81.

[5] *Goethes und Herders Anteil*, pp. 223–5.   [6] Bied. I, p. 37.

[7] WA. 37, p. 339 and letter to Lavater, Jan. 1775 (WA. IV, 2, p. 227).

[8] MM. V, p. 273.

and supporter of Breitinger, who in those far-off childish days, thirty years and more before, had helped to rescue Homer from the Versailles vultures. In these five years Goethe laid the foundation of that knowledge of Homer which was to grow with the years, until he knew him in his own way as thoroughly, and understood him as deeply, as any scholar could do.

In January of 1775 Zimmermann wrote of Goethe to Frau von Stein that he was "connoisseur and reader of the ancients, especially of the Greeks".[1] By the standards of those days the tribute was justified. Goethe could read Homer with ease in the Greek and knew both *Iliad* and *Odyssey* well. He had read some, perhaps all, of Theocritus. He had wrestled with Pindar all one spring and summer and had translated one ode into his own free-verse. He still knew little of the tragedians, but there too he had made a beginning. Some dialogues of Plato he had read—not for their philosophy—and Xenophon's *mémoires* of Socrates; Thucydides and Herodotus he had not touched, nor any of the orators. But Orpheus was a real figure to him and the Orphic hymns conveyed to him real ideas, not, as they do to most of us, a jangle of sounds without sense. This was the achievement of the five years that had passed since Herder arrived in Strassburg and Goethe had gone visiting to Sesenheim.[2]

Zimmermann had called Goethe a "Kenner" as well as a reader of the ancients, by which he meant that Goethe's interest was directed to the art of the ancients as well as to their literature. His interest in ancient art was indeed always keen, but for some time after that fruitful visit to Mannheim in 1769 the chances of increasing his knowledge were scarce and his progress slow. If we assume that he did not visit the Mannheim collection again in August 1771,[3] there is a gap of nearly two years during which his occupation with ancient art seems to have been suspended. During the winter of 1770–1771 he probably heard from Herder most of those ideas on the nature of Greek sculpture which were later published in Herder's

---

[1] Bied. I, p. 52: "Kenner und Leser der Alten, besonders der Griechen."
[2] The review of *Bergsträssers Realwörterbuch* (Morris, *Goethes und Herders Anteil*, p. 247) shows knowledge of Plutarch and Theophrastus's *Characters*.
[3] See above, p. 38, note 2.

essay *Plastik*;[1] but only his ideas, not his visual knowledge, were helped by these talks. From then on during his last summer in Alsace through the winter and spring of 1771–1772 in Frankfurt, the following summer in Wetzlar and the last months of 1772, which he spent again at home, he had no contact with Greek art. Not that the visions which he had from Mannheim faded altogether. Apollo especially stood clear and rather terrible in his mind.[2] But through all these months there is no sign that he ever set eyes on any Greek art, nor even that he felt the need of such contemplation. By February of 1773 however he possessed casts of three antique heads—a Paris, a Venus and a Mercury—who stood beside him on his desk as he wrote.[3] Perhaps his interest had been revived by reading Heyne's *Einleitung in das Studium der Antike*, which he reviewed for the *Frankfurter Gelehrte Anzeigen* in October 1772.[4] From now on at any rate he continued to collect both casts and engravings of Greek works, until by the end of 1774 he had a small collection, which in those days would have been coveted by any amateur of the Greek. At the Easter Fair of 1773 he got from Italian pedlars good casts of the heads of the Laocoön group and of the daughters of Niobe.[5] During the course of the same year he took a favourable opportunity and bought some good engravings of the most famous antiques, and these he hung around his room.[6] In April of the following year he was trying to add to his collection of casts through the good offices of Raspe, inspector of the Cassel art galleries, and of his friend Höpfner,[7] and in December he wrote to Boie asking him "to send the Niobe in part payment".[8] His enjoyment of all these works of Greek art was not only passive. He made drawings of heads of Apollo and Laocoön[9] during the summer and autumn of 1773, and began, perhaps in con-

---

[1] *Werke*, VIII, pp. vii, viii, 116 foll.

[2] See the letter to Herder (WA. IV, 1, p. 264) quoted above, note to p. 38, and *Wandrers Sturmlied*, for which Apollo Belvedere and *Iliad*, I, 43–52 were both in his thoughts.

[3] Letter to Kestner (WA. IV, 2, p. 62).

[4] WA. 38, p. 374.   [5] WA. 28, p. 188.

[6] *Ibid.* p. 189 and Bied. I, p. 27.   [7] MM. IV, p. 77.

[8] WA. IV, 2, p. 220: "Und schicken mir doch indess auf Abschlag die Niobe."

[9] *Ibid.* pp. 102, 118; MM. VI, p. 274 and Düntzer, *Zur Goetheforschung*, p. 29.

nexion with this drawing, a critical discussion of the heads of the Laocoön group.[1]

During these five years, between his meeting with Herder and his departure for Weimar, he advanced very far in knowledge and understanding of Greek art. He did not come to know many other statues than those he had seen at Mannheim in 1769; but now, by making a collection of his own, of all the reproductions in plaster and engravings that he could lay hands on, he made it possible for himself to contemplate and study much of the best Greek sculpture that was then known, and so to get a firm basis of visual knowledge for whatever ideas his contemplation might bring him. Even so the material that he could provide for himself, had serious limitations. Reproductions of full-length statues or whole groups could only be in the form of engravings, which, even if they were as fine as the plates of Apollo Belvedere and the Medici Venus in Spence's *Polymetis*, could not convey as true an effect of plasticity as any reproduction in the round could do. His casts were all of heads detached from the torso; and this fact tended, as his Laocoön fragment shows, to concentrate his attention on the power of emotional expression in Greek art rather than on its greatness and perfection in representation of the human form. For all that, he had done as much as any man could do, who was not solely an archaeologist and who had to live in Germany, to gain knowledge and understanding of Greek art.

From time to time still his thoughts turned with longing towards Italy. Already in the autumn of 1773 he spoke of this wish to Schönborn.[2] Then in the summer of 1775 he stood with one friend on the summit of the St Gothard and looked over the snow-streaked precipices towards the sunny plains. How easy the descent!—to Milan, to Florence—to Rome! But love and Fate drew him back—northwards to another destiny. During the agonised months that followed, a journey to Italy seemed at times the only escape.[3] But it was not yet to be. Eleven years were to pass before he could walk in daily worship among the great forms that already filled him with such longing.

---

[1] A fragment of this essay is preserved WA. 48, p. 235. For date see v. Lücken, *Natalicium*, p. 88.

[2] Bied. I, p. 27.   [3] WA. IV, 2, p. 278; Bied. I, p. 63.

B. IDEAS

In his youth Goethe never sought knowledge for its own sake. He laboured to know the Greeks, not that he might acquire learning in a field where learning was still rare, but because he knew that knowledge of the Greeks would help him to fulfil his great task. Before we consider how he put his new knowledge to use, it will be well to make clear what picture of the Greeks grew up in him during the period of his *Sturm und Drang*, and what significance they had for him in his own struggle to come to terms with his genius and the world.

The picture of the Greeks that he had made for himself at Leipzig and afterwards, underwent enormous changes from the moment of his meeting with Herder. Inevitably, in the revolution that his whole being suffered, his conception of the Greeks widened and deepened; he saw in them new forms and new meanings. But for the most part these changes were the development of ideas already present. Only on one point did Goethe reject a conception he had previously held and actively fight against it. This was the Rococo Hellenism of Wieland, Jacobi and the other Anacreontic writers.

Herder made the first assault on Goethe's partiality for this fashionable pseudo-classicism. He was not content to censure the falsity of German imitations of "the Antique". Even Ovid's *Metamorphoses*, one pillar of the German Rococo, became the object of his merciless blows. There was nothing genuine in this poetry. "Here was neither Greece nor Italy.... Everything was imitation of traditional models, a mannered style, such as was only to be expected from an over-sophisticated person."[1] Thus the book which had, more than any other, led young Wolfgang on to dwell with joy in the bright world of ancient Hellas, was held up to scorn by one whose judgment Goethe revered unboundedly. Goethe tells us that it cost him a struggle to give up his Ovid; and it is clear that rejection of the Anacreontic, Wielandish classicism came only gradually. The first Greek poet to whom he turned after learning Greek

[1] WA. 27, p. 320.

from Homer, was Anacreon,[1] and it was only his reading of Pindar that opened his eyes to the fact that Anacreon and Theocritus, the two gods of Rococo classicism, were only "sidestreams" of the true Castalian flow of Greek poetry. In a review in the *Frankfurter Gelehrte Anzeigen*[2] he still credited Wieland with "true Greek feeling", though a few weeks later in the same periodical he scoffed at "our sentimental poetasters with their gilt-paper Cupids and Graces, and their Elysium of charity and love".[3]

It was the publication of Wieland's *Alcestis* and still more of the *Letters on the Alcestis* (in the *Teutscher Merkur*, January to March 1773), that roused him finally to open war on Wieland's and Jacobi's conception of the Greeks. With giant, jovial ruthlessness he ridiculed in *Götter, Helden und Wieland*[4] the tendency of the Rococo to prettify the Greeks, to sentimentalise them or to explain away, where it could not be denied, the uncomfortable directness of their feelings. Traits from *Agathon* and *Musarion* are held up to scorn by the shade of Hercules, and Wieland is contemptuously dismissed as having "not a drop of Greek blood in his veins".[5]

War was declared on Rococo Hellenism; but in the following summer Goethe came into friendly personal relations with three leaders of the younger Rococo—Heinse and the Jacobi brothers, Fritz and Georg. Heinse, the only one of the three with real genius, had just published his novel *Laidion*. Cast, like Wieland's *Agathon*, in Greece of the fourth century, the book portrays Greek figures in the familiar Rococo manner, pretty, sentimental, delicately lascivious.[6] It is surprising therefore to find that Goethe admired it.[7] There were tones however

---

[1] WA. IV, 2, p. 16. What Goethe read was, of course, that body of poems of Alexandrine and later date, now known as the "Anacreontea" or the "Pseudo-Anacreon", which in Goethe's youth was still attributed to the true Anacreon.

[2] Summer, 1772. Morris attributes the whole review to Goethe in *Goethes und Herders Anteil* (p. 211), but the Weimar Ausgabe, while printing parts of it as possibly Goethe's, does not include this passage (WA. 38, p. 360). [3] MM. VI, p. 219.

[4] WA. 38, pp. 10–36. October 1773, published March 1774.

[5] *Ibid.* pp. 36 and 14: "Die keine Ader griechisch Blut im Leibe haben."

[6] See Heinse, *Werke*, ed. Schüddekopf, III, pp. 9, 37.

[7] Goethe's opinion is quoted by Heinse in a letter to Schmidt, 13 Oct. 1774; see also Goethe's letter to Schönborn, 4 July 1774 (WA. IV, 2, p. 176).

in the *Laidion* deeper and stronger than anything that Wieland or Jacobi could produce. It was in these that Goethe found a kinship with his own genius. The praise, implied by ironical censure, of Hercules's superhuman capacity for love[1] showed sympathy with the conception of the Greeks that Goethe had set forth in *Götter, Helden und Wieland*; and the *Stanzen*, which Goethe particularly admired, though told with the light touch of Wieland's *Komische Erzählungen* and *Musarion*, laid bare depths of erotic feeling with a frankness that was alien to Wieland's art and temperament.[2] Here and in the introduction to his translation of Petronius,[3] Heinse attributed this frankness, this open-eyed recognition of the rightness of natural instincts, to the Greeks, just as Goethe had done in *Götter, Helden und Wieland*. Goethe admired Heinse's work in spite of its Rococo manner, not because of it.[4]

How vast a gulf lay open between Goethe's view of the Greeks and that of the Rococo writers is shown by a remark of Georg Jacobi:[5] "Just as I dwell among the ancient Greeks," he wrote in his diary in July 1774, "so Goethe dwells among the ancient Scots, Celts and Germans; only with this difference, that at times I visit his wild hills and crags with pleasure... but he will never walk down into my joyous vales, where a Grace plays upon the lyre." Poor Jacobi! He would have walked through Goethe's Hellas and never known it, because there were no Graces and no cupids!

That Goethe admired the Greeks during these years hardly needs to be affirmed. In every reference to them enthusiastic reverence is expressed or implied. "Greek tragedy... stirred whole, great emotions in their souls, for it was itself whole and great. And in what souls! Greek souls! I cannot make clear what that means, but I feel it and appeal, for brevity, to Homer, Sophocles and Theocritus, who have taught me to feel it."[6] So, already in the autumn of 1771, he tried to give his bursting

---

[1] Heinse, *Werke*, III, p. 26.
[2] Stanzas 24 and 26 and the climax of the seduction.
[3] *Werke*, II, p. 14.
[4] Letter to Jacobi, 21 Aug. 1774 (WA. IV, 2, p. 188).
[5] MM. IV, p. 115.
[6] *Rede zum Shakespeares Tag*, WA. 37, p. 131. See also *Künstlers Morgenlied*, WA. 2, p. 178: "Und lese, wie sich's ziemt, Andacht liturg'scher Lection im heiligen Homer."

thoughts expression, and through the years that followed, his veneration for the Greeks never grew less. Goethe did not exaggerate when, in *Dichtung und Wahrheit*, he spoke of "our idols (Abgötter) the Greeks".[1] He tended to see in them all the qualities of greatness of which he was aware in himself. Just as he based right conduct in life and in art on truth to nature and direct feeling, so for him the fundamental virtue of the Greeks, from which all others sprang, was their closeness to the realities of life. This might reveal itself in various forms. The mystical wisdom of the Orphic hymns showed it no less than the simple directness of manners in the Homeric world, or the practical methods of Greek medicine.[2] They lived rightly by spontaneous instinct, while modern life often lost itself in sophisticated nullity.

This contrast between modern falsity and Greek sincerity is most fully developed in *Götter, Helden und Wieland*. This farce, dashed off with the help of a bottle of Burgundy in a moment of righteous wrath,[3] was a reply to Wieland's operetta *Alceste* and to the letters[4] in which Wieland had compared his own treatment of the theme with that of Euripides, often to the disadvantage of the Greek poet. It will be profitable to examine Wieland's grounds for censuring Euripides and then the lines of Goethe's counter-attack.

On grounds of taste Wieland objected to such "burlesque scenes" as the unseemly quarrel between Admetus and his father, and to Admetus's promise that he will take a statue of Alcestis to bed with him when she is dead. He was shocked that Hercules, model of noble conduct, should be represented as getting drunk in a house of mourning, and he found Admetus's emotions at sight of his marriage-bed slightly too outspoken—natural, of course, and genuine, but still not the sort of thing one could have a hero say nowadays. "We are too far", he admitted, "from the simplicity of unspoiled nature." The chief stumbling-block for Wieland was that Admetus should know all along that Alcestis was going to die for him, should rail at the hardness of her fate, but should never once consider refusing her sacrifice and dying himself. For Wieland—and most of us would agree with him—this conduct robbed Admetus of all claim to respect or sympathy.

[1] WA. 28, p. 326. [2] *Ibid.* p. 339. [3] *Ibid.* p. 327.
[4] *Teutscher Merkur*, 1773, Nos. I–III.

Goethe would have none of this. In a striking series of arguments, which a Greek might have understood, but which would be likely to shock modern Christian-humanitarian susceptibilities, he defended Admetus's conduct and poured scorn on Wieland's false sentimentality. Admetus was a young king in the bloom of his vigour and happiness, "a young, utterly fortunate prince, who had received from his father realm and house and possessions, and dwelt among them in happiness, and enjoyed himself, and was complete, and needed nothing but people to enjoy with him, and found them, as was natural, and was never tired of giving, and loved them all so that they loved him, and so had made gods and men his friends, and Apollo forgot Heaven at his table—should he not wish to live for ever?"[1] Admetus represented life in its highest form, and had therefore the right to expect other less perfect individuals to sacrifice themselves for him. Goethe undoubtedly regarded such a scale of values as one of the fundamental realities of existence. The Greeks recognised it and acted by it, but Wieland—representative of the moderns—bases his morality on "Würde der Menschheit" (dignity of man; that is: all individuals, as men, have the same dignity, or value, before God), "a thing that has been abstracted from God knows where".[2] In comparison with these truly heroic figures, genuine through and through, not afraid to live and die in accordance with the profoundest realities, Wieland's Admetus and Alcestis are "nasty, artificial, thin, pale dollies".[3] When Wieland, bewildered and shocked at such sentiments, exclaims: "You speak like people of another world, a language, of which I hear the words without grasping the meaning", Admetus replies: "We are talking Greek!"[4]

---

[1] WA. 38, p. 25: "Ein junger, ganz glücklicher, wohlbehaglicher Fürst, der von seinem Vater Reich und Erbe und Herde und Güter empfangen hatte, und drinne sass mit Genüglichkeit, und genoss, und ganz war, und nichts bedurfte als Leute die mit ihm genossen, und sie, wie natürlich, fand, und des Hergebens nicht satt wurde, und alle liebte, dass sie ihn lieben sollten, und Götter und Menschen so zu Freunden gemacht hatte, und Apoll den Himmel an seinem Tische vergass—der sollte nicht ewig zu leben wünschen?"

[2] *Ibid.* p. 23.

[3] *Ibid.* p. 16: "Abgeschmackte, gezierte, hagre, blasse Püppchens."

[4] *Ibid.* pp. 24, 25.

In everything else too Euripides's sentiment is real, Wieland's false. Alcestis expresses disgust at "what you call sensibility".[1] Euripides knew why he was writing an *Alcestis*, Wieland did not.[2] Wieland's genius is nothing but "an ability to distort and smooth down nature and truth according to a system of morals, stage conventions and a patchwork of rules".[3] The modern conception of virtue and vice as opposites or extremes is false. It is "a monstrosity, that cannot be reconciled with the nature of things". If anyone could know what Virtue is, it would be the demi-gods and heroes, amongst whom she dwelt.[4] Needless to say, such little lapses from good manners as Hercules's drunkenness did not trouble Goethe.[5]

In Homer too he loved above all his naturalness, not merely the lifelike character-drawing, which he praised to Bodmer,[6] but the closeness to the ideal state of nature, the patriarchal simplicity of manners, which had shocked Versailles.[7] When Werther had been snubbed as mere bourgeois by the noble company, he took refuge with Odysseus and Eumaeus, who knew of no such false distinctions between man and man.[8] The importance of this new attitude towards Homer is stressed by Goethe himself in *Dichtung und Wahrheit*.[9] Perhaps in the reaction from French snobbery, Goethe and his friends insisted too one-sidedly on the quality of "nature" in Homer.[10] But at least it was the right starting-point for a sound understanding. Recognition of the other qualities could come with time and study.

Goethe's appreciation of the Greek closeness to Nature and reality grew from that reverence for natural values that Herder had first planted in him. Doubtless Herder had convinced him, before he knew even Homer at first-hand, that this was the fundamental quality in the Greek genius. It is clear,

---

[1] "Rührung", WA. 38, p. 21. [2] *Ibid.* p. 22.
[3] *Ibid.* p. 28: "Eine Fähigkeit, nach Sitten und Theaterconventionen und nach und nach aufgeflickten Statuten Natur und Wahrheit zu verschneiden und einzugleichen."
[4] *Ibid.* pp. 32–34. Cf. Morris, *Goethes und Herders Anteil*, p. 225.
[5] *Ibid.* p. 35.
[6] Bodmer's letter to Schinz, June 1775 (Bied. i, p. 58).
[7] See especially in *Werther*, WA. 19, pp. 39–40, 103, 110.
[8] *Ibid.* p. 103. [9] WA. 28, p. 188.
[10] Lücke, *Goethe und Homer*, Nordhausen, 1884.

however, from *Götter, Helden und Wieland* and from his references to Homer, that Goethe was not content to take his opinion on trust from Herder but confirmed it by his own reading. One idea, a development of that of Greek "naturalness", he took more probably at second-hand from Herder and from reading of Hamann. This was the conception of "theopneustia", the special susceptibility of the great poet or artist to the "divine breath". This idea, common in the ancient world, most clearly expressed in Plato's *Ion*, was fundamental in Goethe's conception of his own genius. Once again, even in a matter that touched the most mysterious facts of his existence, he found that the great Greeks had gone before him in experience.[1]

Sincerity or naturalness was the basic quality which Goethe saw in the Greeks under all circumstances. A close examination of his references to them shows that he was not always so consistent in his attribution of other qualities. At one moment he saw this virtue in them, at another that; and the two might be mutually contradictory. He was still open to influences from all aspects of the many-sided genius of Hellas. He had not, as Winckelmann had, a dogmatically fixed conception of them, to which he forced himself to fit the facts.

He nearly always saw the Greeks as great—great in spirit and in physical size. In his earliest picture of the Homeric heroes as "storks, wading large and free";[2] onwards through his conception of Socrates as the great man, heroic fighter for truth and chastiser of error;[3] in his vision of Jove's dwelling towering to the skies;[4] in his impassioned appreciation of Greek lyric poetry—"so strong, so fiery, so great";[5] in his Alcestis, who shocks poor Wieland with her heroic stature;[6] in Deucalion "sowing on over the fruitful soil of the unending earth";[7] in Homer, beneath whose forehead "the mighty Gods and heroes have as much space as in the wide heavens and the endless earth":[8] everywhere there is the same striving to

---

[1] See Sudheimer, *op. cit.* pp. 17, 19, 20, 45.

[2] "Gross und frei watende Störche."

[3] WA. iv, 2, p. 12.   [4] *Ibid.* p. 25.

[5] Review of *Lyrische Gedichte von Blum* in the *Frankfurter Gelehrte Anzeigen*, June 1772, WA. 37, p. 217.   [6] WA. 38, p. 18.

[7] WA. iv, 2, p. 119 and see MM. vi, p. 272.

[8] *Physiognomische Fragmente*, WA. 37, p. 339.

express the vastness that the Greek genius lent to everything it
touched.[1]

At times he let his Greek figures grow till they took on forms
and feelings vaster than the measure of humanity. In sheer size
Hercules far exceeds the human norm. He is not like Wieland's
Hercules, "a well-proportioned man of middle height". He is
a colossus, a monster, a shape such as has never appeared to
Wieland even in dream. Yet he is only the greatest of those
"giant figures of the vigorous world of fable".[2] Energy too,
sheer physical life-force, is possessed in superhuman measure
by his Hercules, who could lie with fifty women in one night.
Coupled with this excess of energy is another trait of the superman (recognised also by Nietzsche)—the right to hurt and
destroy, as well as to build and order. Hercules claims it in his
description of the "braver Kerl" who forces his love on women
"even against their will".[3] The mystical experience of ecstasy
or direct union with the Deity—a faculty which represents the
highest degree of that abnormal receptivity that was in Goethe's
experience the basic quality of genius—he saw personified in
Ganymede, the beautiful boy who was rapt to Heaven by
Zeus's eagle. Prometheus too knew this ecstasy and called it
death.[4] By his mere nature and through his power to create,
Prometheus is equal to the gods;[5] he defies their every attempt
to impose their overlordship on him by craft or force. Prometheus and even more Goethe's other "saints", Ixion and
Sisyphus, were supermen who had transgressed the bounds of
what is fixed for mortals and had suffered for their reckless-
ness.[6] Here was a wild stormy Greece, full of gigantic figures
struggling with pitiless gods, or of heroes locked in desperate
struggle, of trampling horses, wounds and death.[7] Blackwell,

[1] See also WA. 37, p. 203.
[2] Letter to Schönborn, June 1774 (WA. IV, 2, p. 172). Note that the
Hercules of the Orphic Hymns corresponds to Goethe's picture, not
Wieland's. He is called τιτάν, καρτερόχειρε, ἀδάμαστε, ἀγριόθυμε, παμφάγε,
παγγενέτωρ, ἀθανάτοις πολύπειρος, ἀπείριτος.
[3] "Auch wohl ungebeten": WA. 38, p. 34. For "Genie als Zerstörer"
see Sudheimer, op. cit. pp. 177, 178.
[4] WA. 39, pp. 211, 212. See Butler, Tyranny of Greece, p. 90.
[5] WA. 39, pp. 196, 198, 201–2, 205, 213 foll.
[6] WA. 28, p. 314, and see letter to Kestner, 25 Sept. 1772 (WA. IV, 2,
p. 27).
[7] Künstlers Morgenlied, WA. 2, p. 178.

who had emphasised the lawlessness and violence of Homer's world,[1] helped Goethe to see Greece thus; but chiefly this picture was a reflection of the *Sturm und Drang* in his own bosom.

In all this there seems to be no appreciation of the Greek feeling for measure, proportion, μηδὲν ἄγαν; yet he found this quality in them too, not as a static law of proportion in art or of moderation in life, but as a dynamic tendency to control the too-expansive life-force and concentrate it into defined channels. It was Pindar who inspired him thus to bridle his genius, like the charioteer in the race at Olympia or the Pythian games, who reins and whips and cajoles his wilful team till all are pulling together towards the goal. Pindar had known the danger and had been great enough to keep the disintegrating power of genius in check. He had called it ἐπικρατεῖν δύνασθαι.[2] This power to give form to creative impulses, the essence of the artistic gift, Goethe saw again in Prometheus—especially at the time when he was writing the first two acts of his *Prometheus*. Even the other Prometheus, the Zeus-defying Titan, had "toughness",[3] which is another form of the power to resist the destructive forces of genius. In Homer's face could be seen the same firmness.[4]

So we come round half-circle from the monstrous Hercules, the reckless overweening Tantalus and Ixion, the wild, almost lunatic, lust of battle in *Künstlers Morgenlied*, to the "assured repose" that rests, together with firmness, on Homer's features, and to the wonderful peace that pervades all those glimpses of the Homeric world in *Werther*.[5] Not merely the peacefulness of the *Odyssey* soothes Werther's troubled spirit. The picture of Odysseus' smallness in face of the vast sea and the limitless earth, of the life of those ancient patriarchs, so circumscribed and so fortunate, is to him subtly true, deeply human, a mystery of genius.[6] Winckelmann could have recognised these Greeks, while Hercules would have shocked him, as Lessing was shocked.[7] So too there is a breath from the *Gedanken* in

---

[1] *Enquiry into the life and writings of Homer*, 1735, pp. 16, 23, 35, 65.
[2] Letter to Herder, July 1772 (WA. IV, 2, pp. 16, 17).
[3] "Festigkeit" or "Widerstandskraft", Sudheimer, *op. cit.* p. 58 fol.
[4] WA. 37, p. 340.   [5] WA. 19, pp. 10, 39, 103, 110.
[6] *Ibid.* p. 110.   [7] Lessing, *Werke*, XXII, p. 303.

the picture of the lonely statue that looks down "mourning majestically"[1] on the fragments of the ruined temple. Here Goethe was seeing the Greeks more conventionally though no less sincerely.

To sum up Goethe's view of the Greeks—for this catalogue of conflicting impressions leaves a muddled picture in the mind —we may say that he saw in them a people that had understood better than any other how to give form to life on a great scale. They had had the urge to strike out recklessly and know life to the limit; but they had known also how to keep this urge within bounds so that it never lost itself in formlessness. Greek form might at times be superhumanly vast, but it remained always form.

Goethe's view of the Greeks at this period was conditioned by their significance to him, by the use, that is, to which he felt he could put them. The great problem of his life at this time was: how to live at all under the intolerable stress of the daemonic forces within him. He had discovered that he could save himself by projecting the struggle with the daemon outside himself in artistic form. The secondary problem was then to find means of expression equal to this task. For the solution of both problems the Greeks were indispensable to him. From their mythology, their literature and their art, he saw that the artists and thinkers of Greece had, like him, been racked by the daemon and had been brought by it near to destruction. But they had been strong enough to master (ἐπικρατεῖν) the daemon and to turn his terrible power into peaceful, helpful forms. In Pindar the struggle and the barely won victory were plain to see, in Aeschylus too perhaps, who wrestled darkly with words,[2] and revelled in blasphemous defiance of the ruling Powers. Socrates had yoked the daemon to the cause of truth; and Homer, though shapes of gods and heroes had walked in his mind, had won a serenity of view, a detachment, that belied the soul-shattering experiences he must have known. Why had the *Odyssey* such a special fascination for Werther? Because Werther, who felt himself slipping to destruction through inability to harness his abnormal sensibility to some-

---

[1] "Majestätisch trauernd": *Der Wandrer*, WA. 2, p. 173.
[2] Cf. Winckelmann, *Werke*, I, p. 34, and Sulzer, *Allgemeine Theorie der schönen Künste*, article on Aeschylus.

thing constructive,[1] saw in Odysseus the picture of what he would himself like to be. Odysseus too was a genius, or at least he was for Homer a symbol of genius. He was blown over the length and breadth of the knowable world and even beyond, but he never lost sight of his νόστιμον ἦμαρ—the day of his return to his house and his wife and his young son. Through everything he kept his powers fixed on one objective. He remained steadfast, limited, human. Just so limited and so human Werther would gladly have remained. He could not; and when he knew the struggle was useless, when the powers of destruction had him beyond hope in their grasp, he turned from the comforting clarity of the *Odyssey* to the misty howlings of the ancient Celts. Goethe saved himself from Werther's fate, thanks in part to the example of Pindar and Socrates and Homer.

In the business of composition too the Greeks helped him by their example. Not that he hoped any longer to find in their works absolute models to be copied line for line after a system of rules. He never had used them so in his own compositions, and seems always to have had his doubts about the rightness of this method even in theory. Still more since his contact with Herder, such niggling "imitation" was contrary to all his most holy beliefs—the divine originality of genius, "Nature" as the only model, and the relativity of artistic precepts, which vary from land to land and from age to age. He mocked at the Frenchman and the Italian "who creep over the mighty ruins [of antiquity] to beg 'proportions', patch together summer-houses out of the sacred wreckage, and fancy themselves keepers of the secrets of art, because they can give an account of those giant dwellings by measurements in inches".[2] This French attitude to the works of Greek genius, whether it applied, as here, to architecture, or to sculpture, or, in the insistence on the Unities, to literature,[3] aroused in him the same contemptuous rage. Yet the Greeks were models to him too. He would not

[1] See Sudheimer's analysis of the Werther-symbol, *op. cit.* p. 48.

[2] *Von deutscher Baukunst*, WA. 37, p. 141: "Krochst an den mächtigen Resten Verhältnisse zu betteln, flicktest aus den heiligen Trümmern dir Lusthäuser zusammen, und hältst dich für Verwahrer der Kunstgeheimnisse, weil du auf Zoll und Linie von Riesengebäuden Rechenschaft geben kannst."

[3] WA. 37, p. 131.

imitate them but he would emulate them. He would not produce works like theirs, but he would compose as they had done from the same deep knowledge of humanity, the same store of intense feeling, the same nearness to the basic values. They had known the only laws that any artist has ever needed, just as Shakespeare knew them: truth to nature, sincerity, faith in the unconscious power of genius. Herder had first shown him the way to this truly fruitful relationship with the Greek genius. His own later reading of Hamann, perhaps also a renewed and more understanding study of Winckelmann, deepened his conception of this relationship in some directions.[1] But these theoretical pointers would have been useless, had not his own experience of the ways of genius and his own reading of Homer, Pindar and Euripides confirmed what the great critics had foretold. His admiration of Homer did not lead him on to write epics in hexameters. But the *Iliad* and the *Odyssey* revealed to him much about the nature of man and of the world, and still more about genius and art. From such knowledge then he wrote his *Götz*, *Werther*, *Prometheus* and *Faust*. Pindar came nearest to seducing him to crabbed imitation. Yet even here the only result of his "pindarising" was that he evolved a style of lyric that neither he nor anyone else in Germany (except perhaps Herder) had even dreamed of. The great free-verse odes are not Pindaric. In every line and every syllable they are Goethe and only Goethe.[2] The Greeks and Shakespeare revealed to him what poetry could be. Homer, Pindar and the Tragedians set a standard of truth and power and beauty, to attain which even his vast genius had to exert itself to the full. They were models to him but only in this broadest sense, not at all in the sense that they should be copied in form or style.

So in this way too the Greeks helped Goethe the man to survive. For to him a satisfying creative output was as vitally

[1] See Sudheimer, *op. cit.* pp. 375–9. For Herder's attitude to the Greeks as "Vorbilder" see *Werke*, I, pp. 349, 370, 444; IV, p. 260; VIII, pp. 34, 36, 80.

[2] Carl Olbrich, *Nachahmung der klassischen Sprachen in Goethes Wortstellung und Wortgebrauch*, Leipzig, 1891, p. 11, sees clear evidence of direct imitation of Pindaric expressions in the free-verse odes. There is no doubt that Goethe continued the process that Klopstock had started, of enriching the German language by the introduction of Greek phrases and manners of speech.

necessary as the regular working of the natural functions is to
more ordinary folk. Had it not been for the Greek tradition
in a third matter, he might still have been hard put to it to
give artistic form to the ideas that seethed within him. These
ideas were too vast, too complex, often too mysteriously
irrational to be expressed in the intellectual language of abstract thought. Before they could become poetry, they had to
be made visual, to be given a body, which could live and move
and express by its actions and its appearance every aspect of the
conception which was, as it were, its soul. In short Goethe
needed symbols, images taken from life, which by their richness in association could be made to convey these manifold
meanings, deep or subtle as the case might require. His method
was to ransack the history and mythology of all the peoples of
the world in search of men and women (or for that matter
heroes and even gods, if they were visual enough) who seemed
to have experienced what he had experienced and what he was
then trying to express. He demanded three things of these
symbolic figures: that their experience should fit his own case
not too remotely; that they should be real beings with a life
and a shape of their own, not mere personifications of an
abstraction; and that they should be reasonably familiar,
primarily to himself, secondly to the public, so that there would
be no smell of dust or midnight oil about them. It is not surprising therefore to find that Greek legend and mythology
provided him with more of these figures than any other race
or age, more even than his native Germany. For, as we have
seen, the Greeks had known his problems and fought his
battles; their legendary figures, whether gods or men, have a
quality of clear-seen vitality that is rare in the folk-lore of any
other race;[1] and the names and to a great extent the appearance
and actions of these figures were still familiar to all the educated world. Against the three German figures of Götz,
Hanswurst and Faust, Greece gave him no less than nine,
which he used, some with more, some with less, frequency and
depth of import: Ganymede, Hercules, Prometheus, Apollo,[2]
Bromius,[2] Jupiter,[2] Mercury,[3] Venus,[4] and Minerva.[5]

[1] WA. 28, p. 143.
[2] These three in *Wandrers Sturmlied.*   [3] WA. IV, 2, p. 62.
[4] *Künstlers Erdewallen.*   [5] In *Prometheus.*

That this use of mythology was fundamentally different from his use of it in Leipzig[1] hardly needs to be pointed out. Even then he had half-parodied the traditional use while he followed it; but he had had no conception of how to escape from the dilemma and give the myths new life. The realisation of the true meaning and purpose of mythology, revealed to him, it is safe to assume, by Herder in Strassburg,[2] had at a bound lifted him clear of all such difficulties. Now he could afford to laugh openly at the old way; and he did so in a high-flown, pompous apostrophe of the goddess Boredom, who had stirred up his friends to write to him.[3] Already in the summer and autumn of 1771 Herder's attitude to the Greek myths is implicit in Goethe's references to Apollo[4] and to Prometheus.[5] The first poetical use of Greek figures as symbols occurs then in *Wandrers Sturmlied*[6] (spring, 1772). In the second stanza Goethe desired to give form to all that he felt about the strength and beauty of genius. To define these feelings in a string of adjectives and abstract nouns would not have been poetry and would not have helped to unload his spirit. What he felt, could not be defined in such terms. Instead there rose before his mind's eye the figure of the Archer god, as he had seen him at Mannheim, yet transfigured, glowing, splendid, with superhuman vigour and beauty

> ... χωόμενος κῆρ
> τόξ' ὤμοισιν ἔχων ἀμφηρεφέα τε φαρέτρην,
> ἔκλαγξαν δ' ἄρ' ὀϊστοὶ ἐπ' ὤμων χωομένοιο,

as he went out to slay Pytho, the mud-born dragon,

> Ueber Deukalions Flutschlamm,
> Python tödtend, leicht, gross,
> Pythius Apollo.[7]

Later in the same poem he calls on Bromius and Jupiter

---

[1] See above, p. 41.
[2] See Herder, *Werke*, I, pp. 426–9.
[3] *Concerto Dramatico*, WA. 38, p. 3.
[4] Letter to Herder (WA. IV, 1, p. 264).
[5] In the *Shakespeare-Rede*, WA. 37, p. 133.
[6] WA. 2, pp. 67 foll.
[7] "Over Deukalion's sea of mud, Python-slaying, light, mighty, Pythian Apollo."

Pluvius. What sense can these threadbare names have in a modern poem?

> Vater Bromius!
> Du bist Genius,
> Jahrhunderts Genius,
> Bist was innre Glut
> Pindarn war.[1]

This means, according to Morris,[2] that "our century finds in wine the inspiration which should arise from the inner glow (innre Wärme, Seelenwärme)". Bromius is then simply a label for the effect of wine on the human constitution, just as Bacchus had been in the pretty versifyings of Goethe's Leipzig days.[3] But this is impossible; Goethe would never at this period have put the Greek gods to the old misuse.

> Soll der zurückkehren
> Der kleine, schwarze, feurige Bauer?
> Soll der zurückkehren, erwartend
> Nur deine Gaben, Vater Bromius,
> Und hellleuchtend umwärmend Feuer?[4]

That is Bromius, the universal vitalising power, without whose gifts life in its simplest form would be impossible for man, and without whom there would be no higher inspiration. He is "the god of wine", because wine reveals in mysterious concentration the vital spirit that Bromius provides for all life. To turn such conceptions into poetry Goethe needed symbols and he found them ready to his hand in the Greek myths. So too Jupiter Pluvius is not merely the "god of rain". He is symbol of all the power and energy of storm, the fructifying force that reveals itself in rain or in genius such as Pindar's. So Ganymede came to symbolise the mystical faculty, Hercules the "Sakermentskerl", and Prometheus the artist in his divine self-sufficiency; all were aspects of the daemonic force of genius.

---

[1] "Father Bromius, thou art genius, genius of the age, art what inner glow was to Pindar."

[2] MM. vi, p. 187.   [3] *An Venus*, WA. 4, p. 92.

[4] "Shall he turn back, the little, dark, fiery peasant? Shall he turn back, who looks only for thy gifts, Father Bromius, and for bright-glowing, warming fire?"

These Greek figures enabled him to give poetical expression to the experiences which his daemon brought him, and so to free himself from the baleful consequences of association with the daemon. It is fair to say that at this period Goethe was interested in the Greeks solely from this point of view. He used the figures of Greek history or mythology whenever they were most suitable to his purpose. When some un-Greek figure— Mahomed or Faust—fitted his needs more closely, he would use that figure. The Greeks had as yet no absolute value to him. He had no feeling that it was better to use a Greek symbol simply because it was Greek. Still less did he feel any urge to idealise the Greek world and see in it a Golden Age to be longed for and as far as possible reproduced.

> Nicht in Rom, in Magna Gräcia,
> Dir im Herzen ist die Wonne da!

he wrote to Merck.[1] So with simple consistency his relation to the Greeks was based on just that natural necessity which they had taught him to follow in life and in art. In later years he might know them better, he might admire them more exclusively; but he was never in closer contact with the Greek genius than now in the careless days of *Sturm und Drang*.

[1] 4 Dec. 1774 (WA. IV, 2, p. 328): "Not in Rome or Magna Graecia, but in your own heart is bliss."

CHAPTER III

WEIMAR (1775–1786)

Das Land der Griechen mit der Seele suchend.

IT is customary to regard Goethe's arrival in Weimar in November 1775 as marking the end of his *Sturm und Drang* and the beginning of that period of self-discipline and repose which led eventually to the Italian journey and to classicism. Such sharp dividing lines between the periods of development in a human being are inevitably no better than fences which the biographer establishes for his convenience. It was indeed not long before those influences which finally worked the change in him began to take effect, but *Sturm und Drang* did not die without a struggle; it still found expression in a wild mode of life and in such poems as *Rastlose Liebe*. By the beginning of 1776 the battle was joined, but nearly two years were to pass before the victory of self-discipline was complete. Goethe's relation to the Greeks reflects the conflict and the change in all its stages. The earliest reference to Homer in the Weimar-period reads like a passage from *Werther*. On Christmas Eve 1775 Goethe wrote to the Duke from Waldeck, a hamlet in the woods behind Jena: "I will ask the parson if he has the *Odyssey*. If he has not, I will send to Jena for it. It is impossible to do without it in this simple Homeric world. Especially I have been thinking of those verses that run roughly so: And wrapped in their skins they lay by the glimmering hearth; over them blew the rainy wind through the endless night and they lay and slept refreshing sleep till late-dawning day."[1] Then, only three weeks later, he wrote to Charlotte von Stein, whose influence over him was already powerful: "I am glad to get away, that I may learn to do without you...I wish within my heart it were so clear that I...could make you laugh. But all my fun and all my wit are God knows where! I am taking Homer with me. We shall see what he can do for

[1] WA. IV, 3, p. 9. The quotation seems to be a paraphrase in Homeric style of two passages from *Od.* XIV (lines 457–8 and 518–24).

me."[1] Already Homer was an ally of Charlotte, a power for
light in the darkness of the inner struggle. But this marks as
yet no great revolution in Goethe's view of the Greeks, for
the *Odyssey* had always been an antidote to storm.[2] Goethe's
judgments of Bürger's translation of the fifth and sixth books
of the *Iliad* still show insistence on Homer's "simplicity";
he approved Bürger's choice of the iambic metre rather than
the hexameter, because it was the "true, old, natural metre of
our language", and he encouraged Bürger to use archaic
words so as to give the style an antique, vigorous flavour.[3]
All that is the old view of Homer, the bard of patriarchal
simplicity. But there is also emphasis on a new aspect of
Homer, his "golden, living clarity". He was becoming more
than a mere opiate for storm-wracked nerves. This golden
clarity is an ideal, a vision, something new to put in the place
of old gods soon to be discarded.[4]

During the latter part of 1776 and the beginning of 1777
there is no evidence to show how he regarded the Greeks nor
how he related them to his struggle. But the position of Greek
culture in modern life exercised him much during this period,
both as a personal and as a social problem. His conclusions
are to be found in *der Triumph der Empfindsamkeit* (written
during the winter 1777–1778) and in the monodrama *Proserpina*, which, as he said himself, he "criminally"[5] worked
into the *Triumph*, thereby destroying its emotional and aesthetic
effect. For *Proserpina* is a poem of intense feeling and rare
beauty, while the other is a flippant satire on the fashionable
sensibility of the age. In the *Triumph* the main attack was
directed against the emotional sentimentality that Goethe had
himself helped to unleash with *Stella* and *Werther*. But he was
aiming at all expressions of false sentiment or shallow enthusiasm,
amongst which the passion for grecising was particularly objectionable to him. Not only is ridicule heaped on the fashion

---

[1] *Ibid.* p. 18.   [2] See above, p. 76.
[3] *Diesseitige Antwort auf Bürger's Anfrage wegen Uebersetzung des Homers,*
published in the *Teutscher Merkur*, February 1776 (WA. 37, p. 360) and Bied.
I, pp. 77, 78.
[4] The other references to reading of Homer in these first three years
(*Tagebuch*, 8 Nov. 1776, WA. III, 1, p. 27, and 20 June 1778, *ibid.* p. 68) give
no indication of any attitude.
[5] Goethe's word is "freventlich".

for "monodramas", for which the subject was always chosen
from Greek mythology,[1] but throughout the play those who
use Greek words and expressions without knowing their true
meaning, are delicately laughed at. Merkulo, the affected
major-domo of the languishing prince, is the chief offender.
He explains solemnly that a monodrama is a play with two
characters, a duodrama one with three, and that they are sometimes called "melodrama" because there is neither melody nor
song in them.[2] He is shocked when one of the court ladies
criticises the song he has taken from Aristophanes, and silences
her with the all-powerful word: "It is from the Greek!"[3]
The Prince, who is the embodiment of everything false and
affected, is given to the same senseless use of Greek allusions.
He likens his own condition to the sufferings of Tantalus and
begs "the gods" to give him ease.[4] He abuses the girls who
disturb his rest as "Erinnyes, Maenads!" with complete indifference to the exact use of either term.[5] It may be that
Goethe meant to make fun of these ignorant Greekisers even
in the spelling of the Greek names, which are frequently mis-
spelt in the original manuscript—"Pyriphleyton" for "Peri-
phlegethon", "elisäisch" for "elysisch".[6] The gardener has no
illusions about those who lay out parks in the Greek manner.
"So for instance we hide a pig-stye behind a temple, and
another sort of stye (you understand me!) is nothing less than
a Pantheon."[7]

Goethe hated this shallow enthusiasm for everything Greek,
because to him the relationship of the modern world to ancient
Greece was a problem of the bitterest earnest. During 1777 the
struggle between *Sturm und Drang* and self-discipline was at
its height. Vaguely he was aware that the Greeks could help
him to win to the new ideal in life and in art, but as yet he
could not see how this was to happen. As he wrote even in
June 1778, in the Epilogue to *Die Vögel*: "To get from Athens

---

[1] Rousseau's *Pygmalion*, 1762, was the first, on which followed *Ariadne
auf Naxos* by Brandes, 1774; Bertuch's *Polyxena*, published in the *Teutscher
Merkur*, Oct. 1774; and Gotter's *Medea*, 1775 (Biedermann, *Goethefor-
schungen*, pp. 42-4).

[2] WA. 17, pp. 11-12, 24.   [3] *Ibid.* p. 26.
[4] *Ibid.* p. 65.   [5] *Ibid.* p. 32.
[6] *Ibid.* pp. 342, 343, 340.
[7] *Ibid.* p. 37. Cf. WA. IV, 4, p. 142.

to Ettersburg you need to make a salto mortale."[1] This problem and his temporary failure to find a satisfactory relationship to Greek culture found powerful artistic expression in *Proserpina*. The idea of writing a monodrama on the subject of Proserpina's captivity in Hades may have been suggested to Goethe in the first instance as early as April 1776 by Gluck's request that he should write an ode on the death of the composer's niece, but it must soon have become clear to Goethe that the work as it grew under his hand was not suited to such a purpose. The exact date or dates at which Goethe was working on the monodrama are not known. It was written before the *Triumph der Empfindsamkeit*, of which it came to form the fourth act. It was also published by itself in the *Teutscher Merkur* of February 1778.[2]

In the *Triumph der Empfindsamkeit* the way is prepared for the introduction of Proserpina's monologue by the monologue of the gardener, who has been sent to make the gloomy vales of Hades smile like the Sicilian meadows from which the new queen of the underworld has been snatched. "She seeks among the dead as lovely spots as in Sicilian land; we have such only in poems. Daily she asks for glorious fruits, but we have none to offer. We should have to look far for peaches and grapes; crabs, sloes, hips and haws and suchlike is all that grows with us." (Two sprites of Hell bring a pomegranate tree in a pot.) "So I've had recourse to a hot-house; I hatch out these pomegranates with subterranean fire in a frost-covered house. I'll stick it in the ground" (he does so as he speaks), "put stones, grass and moss around it, so that the Queen will think it is growing from the rock; and when she marks the trick, will praise the artist as befits."[3] The old longing for the southern culture, product of the lands of sun and glorious fruits, of which we in our frosty North know only from the poets of Greece and Rome, was strong in Goethe now, as often before. But still he mocked any attempt to breed this culture by artificial means on northern soil.

Then follows the monodrama *Proserpina*. This curious poem has been interpreted in many ways. One commentator sees in it a symbolic representation of the Duchess Luise's unhappy

[1] WA. 17, p. 114 and WA. IV, 4, p. 249.
[2] Cf. WA. 17, p. 311.   [3] *Ibid.* p. 39.

married life; another, Goethe's cry of anguish at his own loneliness in a world that did not understand him. Others seek in
it no deeper meaning, and regard it as a piece written for
Corona Schröter to enable her to display her talents to their
full advantage. Some of these explanations are clearly inadequate. Others, though they are tenable in the light of the
general circumstances of Goethe's life at the time, yet fail to
coincide in detail with many points in the text of the monologue.

There is only one interpretation which fits the broad lines of
development of Goethe's genius at this period and is also
supported by a line-by-line examination of the text. This land
from which Proserpina has been ravished, to which she looks
back with such intense longing—this paradise of sun and
flowers, of "Alpheus sky-clear stream", of fair youths and
care-free comrades, what is it but Greece? What are the
flowers that the deserted comrades gather up as they gaze
vainly after their lost mistress, but the few remnants that have
come down to us of Greek art and poetry? Proserpina rules
indeed in Hades, as the Greek canons ruled in the art and
literature of Goethe's day; but it is a realm of shadows, a
sovereignty in name alone that both enjoy. Helpless to better
the grim world of reality is the Greek ideal—as helpless as
Proserpina to stay the sufferings of the damned. "Empty and
ever empty" is modern life, on which the once full life of
Greece can only look in pity, impotent to enrich a world with
which it has no connexions. The blest who walk in the Elysian
fields, the visions of an ideal Greece in which some moderns
see salvation, are bloodless and lifeless. They have none of the
vital reality that was the essence of the Greek world. Why does
the dark Northerner long for Greece and drag it down, as
Pluto did Proserpina, into his gloomy world? Why is he not
content with a lesser ideal? Ceres lost her divinity in the loss
of her daughter; so life lost that which made it divine, when
Greece, its glorious youth, passed away. Nothing remains to
do it honour now but weeping, comfortless mortals. Always
men search for Greece as Ceres sought her daughter, but the
search leads them into the wilderness and into the land of death.
Men must seek back to Nature, the spring of life, to Zeus the
father, as the Greeks did. Nevertheless the hope cannot be

beaten down that Proserpina may return to earth, that Greece may live again among men. Proserpina catches sight of the pomegranate. Hope rises again that even in the underworld, in the dark northern world, Greece may be won by merely tasting of Greek culture. Proserpina tastes the fruit. A momentary joy is followed by the frightful realisation that now all escape is impossible. By tasting of the knowledge of the Ideal, which was once living in Greece, we drag the Ideal into our hateful world of darkness and suffering. Both it and we must suffer eternally; we, because we can never now be content and yet are impotent to make our vision real; the Ideal, because it is powerless to change the world, into which it has been dragged. So with a bitterness of despair which is equalled hardly even in Faust, Goethe gave expression to his sense of frustration in face of the Greek ideal. In this bitter mood he had no compunction about inserting the beautiful, tragic monologue into the satirical comedy in such a way as to destroy its whole effect. He knew it was a crime, but he did not care.[1] With less bitterness, but with indescribable longing roused by a mere breath from the lost Hellenic world, he wrote in October 1777 to Frau von Stein: "This evening for the first time in a long while I wrote some Greek words. It is quiet here with me, or rather around me; for in my heart it is not so. Adieu."[2]

Proserpina is not an allegorical figure representing Greek culture. She is a symbol, which Goethe's longing for Greece and his sense of frustration drew over from the world of myths into the more real world of poetry. Through her speaks now the poet's longing for Greece, now merely the picture that he had made for himself of that happy land and race. This very inconsistency proves the depth of feeling out of which the figure of Proserpina arose. It is an answer in itself to the objection which may be offered to this whole interpretation of the *Proserpina*: that the problem of his relation to Greek culture was too special and intellectual a theme to inspire Goethe to a work of such passion. For Goethe, it was no academic problem to be discussed learnedly *pro et contra*. He was engaged in one of the decisive struggles of his life. Was he to continue a victim to the uncontrollable attacks of the daemon

[1] WA. 35, p. 6.   [2] WA. IV, 3, p. 181.

which had often brought him to the edge of destruction, or was he to win through to repose, to self-control, to conscious mastery? In that struggle the Greeks were coming to stand for the ideal of repose and of self-control. It was a matter of vital importance to him to find out how to put their example to practical use. The agony which his failure caused him was quite capable of producing a poem of the deepest feeling.

Goethe had always used some aspects of Greece as an inspiration to endure the attacks of the daemon. Now as his need for symbols of the type of Hercules and Prometheus disappeared, these aspects of Greece, which Winckelmann had stressed, grew in importance. From Herder too he had learnt to think of Greece as the Golden Age, the care-free life of dance and song, of beauty and innocent love.[1] Brighter and brighter this picture shone in his mind. He saw in it all the things for which he longed. Before he was aware, Greece had become an ideal.

It was a change of great significance. In the years of *Sturm und Drang* no land or people, no period in history had meant everything to him. He had admired and made use of certain qualities in each, while Nature and his genius remained his only gods. Now one people and one period were beginning to attain a special position in his thoughts. He was beginning to doubt both Nature and his genius, and to set up in his mind an abstract ideal, of which the incarnation had once been in Greece. The change came from within as a reflexion of the great change that was taking place in Goethe's whole nature. A curious hint of what may have been the first dawning of the new attitude to Greece is contained in Wieland's sketch *Goethe und die jüngste Niobetochter*.[2] With delicate wit and understanding Wieland here dramatised a scene that occurred in his own house in the spring of 1776. Goethe, while visiting there with some other gentlemen from the court, fell into a kind of rapture in contemplation of a bust of one of the Niobids. The courtiers might make what suggestions they liked as to the nature of Goethe's rapture; Wieland, himself not unacquainted

---

[1] Herder, *Werke*, I, p. 285, and VIII, pp. 26, 62. Compare Goethe's Maskenzug, *Die vier Weltalter* (WA. 16, p. 440), 1782.

[2] Published *G-J.* IX, pp. 7-10. For commentary on it see Düntzer, *Zur Goetheforschung*, pp. 26 foll., and P. Weizsäcker, *Vierteljahrschrift für Literaturgeschichte*, vol. VI.

with visions, could see that Goethe was in a visionary trance, in which the beautiful face upturned towards him had ceased to be cold plaster and had become a form that drew his soul after it out of the world into realms of power and beauty. At this moment the Greek spirit, clarified in the simple contours of the childish face, took hold of him as an ideal with such power that for over thirty years he could not be rid of it.

It is clear from *Proserpina* that the first workings of this inoculation were far from pleasant. Goethe was tortured by a vision which he could not realise. In an effort to ban the inconvenient spirit he turned in the autumn of 1777 to Aristophanes. Here he hoped to find the Greeks portrayed as men and women with common everyday emotions, needs and cares. In this way it might be the ideal would lose its power. Through the winter and spring of 1777–1778 he read Aristophanes with some consistency.[1] The last reference is from December 1778 and suggests that he was losing interest. This study of Aristophanes is reflected in the *Triumph der Empfindsamkeit*[2] and still more directly in *Die Vögel* (summer 1780).[3] Here Goethe set out to adapt Aristophanes's *Birds* into a satire on certain contemporary figures in German literature. By then he no longer needed Aristophanes's help against the tormenting vision, but he still found the old Greek a useful guide in some of the lighter tasks of genius.

He gave up the attempt to exorcise the Greek ideal by reading Aristophanes, because by the spring of 1778 such a means of escape was no longer needed. The battle had been won. There might be moments when the old torments returned,[4] but fundamentally Goethe was now sure of himself, sure of his ability to move steadily ahead, in full control of his

---

[1] Merkulo's song in the *Triumph der Empfindsamkeit* (WA. 17, p. 25; probably about Oct. 1777) is taken from the opening lines of the *Ecclesiazusae*; then *Tagebuch*, 1778, 15 Feb., 12 March (the *Frogs*) and 8 Dec. (WA. III, 1, pp. 62, 63, 73).

[2] Cf. Düntzer, *Eine andere Gestalt von Goethes "Triumph der Empfindsamkeit"*. *Blätter für literarische Unterhaltungen*, Jan. 1849, p. 96.

[3] WA. 17, pp. 75–115. There are inconclusive signs of an earlier version of *Die Vögel*. See WA. IV, 4, p. 242 and introduction to W. Arndt's edition of *Die Vögel*, 1886. Cf. also Gräf, *Drama*, IV, pp. 393, 394, who suggests that this earlier version was merely a translation of the *Birds*.

[4] "Lidte Prometheisch": *Tagebuch*, April 1780, WA. III, 1, p. 116.

genius and of his fate, at peace with God. In February he noted
in his diary: "This week much on the ice, in always the same,
almost too untroubled mood.... Stillness and premonition of
wisdom.... More definite feeling of limitation and through it
of true expansion."[1] Just a year after that entry in his diary, on
14 February 1779, he began to write *Iphigenie*. The struggle and
the final victory were by then far enough in the past for Goethe
to reconstruct them in a poetic image. *Iphigenie* is the poetical
expression of his victory over the Furies of *Sturm und Drang*.
At the same time it was the fruit of a new relationship to Greece.
It can hardly be doubted that Goethe wished to symbolise this
in the fulfilment of Iphigenie's longing to return to her native
Hellas. Just as this return was won by Iphigenie through the
victory over herself which solved at the same time all other
conflicts, so the solution of Goethe's problem in face of the
Greek ideal arose out of the general victory over the forces of
destruction.

Before this moment there had been no aspect of Greece
with which his divided spirit could make contact. He could
admire and revere the great works of Greek genius but they
had seemed to him sprung from a foreign mentality. The
difficulty had lain in fact in the uncertainty of his own feelings
during the period of transition. Now that he was again united
in himself, Greece could give him from her bountiful store a
symbol for his new creed. He saw before him a Greek youth
in naked simplicity and self-assured repose, and knew that this
was the visible expression of his new wisdom.

No external influences could have helped him to this vision
any earlier, for he was not ready to receive it. In this sense it
grew from within him out of the organic development of his
spirit. But when the moment had come, chance threw in his
way certain men and certain ideas that led him quickly to the
end he was seeking. In May 1778, he was in Leipzig, saw his
old master Oeser and had talk with him on the principles of
art.[2] Winckelmann's doctrine of "noble simplicity and quiet

---

[1] WA. III, 1, p. 61: "Diese Woche viel auf dem Eis, in immer gleicher
fast zu reiner Stimmung.... Stille und Vorahndung der Weisheit...
Bestimmteres Gefühl von Einschränkung, und dadurch der wahren Aus-
breitung."
[2] WA. IV, 3, p. 231.

greatness'', and the art on which that doctrine was based, must have been brought vividly to Goethe's mind even if, as seems to have been the case, he did not actually read any of Winckelmann's works.[1] In the July following he read the aesthetic works of Mengs, which may have served as a substitute for Winckelmann. Anton Rafael Mengs, a German painter of considerable repute in his day, had written much about the theory and practice of art.[2] He had been an intimate friend of Winckelmann in Rome, whose maxims he echoed in his own writings. In these essays Goethe found a picture of Greece that had no room for the gigantic figures of old fable, from whom he was trying to escape. Instead he saw a beautiful youth, and an art that made this single figure the centre of all its labour, constantly refining the representation of it until out of perfect balance and proportion grew a thing of perfect beauty. Divine youth! Was not just such balance and proportion the goal towards which Goethe had been struggling for close on three years, the goal at which he had now arrived?

In the same year Herder published his essay *Plastik*. The ideas in it were not new to Goethe. In Strassburg eight years before, he had read as much of the essay as was already written, or had heard the essence of it from Herder himself.[3] But much had changed in those eight years, especially in the knowledge and insight with which Goethe approached the subject. Coming at this moment the essay must have worked as a revelation in his receptive spirit. "A statue", Herder wrote, "stands there complete in itself under the clear sky as it were in Paradise: image of a fair creature of God, and around it is innocence." "The forms of sculpture are simple and eternal"—these forms which the Greeks evolved.[4] The human form with its mystical

---

[1] Herder's *Preisschrift* on Winckelmann, written for the prize competition instituted by the Cassel "Société des Antiquités" and sent in in May 1778, cannot have attracted Goethe's interest back to Winckelmann. It is almost certain that Goethe knew nothing of the essay (see Duncker's edition of it, 1882).

[2] The first edition of Mengs's works (in Italian) appeared in 1780. All that Goethe can have read in 1778 were the *Betrachtungen über die Schönheit*, Zürich, 1765, and the *Letter to Don Antonio Pons*, translated into Italian from the Spanish, 1777.

[3] Cf. Herder, *Werke*, VIII, p. vii.   [4] *Ibid.* pp. 25, 35, 36.

symmetry,[1] stripped of all particularity of time and place as only the Greeks had the wisdom to represent it[2]—this was to be the mediator henceforward between Goethe and God. Herder showed also how this vision of the human form could be used to produce new works of beauty and wisdom. He pointed out how the Greeks had used their ideal forms as means of expression. They were not "masks of a beautiful, eternal inactivity; the breath of life blew through their forms". Apollo Belvedere expresses a noble anger and determination in his attitude. The other gods and heroes speak to us plastically.[3]

Inevitably as he realised the deeper significance of Greek sculpture, Goethe longed for more opportunity to study it. In the years of inner conflict he had felt out of touch with the serenity of Greek art. There were some antiques in his house,[4] probably brought with him from Frankfurt, and in the spring of 1776 he had some antique gem impressions sent from Leipzig by Oeser.[5] This seems to have been his only effort to gain new knowledge of Greek art. From 1779 onwards, however, he took every opportunity to see and contemplate reproductions of the great works of Greek sculpture.[6] In the summer of 1778—just as the inner meaning of Greek art was dawning on him—he began to take an interest in the work of Klauer, the court sculptor,[7] who in time produced several plaster casts and some bronzes of Greek originals. One commission that Goethe gave to Klauer is of particular significance. In December 1778 Klauer began a nude of Fritz v. Stein, Charlotte's six-year-old son; Goethe commented on it in his diary of January 1779:[8] "Klauer at work on the model of Fritz. At last, thank God, he is finding an unending field of study in the beautiful body.... He cannot wonder enough at its beauty. The story of how it

[1] Cf. Herder, *Werke*, VIII, p. 69. [2] *Ibid.* pp. 19–20.
[3] *Ibid.* pp. 57 foll., 61.
[4] Düntzer, *Zur Goetheforschung*, p. 34.
[5] Letter to Oeser, 6 April 1776 (WA. IV, 3, p. 49) and Düntzer, *Zur Goetheforschung*, pp. 34, 35.
[6] See below, pp. 118, 119. [7] See WA. III, 1, pp. 68, 70, 74.
[8] *Ibid.* p. 78. Volbehr (*op. cit.* p. 143) points out the significance of this sudden interest in the human form. See also E. Wolf, *Goethe und die griechische Plastik* in *Neue Jahrbücher für Wissenschaft und Jugendbildung*, I (1925), p. 55.

has all happened from the beginning is worth remembering."[1]
The tone of these words shows that it was his own conversion
rather than Klauer's that excited him. With the help of
Winckelmann, Mengs and Herder, all of whom based their
thought on the tradition of Greek sculpture, he had begun to
realise the inner significance of the human form. The Greeks
had understood this significance as no other race had done, and
had revealed it in the ideal human forms of their sculpture.
This was the principle on which from this moment Goethe
interpreted Greek art. The greater knowledge that he gained
in Italy, and afterwards, did not cause him to change his
attitude; he used it only to develop the simple idea in ever
greater detail.

The way was now clear to create through the inspiration
of the Greek ideal. He must reproduce in his poetical medium
the "noble simplicity and quiet greatness" of Greek statuary.
For the great work in which he would portray his struggle and
his victory, such a style was aesthetically inevitable. Only thus
in fact could the aesthetic significance of the new wisdom be
expressed. So *Iphigenie* took shape in his mind during the last
weeks of 1778,[2] and was brought to paper in the intervals of
administrative duties during the February and March following.
In the statuesque simplicity, the grave restraint, the perfect
humanity of the characters, Goethe was trying to re-create in
words his vision of the Hellenic man. It may be maintained
that he was not successful, that the characters in *Iphigenie* lack
real plasticity. It is true we learn to know them entirely
through their thoughts and feelings; their physical appearance is
not portrayed. Such description seemed unnecessary to Goethe.
Their physical attributes were those of Greek sculpture, which
were well known and needed no description. He was concerned to portray the deeper significance of Greek contour and

---

[1] "Klauer an Fritzens Modell gearbeitet. Er findet doch endlich, Gott sei
Dank, an dem schönen Körper ein übergros Studium....Er kann jetzt nicht
genug dessen Schönheit bewundern. Die Geschichte, wie es damit von
Anfang gegangen ist, muss ich nicht vergessen."

[2] Some have held that Goethe began to think over a plan to *Iphigenie* in
1776 (see Düntzer, *Die drei ältesten Bearbeitungen von Goethes "Iphigenie"*, 1854,
p. 143), but this view is not generally accepted. Even if this were so it is
significant that he could not bring his plan to fruition until he had found a
new line of approach to the Greek genius.

Greek proportion, as he understood it, and in this he certainly succeeded.

His use of the Greek sculptural ideal involved a reproduction in the poetic medium of certain qualities of Greek plastic art. It was in a sense "imitation"—a thing that he had never allowed himself in the days of *Sturm und Drang*. How far had he accepted the principle of imitation in other matters? How far in fact should *Iphigenie* be regarded as an attempt to write a Greek tragedy? Before this question can be answered it is essential first to establish how well Goethe knew the body of Attic tragedy from personal study. Before he came to Weimar he had read the *Alcestis* and probably the *Prometheus Vinctus*, and was familiar at least with the story of the *Philoctetes*.[1] For the first five years after his arrival in Weimar—until September 1780—there is no direct evidence of any interest in the tragedians, except a reference to Sophocles in a letter to his mother, which might or might not mean that Goethe had been reading him.[2] In letters and diaries there is no indication that Goethe read a single Greek play in preparation for his own *Iphigenie*. Negative evidence, however, can prove nothing, and in this case it is contradicted by strong evidence from other sources. In 1811 Goethe said to Riemer: "Incompleteness is productive. I wrote my *Iphigenie* from a study of the Greek works, which was however incomplete. If it had been exhaustive, the play would have remained unwritten."[3] The evidence of this categorical statement is supported by an examination of the text of *Iphigenie*. A number of phrases and images in it are strongly reminiscent of passages in various Greek tragedies. When Goethe made Iphigenie say: "I came here young, yet old enough to remember those heroes, who, like the gods in the glory of their armament, went forth to fairest renown",[4] he may well have had in his mind's eye the picture drawn at much greater length by Euripides in the *Iphigenia in Aulis* (lines 171-300). Orestes describes how

[1] See above, pp. 59, 61.
[2] 16 Nov. 1777 (WA. IV, 3, p. 187).
[3] Gräf, *Drama*, III, p. 211: "Das Unzulängliche ist produktiv. Ich schrieb meine *Iphigenie* aus einem Studium der griechischen Sachen das aber unzulänglich war. Wenn es erschöpfend gewesen wäre, so wäre das Stuck ungeschrieben geblieben."
[4] WA. 39, p. 358.

Electra goaded him on to slay his mother as his resolution began to waver.[1] This corresponds exactly with the part played by Electra in Euripides's *Electra* (lines 967–84 and 1221–4) and in *Orestes* (line 616).[2] The "faint trace of blood that seemed to shine from out the oft-washed stone" may have been suggested by line 318 of Euripides's *Electra*.[3] Goethe took the "artfully entangling garment"[4] which Clytemnestra used for the murder of Agamemnon from the *Choephori* and the *Eumenides*.[5] These passages and others which it is unnecessary to quote[6] are all derived from those Greek tragedies which deal with the story of the Tantalid house. One sentence—"Like Hercules will I unworthy die, full of shame and shut up within myself"[7]—is strongly reminiscent of the *Trachiniae* (lines 1259–63).

It may be argued that the correspondence between Goethe's words and the Greek passages quoted is in no case so strong as to prove that Goethe had the Greek words in mind. It is possible moreover to prove the same kind of correspondence between Goethe's *Iphigenie* and other plays on the same theme, in which he is most unlikely to have sought inspiration, namely J. E. Schlegel's *Geschwister auf Taurien*, and—even dustier—Lagrange's *Oreste et Pylade*, written in 1699.[8] Why should not a similar theme suggest similar images and turns of phrase to every poet who handles it? Granted that no one of these instances by itself is conclusive proof, yet the accumulation of similarities cannot reasonably be explained as coincidence.

The version of the myth adopted by Goethe does not always correspond with that used by the tragedians. This is not sur-

[1] *Ibid.* p. 361.
[2] Neither Pomey nor Hyginus refers to this.   [3] Also *Choephori*, 59.
[4] WA. 39, p. 355: "Ein künstlich sich verwirrend Kleid."
[5] *Choephori*, 483, 967–71, 984–7, and *Eumenides*, 604, 605: ἀτέρμονι δαιδάλῳ πέπλῳ. Also *Orestes*, 1353–4.
[6] WA. 39, p. 365, lines 14, 15 = *Orestes*, 264; *ibid.* p. 373, lines 6, 7 = *Orestes*, 1155; *ibid.* p. 401, lines 10–14; cf. Euripides's *Electra*, 573. See also Emil Müller, *Antike Reminiszenen in Goethe's Iphigenie*, Zittau, 1888, and Karl Heinemann in *G-J.* XIX, pp. 212 foll. It is very noticeable that the correspondences are far more exact in the final versified form of *Iphigenie* than in the prose version with which I am here dealing.
[7] WA. 39, p. 366: "Wie Herkul will ich Unwürdiger am Tod voll Schmach in mich verschlossen sterben."
[8] Morsch, *Vorgeschichte von Goethe's "Iphigenie"* in *Vierteljahrschrift für Literaturgeschichte*, IV, pp. 80 foll.

prising, since the tragedians themselves used different versions in different plays. Goethe certainly used the *Fables* of Hyginus and other sources, such as Ovid's *Metamorphoses*, from which to draw his material. In these circumstances any occasion on which he follows exclusively the version used in one particular tragedy is evidence of his having read that tragedy. Such a case is found in Orestes's description of the events following Agamemnon's murder until his own return to Mycenae,[1] which corresponds exactly with the version used by Sophocles in his *Electra*. The account of the sins of Tantalus and his descendants in Goethe's *Iphigenie*[2] is fuller than the same account in Euripides's *Orestes* (lines 4–24); Goethe used other sources besides this passage. But the similarity of style in both— the concise narrative interrupted by brief moralising—is hardly due to a coincidence.

In characterisation Goethe generally did not follow his Greek predecessors; but his Pylades corresponds very closely to the Pylades of the Euripidean plays. He is not merely the faithful friend, well known to all by tradition, he is the schemer too, the brains of the party, as in the *Orestes*.

In face of all this internal evidence and of Goethe's statement to Riemer there can be no reason to doubt what is after all inherently likely: that Goethe read a number of Greek tragedies —probably all the Tantalid cycle and perhaps one or two others—in conjunction with his writing of *Iphigenie*. It is impossible to know whether or not he read them in the Greek, but it may be assumed that he had a Greek text before him while relying chiefly upon some translation.[3] In this case he was well acquainted with the form of the Attic tragedy by the time he began to write his *Iphigenie*. He was familiar with the peculiar rhythm of the trimeter, and had been able to observe the function of the chorus, and to gain a true impression of the background of moral ideas out of which the Attic drama arose. With these facts established, it will be possible to decide how

---

[1] WA. 39, pp. 360–1.   [2] *Ibid.* pp. 334–7.

[3] Besides Brumoy and Steinbrüchel (see above, p. 60) there had appeared before 1779 a new translation of Sophocles by E. M. Goldhagen, Mietau, 1777 (see *Teutscher Merkur*, Nov. 1777); one of *Iphigeneia in Aulis* by J. B. Köhler, Berlin, 1779; *Alcestis*, Greek and Latin, by Buchanan, Gotha, 1776.

much he imitated from his Greek predecessors, and whether *Iphigenie* is to be regarded as an attempt to transplant Greek tragedy to German soil.

The first thing that strikes anyone who reads the first version of *Iphigenie* with these questions in mind, is that in its form it does not imitate the Greek tragedy in two matters of fundamental importance. It is not written in trimeters, not in verse at all, but in prose that tends to an iambic rhythm; and there is no chorus. In so far as the play is divided into five acts without choric interludes it follows the form of French tragedy.[1] Perhaps in the passages of stichomythia[2] Goethe was attempting to revive a Greek artifice. But again, this practice cannot be regarded as only Greek, for it is not unknown in Corneille and Racine. Goethe nowhere carried it on for more than a dozen lines whereas in the Greek tragedies eighty or a hundred lines may be written thus. It may be, too, that in the brief *sententiae* with which the play is larded—"Unhappy he, who far from kith and kin leads a deserted life!" "A woman's fortune is hardest of all human lots", "That is not ingratitude, which need commands",[3] and so on—Goethe wished to recapture the Greek simplicity and concentration of expression. In general, however, it is clear that Goethe did not wish to imitate the external form of Greek tragedy. Even had he wished to, his technical knowledge and mastery of Greek forms were unequal to the task. After another twenty years of steeping himself in the Greek tradition he could attempt it, but not yet.

We have seen already that Goethe's vision of Greek sculpture was as much a moral as an aesthetic revelation, and that he used it so in portraying his characters in *Iphigenie*. Perhaps then his relation to Greek tragedy was the same—he was not concerned to imitate the form, but he may have tried to re-create Greek tragedy in its substance and its moral outlook. Yet this theory too is untenable.

Goethe must have realised that all his characters in *Iphigenie* were as unlike the characters of Greek tragedy as could be. With their gentle nobility and unselfishness, their sweet reasonableness, their perfect consideration for each other's feelings,

---

[1] Cf. Kettner, *Preussische Jahrbücher*, LXVII (1891), p. 164.
[2] WA. 39, pp. 329, 339, 359, 376.
[3] *Ibid.* pp. 323, 324, 383.

they are the very antithesis of the passionate, bloodthirsty, ruthlessly selfish Electras and Clytemnestras of the Tantalid cycle.[1] Goethe's own Hercules of five years before could well have mocked at them for being "all of the family of 'Würde der Menschheit'".[2] Not that the characters in *Iphigenie* lack energy or depth of feeling. Late in life Goethe was discussing with Eckermann the problems which *Iphigenie* presented as a stage piece. "It is rich", he said, "in inner life, but poor in action. The difficulty is to reveal this inner life.... The printed word is admittedly only a feeble reflexion of the excitement that I felt while I was composing it. The actor must bring us back to this first glow that inspired the poet in the presence of his subject. We want to see vigorous Greeks and heroes, fresh from the breath of the sea air, who, hard pressed by diverse evils and dangers, give forceful utterance to whatever word the heart in their breast commands."[3] These words, which may be taken to give a true picture of the characters as Goethe conceived them in 1779, show that, in Orestes and Pylades at least, the restraint of the plastic form was not intended to conflict with an Homeric directness of feeling and expression. But they had their passions under control; they respond to the appeal to reason and restraint which Iphigenie makes in the last act. The "noble simplicity and quiet greatness" of Greek sculpture was so blended with the almost Christian humanity of Goethe's new morality, that there was no place for the fiercely self-assertive characters with which the Greek tragedians were wont to create their effects. This lack of contrast between the characters in Goethe's *Iphigenie* is only one form in which the fundamental moral of the play has to express itself. His

[1] Schiller recognised this when he read *Iphigenie* for the second time in Jan. 1802: "It is so extraordinarily modern and unGreek", he wrote to Körner, "that it is hard to conceive how one can ever have compared it to a Greek play. It is purely moral."

[2] See above, p. 72.

[3] Eckermann, *Gespräche*, 1 April 1827: "Es ist reich an innerem Leben aber arm an äusserem.... Das gedruckte Wort ist freilich nur ein matter Wiederschein von dem Leben, das in mir bei der Erfindung rege war. Aber der Schauspieler muss uns zu dieser ersten Glut, die den Dichter seinem Süjet gegenüber beseelte, wieder zurückbringen. Wir wollen von der Meerluft frisch angewehte kraftvolle Griechen und Helden sehen, die, von mannigfaltigen Uebeln und Gefahren geängstigt und bedrängt, stark heraus-reden was ihnen das Herz im Busen gebietet."

characters are at bottom unselfish, straightforward and reasonable, because he wished to teach that reason, truth and unselfishness can in the end solve all conflicts. Can he have believed that this moral was compatible with the Greek view of life, as revealed in those tragedies which he knew?

There are inklings of such a moral in some of these tragedies. One might well sum up the moral of the *Philoctetes* in Goethe's own words: "O Weh der Lüge!"[1] When Neoptolemus restrains Philoctetes from shooting Odysseus, he is, like Iphigenie in the last act, and like Christ in the garden, forbidding the appeal to violence even in a just cause; and the happy ending of the play, brought about indeed only by Hercules's miraculous appearance, justifies him as Iphigenie is justified. In the *Orestes* Euripides seems to be groping towards a similar humane solution of the problem of violence, when Tyndareus maintains that murder should not be paid for in blood but in banishment.[2] It is possible too to interpret *Iphigeneia in Aulis* so as to discover in it a moral similar to that in Goethe's *Iphigenie*, namely that by willing acceptance of her doom Iphigeneia appeals to the highest moral powers and thus wins her own salvation from the goddess.[3] It is impossible to say whether Goethe saw any such moral in the play.

Nevertheless, these glimpses of a humaner morality cannot wipe out the impression which the plays of the Tantalid cycle leave on any receptive mind. The ever-recurring themes of murder, oppression, injustice, selfish passion unrelieved by the least awareness of humaner ideals, fill the mind in time with a stunned horror. But this picture of blood-dabbled wives and sons and daughters, struggling to get the better of each other by every means of violence or trickery, is not in itself so horrible as the presence, behind the human agents, of the gods, who not merely tolerate, but directly enjoin and bring about every new deed of shame. In Aeschylus's Oresteian trilogy Apollo's action in commanding Orestes to kill his mother is indeed called in question by the Furies. But on what grounds? It is not to be

---

[1] "Ah, woe for lying!" WA. 39, p. 374; cf. *Philoctetes*, especially lines 1227-8, 1251 foll.

[2] *Orestes*, 512-17.

[3] *Iphigenia in Aulis*, 1611: σώζουσιν οὓς φιλοῦσιν, but there is little else to support such an interpretation.

expected that they, who represent the unenlightened "old morality", should teach any humane solution of Orestes's problem such as forgiveness or love. They maintain simply that ties of blood as from mother to son are stronger than any duty of vengeance on the father's murderer that would normally apply. When asked why they did not pursue Clytemnestra for murdering Agamemnon, they explain that there is no tie of blood between husband and wife.[1] The case of the "new morality", which is represented by Apollo and is finally victorious, is that a father's murder must be avenged. Orestes's killing of his mother is excused on the grounds that the female is not truly the parent of the child—"she like a stranger preserves the plant for a stranger".[2] In Sophocles's *Electra* there is no suggestion that the murder of Clytemnestra is anything but a just and godly act. Euripides is outspoken in his contempt and hatred of gods who force mortals to commit such crimes.[3] By the pitiless realism with which he portrays the emotions of the unhappy victims of divine inhumanity, he states the moral dilemma more powerfully than either Aeschylus or Sophocles. But he offers no solution of the problem which was so grandly symbolised in the old myth of the house of Tantalus. His *Iphigeneia in Tauris*, in which the house of Tantalus appears for the last time before passing into oblivion, is not concerned with the old question of the fated blood-guilt.

To Goethe the moral to be drawn from the Greek tragedians' handling of the Tantalid myth must have been profoundly unsatisfactory. Aeschylus, in the splendid close of the *Eumenides*, had come nearest to preaching a doctrine of reconciliation akin to Goethe's own, but the moral problem which he recognised, was not such a one as could have any meaning in the modern world. Sophocles had ignored the moral question. Euripides had seen the problem with modern eyes but had failed to suggest any solution. Yet Goethe saw that the Tantalid myth itself provided the material for a solution of the dilemma which would satisfy the highest moral needs of man. The fact that he chose this myth, which had always symbolised for him the superman's "monstrous opposition" to the will of God, to represent his own reconciliation with the moral world-order,

[1] *Eumenides*, 574–5.   [2] *Ibid.* 628–31.
[3] *Iphigenia in Aulis*, 1403; *Orestes*, 162–5, 191 foll.; *Electra*, 1245 foll., 1296.

suggests that he was aware of this failure of the Greek spirit, and was determined to show that it could be put right with Greek material. He would complete the Greek cycle of dramas in his own *Iphigenie*, and provide in it the harmonising close which the Greek spirit had failed to find. His play should be worthy to stand beside those ancient masterpieces; it should be Greek as far as a modern play could profitably be so; but it should teach a moral nobler than anything which the Greek tragedians had conceived. Pylades, not Iphigenie, was Goethe's new symbol for the Greek spirit. The comely, life-loving youth, with the "still soul",[1] who is true and noble in his relations to his friends, but still finds it natural to use trickery and force on the rest of the world, is treated by the poet with gentle respect but in the crisis he is quietly pushed into the background by Iphigenie, whose new morality of universal trust and love resolves the dangerous situation which his code of violence would have aggravated into a catastrophe.

Goethe knew no clearer way than this of expressing his new relationship to the Greeks. Of the fundamental Trinity— Goodness, Truth, Beauty—they had had a unique revelation of Beauty.[2] In their plastic ideal of the beautiful youth they had achieved an absolute, which could still be used as a means of conveying moral ideas. This same feeling for proportioned form had found expression in certain characteristics of their literary style, as well as in their sculpture, and these traits could be imitated to-day. But in the Good and the True they had fallen short of the highest as Goethe then saw it.

Goethe could not yet compose in a spirit of complete surrender to the genius of Greece. Despite the success of *Iphigenie* and the part played by the Greek ideal in its composition, he was still at loggerheads with Greece on some points of capital importance. Greece was not yet synonymous with man. It is not surprising therefore to find that *Iphigenie* does not mark the beginning of a period of fruitful relationship to the Greek spirit. He was still drawn to Greece by a mysterious force; he enlarged his circle of Greek reading and took what

[1] WA. 39, p. 373.

[2] "Denn mein Verlangen steht hinüber nach dem *schönen* Lande der Griechen" and "So seid ihr *schönen* Götterbilder auch zu Staub": WA. 39, pp. 324, 354.

opportunities occurred for the contemplation of Greek sculpture; but there was a lack of method in these studies, and *Elpenor*, the second great attempt to compose under the influence of Greece, ended in failure.

For a time after the completion of *Iphigenie* the influence of Greece served only to confirm the mental peace which was now Goethe's most precious possession. He took every opportunity to make the vision of the Greek youth more living and real by the study of Greek sculpture. So in September 1779 he saw the antiques in the Landgraf's galleries at Cassel, among which were probably some that he had never seen before.[1] In Greek reading he confined his studies to authors who did not raise the problem of humane morality. He did not wish to disturb the visits of "the fairest gods who inhabit the broad Heaven"[2] by any jarring doubts. So on their journey in the Alps in the autumn of 1779 Karl August and he read Homer in the translation that old Bodmer had published the year before.[3] As before in Wetzlar and in the woods behind Jena, it was the relaxing effect of Homer's descriptions of man in his simplest relations with nature, that Goethe sought. With the *naïveté* of his departed youth he read the *Odyssey* aloud to the neatherds in the high valleys, and drew strength, as he toiled up the rough ascents under the precipices and glaciers,[4] from the thought of Odysseus's divine endurance.

As they were about to start out from Zürich on the homeward journey, Goethe was occupied with the thought of a monument to be set up in Weimar to commemorate the whole little adventure, which would, he hoped, bring many blessings to the duchy through its effect on the duke's character. It is indicative of Goethe's new taste in art that this monument was to be in antique style. He conceived it four-sided, rather taller than its width, "quite simple, the way you find monuments of the kind in the remains of antiquity, with an indented roof above. Each of three of the sides should have a single, significant

---

[1] *Tagebuch*, 16 Sept. 1779 (WA. III, 1, p. 99). The *Teutscher Merkur*, Dec. 1780, gives an account of the casts then in the Cassel collection. There is no evidence as to whether he visited the Antikensaal in Mannheim on his way through in either direction.

[2] Letter to Frau von Stein, 4 Sept. 1779 (WA. IV, 4, p. 57) and *Tagebuch*, same date (WA. III, 1, p. 97).

[3] WA. IV, 4, pp. 75, 93; *G-J.* v, p. 209.   [4] Bied. I, p. 100.

figure",[1] the fourth a Latin inscription. On one side should stand Fortune; to her right "Genius, who spurs us on, finds and points the way, bears the torch with bold stride"; on the other Terminus, "the quiet setter of limits, the thoughtful, moderate councillor, standing and pointing with the serpent wand to a boundary stone".[2] It was inevitable for him now to allegorise man's life, with its permitted field of activity and its established limits, in some antique form.

He found the same insistence on the wise limitation that brings man contentment, in the ancient Gnomic wisdom of the Greeks. In Ilmenau, where men and business were often mean beyond endurance, he read "as cleansing and purification" the *Golden Words* of the Pythagorean school and translated a short passage into German hexameters. The lines he chose are significant:

Und wenn du's vollbracht hast,
Wirst du erkennen der Götter und Menschen unänderlich Wesen
Drinne sich alles bewegt und davon alles umgränzt ist,
Stille schaun die Natur sich gleich in allem und allem,
Nichts unmögliches hoffen, und doch dem Leben genug sein.[3]

The translation itself was an exercise in the achieving of perfection within set limits. Unlike the version of this passage published by Gleim a few years before,[4] in which the concentration of the four Greek verses was lost in sixteen lines of watery paraphrase, Goethe followed his text exactly and never allowed the thought to overflow from one half-hexameter into the next.

But the problem of Greek tragedy would not let him rest. Already in March 1780, in the spring following the journey to Switzerland, he was reading Euripides's *Helena* aloud[5] to the

[1] "Ganz einfach, wie man in den alten Ueberbleibseln dergleichen Steine oben mit einem eingekerbten Dach findet."
[2] Letter to Lavater, end of Nov. 1779 (WA. iv, 4, pp. 141–6).
[3] Letter to Charlotte von Stein, 8 Sept. 1780 (WA. iv, 4, pp. 283, 284): "And when you have done it, you will realise the unalterable nature of gods and men, within which all things move, by which all is bounded; you will quietly watch Nature unchanging in all things, will hope for nothing impossible, and yet will do your part in life."
[4] *Teutscher Merkur*, May 1775.
[5] *Tagebuch*, 23 and 24 March (WA. iii, 1, p. 111). This reading assumes the use of a German text, since Brumoy does not translate the *Helena*.

Duchess Anna Amalia; and in September, on a trip in the country with the Duke, he read Euripides while the Duke tried his pistols and the courtiers kicked their heels.[1] Then in the following summer he seized a favourable opportunity to soak himself in Greek tragedy as he had never done before even in preparation for *Iphigenie*. From the beginning of May 1781, until November there was staying in Weimar a young Swiss of the name of Tobler, who had already translated Sophocles into German verse, and who proceeded during his stay in Weimar to translate all the extant plays of Aeschylus and some of Euripides.[2] Already by the end of May Goethe knew some of these translations. He approved them highly.[3] He encouraged Tobler to continue his work and read the translations as they were finished.[4] During this summer and winter Goethe probably came to know several Greek tragedies that he had not read before. If his studies for *Iphigenie* had been confined to the plays of the Tantalid cycle, he must now have come to know Sophocles fully for the first time. It is clear, too, that he felt a profound admiration for Aeschylus.[5] His return to a general conception of the Greeks of which Winckelmann would have approved, did not blind him, as Winckelmann was blind,[6] to the beauty and power of Aeschylus's genius. In fact in 1784 Stolberg declared that, after Homer, Aeschylus was Goethe's favourite poet.[7]

Out of this reading of Greek tragedy there arose in Goethe's mind the idea for a new play—*Elpenor*. The names and setting

---

[1] Letter to Charlotte von Stein, 12 Sept. 1780 (WA. IV, 4, p. 288).

[2] Tobler's Sophocles was published in Basel during 1781. The Aeschylus and Euripides plays are in MS. in the Landesbibliothek in Weimar. They carry the following dates: *Hercules Furens*, May 1781; *Hippolytus*, August; *Ion*, date uncertain (see Knebel's letter to his sister, 10 Feb. 1802, quoted by E. Beutler, *op. cit.* p. 75); *Eumenides*, 28 Aug.; *Agamemnon*, September; *Persae*, October; *Choephori*, *Supplices*, *Prometheus*, *Seven against Thebes*, January 1782. Three of these last four were sent to Goethe in March 1782 (WA. IV, 5, p. 282). In most of these translations the Greek trimeter is rendered into the same metre in German.

[3] Letter to Reich, 30 May 1781 (WA. IV, 5, p. 129).

[4] Letter to Karl August, 4 Nov. 1781 (WA. IV, 5, p. 210) and *Tagebuch*, 29 Aug. 1781 (WA. III, 1, p. 131) *Eumenides*, and 9 Feb. 1782 (WA. III, 1, p. 138) *Agamemnon*.

[5] Cf. WA. IV, 5, p. 210, *Persae*.

[6] *Werke*, I, p. 34.

[7] Bied. I, p. 121.

are Greek,[1] but unlike *Prometheus* and *Iphigenie* the plot is not taken from Greek mythology; it is an invention of Goethe's which he chose to cast in Greek costume.[2] This fact might be taken as being proof of a growing tendency in him to regard Greek art in all its forms as an absolute model. When in the days of *Sturm und Drang* he had used a Greek setting, he had done so because some Greek story best expressed what he wanted to say; for *Iphigenie* too the Tantalid myth was ready to his hand. For his new idea there was no suitable Greek myth; but Goethe was determined to have the setting Greek, so he invented a story and gave the characters Greek names. It is true that he was determined to cast the new play in Greek costume despite the fact that there was no Greek myth available to symbolise the idea, but the reason was not that he was coming to regard a Greek setting as indispensable. Neither of the other two major works which he had in hand at the time, *Wilhelm Meister* and *Tasso*, had anything Greek about them. The reason for his choice of Greek costume lay, as we shall see, in the idea which he was trying to express.

On 11 August 1781, he began to write *Elpenor* and by the 19th two scenes were finished.[3] During the following weeks the work progressed, probably to the end of the first act.[4] Then nothing more was done until February 1783, when the whole plan, which Goethe saw to be "faulty", was revised and a fresh start made.[5] This time two acts were completed,[6] but

---

[1] There can be no doubt that Goethe imagined the setting of *Elpenor* as Greek—the names of the characters and the references to Greek heroes (lines 406, 809) are sufficient proof of that. There are, however, curious touches of un-Greek colour. The sword which Elpenor imagines to himself (lines 206–15, WA. 11, p. 375), with its supple blade, its elaborate hilt, is neither Greek nor Roman; and the "fluttering flags" (line 859, p. 392), at which his horse must not shy, never waved above a Greek battle. It is true the Roman cavalry standard—the vexillum—was more like a flag than any other ancient standard. It is conceivable that Goethe was thinking of this, but it is more likely that he did not think about it at all.

[2] For the sources which Goethe adapted to make his plot, see Fr. Strehlke, *Ueber Goethes Elpenor und Achilleis*, Marienburg, 1870; Seuffert in *Vierteljahrschrift für Literaturgeschichte*, IV, p. 115; Dalmeyda, *Un Fragment de Tragédie antique de Goethe*, 1898; Zarncke, *Kleine Schriften*, I, pp. 230 foll.

[3] *Tagebuch* (WA. III, 1, pp. 130, 131) and letter to Charlotte von Stein (WA. IV, 5, p. 183). [4] Cf. Gräf, *Drama*, I, pp. 282, 283.

[5] Letter to Knebel, 3 March 1783 (WA. IV, 6, p. 133).

[6] Letter to Charlotte von Stein, 5 March 1783 (*ibid.* p. 135).

by September of the following year he had realised that he would never finish the play,[1] and in fact no more was ever written. The two acts that survive are therefore the working out of the revised plan. It is unfortunate that we know nothing about the original plan and the scenes that were completed in 1781. These, conceived and written under the immediate influence of Sophocles's genius, would reveal far more clearly than the present text Goethe's new attitude to Attic tragedy. We should see the extent to which it had changed since *Iphigenie* on the questions of imitation and of Greek inhumanity. From the text as we have it, it is clear that the impressions left on Goethe's mind by his reading of Greek tragedies in 1781 had become dim by the time he set out to rewrite the play. His reason for taking it up again was not that his interest in Greek tragedy had been rekindled by recent reading (he had read no Greek tragedy for a year); he wished merely to have some suitable piece ready to celebrate the expected birth of a royal heir.[2]

As Seuffert says, the style of *Elpenor* is "less antique" than that of *Iphigenie*.[3] It is hard to define wherein the difference lies. It is most conspicuous in the lack of *sententiae*; the style is in general less concentrated.[4] There is practically no stichomythia. There are also fewer reminiscences from Greek tragedy than in *Iphigenie*: Antiope's ritual washing[5] might be suggested by line 201 of the *Persae*; the ghosts of the dead who watch and try to help their dear ones on earth[6] could also be an echo from the *Persae* (line 220). Otherwise there is little. As many touches are taken from the *Odyssey* as from the tragedians: the bow that Elpenor cannot yet draw is a clear reminiscence of Telemachus's attempt to string his father's bow;[7] Antiope, like Penelope, was plagued by suitors after her husband's death;[8] and the names Elpenor and Polymetis derive from the *Odyssey*.[9]

---

[1] See WA. 11, p. 368.
[2] WA. IV, 6, p. 133.
[3] *Vierteljahrschrift für Literaturgeschichte*, IV, p. 115.
[4] "Der Diener eines Glücklichen, nicht glücklich" might be cited as the only example of a recognisable imitation of a Greek idiom (WA. 11, p. 390).
[5] WA. 11, p. 387.   [6] *Ibid.* p. 385.
[7] *Ibid.* p. 373 and *Od.* XXI, 124 foll.
[8] WA. 11, p. 382.
[9] *Elpenor, Od.* X, 552.

On the other hand there are traces in *Elpenor* of a closer imitation of Greek tragedy in some regards than can be found in *Iphigenie*. The fact that the play was to have a chorus of youths and maidens is perhaps of no great significance. The girls, who appear in the first scene, are dismissed without being given the chance to utter their feelings in a choric song; and it is not likely that the twelve boys, all hardly more than children, could have been intended to play a part at all comparable to that of a Greek chorus. In certain passages, on the other hand, in which Goethe deserts the iambic rhythm of the greater part of the play, it is not fanciful to see a loose imitation of Greek practice. The most notable example is to be found in the two speeches in which Antiope demands that Elpenor accept the duty of vengeance and the speech in which he replies.[1] As at the end of the *Agamemnon* and in the *Persae*, when the ghost of Darius appears,[2] and in other places in Greek tragedy, the heightened emotional tension is expressed by a change from iambic to trochaic metre. It is true that the metre used by the Greeks is an eight-footed trochaic (trochaic tetrameter catalectic) whereas Goethe's trochaic prose, in so far as it can be divided into periods, falls generally into lines of five feet. But this difference is typical of his attitude to the imitation of Greek form at the time. He was glad to take a good idea from the Greeks, but he would not carry it out in detail as the Greeks had done. In the last four lines of the text also[3] the iambic rhythm disappears, and a tendency to anapaests takes its place. It is possible that Polymetis's invocation of destruction that is to fall like a thunderbolt on the house of Lycus, reminded Goethe of the close of the *Prometheus Vinctus*, where earth and heaven crash in ruin about Prometheus's head, and he thought it fitting to fall, as Aeschylus had done, into anapaests. The plot of *Elpenor*, although it is not taken directly from any Greek play or fable, reflects the influence of the *Oedipus Rex* in the unexpected disclosure of old misdeeds, and of the *Ion* in the concealed relationship of mother and son. Goethe probably read both of these plays for the first time just before he began *Elpenor*.

More important than any similarities of technique or of plot

[1] WA. 11, pp. 385-6, lines 573-660.
[2] *Agamemnon*, 1628 to end; *Persae*, 697 foll.   [3] WA. 11, p. 396.

between *Elpenor* and Greek tragedy is the type of character
upon which Goethe intended to build the action and the
interest of the play. All four leading characters—Elpenor,
Antiope, Polymetis and Lycus—are, in their ruthless assertion
of selfhood, far nearer to the characters of Greek tragedy than
to those of Goethe's *Iphigenie*. Antiope, like Clytemnestra and
Electra, nurses her vengeance through years of silent suffering
until the opportunity for its fulfilment occurs. Then with the
concentration of her pent-up hatred she drives Elpenor to take
on the duty of vengeance. He is to show no mercy to the
murderer of her child but is to "count out her years of anguish
slowly on his defenceless head". If the murderer is already dead,
Elpenor is to lead his children and grandchildren to his tomb,
and there pour out their blood, that his ghost may drink it and
be disturbed from its rest by the company of the slain[1]—
extraordinary sentiments in the mouth of a Goethean heroine!
Lycus, a kind of Creon who did his own brother, Antiope's
husband, to death, and stole her son with violence, so that she
thinks him dead, is so painted that we expect to see a wolf
indeed when he appears. Polymetis determines to plunge the
house in feud and ruin, so that he may regain the influence of
earlier years.[2] Against these dark figures of selfish passion
Elpenor stands out with sunny lovableness. His selfishness is
that of a child, naïve and blameless. But his first responsibility
as a grown man is to pursue another human being to death in
vengeance for an old crime, and he is too young to question
the morality of such action. He is snared in the toils of the
other's passion.

In the two acts which Goethe wrote, the stage was set for a
tragedy in the Greek style. Yet it is certain that the play was to
end in reconciliation.[3] This can only have come about by a

---

[1] WA. 11, p. 386.   [2] *Ibid.* p. 396.

[3] The controversy for and against the "happy ending" in *Elpenor*, which
raged for decades in the world of *Goethephilologie*, has been settled against
those who wished to end the play with a "grande tuerie", as Dalmeyda
called it (*op. cit.* p. 16). Some who took part in the battle were: Cholevius
(*Geschichte der deutschen Poesie nach ihren antiken Elementen*, II, p. 262);
Viehoff (*Archiv für den Unterricht im Deutschen*, 2. Jahrgang, 1. Heft, p. 125);
Biedermann (*Die Quellen und Anlässe einiger dramatischen Dichtungen Goethes*,
p. 9); Strehlke (*Ueber Goethes Elpenor und Achilleis*, Marienburg, 1870);
Henry Wood (*Goethes Elpenor*, *Vierteljahrschrift der Literaturgeschichte*, VI);

change in the characters of the principals, or rather by the victory of humane ideals (what one might call "Iphigenie-morality") in characters whîch appear to make such a victory impossible. There is sufficient evidence that a victory of reason and love over passion and hatred was in Goethe's mind. As has been pointed out in the Jubiläums-Ausgabe, Antiope's ritual washing is an outward and visible sign of an inward change of heart. She says expressly that she has "washed away the soiling touch of the goddesses of vengeance".[1] It may be assumed that hereafter in any crisis her natural tendency to love and understanding, which has been crippled by misfortune,[2] will assert itself on the side of reconciliation. That Lycus should turn out to be anything but a villain, is harder to believe. Yet Goethe seems to have intended even this. During the first period of work on the play he wrote to Charlotte telling her he hoped to have the second scene finished that day, and added: "It is good that your fancy identifies me with the uncle."[3] Lycus, the uncle, was to be an aspect of Goethe himself, perhaps a less attractive aspect, but not wholly bad nor incapable of betterment. Elpenor, still unformed but open to any noble influence, could easily be turned to accept the higher ideal of reconciliation. He seems to represent the idealism of Goethe's own youth. Like Hercules's "braver Kerl" in *Götter, Helden und Wieland* he is ready to give generously to all from his abundance.[4] The old heroes, the mighty doers of doughty deeds, Hercules, Theseus, Jason, stand to him for the noblest way of life;[5] and in the spirited horse for which he longs[6] there seems to be a reminiscence of that Pindaric figure from which the young Goethe learnt to ἐπικρατεῖν δύνασθαι.[7] Elpenor was to suffer just the inner change that Goethe had experienced

---

Dalmeyda (*op. cit.*); Köster (*Archiv für das Studium der neueren Sprachen und Literatur*, CI, pp. 257 foll.); Gundolf (*Goethe*, pp. 320 foll.); Schlösser (*Euphorion*, II). The whole problem is excellently summed up in the Jubiläums-Ausgabe, XV, pp. 342 foll.

[1] WA. 11, p. 387.   [2] *Ibid.* p. 384, lines 533–6.

[3] 19 Aug. 1781 (WA. IV, 5, p. 184): "Es ist schön dass deine Phantasie mich mit dem Onkle zusammenschmilzt."

[4] WA. 11, p. 376, lines 225–7, and WA. 38, pp. 33, 34.

[5] WA. 11, p. 381, lines 404–9.

[6] *Ibid.* p. 375, lines 198, 199, and p. 392, line 856.

[7] See above, p. 76.

when he passed from *Sturm und Drang* to the new morality of repose, self-discipline and *Humanität*.

Elpenor then was to end like *Iphigenie* in a victory for the new morality. In *Iphigenie* the happy ending was a foregone conclusion, for the characters were all, with the exception perhaps of Pylades, by nature humane and non-violent. In this, as we have seen, Goethe deliberately went against the practice of Greek tragedy. But the problem of Greek inhumanity was not solved by being ignored. In his intensive reading of the Greek tragedians during the summer of 1781 it forced itself upon him with renewed insistence. As a result he had conceived the idea of writing a play in which the characters should stand on the moral level of Electra and Creon, and in which "Iphigenie-morality" should yet triumph. The conflict between Greek and modern morality was to be resolved in *Elpenor*.

There may have been external reasons for the failure to complete the play, but the fundamental reason was that Electra-morality and Iphigenie-morality could not be reconciled. On the technical plane the motivation of the psychological changes was impossible. It is probable that this was the reason why the first plan was abandoned: Goethe, under the influence of Sophocles and Euripides, had conceived the characters as uncompromisingly inhumane. As soon as he came to work out his plan he saw that it would be impossible to bring about a reconciliation with such characters. He let the play lie for eighteen months, by which time the impressions of Greek tragedy had grown a little dim, and then made a new plan based on compromise characters, who should seem to be Greek in their morals although in their deepest nature capable of rising to the demands of the highest modern ideals. Such a plan was foredoomed to failure. It destroyed the point of the original conception, which was to write a play with truly Greek characters that should end in reconciliation. It could only result in such unconvincing character-drawing as is displayed in Antiope. Her lust for blood and vengeance is psychologically incompatible with the rest of her character. It is artificially grafted on to her natural goodness because the conflict on which the play was to be built demanded it. Her Greekness is a sham.

Goethe had set his hand to an impossible task. There could

be no reconciliation between his own almost Christian faith in forbearance and understanding, and the crude Aeschylean morality, survival of an age of violence, or the cynicism of Euripides's more refined views. Much of the moral teaching of Greek tragedy he could revere with his whole heart. The oft-recurring theme of ὕβρις, the over-stepping of the bounds set for man and the terrible results of such transgression, fitted exactly with his own new ideal of limitation; and it was probably for this reason that he had a "special preference" for the *Persae*.[1] But he had to realise that the Greeks had failed to find a solution to the problem of violence. Upon this one point he was aware of a gulf between his own view and theirs. Inevitably he tried to prove to himself that the gulf could be bridged; inevitably he failed.

Tobler's presence in Weimar caused an interest in other works of Greek literature besides Greek tragedy. Beutler[2] has shown that the Orphic hymns were again to the fore, and has attributed to their influence the composition of Goethe's prose-hymn to Nature.[3] A comparison of its text with the Orphic hymn to Nature confirms this suggestion strongly: ἄψοφον ἀστραγάλοισι ποδῶν ἴχνος εἰλίσσουσα becomes with Goethe "ungebeten und ungewarnt nimmt sie uns in den Kreislauf ihres Tanzes auf und treibt sich mit uns fort".[4] αὐξιτρόφων πίειρα, πεπαινομένων δὲ λύτειρα is equivalent in thought to Goethe's "Sie baut immer und zerstört immer".[5] The single word ἀλλοτριομορφοδίαιτε is expanded by Goethe thus: "Sie schafft ewig neue Gestalten; was da ist, war noch nie; was war, kommt nicht wieder—alles ist neu und doch immer das

---

[1] WA. IV, 5, p. 210. Cf. *Königlich Gebet*, WA. 2, p. 86, probably written about 1780 (Gräf, *Lyrik*, II, 2, p. 881).

[2] Beutler, *op. cit.* pp. 121–3.

[3] JA. XXXIX, pp. 3 foll. Written probably late 1781, published in *Tiefurter Journal*, 32. Stück, end of 1782. I accept the *Naturaufsatz* as a product of Goethe's mind, if not of his pen. On the question of authorship see WA. IV, 6, p. 440 and E. Beutler, *op. cit.*

[4] Greek = whirling thy noiseless step with the ankles of thy feet. German = "unasked and without warning she catches us up in the whirl of her dance and flies onward with us."

[5] Greek = fat with growing things, but dissolver of ripe things. German = "she builds up ever and destroys ever."

Alte."[1] The contrast: κοινὴ μὲν πάντεσσιν, ἀκοινώνητε δὲ μούνη, appears with Goethe in many forms. "Sie lebt in lauter Kindern, und die Mutter, wo ist sie?" "Wir leben mitten in ihr und sind ihr fremde", "Die Menschen sind all in ihr und sie in allen", but "Sie hat sich einen eigenen allumfassenden Sinn vorbehalten, den ihr niemand abmerken kann".[2] More striking than similarities of phrase, which are often obscured by Goethe's tendency to develop and clarify a thought only suggested in the Greek, is the resemblance of style between Goethe's fragment and the Orphic hymns. The tendency to aphorisms, to accumulated epithets ("She is rough and gentle, kind and dreadful, weak and all-powerful"),[3] above all the constant use of paradox, are all of the essence of the Orphic style. It is curious to find these mystical writings still exercising their influence on Goethe's thought at a time when in other ways his relations to Greece were becoming more and more dependent on the intellectual assimilation of knowledge. But his conscious admiration of Greece was always founded on perceptions which lay deeper than the intellectual plane and could not find full expression in terms of intellectual thought. There was to him nothing strange in the fact that the Greeks, for all their sunny self-consciousness, had had their own tradition of intuitive wisdom, and it was natural that, in his search for points of contact with the Greek genius, he should make use of both the matter and the style of the Orphic hymns when attempting to express his own intuitions on such subjects as the nature of life and of the world.[4]

The Greek anthology—a very different type of poetry—

[1] Greek = living in ever new forms. German = "She creates ever new forms; what is, was never yet; what was, never returns—all is new and yet ever the old."

[2] Greek = common to all, yet alone unshared. German = "She lives only in her children, and the mother, where is she?" "We live in the midst of her and are strangers to her." "Men are all in her and she in all", "She has reserved to herself an all-embracing meaning of her own, which no one can learn from her."

[3] "Sie ist rauh und gelinde, lieblich und schrecklich, kraftlos und allge-waltig."

[4] C. Bapp, *Aus Goethes griechischer Gedankenwelt*, Leipzig, 1921, has pointed out a close resemblance between the thought of Goethe's *Naturaufsatz* and that of Heraclitus. He advances no evidence to suggest that Goethe knew anything directly of Heraclitus at this date.

was also to the fore during Tobler's stay in Weimar. Herder had started the vogue in the previous autumn (1780) by circulating translations of thirty epigrams among the friends in Weimar.[1] Goethe probably saw these, but it was not until the following summer that his interest became strong enough to rouse him to imitations and adaptations of his own. His earliest epigram in elegiac metre dates from 1 June 1781.[2] Another ("Arm an Geiste kommt heut spät dein Geliebter vor dich...") may well be as early[3]; its crudely faulty versification suggests that it was one of Goethe's first attempts. Der Becher (September 1781),[4] though not in elegiacs, takes its images from the Anthology. Beutler supposes that Tobler, Herder and Goethe pursued an interest in the Anthology in common during 1781. In March of the next year Tobler sent a number of translations from it to Goethe,[5] who now turned with enthusiasm to the composition of epigrams in elegiac metre. Ten of the epigrams which survive took shape during the early summer of 1782.[6] After this burst of activity there was a lull during the rest of 1782 and the following year.[7] Herder however continued to work at the Anthology with growing seriousness and by 1784 his enthusiasm had again infected Goethe. Eleven elegiac epigrams and one in hexameters date from this year and the next.[8]

None of Goethe's epigrams are translations from the Greek.[9]

[1] Herder, Werke, XXVI, p. x and Beutler, op. cit. p. 71.

[2] Versuchung, WA. 2, p. 130 and 5, 1, p. 66. Cf. JA. 1, p. 367.

[3] WA. 4, p. 121 (cf. JA. III, p. 323), where it is dated 1782.

[4] WA. 2, p. 106. Gräf puts it in the spring 1782; cf. Schr. der G-G. VII, p. 371.

[5] WA. IV, 5, p. 282.

[6] WA. 2, pp. 126–9, 131. These are: Einsamkeit, Erkanntes Glück, Erwählter Fels, Ländliches Glück, Philomele, Geweihter Platz (in hexameters), Der Park, Ferne (p. 108), and Nos. 1 and 2 of the Sechzehn Epigramme (WA. 4, p. 119).

[7] Heilige Familie and Entschuldigung, 1782 (WA. 2, p. 131), No. 3 of the Sechzehn Epigramme, Aug. 1783, and "Will der Knabe nicht hören", Oct. 1782 (WA. 5, 2, p. 360), according to Gräf, Oct. 1783.

[8] Dem Ackermann, Anakreons Grab, Die Geschwister, Zeitmass, Warnung (WA. 2, pp. 123–5), Die Lehrer (ibid. p. 129), Epigramm and Ein Anderes, Pauper ubique iacet, Die Wahrheit and "Unglück bildet den Menschen" (WA. 4, pp. 119–21), Der Gräfin Brühl (ibid. p. 223). Two epigrams, Ungleiche Heirat (WA. 2, p. 130) and "Als der Undankbare floh" (WA. 4, p. 121), also date from the early 'eighties.

[9] Beutler, op. cit. pp. 80, 83.

Some, as *Zeitmass* and *Warnung*, are developments of translations by Herder. Others are free variations on antique themes—*die Geschwister* being the most remarkable example of this.[1] The majority are simply occasional poems in the Greek epigrammatic form with no particularly Greek association. In such cases the subject chosen is of a kind which a Greek epigrammatist might well have treated. For the first time Goethe was attracted by the form of a Greek *genre*. Previously it had been the symbolism of their mythology, their plastic ideal or the unbending strength of their tragic characters, which he had tried to reproduce in his own poetry; in doing so he had not thought it necessary to imitate Greek literary forms. Now in the elegiac couplet he found a verse form which by its sensuous shape favoured the expression of a particular type of thought or feeling. So Goethe used the form. He did not archaise with it; in many of his epigrams the local colour is unmistakably modern. The metre was to him a universal form, invented by the Greeks, but suitable for use in all times and countries whenever a particular type of thought had to be expressed. Little by little he was coming to regard the Greek forms as archetypes of all forms of thought and expression.

This was the first sustained effort that Goethe made to imitate an antique metre. At times during his first years at Weimar he had experimented with short passages of German hexameters. The earliest of these passages that survives is the *Physiognomische Reisen*, fifteen hexameters, written in 1778 or 1779.[2] The four lines of translation from the *Golden Words* of Pythagoras (September 1780) have already been mentioned.[3] The problem of adapting Greek metres to the German language was therefore not new to Goethe when he set his hand to the Greek elegiac form. He solved the problem in the same simple fashion as Klopstock before him—by substituting alternations of light and heavy stress accents for the alternations of long and short syllables upon which all Greek and Roman metres are based. Goethe's hexameters and pentameters were at this period

[1] See Baumgart, *Goethes lyrische Dichtung*, II, p. 190.
[2] WA. 2, p. 264; see also JA. I, p. 369 and Baumgart, *op. cit.* II, p. 197. Gleim heard Goethe extemporise hexameters in the summer of 1777 (Bied. I, p. 87).
[3] WA. IV, 4, 284; see above, p. 105.

primarily accentual and had little or no regard for quantity. Let us take the earliest of Goethe's hexameters that has survived, the first line of *Physiognomische Reisen*, and scan it first by accent as he meant it to be scanned and then by quantity as a Greek would have scanned it.

Sóllt'es | wáhr sein was | úns der | róhe | Wándrer ver|kündet.

It will be seen that Goethe was quite indifferent to the length or quantity of the unaccented syllables. In Greek metrical theory the second and third syllables of a dactyl must be short, the second syllable of a spondee long. But Goethe puts "sein", a diphthong and therefore long by nature, as the second syllable of a dactyl, and makes "rohe" into a spondee, although the second syllable is short by nature and by position. Scanned by quantity the line appears thus:

Sōllt'ēs | wāhr sēin wăs | ūns dēr | rōhĕ | Wāndrēr vēr|kündĕt.

In a Greek hexameter each foot is two beats long whether it be formed of two syllables (spondee) each one beat long, or three (dactyl), the first syllable having one beat, the other two a half each. In this line of Goethe's the second foot has two-and-a-half beats, the fourth one-and-a-half, and the fifth three. Goethe's elegiacs in his epigrams of 1782 and 1784-1785 show the same treatment of the Greek model.

In fact Goethe was making no attempt to write quantitative verse. As he said himself of his *Reinecke Fuchs*, he followed Klopstock in writing hexameters simply "by ear". This shows that, like most of us Northern barbarians, he read Homer and Virgil, Ovid and the anthology accentually not quantitatively. He may not yet have realised that ancient verse was scanned on a different principle from modern verse. Most likely, however, he was aware of the difference (Herder, who was a great Greek scholar, also wrote accentual not quantitative elegiacs),[1] but preferred to bow to the genius of the German language and not try to write quantitative verse in so recalcitrant a medium.[2]

The urbanity of the Greek epigrams, their refined variety of subject and mood and the thoughtful daintiness of their ex-

---

[1] *Werke*, XXVI, pp. 11-147.
[2] For a further discussion of Goethe's practice in adapting the ancient hexameter to German see Appendix B, pp. 295-300.

pression, all attracted Goethe.[1] Here was the voice of a society at the peak of civilisation. They helped to ban the ghost of Electra whose cries for blood and vengeance still disturbed his good relations with the Greek genius. They helped him to forget the truth that he had once realised so clearly, that Greek greatness was founded on strength, and to regard delicacy of thought and outline as an essential quality of Greek formal perfection. Even the once despised Anacreontics were now held in honour and thought worthy of translation.[2] It was the lack of just this delicacy which shocked Goethe when for the first time in his life he set eyes on a Greek temple.[3]

A continued study of Greek plastic art also helped to allay his doubts about the validity of the moral message of Greece. Already in the summer of 1780 a cast of Apollo dominated his dining-room.[4] Perhaps this was one of the many casts of antique statues made by Klauer during the early 'eighties. Amongst others in Weimar were the Laocoön group, Niobe and daughter, the Medici Venus and the Antinous.[5] In January 1782, two months before Tobler sent his last translations of Aeschylus, a cast of the Apollo Belvedere arrived from Gotha,[6] and in June of the following year Goethe saw the casts that the Duke of Gotha had collected.[7] In September 1781 Herder's essay on Winckelmann appeared[8] in the *Teutscher Merkur*. It would have been natural, if Herder's enthusiastic appreciation of the man and his work had fired Goethe at last to undertake a proper study of the *Geschichte der Kunst des Altertums*. He had by now seen so much of the great statues of antiquity that such a study would have been profitable. But apparently he still left the *Geschichte der Kunst* unopened, as he had done in his student days at Leipzig, and only three years before when the Greek youth had first appeared to him. In the following February and March he was reading Mengs,[9] a complete edition of whose works, in Italian, had appeared in 1780. Again as in 1778 Mengs acted as proxy for Winckelmann.

[1] Letter to Herder, late Nov. 1784 (WA. IV, 6, p. 400).
[2] *An die Cicade*, WA. 2, p. 110. Cf. WA. IV, 6, p. 165.
[3] See below, p. 152.   [4] Bied. I, p. 106.
[5] *Teutscher Merkur*, March 1785.
[6] WA. III, 1, p. 136.   [7] WA. IV, 6, p. 171.
[8] *Werke*, xv, pp. 35 foll.   [9] WA. III, 1, p. 140.

The better he came to know the remains of Greek sculpture, the more certainly he saw in them a visible expression of the highest moral and aesthetic ideal.

Und Marmorbilder stehn und sehn mich an:
Was hat man dir, du armes Kind, getan?[1]

Thus he summed up his feelings in the presence of a Greek statue. How was it possible that he, the modern, northern man, could have fallen so far below the physical and spiritual standard, that here stood, visible and tangible, not a mere idea, before him? In 1778 he had first fully realised the significance of Greek sculpture. The years passed and the vision never left him, but it was hard to keep it productive in a northern land. A few casts in Weimar, an occasional sight of some better equipped princely collection, a description of the Acropolis and its treasures from the pen of some travelling Englishman[2]— thus sparingly did the sunshine of the ideal filter through the Cimmerian cloud-rack to warm the seed that longed to flower. Except for these glimpses, his life was spent among the fir-forests and bare cornlands of Thüringen, in a town of narrow gables and dark streets, among men and women without beauty, surrounded by an art without sense for the ideal. The vision was there but in such circumstances it could never be realised. It turned instead into a longing so violent that it became in time a sickness.[3] It no longer found expression directly, as it had done in *Iphigenie* in the first strength of realisation. The longing for the ideal, not the ideal itself, became poetically active and produced a symbol of itself—not Pylades, a vigorous, beautiful youth, but Mignon, a frail child, pining for its sunny home, misunderstood, at times mishandled, by barbarian masters. Strangely Mignon resembles Proserpina. Both, condemned to wander in a dark land, pine with longing for the sunny country they have once known. In those last

---

[1] "And marble statues stand and gaze at me:
'What have they done to you, poor child?'"
[2] Richard Chandler's *Travels in Asia Minor and Greece* (Chaps. VIII and IX), read by Goethe in a German edition in April 1781 (cf. WA. IV, 5, p. 119).
[3] WA. III, 1, p. 290, and letter to Kayser, 24 June 1784 (WA. IV, 6, p. 314).

years in Weimar before the flight to Italy[1] Goethe was back almost where he had started in his relationship to the Greek genius. Mignon symbolises a frustration almost as complete as that for which Proserpina had stood. There is but one difference. Proserpina's longing was utterly hopeless. "What thou seek'st, lies ever behind thee", she had told herself. At that time it seemed to Goethe that Greece was gone for ever, because it was past in time. Mignon is not without hope. The land of longing is not gone for ever. It is not here, but neither is it nowhere. It is there, just beyond the Alps, removed only in space not in time. The cloudy path that leads away can also lead back. The mules pass over with their loads, then why not she and her protector?

Why not? Why not? The question hammered in his head, until to fight it down almost cost him his reason. He could not read a Latin book; he avoided the contemplation of Greek sculpture;[2] except for the novel in which his Mignon lived, his poetical vein was almost dead; he turned the energy of his genius to exploring the secrets of Nature. He had seen Greece from afar, but, living as and where he did, he could never possess the holy land. The beautiful youth held out his hand to him and he could not take it. As the winter of 1783 closed down he asked his friend for maps of Italy.[3] For two more summers and two more winters he endured. As the third spring tarried he could hold out no longer, and when in July he went to take the waters at Carlsbad, he knew—he and his secretary, but no one else—that he would not come back to another winter of living death in Thüringen. Proserpina would be free, Mignon would be free, and Pylades would welcome them with quiet greatness as they came down from the Alps into the sunny land.

[1] Mignon first appears in the third book of *Wilhelm Meister's Theatralische Sendung*, which was finished in Nov. 1782 (WA. IV, 6, p. 88). The poem *Nur wer die Sehnsucht kennt* (Book VI, chap. VII, WA. 52, p. 225) was sent to Charlotte von Stein in June 1785 (WA. IV, 7, p. 67).

[2] The visit to Gotha in June 1783 is the last indication of any interest in Greek art.

[3] Letter to Charlotte von Stein, 26 Nov. 1783 (*Ibid.* 6, p. 217).

CHAPTER IV

ITALY

Hier! durch ein Wunder, hier in Griechenland!
Ich fühlte gleich den Boden, wo ich stand;
Wie mich, den Schläfer, frisch ein Geist durchglühte,
So steh ich, ein Antäus an Gemüte.

A. TOWARDS ROME

"ON the 3rd of September at three o'clock of the morning, I stole out of Carlsbad; they would not otherwise have let me go."[1] With the swiftness and secrecy of an escaped prisoner Goethe pursued his journey southward, through Munich and Innsbruck, over the Brenner, down along the shores of Garda to Verona, where for the first time he paused. From there he wrote to the friends in Weimar, but still gave them no hint of where he was. Even in Venice, where he stayed nearly three weeks, he still concealed his whereabouts, as though to reveal it before he had reached Rome might in some way jeopardise his whole plan. At last, two months after leaving Carlsbad, he wrote from Rome to tell his Duke and his other friends where he was and what had been the object of his unaccountable flight. This strange stealth, quite unjustified on rational consideration of the circumstances, is proof enough that Goethe was in no normal state during the summer and autumn of 1786. Suspicions and fears, the product only of his own strained phantasy, hunted him and would not be shaken off. He was in fact in danger of suffering some irremediable catastrophe such as has overtaken many of the noblest minds of German literature. "Forgive me!" he wrote to Charlotte, "I was in a life-and-death struggle and no tongue can tell what was going on within me."[2] It was not merely that he needed a holiday with sun, as many of us do after a northern winter, nor that Charlotte was holding him with too tight a rein, nor that society in Weimar had come to seem intolerably petty to

[1] *Tagebuch*, 1786 (WA. III, 1, p. 147).
[2] 23 Dec. 1786 (WA. IV, 8, p. 102): "Ich kämpfte selbst mit Tod und Leben, und keine Zunge spricht aus was in mir vorging."

him. All these were only symptoms of a fundamental maladjustment. We must seek deeper for the cause of Goethe's flight to Italy. "His genius, his daimon drove him", Miss Butler says,[1] and thus expresses excellently the terrifying power of the forces that were at work. Gundolf, less picturesquely but with no less appreciation of the vast emotional tensions which Goethe had somehow to keep under control, speaks of his "urge to give form to great impressions",[2] and defines the cause of his mental sickness as the lack of a world which could provide these "great impressions". In Weimar his artistic genius was starved for subjects worthy of its power. He believed he could find the "great world" in Italy, and so he fled.

He did not expect to be inspired by everything he found in Italy. There, no less than in the rest of Europe, the Middle Ages had represented, in his opinion, a relapse into barbarism, and the culture of medieval Italy repelled him no less than a German fir-forest. In Assisi St Francis and Giotto were nothing to him. He climbed the hill straight to the piazza, where a Roman temple of Minerva still stands, worshipped there in his own way the wisdom of the ancients—and strode on to Foligno. For us it is important to ascertain to what extent Goethe regarded the rest of what he was to see in Italy as equivalent to the Greek tradition in art and in life. Was he seeking solely, or even primarily, the secret of Greek supremacy? Or were the statues in Rome, the only remnant, as was then thought, of Greek art, only one "great impression" among many that awaited him? Certainly it was not these statues alone that attracted him to Rome, like a needle to a magnet. On his journey thither Renaissance painting drew from him more comment than the examples of antique sculpture which he saw; and throughout his eighteen months in Italy the study of Raphael, Michelangelo and other modern masters took up a large part of his time. Furthermore, no art however noble would have constituted for him a "great world", unless seen against the ennobling background of Italian landscape, Italian climate and Italian vegetation. On the shores of Garda, on the Lido at first sight of the sea, among the Apennines or the Alban Hills, in Naples and in Sicily, Nature revealed herself to him on a scale

[1] WA. IV, 8, pp. 104 foll.
[2] *Goethe*, p. 363: "Trieb nach Gestaltung grosser Eindrücke."

and with a meaning that was new to him. This "grosse Natur" was one of the most powerful of the great impressions that he received. He had always expected that it would be so.

In these two ways it was not Greece but modern Italy that gave him what he was seeking. In a third category were all those impressions of grandeur and truth which came to him from the works of "the ancients". On innumerable occasions Goethe wrote thus ambiguously of "die Alten", in such a way as to suggest that he had no clear idea of the difference between Greek civilisation and Roman. At times he undoubtedly thought in terms of two civilisations—the ancient and the modern—more or less opposed to each other in ideals and practice, and was not concerned to define how much of what was ancient was also Greek. In architecture especially such purely Roman works as the Amphitheatre at Verona and the aqueduct near Spoleto impressed him profoundly, and led him to generalise on the mighty conceptions and superb execution of "the ancients".[1] It is hard to say whether he was aware that the Greeks had known nothing of such giant structures, which were the product of a purely Roman spirit. The relative merits of Greek and Roman sculpture had been pointed out clearly enough by Winckelmann[2] and were by now well understood; but in architecture, the same distinction was far less clearly established. Examples of Greek architecture were practically unknown—even the temples of Paestum, only sixty miles from Naples, had hardly begun to attract attention in Winckelmann's day.[3] Goethe used Palladio as guide in architectural matters, who founded his practice on that of "the ancients", but to whom the true Greek Doric with its sturdy proportions was unknown.[4]

There were moments however, even in the first days of his Italian journey, when Goethe realised that "die Alten" were not enough, and that even in Italy there were still veils between him and the light that had once streamed out from Greece. Italian art was crippled by its Christian subject-matter,[5] and

---

[1] WA. III, I, pp. 197, 327.   [2] *Werke*, V, pp. 282, 290, 292.
[3] Winckelmann, *Werke*, I, pp. 330 foll.
[4] *The First Book of Andrea Palladio's Architecture*, London, 1742, p. 28.
Cf. Winckelmann, *Werke*, I, pp. 289, 292.
[5] WA. III, I, pp. 283, 308.

even the Romans were barbarians, who plundered the world of its beautiful things, and yet were always dependent on Greek craftsmen to help them use what they had robbed.[1] At bottom he was seeking the Greek tradition in life and in art, and had no patience with the "modern", "Christian" or "northern" tendencies which obscured it even in Italy. At times he found the true Greek or "southern" nature in the common people: the *Odyssey* he saw embodied in a Venetian beggar; Italian love of rhetoric, though only a feeble survival of the Athenian passion for all the forensic arts, explained to him the long harangues of Greek tragedy;[2] and when he said that the common people of Italy still displayed the mentality and customs that are to be found in the "ancient" writers,[3] he must have been thinking primarily of Homer: nowhere in Latin literature are those qualities as vividly painted, which astounded Goethe when he first met them in Venice. The unreflecting naturalness, the passionate absorption in the business of living, the singing, the quarrelling, the chaffering, the law-suits in the open air, the rhapsodist's intent audience[4]—this was life, direct, simple, intense, free from the distortions, the uncertainties, the impotence that had gathered round it in the two thousand years that had passed since Homer was the Bible of the Western world.

In Germany and as he crossed the Alps, Goethe may not have realised how sharply he would have to distinguish between merely Italian or even "ancient" culture and the Grecian core in which the pure essence of what he was seeking was preserved. From his earliest childhood he had dreamed of Italy as the land where all longing would be stilled, and he never ceased throughout his life to speak of Rome as the capital of the world, or even as a world in itself. Even in Italy his desire to reach Rome was so great that he hurried through Florence with hardly a glance at its artistic treasures; and when he had at last to leave the Eternal City and return to the Cimmerian forests, he wept in anguish. Yet the longer he stayed in Italy the more clearly he saw that Rome too could not satisfy him. In so far as it was not Greece it was nothing, and in many ways

[1] WA. III, 1, p. 308.　　　　　　　　　　[2] *Ibid.* pp. 248, 271.
[3] Bied. I, p. 179 (8 Oct. 1791). Cf. WA. 31, p. 39.
[4] WA. III, 1, pp. 248, 249, 250, 260.

it was very far from being Greece. Why then, if he knew that Greece alone would satisfy him and that Greece was not to be found in Rome—why did he not go to Greece? The journey, though difficult, was not impossible. He had an opportunity to go and refused it. Was it simply lack of enterprise, inertia, fearfulness of the physical dangers and inconveniences? Partly perhaps, but not at bottom. There was in fact no reason why he should go. As far as he knew, all the remains of Greek sculpture were in Italy—most of them concentrated in Rome. The Olympian pediment figures, the Hermes of Praxiteles, the Aeginetan marbles and innumerable other works were still buried. The Parthenon marbles had been seen by travellers; their existence was realised,[1] but not their importance. Historically Greece did not interest him. It would have meant little to him to stand on the Pnyx and reflect that here Themistocles and Pericles and Demosthenes had swayed the Athenian Demos with the magic of words, or to look out from the Acropolis over the Saronic Gulf, and to think of all the famous events that had taken place on its waters or around its shores. This was not the kind of "great impression" which Goethe was seeking. In short there was nothing to induce him to make a hazardous sea voyage to a barbarous outpost of the Turkish empire. But though he never went to Greece, he did at one moment escape from Rome and make a journey that amounted in his mind to "going to Greece". In Sicily he found at last what he was looking for—essential Hellas, free of northern mists, of Roman vulgarity, and of Christian other-worldliness.

Great impressions with which to feed his creative genius were what he sought as an artist. As seer or seeker after truth he crossed the Alps in the hope that in Italy he would find life in closest contact with ideal reality. In northern lands there seemed to be a veil over the process of manifestation, so that neither Nature nor human life, and therefore also not art, could reveal themselves in great, simple forms of ideal signifi-

[1] Goethe first saw drawings of the Parthenon marbles in August 1787, during his second stay in Rome (WA. 32, p. 63). They had been brought back from Athens by Richard Worsley (Goethe wrote Worthley), and were later published in the *Museum Worsleyanum*, 1794–1803. The *Museum* contains engravings of some metopes, much but not all of the frieze, and none of the pediment figures.

cance. In Italy he knew it would be otherwise, and so it proved. Even the Alps, the barrier between north and south, were to him the "fairest and grandest natural phenomena of the land".[1] On the shores of Garda, with a strong wind driving great waves against the strand and with the sun streaming down in southern strength,[1] he was aware of a new power in Nature to carry through great ideas, without faltering, in simple immediacy. Next at Verona, as he stood in the Roman amphitheatre and filled it in imagination with a thronging multitude, as it was meant to be seen, there came to him a revelation of what man could do, when he worked like Nature directly, unfalteringly, from a vast and simple idea to its vast and simple fulfilment.[2] It was thus that the ancients had worked; the temple at Assisi and the aqueduct at Spoleto confirmed this first impression;[3] and it was thus that he must learn to work. The conception did not need to be vast (the temple of Minerva was modest in proportions, befitting a small town), so long as it were true in itself and were carried out with a simple attention to the expedient means. The antique stelae in Verona exemplified this "true purposefulness" of ancient art most perfectly.[4] Here was no armoured knight, awaiting on his knees a blissful resurrection, no folded hands, no heavenward glances; such other-worldly nonsense, Goethe implied, was foreign to the ancient way of thought. Instead: "There stand the father and mother, their son between them, and look at each other with indescribable naturalness; another pair clasp hands. There a father seems to bid his family adieu, as he lies on his death-bed.... The artist has just portrayed the simple presence of these men and women, and so prolonged their existence and made it eternal.... They are what they were, they stand beside each other, they are concerned with one another, they love each other." Despite often inadequate craftsmanship these simple ideas were so movingly expressed, that Goethe wept as he gazed on them.

It is remarkable how little Goethe commented on the other works of antique sculpture which he saw on his way to Rome, although he dutifully visited the galleries and checked off the

---

[1] WA. III, 1, p. 182.
[2] *Ibid.* pp. 194 foll., 197.
[3] *Ibid.* pp. 323 foll., 327.
[4] *Ibid.* pp. 199 foll.: "Wahre Zweckmässigkeit."

antiques in his guide-book. A Ganymede attributed to Phidias received a laconic "good"; a Leda in the same collection in Venice he found to be "nobly sensuous in conception".[1] The antiques in Verona were "schön", those in Ferrara "köstlich".[2] Only the collection of antique sculpture in the Casa Farsetti in Venice drew from him any general comment: "These are works in which the world can rejoice for thousands of years and still will never exhaust the artist's worth."[3] He probably saw little of importance that he did not know already, except perhaps the Niobe and daughter.[4] In his haste to reach Rome he neglected the antiques in Florence, among them the Medici Venus, which moved him to such admiration on his return journey eighteen months later. More important than any lack of material was the fact that his eye was not trained to the appreciation of these more impersonal works of antiquity.[5] They did not yet reveal to him any fundamental idea. He was disappointed, for he had come to Italy in search of revelations, among the most important of which was to be that which showed him the ideal significance of Greek art. That first revelation, which had produced *Iphigenie*, was too limited, too narrowly moral. It had fitted the stage of development at which he had arrived eight years ago. Now he was ready for something greater, something more profoundly simple, more subtly complex. On the hurried journey to Rome there was no opportunity for the intensive study and the undisturbed contemplation which alone would compel the vision to appear. In Venice he thought that the analogy with architecture was setting him on the right road,[6] but it was not until a year later that he really saw and knew and understood.

Nature revealing herself with simple power; ancient architecture that followed Nature in its immediate expression of great ideas; the life of the common people, unself-conscious, passionate, directly expressive, like that of men and women in Homer—these were three "great impressions" which Goethe

---

[1] *Ibid.* p. 255: "Von hohem sinnlichen Sinn."
[2] *Ibid.* pp. 208, 299: "Beautiful" and "delightful".   [3] *Ibid.* p. 261.
[4] In the *Teutscher Merkur*, March 1785, this group is mentioned as being among the casts of antique statues in Weimar, yet Goethe mentions it in his diary (WA. III, 1, p. 260) among the works seen by him for the first time.
[5] *Ibid.* pp. 153, 261.   [6] *Ibid.* p. 261.

received before he reached Rome. Each of these showed him
the idea revealing itself without distortion or waste; and the
example of ancient architecture taught him that man could find
the way to such direct expression, as well as Nature. This
example he must follow. He must learn to feel and think and
produce as the ancients had done. He must make their power
of vast conception and their methods of execution his own.
Yet imitation, mere copying, was not enough. He was a
modern man. The world that he knew was not Homer's world.
He could not write an epic poem full of bloody and heroic
deeds, nor of mariners' tales of ships and storms and giants and
sorceresses. He had never seen blood spilt in anger, had never
set foot on a ship; and in the modern world giants and sorceresses
were only pretty fictions, not, as in Homer's day, awful possibilities. Nor could he write a Greek tragedy of blood and
hatred, larded with rhetorical harangues. He must draw his
material from his own experience and in handling it remain
true to his own nature. Only in interpreting and giving form
to the world around him, he must rival the ancients in power
and directness of expression. This principle was easy enough
to state; in its application, it raised problems to which solutions
were hard to find. How much, for instance, was the success
of the ancients in giving expression to the idea due to the forms
of expression which they had evolved? Was it possible to
achieve equally powerful expression without using these forms?
If they were to be used, how would modern material fit itself
into them? Was it possible to write iambic trimeters in German?
Herder had advised against it,[1] and he was probably right. But
could blank-verse ever convey the impression of dignity and
restrained power which the trimeter gave? Again, could the
greater emotional complexity of the modern world ever be
expressed as directly as the Greeks had expressed their simpler,
but more powerful ideas? Would not the attempt to press this
modern material into the old forms produce something
monstrous, something half bull, half man, and neither quite?
These were the problems which Goethe brought with him to
Italy. His failure with *Elpenor*, the success of his epigrams, and
the work of versifying *Iphigenie*, had given him conflicting
experience. The sight of the amphitheatre at Verona impressed

[1] See below, p. 131.

him again with the vital importance of finding some way to interpret Nature as the ancients had done. At this critical moment he found a guide, one who had faced the same problem, had made the same mistakes, and had found at last a working solution.

It was in Vicenza that Goethe first saw examples of Palladio's work.[1] At once he was filled with wonder and recognised a companion in genius.[2] Palladio too, he saw, had struggled with the problem of combining the tradition of antiquity with modern needs, and had not always been successful. These buildings in Vicenza showed plainly how he had experimented, first on this theory then on that. His attempt to use pillars in the ancient style on the fixed forms of modern domestic architecture was imposing, it revealed the force of Palladio's genius, but the result was a monstrosity. In the Olympic Theatre, on the other hand, he had cut loose from all modern tradition and sentiment, and had reproduced an ancient theatre. The result was "indescribably beautiful". But it did not suit modern needs. It was too lofty a conception for everyday life. In the Rotonda Palladio had tried another solution of the problem.[3] He had been free to build in any form he pleased. Instead of copying some ancient building, he had chosen to give expression to his complex, modern genius. Only the parts, not the whole, took their forms from the tradition of antiquity, and the result was "a bit wild".[4]

By a curious chance Goethe heard his own and Palladio's problem debated in the Academy of the Olympians in Vicenza. The question for debate was: "Whether invention or imitation is more advantageous to the fine arts."[5] Goethe had no sympathy with the supporters of imitation. Their arguments were just such specious sophistries as the many can appreciate. But in fact there could be no conclusion to a debate in which imitation and invention were set up as opposing, hostile principles. Goethe had long realised that the only solution of the problem lay in making a synthesis of the two. His difficulty

[1] WA. III, 1, p. 213.
[2] *Ibid.* p. 214: "Palladio ist ein recht innerlich und von innen heraus grosser Mensch gewesen."
[3] *Ibid.* p. 218.   [4] "Ein wenig toll."
[5] *Ibid.* pp. 222 foll.

was to find means for putting the synthesis into practice. It was significant that Palladio was cited by both sides in the debate.

In Padua Goethe bought Palladio's great treatise on the theory and practice of architecture. In Venice, where he arrived on 28 September 1786, he studied it, his eyes were opened, and he saw the goal that he had come to seek. "The revolution that is going on in me, is that which has taken place in every artist, who has studied Nature long and diligently and now sees the remains of the great spirit of antiquity; his soul wells up, he feels a transfiguration of himself from within, a feeling of freer life, higher existence, lightness and grace."[1] Goethe does not tell what it was in Palladio's book which revealed to him the secret of production in the manner of the ancients. It may however be hazarded that it was the sureness with which Palladio prescribed the proportion for every part in relation to every other part, and the unquestioning assumption that the product of these proportions would be beauty. These laws of beauty Palladio had from Vitruvius and from his study of ancient buildings. It was they which enabled the ancients to give complete, unfaltering expression to their great ideas. This system of proportions, worked out and perfected through centuries of diligent experiment, was the key to the greatness of the ancients in architecture. But merely to follow these specific laws—proportion of diameter to height in columns, height of pedestal to height of column and so on— would be imitation. The modern artist with modern emotions and material would not be helped by such superficial knowledge of ancient practice. It must be possible—Palladio had probably done it—to discover the fundamental law of proportion, upon which the ancients had worked in evolving all the specific laws, and from this fundamental law to evolve new specific laws for the creation of forms fitted to modern needs. Here was the key to the modern artist's dilemma. If the ancients had had these laws for architecture, they had them

[1] WA. III, 1, pp. 250 foll.: "Die Revolution, die jetzt in mir vorgeht, ist die in jedem Künstler entstand, der lang emsig der Natur treu gewesen und nun die Ueberbleibsel des alten grossen Geists erblickte, die Seele quoll auf und er fühlte eine innere Art von Verklärung sein selbst, ein Gefühl von freierem Leben, höherer Existenz, Leichtigkeit und Grazie."

also for sculpture and for poetry. Hard work and intuition would reveal them—first the specific laws, then the fundamental, and from that could be evolved new laws for use when modern needs demanded forms unknown to the ancients. No wonder Goethe spoke of Palladio with reverence and gratitude. He had learnt from him the method which in future he always used, to win from ancient art the secret of its ideal significance.

In the meantime Goethe was confronted with a self-imposed task, whose completion he could not long postpone. *Iphigenie* in its loosely iambic prose had never satisfied him. He had polished it at intervals during the last seven years,[1] especially during the summer of 1781, when he was reading much Greek tragedy, but had undertaken no radical change in the form. The decision to publish it in the first complete edition of his works forced him in 1786 to apply himself with energy to the task of giving *Iphigenie* an outward form worthy of its content. Encouraged in this decision by Wieland and Herder, he had taken the manuscript with him to Carlsbad and had set to work, with Herder's active help in the solution of questions of prosody, to recast the whole in blank-verse. The task had proved more formidable than he had thought. He was perhaps glad to have to take the "sweet burden" with him over the Alps. On the shore of Garda, in Verona, Vicenza and Venice he had worked on. Now, after a week in Venice, he found it impossible to continue. Not till he had been ten days in Rome did he return to the charge, and two months more passed before in January 1787 the perfected fair copy was dispatched to the friends in Weimar.

During this work on *Iphigenie* Goethe had the Greek tragedians always at his elbow. In Carlsbad he read the *Electra* of Sophocles in the Greek. The "strange rolling and turning" of the pauseless six-footed iambics made so strong a sensual impression on him, that he at once determined to recast his *Iphigenie* in trimeters rather than blank-verse.[2] He even set to work to rewrite the first scene. But the idea was soon given up, probably on Herder's advice, and the work on *Iphigenie* was continued in the simpler metre. Goethe took the tragedians in a Greek

[1] For the full history of the text see WA. 39, pp. 449 foll.
[2] Letter to Herder, late Aug. 1786 (WA. IV, 8, p. 8).

text with him to Italy.[1] In a letter to Herder from Venice he quoted the last lines of the *Ajax* in Greek;[2] and the final version of *Iphigenie* shows indubitable traces of recent reading of many Greek tragedies. Iphigenie's reflexions on woman's lot in her opening speech[3] are a close parallel to a passage in the *Medea*;[4] "the shy glance" that Iphigenie cast at the departing heroes— a visual touch not in the first version—is taken directly from *Iphigenia in Aulis* (lines 187, 188); and Iphigenie's appeal to Diana to save Orestes from madness (lines 1317–31) corresponds so closely to the similar appeal in Euripides's *Iphigenia in Tauris*, that one line of Goethe's text is actually a translation from the Greek.[5] Already in the prose version these three passages show a vague resemblance to the Greek passages cited. The last two were probably suggested by reading of the two *Iphigenias*. But in the verse text the resemblance is one not merely of thought but of concrete images, in one case of actual words. These passages, and others in the final version of *Iphigenie*,[6] prove beyond a doubt that Goethe had the Greek tragedians at hand, while he was engaged on the work of re-writing.

Goethe hoped no doubt that a new soaking in Greek tragedy, combined with the great impressions of ancient art and southern life, would rid *Iphigenie* of its northern mistiness and make it worthily antique. In fact the influence of the amphitheatre at Verona and of the Attic tragedians can be plainly discerned in the finished play. Already in 1781 Goethe had added touches which made the story of the house of Tantalus still more dark and terrible,[7] and emphasised the helplessness of mankind in struggling against implacable gods. In the final version the horror of the bloody deeds and their terrible punishment is made more present and compelling by a number of finely visual passages.[8] Therewith the conflict is sharpened between Iphigenie's lofty trust in goodness and the despairing philosophy

[1] Ernst Maass, *Goethe und die Antike*, p. 168 and *Schr. der G.G.* ii, pp. 319, 439. Cf. also *Egmont*, Act v, WA. 8, p. 302, and *Trachiniae*, lines 1222 foll.
[2] WA. iv, 8, p. 31.   [3] WA. 10, p. 4, lines 24–34.
[4] *Medea*, 230–54.   [5] *Iph.* 1321 = *Iph. Taur.* 1401.
[6] Cf. especially *Iph.* 307 and *Ag.* 629.
[7] Especially WA. 39, p. 472, lines 8, 9.
[8] Especially lines 384–7, 751–2, 1036, 1057–65, 1726–66 (the *Parzenlied* re-cast in verse).

which sees the world governed by gods who "kill us for their sport". The conflict comes to its crisis in Iphigenie's heart and finds expression in those famous lines:

> O dass in meinem Busen nicht zuletzt
> Ein Widerwille keime! der Titanen
> Der alten Götter tiefer Hass auf euch,
> Olympier, nicht auch die zarte Brust
> Mit Geierklauen fasse! Rettet mich,
> Und rettet euer Bild in meiner Seele.[1]

In the first version the conflict and the danger are only implied, not stated.

In Carlsbad Goethe may have wished merely to give *Iphigenie* a more worthy outward form before publishing it. The re-reading of Greek tragedy and the sight of ancient works of art, especially the amphitheatre and the stelae, made him see that profounder changes must be made. The idea of *Iphigenie* must be expressed with the directness of an ancient work of art. The contrast of dark and light must be intensified, the whole made more visual, less abstract. So to Herder he wrote: "It is tending towards complete crystallisation. The fourth act", in which the crisis of the play is reached, "is turning out almost completely new."[2]

So he progressed, with ever deepening insight into the nature of the problem, until he had been almost a month in Italy, one week in Venice. Then on 7 October he noted in his diary that he had been unable to compose a single line, and by the 10th he realised that he was not destined to finish *Iphigenie* immediately.[3] He gave no reasons to explain this sudden impotence, but it was in fact inevitable that he should have to pause in his work on *Iphigenie*. His attitude to the problem of composition in the antique manner was changing daily. Great new impressions had thrown his ideas into confusion. Palladio's ex-

---

[1] Lines 1712–17: "Oh! may no opposition grow at last in my breast! May the deep hatred which the Titans and the old gods feel for you, Olympians, not seize my tender heart too with vulture-claws! Save me, and save your image in my soul!"

[2] WA. IV, 8, p. 32.

[3] WA. III, 1, p. 289. The letter to Herder (WA. IV, 8, p. 31), dated 14 Oct., was only sent on that date. It was written probably soon after Goethe's arrival in Venice.

ample had shown him the pitfalls that awaited the modern artist. Finally on 2 October he had seen something which made him despair of ever making anything but a "monstrosity" out of his attempt to give antique expression to so modern a conception as that of *Iphigenie*. It was a building by Palladio,[1] the reproduction of an ancient dwelling-house. Goethe was carried away. He had seen nothing more sublime, he wrote. Here at last "the artist with the in-born sense for greatness...had had an opportunity to execute a favourite idea...in circumstances where the conception was entirely suitable. There was nothing to cramp him and he acted accordingly."[2] In contrast to this Goethe saw on the same day and the next fresh examples of Palladio's failure, when attempting to combine ancient forms with modern conceptions.[3] The lesson was all too clear. He would himself produce nothing truly in the style of the ancients, until he could set to work on a subject of his own choosing. He must be uncramped, like Palladio. All his tinkering at *Iphigenie* would produce at best a "beautiful monster", neither truly northern nor truly southern.[4]

At first this realisation seems to have produced in him a resigned despair. On 5 October he wrote: "On this journey I hope I shall bring my mind repose on the matter of the arts. I want to stamp their holy image indelibly into my soul and keep it there for my own silent enjoyment. Then I shall apply myself to handicrafts, and when I come back, study chemistry and mechanics. For the day of beauty is past; our age demands only stern necessity."[5] In Palladio's day, in that wonderful second blooming of the spirit of antiquity, it had still been possible, if only occasionally, for the great artist to achieve perfection. What hope was there that his own modern genius would ever discover for him a subject that would enable him to repeat Palladio's experience with the ancient dwelling-

---

[1] In the Convent of Santa Maria della Carità, now the Accademia di Belle Arti.

[2] WA. III, 1, pp. 254, 268, 292: "Der treffliche Künstler mit dem innerlichen Sinn fürs Grosse geboren,...findet Gelegenheit einen Lieblingsgedanken auszuführen, eine Wohnung der Alten nachzubilden, Gelegenheit da wo der Gedanke ganz passt. Er ist in nichts geniert und lässt sich von nichts genieren."

[3] *Ibid.* pp. 257 foll.

[4] *Ibid.* p. 275.   [5] *Ibid.* p. 266.

house? Better to resign himself in time and turn his energies to work that could be profitable. Thus once again Goethe's spirit failed at the vastness of the task that had been thrust upon it. During those days in Venice he first fully realised the difficulty of making Greece live again in a world that had forgotten every ideal for which Greece had once stood. He saw that the attempt was foolishness and resolved to give it up. But his human common sense was no match for his genius and his destiny. The stone must be rolled to the top of the hill; the gods alone would decide whether the labour should be crowned with achievement, or the stone roll back and all be lost.

His genius allowed him only a short breathing space. Two weeks later it revealed to him the new subject to which he could apply his antique manner "ungeniert". "Early this morning," Goethe wrote in his diary,[1] "on the way here from Cento, I had the good fortune, between sleep and waking, to find the plan to *Iphigeneia at Delphi* complete. There is a fifth act and a recognition-scene that few can equal. I cried over it myself like a child, and in the treatment of it the southern quality[2] will, I hope, be recognisable enough." Next day in Bologna he saw a St Agatha by Raphael. The "healthy sure maidenliness without coquetry, but without frigidity or coarseness"[3] of the saint seemed to him to be the visual realisation of his Iphigenie. He resolved to "read his *Iphigenie* aloud to this ideal and let his heroine say nothing that this saint could not say". It is usually assumed that the *Iphigenie* here referred to was the old one, the *Iphigenie auf Tauris*. Goethe himself states as much in the *Italienische Reise*.[4] Nevertheless it is not impossible that he was there exercising his right of "*Dichtung*" at the expense of "*Wahrheit*": the straightforward sequence of events of the diary is altered at this point so as to bring the two *Iphigenies* into more striking juxtaposition, and emphasise the inner struggle which their rival claims on his time and energies caused him.[5] It is far more natural to suppose that Goethe was

---

[1] Bologna, 18 Oct. (*Ibid.* p. 304).　　　　　[2] "Das Tramontane."
[3] "Eine gesunde, sichre Jungfräulichkeit ohne Reiz, doch ohne Kälte und Roheit": *Ibid.* p. 306.
[4] WA. 30, p. 167.
[5] Cf. also *Italienische Reise*, 6 Jan. 1787 (*Ibid.* p. 244).

still full of the *Iphigenie auf Delphos* when he saw St Agatha, and that it was his new play that he intended to read aloud to her as he composed it. An inspiration that had moved him so deeply only the day before, and that offered the opportunity of making the perfect modern work of art, can hardly have been forgotten or even deliberately laid aside so soon. It is more probable that *Iphigenie auf Delphos* continued to occupy him during the remaining ten days of his journey to Rome, and that it was at some point during the first days or weeks in Rome that his feeling of duty towards the old *Iphigenie* finally triumphed.[1]

Yet if this *Iphigenie auf Delphos* was the longed-for new subject in which Goethe was to be "ungeniert", free of the cramping demands of modern-northern traditions, as Palladio had been when he made his ancient dwelling-house, how could the heroine of the new piece find her visual embodiment in the picture of a Christian saint? Surely there could be no hope of making anything antique out of such a character. Let us examine the action of the play as Goethe intended it to be, and try to see how he hoped to make out of it something truly "in the style of the ancients".[2]

Nothing of the new *Iphigenie* was ever written down; at least no fragment of it has survived for posterity. All that is known about it is contained in the passage from Goethe's diary quoted above, and in the synopsis of the plot which he inserted from memory into the *Italienische Reise* nearly thirty years later.[3] This synopsis runs as follows: "Electra, confident that Orestes will bring the ikon of the Taurian Diana to Delphi, appears in the temple of Apollo and dedicates the fatal axe that has caused so much woe in Pelops's house, to the god as final offering of expiation. Unfortunately she is met by one of the Greeks, who tells her how he accompanied Orestes and Pylades to Tauris, how he saw the two friends led to death, and how he himself was fortunate enough to escape. The passionate Electra is beside herself, and does not know whether to direct her rage against gods or men. In the meanwhile Iphigeneia, Orestes and Pylades have also arrived in Delphi. Iphigeneia's saintly

---

[1] Other references to *Iphigenie* in the diary—whether the Delphic or the Taurian is not indicated—occur: WA. III, 1, pp. 314, 315.
[2] "Im Sinne der Alten."   [3] WA. 30, pp. 167 foll.

calm contrasts most strangely with Electra's earthly passion as the two figures meet without recognising each other. The Greek who escaped sees Iphigeneia, recognises in her the priestess who sacrificed the friends, and reveals it to Electra. She is about to murder Iphigeneia with the self-same axe, which she seizes up from the altar, when a fortunate turn saves the three from this last frightful calamity. If this scene comes off, it would be as noble and moving as anything that has ever been seen on the stage."

It is easy to see how this plot would provide Goethe with opportunity for treatment in the Greek manner, despite Iphigenie's modern-Christian character. Electra was to be in every way the Electra of Greek tragedy, passionate, ruthless, bloodthirsty in revenge. In her rage against the gods she could blaspheme with Euripidean bitterness, and in her hatred of her brother's murderess and in her resolve to requite blood with blood, she would reveal herself as one of those characters compounded of flint and fire, to which, as Goethe well knew, Greek tragedy owes its powerful effect. With this character as a foil even the gentleness of Iphigenie-Agatha would be compatible with the antique style of expression; by the powerful contrast of these two characters the idea of the play would be expressed with the direct simplicity that Goethe had learnt to wonder at in ancient works of art. The problem that Goethe was attempting once again to state and to solve in dramatic symbolism was the same that had inspired *Elpenor*: the problem of Greek inhumanity. Fresh reading of the Greek tragedians in juxtaposition with intensive work on his own *Iphigenie* had stirred up the old question. Now his genius had shown him the means, antique in their simplicity, of dramatising the problem and its solution. The two moralities were to meet, to come into conflict, the one was nearly to destroy the other; but they were to find reconciliation in the realisation that they were sisters, co-equals, diverse but not opposed, who had never wronged each other. This was to be the deeper meaning that underlay the moving drama of human emotions, hopes and fears.

It will be objected that a reconciliation on this basis is still no solution. "Iphigenie-morality" and "Electra-morality" cannot hold sway together as co-equals in one mind; and so long as Goethe was so much a modern at heart as to see his ideal in

Iphigenie, he must continue to reject Electra. In fact the moral of *Iphigenie auf Delphos* is a rebuke for Electra. She is proved fundamentally wrong in her belief that the gods deliberately lead human beings to destruction; and only this belief can justify her recourse to violence. In Goethe's mind the Greeks were still condemned for their belief in an inhumane world-order.

Had Goethe set to work at once to write his new *Iphigenie*, he might have finished it. He delayed to do so, allowed himself to be caught up in all the wonder of Rome, and returned to the more mechanical task of versifying his old play; in the meantime that change began in his whole *Weltanschauung* which caused him to turn his back on the gentle Iphigenie, calmly trusting in the goodness of humane gods, and to dismiss the morality for which she stood as "quite devilish humane".[1] As soon as that process had started, *Iphigenie auf Delphos* could never be finished. Goethe would have been condemning a view of life that he was himself coming to adopt. So the first great opportunity to compose in the style of the ancients was lost, because Goethe's mind was still developing faster than his genius could gather the fruits of his experience.

B. ROME

Goethe arrived in Rome on 29 October 1786. Next day he visited the chief ruins of ancient Rome, and St Peter's.[2] So began the most intensive and penetrating sight-seeing that the Eternal City has ever experienced. For the first six weeks he saw and saw without method, anxious only to obtain as quickly as possible a general impression of the city and all it contained. Ruins, statues, Renaissance painting and architecture occupied his time and energy equally. Only medieval Rome, like medieval Assisi, was neglected. New impressions of grandeur and beauty poured in on him daily, almost hourly. He made no attempt as yet to order them or reflect on them; but a few were so powerful that of themselves they took possession of

[1] Letter to Schiller, 19 Jan. 1802 (WA. IV, 16, p. 11): "Ganz verteufelt human."
[2] WA. III, 1, p. 331.

his mind to the temporary exclusion of everything else. The Apollo Belvedere, seen at last in the living warmth of the marble, seemed to him the most inspired work of art in the world.[1] The vast ruins of ancient Rome—the Colosseum, the baths of Diocletian, the imperial palaces on the Palatine, "that stand like cliffs", the façade of the Pantheon—impressed him profoundly.[2] He began to feel "a solidity of spirit...earnestness without dryness, and a firm but joyful nature".[3] These were the Greek virtues as Winckelmann had described them.[4] It is significant that Goethe connected their growth in himself with the influence and example of Roman architecture.

Apart from the Apollo Belvedere and the Ludovisi Juno,[5] works of ancient art drew from him less exclamations of enthusiasm during these first weeks than did Roman architecture and Renaissance painting. During the last days of November he could think and speak of little but of the Sistine Chapel. Michelangelo's frescoes overwhelmed him, so that even Raphael and the ancient sculptors faded for the time from the forefront of his interest.[6] Not that he was in any doubt as to the supreme excellence of ancient art. His naïve certainty on this point is illustrated by a passage in a letter to Frau v. Stein.[7] There was a picture in Rome which had been held to be "antique", until Mengs on his deathbed confessed that he had painted it. Goethe sided with those who still believed it to be genuine or at least a copy of an "antique",[8] on the grounds that the unrestored parts of it were "too beautiful even for Raphael". Goethe presumably knew that the picture, if antique at all, was at best the work of a Greek artist of the early Roman Empire. Yet such magic lay in the word "antique" that even the nameless products of this decadent period were assumed to be superior to those of the greatest artist of the Italian Renaissance. It is true that in November 1786, when Goethe gave his opinion on this picture, he had not yet studied

---

[1] WA. IV, 8, p. 45.   [2] *Ibid.* pp. 46, 51, 75.
[3] "Eine innere Solidität...Ernst ohne Trockenheit, und ein gesetztes Wesen mit Freude": *Ibid.* p. 51.
[4] Winckelmann, *Werke*, I, pp. 31, 161.   [5] WA. IV, 8, p. 117.
[6] *Ibid.* pp. 63, 71, 75.   [7] *Ibid.* p. 56.
[8] I thus interpret Goethe's remark: "Ich habe eine Hypothese wie das Bild entstanden."

Winckelmann's *Geschichte der Kunst*, and had little idea of the historical development of ancient art or of the inferiority of Romano-Greek work.[1] In later years an exacter knowledge of periods and styles gave his opinions more proportion; but throughout his classical period he tended to a habit of mind, exemplified by this judgment of Mengs's "antique" picture, which divided culture into "ancient" and "modern", and attributed all good qualities to the former and at best a power of imperfect imitation to the latter.

By the middle of December he had obtained his general view, and could turn with deliberation to a deeper study of whatever seemed most worthy.[2] At once he threw himself onto the remains of Greek sculpture. The Apollo renewed in him inarticulate wonder. The mask of a Medusa now for the first time attracted him;[3] it remained throughout his life one of his dearest impressions. He began to buy casts of those works that delighted him most: first in mid-December a colossal head of Jove,[4] three weeks later the Ludovisi Juno to match,[5] and about the same time another Juno head and the head of the Apollo.[6] In the first days of the new year he began to study Winckelmann's *Geschichte der Kunst des Altertums*.[7] He had bought it soon after his arrival in Rome[8] (from his reference to it in a letter to Herder it is clear he had never read it before), and had used it as a guide-book to the museums;[9] now at last, when he had seen with his own eyes the statues of which Winckelmann was writing, he felt himself ready to take Winckelmann as a guide in the task of ordering his impressions and deducing from their multiplicity the single ruling idea.

Late in life Goethe said to Eckermann: "One learns nothing when one reads Winckelmann, but one becomes something."[10] He had forgotten how little he had known of Greek art when he came to Rome, and how hard it would have been for him to find his way among that forest of undated statues, if he had not had Winckelmann to guide him. He learnt in fact from the *Geschichte der Kunst* the very fundamentals of an exacter

[1] Cf. Winckelmann, *Werke*, v, p. 186.
[2] WA. iv, 8, pp. 96, 100.   [3] *Ibid.* p. 100.
[4] *Ibid.* p. 101.   [5] *Ibid.* p. 117.   [6] *Ibid.* p. 135.
[7] *Ibid.* p. 119.   [8] WA. 30, p. 232.   [9] WA. iv, 8, p. 76.
[10] Eckermann, 16 Feb. 1827.

knowledge of ancient art. Before January 1787 he had no clear conception of its historical development or of the relation of schools and artists one to another; as soon as he started to study the *Geschichte der Kunst* he realised the basic importance of Winckelmann's "periods".[1] They became the framework into which he fitted all the vast knowledge that came to him through years of observation and study.

Winckelmann devoted one of the books of his *Geschichte der Kunst* to an account of the rise and fall of Greek art. He recognised four distinct styles: the archaic, in works dating from the earliest beginnings down to Phidias; the grand or lofty, with Phidias, Polyclitus, Scopas and Myron as its great exponents; the beautiful, from Praxiteles to Lysippus and Apelles; and the period of the imitators, in which ancient art (in Winckelmann's opinion the Romans had no art independent of the Greek)[2] slowly declined until it disappeared in barbarism.[3] For Winckelmann Greek art reached its highest excellence in the period of the "beautiful style". The "lofty style" was indeed worthy of profound admiration; it was great and powerful, nobly simple in conception and execution; but it lacked a certain "grace and charm";[4] beauty was sometimes sacrificed in it to an austere correctness of proportions. The works of Praxiteles and Lysippus had a delicacy of thought and softness of contour which made them the perfection of artistic achievement.[5]

Of all the ancient works of art in Rome Winckelmann recognised only two as dating from the period of the "lofty style". These were a Pallas in the Villa Albani and the famous group of Niobe shielding her daughter from the shafts of Apollo. This work, now assigned to the late fourth or early third century, a product, according to the *Encyclopaedia Britannica*, of "the pathetic school", appeared to Winckelmann to typify all the qualities of the lofty style (fifth century). The sublime simplicity of the idea executed with effortless perfection, as it were "blown by a breath", could, according to Winckelmann, have been achieved only by a contemporary of Phidias.[6] No work nor copy of a work by Phidias, Polyclitus

---

[1] WA. iv, 8, p. 137 and WA. 30, p. 264.
[2] *Werke*, v, pp. 282, 290, 292.   [3] *Ibid.* pp. 210, 236.
[4] "Grazie und Gefälligkeit."   [5] *Ibid.* v, pp. 236–45.
[6] *Ibid.* pp. 239 foll.: "Von einem Hauche geblasen."

or Myron was known. Goethe believed he had discovered another example of the lofty style, overlooked by Winckelmann, in an Athene in the Giustiniani palace.[1] The beautiful style was better represented in Rome. Outstanding among examples of it, and in their different ways the most perfect works of all ancient sculpture, were the Apollo Belvedere and the Laocoön group. Lessing and others had doubted whether the Laocoön could date from so early a period, but Winckelmann placed it in the fourth century on the grounds solely of its supreme perfection.[2] It is now known to be Rhodian work of the first century B.C.

It is not surprising that Winckelmann was often wrong in his attempts to date the remnants of ancient art. He was the first to try to arrange these remnants in chronological periods. There were no criteria, established by a tradition of scholarly investigation. He had to evolve his criteria for himself, and inevitably he was forced to rely rather on intuition than on reasoning from observation. It was unfortunate that his taste led him to stress the excellence of such works as the Apollo, the Niobe and the Laocoön, which give no idea of what Greek sculpture at its highest could achieve. His fault here was due partly to the age in which he lived, in which grace and delicacy were held in higher esteem than to-day, but still more to the fact that the greatest works of Greek sculpture, such as the Parthenon marbles, the pediment figures from Olympia, and innumerable others, were unknown to him. He did not know the best and so was forced to commend the second best. His merit was that he defined the characteristics of the different periods so truly, that later discoveries of Greek works of art of the best period did not disturb the picture which men had learnt from him, but merely confirmed it. He sensed, as it were, the existence of the Elgin Marbles. It was they that he unwittingly described when he wrote of the lofty style. Only in looking round for an example of this style to which he could point, he was forced to light on an inferior work such as the Niobe. Winckelmann's importance for Goethe was just this: he established the periods of Greek art and the characteristics of each so rightly, that Goethe was able to fit all his knowledge, as it accumulated, into this framework; and when thirty years

[1] WA. IV, 8, pp. 130, 131. [2] *Werke*, VI, I, p. 101.

later the Parthenon sculptures came at last to be fully known,
their qualities were not strange or unexpected, as the temples
at Paestum had been at first sight; they were the fulfilment
which Winckelmann had foretold and for which Goethe had
been waiting. In the meantime, it is true, Goethe worshipped
the Apollo Belvedere and the Laocoön, but that was inevitable
in the state of knowledge of those days.

The *Geschichte der Kunst* suggested to Goethe a second line
of enquiry which led him in time to strange depths of contemplation. The problem was to discover what the Greeks had
intended to express in the statues of their gods and heroes. In
writing up the *Italienische Reise* he defined the problem thus:
"to find out how those incomparable artists set to work, in
order to reveal, through the medium of the human form, the
circle of the divine nature, which is completely closed, and in
which no primary character is lacking any more than the intermediary stages and connecting links.[1] I have an idea they
followed just those laws which Nature follows and of which
I am on the track. Only there is something else there, which I
would be at a loss to define."[2] It is not likely that in January
1787 Goethe was already so clearly aware of the nature of the
problem. The passage is probably an interpolation, made at the
time when he was working up his letters and diaries for publication as the *Italienische Reise*. But there can be no doubt that,
during the last weeks of his first stay in Rome, he was beginning
to realise the capital importance of the question and to make his
own studies and observations. Winckelmann had not attempted
to define the significance which the Greeks attached to the
statues of the gods, but he had emphasised an important fact,
which Lessing had already pointed out,[3] namely that each god
was represented in a stereotyped form which was recognisable
through the individual variations of each statue. Thus Mercury
could be distinguished from Apollo by a "special fineness in
the face";[4] the elder gods, Jupiter, Neptune, Pluto, Vulcan

---

[1] German: "zu erforschen wie jene unvergleichlichen Künstler verfuhren,
um aus der menschlichen Gestalt den Kreis göttlicher Bildung zu entwickeln,
welcher vollkommen abgeschlossen ist und worin kein Hauptcharakter so
wenig als die Uebergänge und Vermittlungen fehlen."

[2] WA. 30, pp. 264-5 (28 Jan. 1787).

[3] *Wie die Alten den Tod gebildet, Werke*, XI, p. 8.

[4] Winckelmann, *Werke*, IV, p. 84.

are as easily recognised and distinguished as the portraits of
famous men of antiquity;[1] Juno can be known by the large eyes,
Pallas by the thoughtful look in half-closed eyes and gently
bowed head.[2] Lessing had attributed the origin of these different
forms to chance, their general acceptance and continued use to
convenience; Winckelmann had indicated that they were held
in antiquity to be the result of special revelations received by
the great artists,[3] but he had not gone more deeply into their
significance. Goethe could not rest until he had probed the
matter to the bottom, for in the solution might lie the key to
the meaning of Greek art, even perhaps to the whole Greek
genius. He surrounded himself with heads of the great gods,
in the hope that in their constant presence he might be granted
the revelation of their secret.[4] He applied himself to the study
of antique gems and coins,[5] which offered the richest material
for a study of the forms of the gods. He wrote to Herder that
he was practising himself in the study of the different gods and
heroes. "What the ancients accomplished in this line, has
never been told and never could be told. I won't speak of it,
but will demonstrate it to my friends when I have made myself
sure of it."[6] His interest in the second part of Herder's *Zer-
streute Blätter*, which he read aloud to his artist friends,[7] lay
partly in the fact that in the essay on Nemesis Herder was
attempting to re-define the characteristics of one of the Greek
goddesses from the picture that the Greeks had made of her in
their literature and their art.[8] During the last days of January
and the beginning of February Goethe was indefatigable in
visiting and re-visiting the museums, seeking out anything that
he had missed, seeing the great works again and again.[9] A new
conception of the significance of Greek art was beginning to
take shape in him,[10] but he was still far from having evolved a

---

[1] Winckelmann, *Werke*, IV, pp. 96, 98, 102.   [2] *Ibid.* pp. 115 foll.
[3] *Ibid.* p. 135.
[4] It is true that Goethe bought the Jupiter and the Juno before he started
his systematic reading of the *Geschichte der Kunst*. But he had been using
it ever since his arrival in Rome, and he had probably come across what
Winckelmann says about the Greek gods during the earlier reading.
[5] WA. IV, 8, pp. 135, 150 (13 and 25 Jan.).   [6] *Ibid.* p. 153.
[7] *Ibid.* p. 155.
[8] Herder, *Werke*, XV, pp. 395–428.
[9] *Ibid.* pp. 156, 170, and WA. 30, p. 270.   [10] WA. IV, 8, p. 150.

system of interpretation, which would enable him to judge clearly and formulate his judgments.[1]

At this moment he found a companion whose kindred mind was at work on the same problems. Karl Philipp Moritz had become known to Goethe in the previous November. A relationship of extraordinary intimacy sprang up between them. Goethe described himself as Moritz's "father-confessor and confidant, finance-minister and private secretary", and looked on Moritz as his younger brother; for the story of Moritz's life seemed a replica of Goethe's own, save that fortune had always been hard on Moritz while she had smiled on Goethe.[2] Moritz had an active and sensitive mind. His theories of prosody were of great value to Goethe in the final work on *Iphigenie*.[3] At the beginning of 1787 he began, perhaps at Goethe's suggestion, to occupy himself with Greek mythology. His object was to re-interpret the myths in such a way as to make them once again a source of living symbols for artist and poet. He worked throughout in close co-operation with Goethe and the result of his labours, *Die Götterlehre*, undoubtedly sets forth essentially Goethe's own views on the origin and significance of the Greek myths.[4] *Die Götterlehre* was not published until 1791; Goethe and Moritz were most actively engaged on it in the summer of 1787, after Goethe's return from Sicily;[5] but it will not be out of place to quote from it at this point, since the interpretation of mythology which it sets forth was already forming in Goethe's mind. By 17 February 1787, when he wrote to Herder asking him to help Moritz in his "antiquarian undertaking",[6] Goethe had already passed into a new stage of his unending development. He had freed himself at last from Iphigenie and Charlotte. He had become a pagan.

In Moritz's view the myths reveal, through the medium of the poetical faculty ("*Phantasie*"), the nature of the funda-mental forces which create and maintain the world. The gods are these forces made visible by poetry to human understanding. Moritz hoped that his book would be the evangel of a new

---

[1] Cf. E. Wolf, *Goethe und die griechische Plastik*, p. 57.
[2] WA. IV, 8, p. 115 and p. 94.   [3] WA. 30, p. 248.
[4] This is denied by Rudolf Fahrner in his essay *Karl Philipp Moritz Götterlehre*, Marburg, 1932.
[5] WA. 30, p. 70.   [6] WA. IV, 8, p. 189.

religion, based on the pagan tradition, which Christianity had destroyed. He speaks of the "new dawn" that will come if the myths are properly understood.[1] All the myths, even the most primitive, are full of the eternal wisdom that has significance for men of all ages. According to the Greeks Night enfolded within her "all the forms which the light of day reveals to our eyes".[2] This is the Neo-Platonic conception of the world of Ideas, as active in our day as three thousand years ago; it is Goethe's "Realm of the Mothers", where Faust sought the magic tripod. The war of the old gods against the new was not just a strange old tale to the Greeks; it symbolised the victory of proportion and form over the monstrous and unformed.[3] Most significant of all is a defence of anthropomorphism in religion. Nature created mankind in order that she might be conscious of herself. In return mankind has learnt how to re-express Nature in his own form. "For the expression of the divine form, nothing nobler could be found than eye and nose, brow and eyebrow, cheek, mouth and chin; since only from a living thing which has this form, can we know that it has conceptions like ours, and that we can exchange thoughts and words with it."[4] The Greeks it was who in their art reached the summit of achievement in this holy work; they created forms of gods, that were human yet raised above human stature, forms from which everything accidental was excluded, in which all essential characteristics of power and sublimity were combined.[5]

It was wrong in Moritz's opinion to seek ethical precepts in the myths. In them "man is of such secondary importance that little regard is taken of him or his moral needs. He is often nothing but a sport of the higher powers." The gods punish not so much injuries done by man to man, as "every appearance of encroachment on the prerogatives of the gods". (This was the sin of Tantalus.) In fact these higher powers are not moral beings. Their attribute is power. Each one of them represents Nature with all her "luxuriant, wanton growths", and is therefore above morality.[6] Conflict between the gods, often

---

[1] *Die Götterlehre*, 3. unveränderte Ausgabe, 1804, p. 6.
[2] *Ibid.* p. 9.   [3] *Ibid.* p. 16.
[4] *Ibid.* p. 22.   [5] *Ibid.* p. 73; cf. also pp. 38, 81–2.
[6] *Ibid.* pp. 5, 6: "Üppigen Auswüchsen."

portrayed in Greek mythology, is not a barbarous conception, fit only for primitive religions. All these higher powers coexist in Nature, so that conflict between them is inevitable, a basic law of Nature. Conflict such as that between the young gods and the Titans was not a conflict of Good against Evil, but simply of Power against Power.[1] The young gods won, because they were more "gebildet", their being was more firmly established and defined. But the vanquished gods remain great and venerable. They are part of Nature and cannot be destroyed. The younger gods—Zeus, Hera, Mars, Apollo "the destroyer"—are anything but humane in the sense in which Iphigenie's gods were humane. "Jupiter begot with Juno implacable Mars, the dreadful god of war. Jupiter was often wroth with him, and threatened to fling him from Heaven, but spared him, because he was his own son."[2] Conflict and violent destruction are part of the order of Nature. Though they may seem at times to disturb the plan of the supreme deity, the Greeks knew they must be allowed to play their part in the world. Hera's jealousy is not ridiculous but noble and beautiful; for it is not impotent, but is armed with divine might, and successfully opposes the Thunderer himself on the highest summit of his power.[3] It is entirely fitting that the heroes should result from secret matings that Zeus enjoys only with difficulty, for the Greeks well knew that "everything beautiful and strong...must struggle against opposition and difficulties and must go through many a trial and danger".[4] The Greeks fully realised the implacable essence of life. They depicted it in the Fates and the Furies. But even to these dreadful, and to human beings hateful, powers they gave beautiful forms; not because on aesthetic grounds they avoided the hideous in art, but because in their deep wisdom they knew that these highest powers, who ruled even the gods, were beautiful. "The Fates represent the terrible Power to which even the gods are subject, and yet they are portrayed as beautiful women.... Everything is light and easy for the unlimited highest Power. Nothing laborious or difficult exists on this plane; all opposition ceases at this culminating point."[5] Gods, and still more mortals, know pain and trouble, but on the highest plane of being there

[1] *Ibid.* p. 17.   [2] *Ibid.* p. 61.
[3] *Ibid.* p. 62.   [4] *Ibid.* p. 64.   [5] *Ibid.* p. 34.

is nothing but unimpeded power. For an existence so perfect and so easy the only possible symbol was the youthful female form in idealised perfection.

Iphigenie's gentle doctrine of understanding, non-violence and trust in the goodness of God has no place in this interpretation of the world. The gods had turned out to be inhumane and cruel, as Iphigenie had feared but had refused to believe. "Every attempt of a mortal to measure himself against their lordly power, is terribly punished", Moritz wrote,[1] and quoted the *Parzenlied* from *Iphigenie*, to illustrate the Greek conception of the relation of men and gods. Iphigenie's doubts had conquered; her faith had been misplaced. The sight of the Apollo Belvedere, the Zeus of Otricoli and the Ludovisi Juno had carried Goethe past the barrier that we know as the problem of good and evil. He had seen the inner meaning of conflict, the justification of "Electra-morality". The tendency that was fundamental in him, to admire what was great, beautiful and powerful, though it might be in no way beneficent on the human plane, now found itself supported and justified by the wisdom of the Greeks, which they had incorporated in their myths, their poetry and their art. Already on 23 December 1786 he wrote to Charlotte that his moral sense was undergoing as great changes as his aesthetic ideas.[2] The new wisdom was breaking through. During the next two months his intense study of the remains of ancient art and his talks with Moritz on mythology, helped it to take root, to grow and to gain shape, so that when on 21 February he left Rome for Naples, he went a pagan, with eyes open to see the world as it is, in its beauty and its terror.

C. NAPLES AND SICILY

Already in the middle of December Goethe had made up his mind to leave Rome at the New Year and spend some weeks in Naples. His object was "to enjoy the glorious countryside, wash my mind clean of so many mournful ruins, and to get relief from over-austere aesthetic conceptions".[3] He stayed

[1] *Götterlehre*, p. 263.   [2] WA. IV, 8, p. 101.
[3] *Ibid.* p. 33: "Mich der herrlichen Natur erfreuen und meine Seele von der Idee sovieler traurigen Ruinen reinspülen, und die allzustrengen Begriffe der Kunst lindern."

six weeks longer in Rome than he had intended, because his study of Greek sculpture had brought him to the problem of the Greek gods and their significance. But his objects, when he did start out for Naples, were the same as they had been two months before. After five months in Italy, of which three and a half had been spent in Rome, he realised that he had not got to the heart of what he was seeking. None of the country that he had seen quite fulfilled his expectations as a direct manifestation of the forces of Nature. He hoped that the landscape and the vegetation round Naples would show him what he wanted: Nature revealing herself unhindered in great and simple forms, that were perfect expressions of the ideas behind them. His search for the same quality in human culture, which he had expected to find in Rome in the remains of "ancient" civilisation, had also not been entirely successful. Much of what he had seen was indeed of the highest conceivable excellence and value; but Rome itself, he was coming to see, contained too much that blurred the outlines of his "great impressions". Already in December he had begun to have a horror of the "mournful ruins", and to see that their interest was little more than historical. His study of Greek art during January and February and his reading of Winckelmann made him realise, more and more clearly, that the Romans had left behind little or nothing that could help him in his search for aesthetic-philosophical truth. In art the Romans had been nothing but imitators. Their importance lay in their history, which Goethe studied in Livy during January,[1] and in their political achievement; their significance for later generations was therefore conditioned by the changing circumstances of human life. Goethe was seeking eternal ideas, which should be as valid now as they had been two thousand years ago. For these, he now saw, the Greeks had been the sole fountain-head. Did he know that he would find Greece, if he journeyed farther south to Naples and Sicily? He could hope at least to come nearer to the forms he was seeking, if he got away from "form-confusing Rome"[2] to a land where Nature was great and simple, and where the memories of wars, of consuls and of emperors were not so oppressively present.

[1] *Ibid.* pp. 143, 146, 152.
[2] WA. 31, p. 120: "das gestaltverwirrende Rom."

It was natural too that, after two months' intensive study of Greek sculpture, he should feel the need of a period of contemplation during which to set in order the crowd of impressions that he had received. He must strive to find the idea that governed this mass of phenomena and gave to each and all their pure significance. This effort to lay bare the kernel of Greek art would lead him, he knew, to strange planes of thought; the pursuit of the new-found problem of the Greek gods would link the contemplation of art with the contemplation of Nature. There could be no better background for this aesthetic enquiry than the "herrliche Natur" of the Neapolitan countryside.

During his stay in Naples, where he remained until the end of March 1787, Goethe gave himself a holiday from the study of Greek sculpture. Except for an antique horsehead, the coin collection of Prince Waldeck, and the decorated household utensils that had been brought from Pompeii,[1] he did not take special notice of any of the ancient works of art in Naples. He spent his time observing the way of life of the Neapolitans and in making expeditions to the places of interest in the neighbourhood—Pozzuoli, Vesuvius, Pompeii and Herculaneum, Capua, Paestum. On these expeditions he was surrounded by the splendour of Nature, and he was not disappointed by what he saw. The situation of Naples, the sweep of the gulf, Vesuvius, the rich lands sloping to the sea, the sea itself—real sea with real waves and storms—the islands, the luxuriant vegetation, and over all the blue Heaven—here was nothing half-expressed, veiled, distorted.[2] As Goethe and the artist Kniep were driving back from Paestum and came over the high ground that lies between Salerno and the Bay of Naples, the whole picture lay before them in all its nobility and beauty. Suddenly their ecstatic contemplation was interrupted by a "ghastly singing or rather shrieking and howling of joy". It was the Neapolitan lad who had accompanied them. Goethe rebuked him sharply. "For a while he never moved; then he touched me gently on the shoulder, stretched his right arm between us pointing and said 'Signor, perdonate! questa è la mia patria!'—Poor Northerner that I am, something like tears came into my eyes!"[3]

[1] WA. 31, pp. 33, 35, 60.
[2] Ibid. pp. 23, 24, 34, 47, 48, 75.   [3] Ibid. p. 73.

In Naples he felt, for the first time, what it could mean to be a "Southerner". The happy-go-lucky way of living, that in Northern Italy and Rome had repelled him as often as not, here seemed to him utterly good. "Naples is a paradise; everyone lives in a sort of drunken half-consciousness. I feel the same. I hardly know myself; I seem to be another being altogether. Yesterday I thought: either you were mad before, or you are mad now."[1] The Neapolitans, even those of the educated class, had a *naïveté* that brought them near to being the unspoilt *hommes naturels*, of whom so many in Goethe's day dreamed.[2] Goethe felt himself turning natural in spite of himself.[3] He had now seen with his own eyes that marvellous background of sky and landscape from which the Greek civilisation had sprung, and had experienced something of that happy carelessness, that capacity to live without thinking, without problems, without "Thou-shalt-nots", which he and his contemporaries held to be one of the basic qualities of the Greek character.[4] Here too Goethe saw the idea finding expression directly; even these modern southerners had something "elementally human" about them.[5] How much more nearly "*Urmenschen*" must the ancients have been, above all the Greeks!

By coming to Naples he had come closer to Greece. He was enchanted by the "passion for art and pictures displayed by a whole people" which the painted walls and household things of ruined Pompeii revealed.[6] He did not regard Winckelmann's warning voice, who had condemned the wall decorations in Herculaneum as being "of a period, in which good taste no longer ruled".[7] These ancients with their simple spontaneous joy in life had known how to use art, so as to "cheer the spirit and give it breadth".[8] Goethe knew of course that the inhabitants of Pompeii had not been Greeks, but he had no difficulty in regarding this riot of daintiness as in keeping with the Greek spirit. He greeted it as confirmation of his belief in the "*Heiterkeit*", the productive cheerfulness, of the Greek way of life.

---

[1] *Ibid.* p. 52.   [2] *Ibid.* p. 49.
[3] *Ibid.* p. 63.   [4] Cf. *Ibid.* p. 260.
[5] "Ursprüngliches der Menschengattung": *Ibid.* p. 49.
[6] *Ibid.* pp. 38, 60: "Kunst- und Bilderlust eines ganzen Volks."
[7] *Werke*, v, p. 186.   [8] WA. 31, p. 60.

How strangely then was his belief upset when for the first time he stood before a Greek temple! In the second half of March he visited Paestum with Kniep. In the marshy barrens by the sea three temples stand, as the Greek settlers built them five hundred years before the birth of Christ. Two of them date from the early days of the colony when the Greek temple form was still evolving. The middle temple, a little later than the Parthenon and the temple of Zeus at Olympia, represents the perfection of the Doric style.[1] These were the first buildings which Goethe had seen, in which the voice of Hellas spoke to him directly, undistorted by Roman or Renaissance imitators. "The first impression could rouse only astonishment. I found myself in an utterly unfamiliar world. For as the centuries progress from the severe to the pleasing, so they modify mankind with them, indeed they create him so.[2] Now our eyes, and through them our whole inner being, is adapted and accustomed to slenderer architecture, so that these squat, tapering column-masses, pressed close one against another, seem to us oppressive, even terrifying. Yet I quickly pulled myself together, remembered the history of art, thought of the age which found such a style fitting, called to mind the austere [i.e. Winckelmann's 'lofty'] style of sculpture, and in less than an hour I felt myself at home."[3] Thus Goethe describes his feelings in the *Italienische Reise*. There is no record in letter or diary of the first visit to Paestum, but there is no reason to doubt that this account of the impression which the temples made upon Goethe is essentially true. It was a profound shock to his whole conception of the "ancient" attitude to life. The "Bilderlust" of the old Pompeians, which had survived even to the present day among the Neapolitan peasantry,[4] the care-free life and the untrammelled flourishing of Nature, had all emphasised in his mind the ease and joyousness of existence in ancient times. The Rococo element in ancient art was beginning to mean too much to him.[5] Roman superficiality had seduced him, though he had left Rome to escape just such

---

[1] *Encyclopaedia Britannica*, eleventh edition, Paestum.
[2] "Denn wie die Jahrhunderte sich aus dem Ernsten in das Gefällige bilden, so bilden sie den Menschen mit, ja sie erzeugen ihn so."
[3] WA. 31, pp. 71 foll.
[4] *Ibid.* p. 39.
[5] *Ibid.* p. 60.

dilution of the true Greek spirit. Now these stark temples, utterly lacking in ornament, scorning all elegance save that of solidity and proportion, reminded him of the austerity of his quest, and revealed to him how far he still was from feeling and seeing as a Greek. Since January, when he had read the *Geschichte der Kunst*, he had been needing some visible example that should demonstrate the difference between Roman and Greek culture. He had found it in the temples of Paestum. He saw now that Palladio had known nothing of Greek architecture, that his "ancients" were merely Romans.[1] It was essential for him to avoid the same mistake.

Since the early days of his stay in Naples he had been thinking of making a journey to Sicily. In Naples he felt the same kind of longing for the little-known island as in Germany he had felt for Rome and all Italy.[2] He had not yet found what he had come to find. Yet for many days he could not decide to go. The decision, whether to go or stay, he felt to be of profound importance to his whole life. He seemed to himself hardly a free agent: "Two spirits are fighting over me."[3] When at last he had made up his mind to go, he felt immense relief, and knew that the journey would be "decisive" for him.[4]

What did Goethe expect to find in Sicily? The hints that he gives us in the *Italienische Reise* are confusing, and the letters and diary help but little. Sicily, he said, pointed on to Asia and Africa. It would be an experience to stand on "the remarkable point, where so many radii of the world's history are focussed".[5] Later he spoke of his hope that Sicily and "Neugriechenland" (presumably Magna Graecia) would free him from the evils of an education based on "formless Palestine and form-confusing Rome";[6] and in the only letter from Palermo which has survived, he told Fritz v. Stein: "I have seen an enormous amount that was new to me; only here does one get to know Italy."[7] Before he left Naples he announced his intention of being back in Rome before the end of June. "Since I have missed Easter, I must at least celebrate St Peter's Day there. My Sicilian journey must not distract me too far from my original purpose."[8]

[1] Cf. WA. IV, 45, p. 115.
[2] WA. 31, pp. 23, 24.
[3] *Ibid.* p. 53; cf. p. 57.
[4] *Ibid.* pp. 76, 90.   [5] *Ibid.* p. 76.
[6] *Ibid.* p. 121.
[7] WA. IV, 8, p. 211.
[8] WA. 31, p. 76.

It was not Goethe's way in his autobiography to reveal the inner springs of action that led him to adopt this course or that. That sentence for instance, in a letter to Charlotte—"Ich kämpfte selbst mit Tod und Leben"—which shows the whole seriousness of Goethe's condition before the flight to Italy, does not appear in the *Italienische Reise*. So we should not expect to be told the exact nature of the hopes that drew Goethe to Sicily, and of the fears that nearly held him back. Nor should we be surprised, if some of the hints given are hard to reconcile with the main body of the evidence. Deliberate mystification was not Goethe's intention, but it often happened that in working up his letters, he gave as much prominence to what had at the time been a secondary consideration, as he did to any hints of his fundamental motive. It is highly improbable that Sicily was of much importance to him as a stepping-stone to Asia and Africa or as the scene of so much of the world's history. It is hard to know what interest he can have felt in Asia at that time, unless it were in Asia Minor as the land of the Ionian Greek cities, of Troy and of the probable birthplace of Homer. His reading of Livy had shown him the important part played by Sicily in the Punic Wars as no-man's land between Rome and Carthage. As Meinecke points out,[1] Goethe's interest in a focal point of history of this sort was not purely historical. He derived rather an aesthetic satisfaction from being able "to scan all the roads that once led outwards from such a centre of mighty events into the world around". That he undertook the Sicilian journey primarily in order to taste this pleasure is obviously impossible. He was seeking a far deeper spiritual experience than this.

He went to Sicily in order to see two things: Greek culture untouched by any Roman influence, and above all the land on which this culture had grown.[2] With these things seen and understood he was confident that the revelations which he was seeking would soon come to him, and his quest would be at an end. When he said that one had to go to Sicily in order to understand Italy, he meant that Sicily revealed the quintessence of the southern spirit, without any of those impurities and complications that had made him dissatisfied with the im-

[1] *Die Entstehung des Historismus*, II, p. 515.
[2] Cf. Rehm, *op. cit.* p. 144.

pression that Rome and Italy had made on him. Italy without
Sicily, he said, "makes no picture in the mind".[1] The purity
and the simplicity of the impressions which he expected to
receive in Sicily, would drive out the confusion of his Roman
impressions. Yet one more problem remains. If in Sicily he
hoped to come to the end of his quest, to find at last in its
purest essence the knowledge that as a northerner he lacked,
why did he speak of the journey to Sicily as leading him aside
from his original purpose? Surely his original purpose had
been to find this essential knowledge. No doubt it had been:
but inextricably bound up with this fundamental purpose had
been the longing to see Rome. When he left Germany, Goethe
never doubted that he would find in Rome complete satisfaction
of all his desires.[2] For thirty years his mind had been acquiring
a habit of veneration and longing for Rome. The realisation
that Rome was not enough, was unwelcome. Mental inertia
resented the necessity of modifying this habit, and opposed any
step, such as the Sicilian journey, which this necessity brought
about. The lesson of Paestum had been accepted; but it had
been a shock, not only to his preconceived notions, but to his
pride. It left him curiously touchy, on the defensive against
any demands which the new realisation might make on him.
The Sicilian journey was as far as he would go in altering his
plans for the sake of ancient Hellas. "The Prince of Waldeck",
he wrote the day before he sailed for Sicily, "unsettled me just
as I was saying good-bye. He actually suggested that I should
be ready on my return to go with him to Greece and Dalmatia.
When once you set out into the world and get entangled with
it, you must be on your guard that you don't get led astray,
or even driven crazy by it. I am incapable of another word."[3]
Strange outburst! He longed to go and knew he ought to.
But it would have meant another change of plans; he might
encounter more shocks like that of Paestum. He knew in his
heart that these objections were worthless, and sought to hide

---

[1] "Macht kein Bild in der Seele": WA. 31, p. 124.
[2] WA. IV, 8, p. 37.
[3] WA. 31, p. 78, last two sentences: "Wenn man sich einmal in die Welt
macht und sich mit der Welt einlässt, so mag man sich ja hüten, dass man
nicht entrückt oder wohl gar verrückt wird. Zu keiner Silbe weiter bin
ich fähig."

his weakness behind a spurt of annoyance against the Prince and "the world".

On 2 April Goethe arrived in Palermo, after a rough crossing made in the face of contrary winds. As in Naples, his interest in Greek art was secondary to other interests. Not until 11 April did he visit the antiques, then housed in the Palazzo. He was disappointed to find the statues in confusion, owing to redecoration of the gallery, but he was delighted by the two bronze rams, "mighty figures of the mythological family, worthy to bear Phrixus and Helle".[1] He attributed them to the "best Greek period". With some reluctance he allowed himself to be taken to see a collection of antique coins. He knew so little of the subject and did not want to be troubled by a new branch of learning just at that moment. In the end he was glad to have gone, for he gained a vivid new impression of the wealth and high culture of the old Siceliot cities, and a fresh proof of the superiority of Greek things over Roman.[2] But the problems of ancient art were not in the forefront of his mind. On the 15th, on a last sight-seeing trip around the city, he happened on some statues, much damaged and badly placed for investigation. "We had not the patience to make out what they were."[3]

On 18 April Goethe left Palermo, accompanied by the German artist Kniep, whom he had engaged to go with him and sketch whatever of landscape and ruins was worth preserving. On the third day they visited the temple of Segesta, a Doric building of the late fifth century B.C. The temple stands below the ancient city on a small hill in the cup of a great valley. It was never finished, but all that was completed—the outer rectangle of columns with their architraves and the pediments—is still standing. The columns were left unfluted. Goethe's description of the temple in his diary is matter of fact in the extreme. Not a word of praise, not a touch of enthusiasm; and one suggestion of criticism. As at Paestum he felt a forbidding austerity, a lack of charm. "The wind whistled through the columns as through a wood, and birds of prey wheeled screaming above the entablature. I suppose they had young in the crevices."[4] The sense of transience, of destruction, of the past

---

[1] WA. 31, p. 119.   [2] *Ibid.* p. 120.   [3] *Ibid.* p. 146.
[4] WA. III, 1, p. 341.

as something irrevocably gone, oppressed him, the more so as these Greek temples should have pointed him to the eternal ideas that he was seeking. The proportions of the Greek temple were still so strange to him, that he could not see in them the timeless truth that conquers the destruction of the centuries. At Selinus, a few miles away, there were remains of other great temples of the fifth century. But of them not even the columns stand. He left them unvisited. He was seeking "*Anschauung*", a picture for his mind's eye. Foundations and tumbled drums could not help him. So too at Girgenti, where he spent five days (23 to 28 April), the vast ruins of the temple of Zeus impressed him by their size—he could stand comfortably inside the fluting of the fallen columns—but the "shapeless chaos" gave him no pleasure. When he had viewed it, he felt that he had "seen nothing and gained nothing".[1] The temple of Concord on the other hand, again a Doric structure of the late fifth century, which has been preserved almost intact, spoke to him a language that he understood. "Its slender style approaches our standard of what is beautiful and graceful. It compares with the temples at Paestum as a god's form with that of a giant."[2] It is true that the columns of the temple of Concord are taller in proportion to their breadth at the base than those of the temple of Neptune at Paestum. In the former temple the relation is 5 to 1, in the latter about $4\frac{1}{3}$ to 1.[3] But by Palladio's standards, who gives the proportion for Doric pillars as $7\frac{1}{2}$ or 8 to 1, the columns of the temple of Concord are still absurdly stocky. In the case of the Paestum temples Goethe had also complained that the columns were set too close together.[4] In fact the columns of the temple of Concord are set closer than the temple of Neptune (Concord: 13 columns in 130 feet; 6 feet between each. Neptune: 14 columns in 197 feet; 9 feet between each). Goethe's eye, helped by the enthusiasm with which his guidebook[5] described these ruins, was beginning to become accustomed to Greek proportions. But still he derived most pleasure

---

[1] WA. 31, p. 163 and WA. IV, 44, p. 84.   [2] WA. 31, p. 162.
[3] Measurements taken from the *Encyclopaedia Britannica*.
[4] "Enggedrängt."
[5] Riedesel's *Reise durch Sicilien und Grossgriechenland*, Zürich, 1771; cf. pp. 40–1.

from the sight of the Tomb of Theron, a work of the Hellenistic period.[1]

In the cathedral at Girgenti Goethe admired the relief-work on a marble sarcophagus as the finest he had seen, and noted it as "an example of the most graceful period of Greek art".[2] Actually it is late Roman work, though perhaps a copy of a fourth-century Greek original.[3] From Girgenti Goethe and his companion struck inland and made a four days' journey across the island to Catania. To do this they had to give up their intended visit to Syracuse. Riedesel mentions a well-preserved temple at Syracuse in the Doric order, like those at Paestum and Girgenti,[4] but this was no attraction to Goethe in comparison with the chance of seeing the rich cornlands of the interior. He probably knew nothing of the Athenian siege of Syracuse in the Peloponnesian War (Riedesel does not mention it, and Goethe had never read Thucydides); Nicias, Epipolae, the fateful quarries were not even names to him. But even had he known, he would not have greatly cared.

In Catania Goethe viewed the antiques in the palace of the Biscari family, but found little of interest. The Prince's coin collection on the other hand gave him opportunity to continue the study that he had begun in Palermo. Here, as always now, he found Winckelmann's periods an infallible guide.[5]

On 12 May Goethe sailed from Messina and arrived in Naples on the 15th.[6] On the crossing he looked back over his Sicilian journey and summed up its results. Sea-sickness made him overrate the failures and forget the achievements. "We had really seen nothing but the vain efforts of men to maintain themselves against the violence of Nature, the malicious caprice of time, and their own quarrels and dissensions. The Carthaginians, the Greeks, the Romans and innumerable races that followed them, had built and cast down. Selinus lies deliberately destroyed: two thousand years had not sufficed to reduce the temples of Girgenti to ruins, but a few hours, nay moments, had been enough to wipe out Catania and Messina."[7] The

[1] WA. 31, p. 164.   [2] *Ibid.* p. 159.
[3] Cf. Eduard Castle, *In Goethes Geist*, Vienna, 1926, p. 201.
[4] *Op. cit.* p. 85.   [5] WA. 31, p. 187.
[6] For the problem of the dates at this point see *Ibid.* pp. 306, 340.
[7] *Ibid.* p. 224.

Greek temples had not succeeded in giving him that vision of
eternity which he had hoped for. They had come nearer to
doing so than he yet realised; but still on this score he was
perhaps justified in feeling disappointment. Fortunately his
Sicilian journey had had another goal, and this had been
attained with a richness of fulfilment that amazed and awed
him. He felt deep happiness at "possessing the great, beautiful,
incomparable conception of Sicily so clear, complete and pure"
in his mind.[1] To the Duke he wrote that his vision of Sicily
was an "indestructible treasure" for his whole life.[2]

In the Sicilian landscape he had hoped to find that unthwarted Nature which he had been seeking ever since he left
Germany. He found it and he found much more—the link
between this vision and that of the "*Urmensch*", which he had
been approaching in Rome and in Naples. This link was the
Odyssey. With profound insight Rehm has pointed out,[3] that
the understanding of Greece and the understanding of Nature
were two aspects of the same problem for Goethe. If he had
not seen the "*Urlandschaft*" in Naples and Sicily, Greece would
have remained a riddle; if he had not re-read the *Odyssey* and
known what he did of Greek art and culture, the deepest
significance of the "*Urlandschaft*" would have been lost to him.

The voyage from Naples to Palermo introduced him into
the world of Odysseus. There was a storm; the ship was driven
out of her course, and had to go far about to reach Palermo.
For the first time in his life Goethe saw islands on the horizon,
as Odysseus had often seen them as he sailed to and from Ithaca.[4]
It affected him deeply, so that he often spoke of his journey
through Sicily, which was really confined to the single main
island, as a journey to "the islands".[5] As the vessel approached
Palermo, Goethe first observed that "hazy clarity", which
transfigured hills and sea.[6] Later he described it poetically:

> Ein weisser Glanz ruht über Land und Meer,
> Und duftend schwebt der Aether ohne Wolken,[7]

---

[1] *Ibid.* p. 237.
[2] WA. IV, 8, p. 221.   [3] *Op. cit.* pp. 144 foll.
[4] WA. 31, p. 84 and *Od.* IX, 26.   [5] WA. 31, p. 237; cf. p. 198.
[6] *Ibid.* p. 91: "Dunstige Klarheit."
[7] WA. 10, p. 423: "A white radiance rests on land and sea, and fragrant
and cloudless hang the heavens."

and had in mind the abode of the Olympians as Homer describes it:

$$\text{ἀλλὰ μάλ' αἴθρη}$$
$$\text{πέπταται ἀνέφελος, λευκὴ δ' ἐπιδέδρομεν αἴγλη.}[1]$$

In Palermo the presence of the sea never let him forget the *Odyssey*. The dark waves sweeping in on the bays and headlands, the smell of the sea, carried him in spirit to the island of the Phaeacians.[2] And when in the public gardens by the sea he saw around him the full luxuriance of southern vegetation in its unbroken fruitfulness, he felt himself to be in the gardens of Alcinous.[3] He had no Homer with him, but on 15 April, after nearly two weeks in Palermo, he bought a copy, Greek with Latin version.[4] He sat in the public gardens and read again with wonder and joy of that enchanted island of the Phaeacians. But now he saw that it was not enchanted, not a fairyland that could never exist. Homer had described the world that he saw around him.[5] That world—its hills, its plants, its colours, the sea, the men—was an "ideal" world, but not in the sense that it existed only in the beautifying imagination of the poet. It was ideal because in it all Nature's intentions were perfectly realised. Nothing was half-expressed or distorted. Homer's greatness, like that of all the Greek writers, had lain solely in his power of seeing this world in all its grandeur, its beauty, its outward forms and inner relationships, and in describing what he saw in such a way that nothing remained half-expressed. By doing so he had himself made Nature's intentions manifest; he had created as even Nature could only sometimes create. For Goethe the *Odyssey* ceased at this moment to be a poem; it seemed to be Nature herself.[6]

In Naples and Sicily Goethe saw with his own eyes the same ideal landscape that Homer had known.[7] The summits of the hills were as "eternally classical"[8] as in Homer's day; the sea was as fascinating to him in its manifold beauty, as terrible in its

---

[1] *Od.* VI, 44. [2] WA. 31, p. 106.
[3] WA. IV, 8, p. 211; WA. 31, pp. 105, 106.
[4] Cf. WA. 10, p. 413.
[5] Goethe once suggested that the *Odyssey* was composed in Sicily (Spring, 1795: Bied. I, p. 229).
[6] Letter to Schiller, 14 Feb. 1798 (WA. IV, 13, p. 66).
[7] Rehm, *op. cit.* p. 147. [8] WA. 31, p. 95.

latent power as it had been to Homer;[1] the journey through the
interior from Girgenti to Catania had shown him what fruitfulness in Nature could be: he had seen Ceres manifest; and in
the "gardens of Alcinous" at Palermo he had hoped that he
might find that imaginary plant which Schiller saw was "only
an Idea"—the "*Urpflanze*". With this picture in his soul he
hoped to be able to reproduce, even when back at home in the
north, "shadow pictures of this blest abode".[2] If he could keep
what he had seen, he would be able to create as the Greeks had
done, by merely describing this ideal nature.

But Goethe could never depend solely on the beauties of
Nature for his poetic material. His poetry had to be primarily
human. To create as the Greeks had done he must have seen
and known ideal men and women as well as ideal Nature. The
vision of the "*Urmensch*" was even more necessary to him than
that of the "*Urlandschaft*". The modern Italians had not
satisfied him. In Venice they had shown some qualities that
had marked them as decadent descendants of true "natural
men". Still more had the carefree life of the Neapolitans
seemed to give a hint of what the existence of the "*Urmensch*"
would be like. But Goethe never supposed for a moment that
the modern Neapolitans expressed fully and undistorted God's
idea of man. In Sicily too he found nothing that brought him
nearer his goal. The "*Urlandschaft*" was there, and perhaps the
"*Urpflanze*"; but the "*Urmensch*" no longer walked those hills
or sailed those bays. He, it was all too plain, was only an idea.
Yet he had once been real, for Homer had described him; and
Homer did not invent or idealise—he described what he saw
"with a terrifying clarity and inner understanding".[3] The
picture that Goethe needed, of man as he is, with all his essential
qualities, passions and abilities, free to develop within his set
limits, unhampered by unfavourable natural surroundings, by
cramping customs or religious taboos, this picture Goethe
found in Homer, at present in the *Odyssey*, especially in the

[1] WA. 31, pp. 89, 90, 106, 198 foll., 203, and WA. 10, p. 419. Cf. *Od.*
vIII, 138, 139, underlined by Goethe in the copy bought at Palermo (cf.
WA. 10, p. 413).

[2] WA. 31, p. 91: "Schattenbilder dieser glücklichen Wohnung."

[3] *Ibid.* p. 239: "Mit einer Reinheit und Innigkeit gezeichnet, vor der man
erschrickt."

description of the Phaeacians, and later with undiminished truth in the *Iliad*.

Already in the days of *Sturm und Drang* Homeric man had been something of an "*Urmensch*" to Goethe. He had represented man stripped of the falsities of civilisation, simple in habits, sincere in feeling. It had been a limited ideal, because it had contained in it a negative idea: hostility to civilised life. In the new conception of the Homeric man as the "*Urmensch*" none of the positive qualities of the human spirit could be excluded. The passages which Goethe marked in his Sicilian *Odyssey*[1] show how his appreciation of Homer's men and women had developed since Wetzlar. The simile of the ploughman who longs for his supper[2] would have delighted the author of *Werther* no less than the mature Goethe. This is the "*Urmensch*" as "*Naturmensch*". The same sensual appreciation of the value of meat and drink attracted him also in the marked passage at the beginning of the ninth book (lines 5–11). But here the earthly pleasures of palate and belly are secondary to the artistic pleasure of listening to the divine minstrel. This was the new emphasis in Goethe's reading of Homer. The "*Urmensch*" had known that without art life was incomplete. He did not take delight in living primitively, as Werther imagined the Homeric heroes to have done. The Phaeacians (in another marked passage)[3] boast modestly of their love of "banquets, music, dancing, changes of raiment, warm baths and the couch". These Homeric men were sensual, but not coarsely so. They delighted in all the sensations of life and prized art as the noblest of these. No doubt Goethe thought of the Pompeians as he read this passage. They too had used art to set the peak of joyfulness on a life of vigorous sensuality. And as with the Phaeacians (did Goethe think of this?), their lovely city had been buried by a mountain.

This then was the realisation that the Sicilian journey and the *Odyssey*, re-read in that setting, brought to Goethe:[4] the Greeks had been perfect men living in perfect natural surroundings. That had been their good fortune. Their merit, which made their art and their literature pre-eminent, had lain in their

[1] Cf. WA. 10, p. 413. [2] *Od.* XIII, 31 foll.
[3] *Od.* VIII, 246–9.
[4] Cf. letter to W. v. Humboldt, 26 May 1799 (WA. IV, 14, p. 95).

capacity to know and to understand the perfection of the world
they lived in, and in their simplicity of soul, which made them
content merely to describe what they saw, not what they felt.
"They portrayed the reality, we usually its effect; they described terrible things, we describe terribly; they pleasant
things, we pleasantly, and so on."[1] In this way they had
achieved the highest of which art is capable. They had made
manifest the ideas of God more directly and more perfectly
than Nature herself is usually capable of doing. In old age he
said to Eckermann:[2] "He who would make something great,
must have trained himself to such a pitch, that he is able like
the Greeks to raise the less perfect actual world to the level of
his own spirit, and to make actual that which in the world of
phenomena has remained unfulfilled, whether owing to inner
weakness or thwarting from without." It was in Sicily that
he first clearly understood that this was the nature of Greek
art, and that his own production must in future be based on the
same principles.

As soon as he arrived in Palermo, Goethe began to put on
paper a poetical project that had occupied his thoughts from
time to time for some months. The idea of dramatising
Odysseus's stay among the Phaeacians had come to him first
on the last stage of his journey to Rome, in October of the
previous year. He had then called the tragedy *Ulysses auf
Phäa*.[3] Scherer suggests that the plan was again in his mind in
Naples,[4] and it is likely he gave it more thought during the
voyage to Palermo.[5] Some time before 15 April (when Goethe
bought a Homer)[6] the whole plan was written down, the
subject of each scene being indicated in a few words. This
scheme is preserved.[7] The first scene[8] was also written before
Goethe began to read Homer.[9] The other fragments that have
been preserved, he wrote with the *Odyssey* open at his

---

[1] WA. 31, p. 239: "Sie stellten die Existenz dar, wir gewöhnlich den
Effekt; sie schilderten das Fürchterliche, wir schildern fürchterlich; sie das
Angenehme, wir angenehm, usw."

[2] 20 Oct. 1828.

[3] WA. III, 1, p. 315.   [4] *Goethe-Aufsätze*, p. 209.

[5] Cf. WA. 10, p. 412, and Ernst Maass, *Goethe und die Antike*, p. 188.

[6] Cf. JA. xv, p. 352; also WA. 10, pp. 412 foll. and 31, p. 147.

[7] WA. 10, pp. 417 foll.   [8] *Ibid.* pp. 99 foll.

[9] *Ibid.* p. 413.

side.[1] Most was written in the public gardens during his last three days in Palermo. Only at this stage did the tragedy receive the name *Nausikaa* by which it is always known. More would have been written had not the luxuriant vegetation of the gardens distracted his interest from his poetical plans to the search for the "*Urpflanze*".[2] But the interruption was only momentary. At times during his journey through the island, Goethe pondered the detailed execution of his plan and jotted down a line or two.[3] Especially in Taormina *Nausikaa* was much in his mind.[4] Scherer suggested[5] that the plan as first written down in Palermo was considerably changed in Taormina, and that this second plan is contained in the version given in the *Italienische Reise*.[6] Morris has shown[7] that this view is not tenable, and that the plan in the *Italienische Reise* was, as Goethe indicated, composed from memory thirty years later,[8] and can therefore not be considered in any reconstruction of Goethe's intentions for *Nausikaa*. All the hundred and seventy-five lines and fragments of lines of *Nausikaa* that were ever written, were written in Sicily. Once Goethe had left the island where Homer had become for him "a living word",[9] the figures of his Homeric tragedy faded from his mind, and never returned to disquiet him or bring him joy.

It may be questioned whether Homer meant to hint that Nausicaa had fallen in love with Odysseus, when she found him sea-battered on the shore, and won him her father's protection and favour. A modern reader is inclined to conclude as much, and to wonder at Homer's restraint in not treating in more detail so promising a motive. Goethe saw in this unfulfilled episode all the material for a tragedy. Nausicaa was to fall in love with Odysseus; ignorant of his name and of the fact that he was married, she was to make an avowal of her

---

[1] WA. 10, p. 409, lines 16–20: *Od.* v, 483, 488; *ibid.* p. 416, line 24: *Od.* vi, 20 foll.; *ibid.* p. 418, lines 7–11: *Od.* vii, 114–21; lines 16–18: *Od.* vii, 129; *ibid.* p. 422 (*a*): *Od.* xi, 363–8; (*b*) *Od.* vi, 44.

[2] WA. 31, p. 147.

[3] WA. 31, p. 201; WA. 10, p. 418, line 15; cf. *ibid.* p. 419, line 4; *ibid.* p. 418, lines 23–4, Girgenti to Catania; p. 420, line 5*b* [IV], Etna, but cf. WA. IV, 8, p. 91.

[4] WA. 10, p. 414; 31, p. 198.
[5] *Goethe-Aufsätze*, p. 213.
[6] WA. 31, pp. 200 foll.
[7] *G-J.* xxv, pp. 109 foll.
[8] Cf. WA. 10, p. 415; JA. xv, p. 353.
[9] WA. 31, p. 239.

love, only to find that he was about to return to his native land and his wife. Partly from shame at having compromised herself, but chiefly owing to the realisation that her passion was hopeless, Nausicaa was to kill herself.[1]

Morris may be right in maintaining that such romantic love, for which life loses all value except in relation to the beloved, is a human passion unknown to Homer. Goethe probably did not feel that his central theme was unantique: Sappho's leap and Phaedra's suicide would have been sufficient warrant for him that it was antique enough, if he considered the question at all. Moreover since he regarded Homer's men and women as "*Urmenschen*", he can hardly have believed that they were ignorant of an emotion so fundamental in modern man.[2] Be that as it may, the theme of *Nausikaa* was taken from Goethe's own experience. All too often his personality had roused a woman's love, and always his fate had made it necessary for him to desert her. There may have been recent flirtations in Rome and Naples, as is suggested in the *Italienische Reise*,[3] but the immediate experience which provided the material for *Nausikaa* was undoubtedly his own breaking away from Charlotte, and the suffering that he knew he had caused her.

The treatment of this very personal theme was to show the effects of his new insight into the nature of Greek wisdom and art. In the first place the play was to be a real tragedy. No lofty trust in the goodness of God could here avert the fatal conflict of natural forces. Ulysses's share of guilt was to be a very minor one, deriving from his having told Nausicaa that he was unmarried. The catastrophe would be represented as a "misfortune sent from God".[4] The world-order would be revealed as inhumane: inhumane the daemonic power of attraction in Ulysses's character; inhumane the love that drives the girl to destruction. Had Goethe wished to use the conventions of Greek tragedy, he could have let Aphrodite foretell

---

[1] There have been various attempts to reconstruct the action of *Nausikaa*. Scherer's essay in *Goethe-Aufsätze* and Max Morris's in the *Goethe-Jahrbuch*, xxv are the most important.

[2] Compare his discussion of this question in *Winckelmann und sein Jahrhundert*, WA. 46, p. 26.

[3] WA. 31, p. 201.   [4] "Gottgesendet Uebel": WA. 10, p. 422.

Nausicaa's doom in a grim speech modelled on the prologue
to *Hippolytus*.

In this way *Nausikaa* was nearer to the spirit of Greek
tragedy than either *Iphigenie* or *Elpenor*. The form was still to
be modern: five-footed iambic lines, five acts, no chorus. It
was in the style, that the new closeness to Greece would emerge
most clearly. It would be a description, carried out with
Homeric "clarity and inner understanding", of the ideal world
of men and Nature, which the Greeks had known and which
Goethe now believed he had seen. He would "portray the
reality", not, as modern writers do, the effect;[1] and so having
ideal man and ideal Nature for his subject, he would give
perfect manifestation to ideas that often lie unfulfilled in
Nature. The fragments that he wrote down contain examples
of this new style of "*naiv*", not "sentimental", description.
In the most successful he crystallised his observations of that
phenomenon of "hazy clarity" that filled him with such
wonder:

> Ein weisser Glanz ruht über Land und Meer,
> Und duftend schwebt der Aether ohne Wolken.[2]

Description of the "*Urlandschaft*"—the sea, the coast, the
islands, the hills, the vegetation, the harmonising colours—
was to form as important a part of the play as the human action
of which it was the setting.[3] That no essential element might
fail in this microcosm of Nature, a large part of the second
act was to be taken up with a description of a storm and of its
destructive effect on the beauty of the gardens.

The men and women who move in this setting harmonise
with it in the simple perfection of their humanity. Phaeacian
society was to be drawn on the lines of the picture given in the
Odyssey: a simple community, still founded on the essential
needs of man, uncorrupted by over-complication and false
conventions, yet cultured in every way that ennobles the
human spirit. Morris points out[4] that the characters in *Nausikaa*
are psychologically less complicated than those of *Iphigenie*

---

[1] See above, p. 163.
[2] WA. 10, p. 423; see also above, p. 159.
[3] WA. 31, pp. 198 foll. and 10, pp. 417 foll.
[4] G-J. xxv, p. 114.

and *Tasso*. As "*Urmenschen*" they were to have only those basic emotions which are common to all men who have emerged from a state of barbarism. They were to be free of scruples and subtleties such as plague and thwart modern refined society. Perhaps the naïve manner in which Alcinous and Ulysses arrange to marry off Nausikaa to Telemachus was intended as a trait proper to simple humanity, which is more concerned with realities than sentiment.[1] Nausikaa and Ulysses were to represent most clearly this essential, unthwarted humanity. She is unable—perhaps she does not even try—to conceal her passion; nor when it is shown to be hopeless, does she wish to overcome it and drag on a wretched, unsatisfied existence. Ulysses appears first as naked man, stripped of every aid to life but his bare wits. By these he wins back to fortune and to the accomplishment of his single purpose—his return. It is in pursuit of this purpose that he commits the fatal error of concealing his identity.[2] In this undeviating determination to survive and to achieve his end he is "*Urmann*", as much as Nausikaa, by her absorption in her passion, is "*Urweib*".[3] His "manly bearing" was to be stressed by Nausikaa's brother.[4] It is the ideal perfection of these opposed emotions which brings on the catastrophe. Had they been tempered by inhibiting subtleties of feeling, there would have been no storm in the world of men to match that in the world of Nature.

Goethe left Sicily with all his longing stilled. He had seen and he understood. He was confident that he would now be able to create as the Greeks had created. He even hoped that he might live as they had lived. Fear of his old northern self had gone: on his return to Naples he agreed to meet a stranger who wished to discuss *Werther* with him; "six months ago...I should have refused. My acceptance showed me that my Sicilian journey had had a good effect on me."[5] His last misunderstandings with the spirit of Hellas had been removed by what he had seen in Sicily. The day after his return to Naples

---

[1] WA. 10, p. 421. I have already pointed out that Goethe introduced this idea into the last act of *Egmont* (written in Rome during the summer of 1787), and that he may have taken it from the *Trachiniae* (line 1222 foll.).
[2] WA. 10, p. 419.
[3] "Essential man" and "essential woman". See below, p. 171.
[4] WA. 10, p. 420.   [5] WA. 31, p. 241.

he went once more to Paestum. "It is the last and, I might almost say, the most glorious idea, that I now carry northwards with me complete. The middle temple (of Neptune) is in my opinion better than anything that is still to be seen in Sicily."[1] His settled opinion of the Greek Doric[2] was less enthusiastic but still respectful. He granted that its effect was majestic, sometimes even inspiring (reizend), but he took leave to prefer the slenderer Ionic, defending his preference on the ground that it is natural for human taste to develop "even beyond its goal". In other words he could not accept the fifth-century style of architecture as canonic. In order to justify his own taste he was forced, contrary to the tendency of his thought on other matters at the time, to stress the right of aesthetic standards to change and progress. He never came to feel at home in the world of the Doric temple. In his old age he spoke of it with reverence but called it a "fairy world".[3]

Any difficulty that he may still have felt, at fitting Greek tragedy into his picture of the Greeks, was finally dispelled in Sicily. His own experience of a storm at sea had brought vividly home to him the terrifying power of Nature.[4] In the *Odyssey* he had found more perfectly portrayed man's helplessness in the face of implacable natural forces. He had hoped to give expression to this fundamental callousness of life in *Nausikaa*. The Greeks had done the same in their tragedies, and in so doing had given proof not of barbarity of mind and morals, but of their greatness in seeing and depicting the world as it is, not as it might be. "*Humanität*", as he had preached it in *Iphigenie* and as Herder still preached it in his *Ideen*, was to Goethe now only a "fair dream-wish". In a letter to Charlotte from Rome,[5] he mocked at Herder for clinging to the old ideal. "Though I may believe that '*Humanität*'[6] will finally conquer, I fear that at the same moment the world will be one great

---

[1] WA. 31, p. 238.

[2] Contained in the essay *Zur Theorie der bildenden Kunst* (WA. 47, pp. 60 foll.), 1788.

[3] WA. iv, 45, p. 115.

[4] Cf. also WA. 31, p. 203.

[5] 8 June 1787 (WA. iv, 8, p. 233).

[6] *Humanität* cannot be translated by "humanity", nor "humanism". "Humane ethics" is too ambiguous a term. It is simplest to identify *Humanität* with "Iphigenie-morality". See above, p. 137.

hospital, and each will be occupied in being the other's humane nurse."[1]

The ten years' aberration towards a Christian-ethical interpretation of the world was over. Once more Goethe could admire the Greeks as he had done in the days of *Götter, Helden und Wieland*, even for those qualities in which they had run counter to modern sentiment. Having seen, in Sicily and in the *Odyssey*, God's ideas made manifest, he could only say: "That which is, is moral."

D. ROME AGAIN

On 6 June 1787 Goethe was back in his old quarters in Rome. He returned at once to his interrupted studies in art. In order truly to understand the possibilities and the limits of artistic expression, he drew and painted. In the beginning of July he began to copy casts of antique heads.[2] Along with this practical activity went repeated contemplation of the ancient statues.[3] In August he and Moritz returned to those discussions of ancient mythology which resulted in Moritz's *Götterlehre*.[4] On 22 August Goethe saw sketches which an English traveller had brought back from the eastern Mediterranean. Among them were drawings of the Parthenon frieze. "The few simple figures" at once roused Goethe's wonder.[5] It was the first time he had seen any reproduction of the Parthenon sculptures. In the following days he made the final discovery that rounded off what he had learnt in Sicily, so that in future he could say he understood Greek art, as he understood Homer and the world of Nature in which the Greeks had lived.

"The human form", he wrote to Charlotte, "is asserting its rights....I have found a principle which will lead me, like Ariadne's thread, through the labyrinth of the human structure. ...It is as though a veil had suddenly been removed from all statues. I have begun to model a head of Hercules. My artist

---

[1] Cf. WA. 31, p. 238 and WA. IV, 11, p. 100, Herder as "Freund Humanus"; Suphan in *Preussische Jahrbücher*, XLIII, pp. 430 foll.; and Irmgard Taylor, *Kultur, Aufklärung, Bildung, Humanität und verwandte Begriffe bei Herder*, Giessen, 1938, pp. 14 foll.

[2] WA. 32, p. 28. [3] *Ibid.* pp. 6, 32, 35, 39.

[4] *Ibid.* p. 59; see also above, p. 145. Material both to the *Götterlehre* and to *Anthousa*, Moritz's work on the antiquities of Rome (publ. 1791) was probably discussed. [5] WA. 32, p. 32.

friends are amazed, because they think I have hit the likeness
by chance, but I have made it according to my principle and
can make others so, if I have time and industry to develop this
principle."[1] The *Italienische Reise* throws further light on this
revelation. "The alpha and omega of all known things, the
human form, has gripped me and I it, and I say: Lord, I will
not let thee go, till thou bless me, though I be lamed in my
wrestling....I have come on an idea, that makes many things
easier....My obstinate study of Nature, the care with which I
have worked at comparative anatomy, now enable me to see
much as a whole in nature and in antique sculpture, which an
artist has to seek singly and with difficulty."[2] His "principle"
linked up with his old studies in physiognomy.[3]

In the following weeks he applied his principle to the study
of the antiques and also to his drawing and modelling of the
human figure. He found it worked in every case.[4] It was like
Columbus's egg—so simple and so perfect a solution of the
problem. November and December he spent on the study of
the head and face; with the new year he passed on to the body,
working downwards section by section, until by the middle of
March he had reached the foot.[5]

Neither in letters nor in the *Italienische Reise* did Goethe
reveal the nature of his "principle". It is plain from the
manner in which he speaks of it and of his studies of the human

[1] WA. iv, 8, p. 255: "Die menschliche Gestalt tritt in alle ihre Rechte
und das Übrige fällt mir wie Lumpen vom Leibe. Ich habe ein Prinzip
gefunden, das mich wie ein Ariadnischer Faden durch die Labyrinthe der
Menschenbildung durchführen wird....Indess bin ich sehr vergnügt, weil
mir auf einmal wie ein Vorhang vor allen Statuen wegfällt. Ich habe einen
Herkuleskopf angefangen, worüber sie sich alle wundern, weil sie denken
ich hab ihn durch einen Zufall so getroffen, ich hab ihn aber nach meinem
Grundsatz gemacht und wenn ich Zeit und Fleiss habe diesen Grundsatz zu
entwickeln und mich mechanisch zu üben, kann ich andere eben so machen."
[2] WA. 32, p. 62: "Nun hat mich zuletzt das A und O aller uns bekannten
Dinge, die menschliche Figur, angefasst, und ich sie, und ich sage: Herr, ich
lasse dich nicht, du segnest mich denn, und sollt ich mich lahm ringen....
Wenigstens bin ich auf einen Gedanken gekommen, der mir vieles erleich-
tert....Es läuft darauf hinaus: dass mich nun mein hartnäckig Studium der
Natur, meine Sorgfalt, mit der ich in der comparirenden Anatomie zu Werke
gegangen bin, nunmehr in den Stand setzen, in der Natur und den Antiken
manches im Ganzen zu sehn, was den Künstlern im Einzelnen aufzusuchen
schwer wird."   [3] *Ibid.* p. 113.   [4] WA. 32, pp. 73, 77, 81.
[5] WA. iv, 8, pp. 316, 320, 329; WA. 32, pp. 208, 212, 294.

form, that he was occupied with just such an apperception of the nature of things, as had come to him in his vision of the "*Urpflanze*". It was a revelation terrifying in its profundity and its power. He had struggled in thought to win it, as Jacob struggled. It had opened to him the door of the temple,[1] and he knew that if he could follow the thread of Ariadne as the ancient artist had followed it, it would be granted him to see God, the ultimate Necessity.[2] He spoke of receiving revelations, of seeing deep into the nature of things and their relationships, and in clear connexion with this he wrote: "The study of the human body now holds me completely. Everything else is as nothing to it."[3] Formerly he had been unable to bear the brilliance that streamed from the human form, as from the sun, but now he was able to contemplate it and to linger on it with rapture.[4] The human form he called the "non plus ultra of all human knowledge and activity."[5]

There can be no doubt that his study of Greek sculpture, supported by the knowledge of comparative anatomy acquired before he came to Italy, had given him a vision of the "*Urmensch*", just as the southern vegetation had brought him the vision of the "*Urpflanze*". The two conceptions are precisely parallel. The "*Urpflanze*" was, in Platonic language, the Idea of the plant form; that essence common to all plants, by which we know that a plant is a plant and not an animal or a stone; that binding influence that prevents any plant species from straying so far from the norm, that it loses its character as plant. With this ideal plant clear in mind it was possible "to invent plant forms ad infinitum...which, even though they do not exist, yet could exist, and are not merely picturesque or poetical shadows or seemings, but have an inner truth and necessity". Significantly Goethe added: "The same law will be capable of application to the rest of the living world."[7]

[1] WA. 32, p. 77.   [2] *Ibid.* p. 78.   [3] *Ibid.* p. 208 (5 Jan. 1788).
[4] WA. IV, 8, p. 329.   [5] WA. 32, p. 212.
[6] WA. 31, pp. 147–8; cf. WA. 32, pp. 470, 471.
[7] WA. 31, p. 240: "Mit diesem Modell und dem Schlüssel dazu kann man alsdann noch Pflanzen ins Unendliche erfinden, die consequent sein müssen, das heisst: die, wenn sie auch nicht existieren, doch existieren könnten und nicht etwa mahlerische oder dichterische Schatten und Scheine sind, sondern eine innerliche Wahrheit und Notwendigkeit haben. Dasselbe Gesetz wird sich auf alles übrige Lebendige anwenden lassen."

So, in the world of ideas at least, there is an "*Urmensch*", an idea of man, which is present in more or less degree in every race of men and in every individual man. The Homeric men and women of whom Goethe read in Sicily, brought him close to the vision of the ideal man. They had portrayed the moral qualities of the "*Urmensch*". But they lacked that quality which is the essence of the Platonic ideas—form. Goethe could not get the imprint of the form of the "*Urmensch*" from Homer. It was the "*Urmensch*" as visible, tangible, measurable form, that was revealed to him during his second stay in Rome. That he should have wrung this revelation from the grudging hands of Nature, was the supreme achievement of his Italian journey.

It was of course the Greek statues from which he derived the form of the "*Urmensch*". Not abstract speculation alone— "der Betrachtung strenge Lust"—had brought him this revelation; "der Vorwelt silberne Gestalten" had appeared before him and had shown him the way. Thus poetically he described his experience in one of the scenes of *Faust* that were written in Rome.[1] Outside Rome, he said—that is, away from the statues—one could have only an imperfect idea of the human body.[2] In his detailed study of each part of the body he always had before him examples from Nature and from antique works of art. Those from Nature showed him the imperfect expression of the idea, those from the antique the perfect expression, as God conceived it.[3] For, just like Homer, the Greek artists had known Nature from within and without; they had known what her intentions were, even if in the actual world she was seldom able to realise these; and they had created untrammelled according to her laws, so that what they produced was the complete expression of her ideas. "These noble works of art are at the same time the noblest works of Nature, produced by men according to true and natural laws. Everything capricious, everything merely imagined collapses; there is Necessity, there is God."[4]

Not that any one Greek statue was the "*Urmensch*" made

[1] "The silver figures of the past": WA. 14, p. 164 (Wald und Höhle).
[2] WA. IV, 8, p. 320.
[3] *Ibid.* p. 329 and WA. 32, p. 294.
[4] WA. 32, pp. 77 foll., last sentence: "Alles Willkürliche, Eingebildete fällt zusammen, da ist Notwendigkeit, da ist Gott."

visible. No single statue could express all the qualities that
lay in God's idea of man. All that art could do was to express
each one of these qualities in perfection. This the Greeks had
done in their statues of gods and heroes. A statue of Apollo
was the perfect visible expression of a certain aspect of man's
moral and physical existence. Jupiter represented another
aspect or character, Athene another, Mars another, and the
heroes yet others. The moral or spiritual character of each was
expressed in the form and the attitude. In the eleventh *Roman
Elegy*[1] Goethe stressed rather the characteristic attitude, but
the pure form was at least equally important.[2] All were
"*Abweichungen*", variations, from the basic idea; yet behind
each variation, as the Greeks portrayed it, the norm of the
"*Urmensch*" was visible, and the circle of gods and heroes taken
together expressed the idea of man completely.

Already before his journey to Naples and Sicily Goethe had
been investigating this question of the ideal characters of man,
as represented by the statues of the Greek gods.[3] He had learnt
from Winckelmann that the Greek artists had unalterable rules
for the portrayal of each god, but he had not then discovered
the secret of these rules. The vision of the "*Urmensch*" gave
him the secret. He saw the norm, the common denominator,
of all these variations, and so could deduce the rules which the
Greek artists had followed in leaving the norm to produce the
ideal characters.

Goethe told none of his friends in Rome, except Meyer and
Moritz, of the essence of his discovery,[4] nor did he reveal it
in the essays on art which he wrote and published on his return
from Rome. It was a mystery not fit for the ears of any but
the few who could truly understand. But one day in September
after his return to Germany, as he was driving with Caroline
Herder and Fritz v. Stein down the Saale valley from Rudolstadt
to Jena, while the sun shone with mild late-summer radiance,
he was moved by discussion of Schiller's newest poem, *Die
Götter Griechenlands*, to open his heart to the trusted friends.
"Goethe came to speak", Caroline wrote to Herder,[5] "of the

---

[1] WA. 1, p. 246.   [2] Cf. *Schr. der G-G.* v, p. 29.
[3] See above, p. 143.   [4] WA. 32, p. 77.
[5] Bied. 1, p. 150: "Goethe kam auf die Eigenschaften, die die Alten in
ihren Göttern und Helden in der Kunst dargestellt haben, wie es ihm

qualities which the ancients represented in art in their gods and heroes, and of how he has succeeded in finding out how they did it.... The whole idea lies, it seems to me, as a great unfulfilled task in his mind. He said at the end, he believed, if Louis XIV were still alive, he could manage the whole business with his support;...he could work it out in ten years—in Rome of course. The moral implications of his idea moved me extremely.... No single man, he said, could have one character in perfect manifestation; he could not live if he had; he must have mingled qualities in order to exist. As he said all this he was truly in his Heaven, and we had to promise at the end to speak to no one about it." In a later letter to Herder,[1] Caroline gave more details: "I will tell you something about the gods and heroes that I heard from Goethe that time, when he spoke of the characters in statues.... It is hard to find a true head of a god or hero even among the antique works. The artist often took the portrait of someone he wished to honour, as model for a god or hero.... Deep study is necessary to discover the true ideals.... If Goethe were favoured by fortune, money, and artists in Rome, I am sure, he could work out each human character from the crown of the head to the soles of the feet."

Caroline's account gives us a clearer idea of what Goethe meant by "ideal characters". Any human being is compounded

geglückt sei, den Faden des Wie hierin gefunden zu haben....Die ganze Idee liegt wie ein grosser Beruf in seinem Gemüt. Er sagte endlich: Wenn Ludwig XIV. noch lebte, so glaubte er durch seine Unterstützung die ganze Sache ausführen zu können....Er könnte es in zehn Jahren, in Rom versteht sich's, ausführen. Der moralische Sinn darin hat mich sehr gerührt....Gar schön war's, wie er sagte, dass ein einzelner Mensch nie einen Charakter in dem höchsten Ausdruck haben könne; er würde nicht leben können; er müsste vermischte Eigenschaften haben, um zu existieren. Er war in der Stunde, da er dies alles sprach, recht in seinem Himmel, und wir haben ihm endlich versprechen müssen, mit niemand davon zu reden."

[1] Bied. I, p. 151: "Ueber die Götter und Helden will ich dir doch etwas sagen, was ich damals beiläufig von Goethe gehört habe, als er von den Charaktern in den Bildsäulen sprach, als wir von Kochberg zurückfuhren. Es ist selbst schwer einen echten und wahren Götter- und Heldenkopf unter den alten aufzufinden. Der Künstler hat oft, wenn er diesen oder jenen ehren wollte, sein Porträt zum Gott oder Helden, oder jenes Frauenporträt zur Göttin genommen. Dazu gehört ein Studium, die echten Ideale aufzufinden....Wenn Goethe begünstigt würde durch Glück, Geld und Künstler in Rom, so glaube ich gewiss, dass er jeden menschlichen Charakter vom Scheitel bis zur Fusssohle, wie er glaubt, herausbringen könnte."

of a number of spiritual qualities, which influence and interfere with each other so that none appears "im höchsten Ausdruck". In the Idea of man these characters exist side by side in perfection. But so long as they are merely ideas, so long as their manifestation in the actual world is through the imperfect medium of human individuals, Nature has failed in her highest object. Greek art was of supreme value because it had evolved a means of giving complete expression to these ideal characters in the actual world.

In ten years, Goethe thought, he could rediscover the lost tradition that the Greek artists had evolved, and reduce it again to a system that could be handed on from master to pupil. It would involve a minute study of all the antiques in Rome, careful measurements of every statue in all its parts, comparison of the results, deduction of the norm for each god and hero, then of the ultimate norm, the form of the "Ur-mensch". So the vision that came to him in August 1787 would be made actual, given tangible, communicable shape, and art could be re-founded to fulfil its highest mission, as it had done in ancient Hellas.

Already in Rome, immediately after the discovery of his "principle", he started to work out the proportions between the different parts of the body. He learnt from his artist friends what they knew of the matter;[1] he tried to find out from such works as Camper's *Kleinere Schriften*[2] what other moderns had discovered; and he compared all this, as well as he could, with the antiques. Even at night, in the arms of his Faustina, the great problem did not leave him:

Dann versteh' ich den Marmor erst recht; ich denk' und vergleiche.[3]

He noted down the statues that were especially important for his purpose;[4] but he had to leave Rome before the task was one-tenth accomplished. In Weimar he pushed on with his investigation despite the lack of material. He attended lectures on anatomy in Jena "as preparation for the study of characters

---

[1] WA. 32, p. 77.
[2] Cf. *ibid.* p. 113 and Herder, *Werke*, XIV, p. 108.
[3] WA. 1, p. 239: "Only then do I understand the marble aright; I ponder and compare."
[4] WA. 32, p. 454.

in the human body".[1] In December 1788 he wrote to Herder
that he had made good physiognomical discoveries relating to
the formation of ideal characters.[2] In July of the next year he
was at work himself on a profile of Jupiter.[3] Amid unfavourable
surroundings, with the innumerable distractions of his life in
Weimar, his determination flagged at times,[4] but revived again
especially under Meyer's influence. In March 1791 he asked
for Meyer's help in "working out a canon of male and female
proportion; seeking the variations through which characters
arise; studying the anatomical structure more closely and
seeking the beautiful forms which make outward perfection".[5]
It is impossible to say how far the two friends progressed at
this attempt. Three years later there was much still to do.
Meyer spent the summer of 1794 in Dresden at work in the art
gallery. He asked leave not merely to copy the antiques but
to take measurements. This was not permitted, and he wrote
to Goethe: "I am the most unfortunate of men, for the chief
hope and purpose of my whole journey is thus brought to
naught."[6]

Nevertheless Goethe and Meyer were clear about the general
rules of the Greek tradition for portraying ideal characters by
the mere form. Winckelmann had observed some of them:
Mercury's greater fineness of feature in comparison with
Apollo;[7] Juno's large eyes;[8] the rounded brow of Hercules,
indicative of his strength and ceaseless labour;[9] Jupiter's cheeks,
less full than those of the younger gods; his loftier brow.[10]
Goethe had observed that Venus's character was expressed by
the smallness of the spaces between her features.[11] Meyer interpreted Odysseus's character from an antique head, in a
manner strongly reminiscent of Lavater's physiognomical

---

[1] Caroline to Herder, 14 Nov. 1788 (W. Bode, *Goethe in vertraulichen
Briefen*, p. 391).
[2] WA. IV, 9, p. 67.
[3] *Ibid.* p. 145. Cf. *Schr. der G-G.* V, p. 14.   [4] Cf. WA. 47, p. 21.
[5] WA. IV, 9, p. 248: "Auf einen Canon männlicher und weiblicher
Proportion loszuarbeiten, die Abweichungen zu suchen wodurch Charaktere
entstehn, das anatomische Gebäude näher zu studieren, und die schönen
Formen, welche die äussere Vollendung sind, zu suchen."
[6] *Schr. der G-G.* XXXII, p. 98, also p. 116; cf. also XXXIII, p. 8.
[7] *Werke*, IV, p. 84.   [8] *Ibid.* p. 115.   [9] *Ibid.* p. 87.
[10] *Ibid.* p. 94.   [11] Bied. I, p. 180.

theories.[1] The character was expressed not only in the face, but equally in the form of the whole body.[2] Apollo's long thighs had significance no less than Bacchus's broad, almost womanish, hips, or Jove's massive solidity of torso. All these proportions had to be discovered by measuring, and the results correlated, before the Greek tradition could be made active in the world again.

In this drudgery of measuring and comparing, the original vision of the ideal form of man was in danger of becoming intellectualised and losing itself in a desert of figures. But while it was fresh and vivid in Goethe's mind, and at times for many years after his return from Rome, it had all the power and the depth of a religious revelation. Through it he had gained far more than a new insight into Greek art, more even than a new understanding of the nature of man. It was a revelation of the ultimate nature of existence, of the forces which govern the whole physical and spiritual universe. The circle of gods, as the Greek sculptors represented them, was Goethe's creed expressed in forms instead of words. To Goethe the Greek gods were as real as they had been to any ancient Greek. They were not allegorical figures, artistic formulae, convenient by reason of their associations for expressing certain intellectual or moral concepts. "Statues of gods in themselves have no meaning outside themselves, but are really what they represent: Jupiter, the image of the loftiest dignity of boundless power; Minerva, the image of reflective wisdom; Hercules, of strength; Venus, of woman created for love; that is, they are characters of the purest kind, or general ideas given form by art. Such representations are called symbols, as distinct from allegories."[3] The Greeks, or at least their poets and artists, had looked into

---

[1] *Schr. der G-G.* xxxii, p. 21.   [2] Cf. *Iliad*, ii, 477, 478.

[3] "Götterbilder aber, an sich selbst, haben keine fernere Beziehung, sondern sind wirklich was sie darstellen: Jupiter, das Bild höchster Würde unumschränkter Macht; Minerva, sinnender Weisheit; Herkules, der Kraft; Venus, des zur Liebe geschaffenen Weibes usw.; also Charaktere von der höchsten Art, oder allgemeine von der Kunst verkörperte Begriffe, und solche Darstellungen nennt man, zum Unterschiede von eigentlichen Allegorien, Symbole" (Winckelmann, *Werke*, ii, p. 684). The notes to this edition were written by Meyer (cf. Justi, *op. cit.* iii, p. 220), and therefore contain Goethe's views of Greek art as finally established in Italy. For Goethe's interest in this edition see Bied. v, p. 67. For symbol and allegory cf. WA. iv, 9, p. 251.

the heart of the universe and had seen there certain vast forces whose action and interaction created and still uphold the world in which we live. The poets, especially Homer, had first personified these forces as gods in human form; later the artists had evolved a means of representing them in visible and tangible shape, also in the medium of the human form. It was possible to express such fundamental forces or ideas by means of the human form, because in man Nature becomes self-conscious, contemplates and reflects herself.[1] Man is a microcosm of the whole universe. While at work on a profile of Jupiter Goethe had "very curious thoughts about anthropomorphism, which is the basis of all religions", and remembered with pleasure the bon mot: "Tous les animaux sont raisonnables, l'homme seul est religieux."[2]

Goethe believed that in Italy the ultimate truth about the nature of things had been revealed to him, as it had been revealed to all the supreme artists of the past, above all to Raphael and to the Greek artists and Homer. The highest art could only be produced by an individual who was in touch with the whole universe, and understood the laws on which it was built. This is the central idea of Moritz's essay *Ueber die bildende Nachahmung des Schönen*, which is the codification of Goethe's new aesthetic ideas.[3] Goethe himself wrote, in his essay on *Einfache Nachahmung, Manier, Stil*, "style [the highest form of artistic expression] rests on the foundations of knowledge, on the nature of things".[4] This knowledge, which he now possessed, had come to him in Italy: first through sight of the "*Urlandschaft*" round Naples and in Sicily, then through reading of Homer in those surroundings, and finally and most completely through study of Greek sculpture, by which he won the vision of the form of man, in unity and variety, a microcosm of the universe, key to the knowledge of God.

[1] *Götterlehre*, p. 22; already quoted above, p. 146.
[2] Letter to Herder, July 1789 (WA. IV, 9, p. 145).
[3] For the *Genie's* relation to the universe cf. especially pp. 25–8, 31–3, 35, 36 (reprinted edition, Heidelberg, 1924). Cf. also Bied. I, pp. 163–5, 173.
[4] WA. 47, p. 80: "So ruht der Stil auf den tiefsten Grundfesten der Erkenntnis, auf dem Wesen der Dinge." This essay appeared in the *Teutscher Merkur*, February 1789.

CHAPTER V

FULL CLASSICISM: 1788–1805

Beim erneuerten Studium Homers empfinde ich erst ganz, welches
unnennbare Unheil der jüdische Prass uns zugefügt hat. Hätten wir
die Sodomitereien und ägyptisch-babylonischen Grillen nie kennen
lernen, und wäre Homer unsere Bibel geblieben, welch' eine ganz
andere Gestalt würde die Menschheit dadurch gewonnen haben.

A. BACK IN WEIMAR

WHEN Goethe returned to Weimar in June 1788, and
settled down to a new life in the old surroundings, he
believed that he had found in Italy the secret of Greek
supremacy in art and in living. In Naples and Sicily he had
seen the conditions of climate and land which had made the
Greek man possible. In the Italian character he had caught
glimpses of this Greek man, but they had been fleeting and
unsatisfying. In Homer then, re-read in Sicily, he had found
the picture for which he was searching: man as God conceived
him, developing with instinctive rightness all his faculties to
their allotted perfection. This "*Urmensch*" lived in harmony
with Nature, however much he might have to battle with her
in many of her manifestations. He did not ask that life should
be other than what it was. Thus, at peace with God, he was
granted exceptional revelations of ultimate truth, and, with
the sure instinct of his nature, found the simplest means of
giving artistic expression to these revelations, by faithful reproduction of the God-filled world around him.

Goethe knew that the Greeks had been exceptionally
favoured by circumstance. It had been enough for them to
reproduce the world around them, because in that world
Nature's intentions were more perfectly expressed than in the
modern world, more so particularly than in the modern world
north of the Alps. It was therefore unlikely that any modern,
northern artist could achieve what the Greeks had achieved.
But Goethe knew of no alternative; the Greek way of artistic
production was the only way by which the artist could fulfil

his function. The attempt must be made to follow the Greeks, despite the unfavourable circumstances of a northern artist's life.

The excellence of Greek art was based on the excellence of the Greek way of life; and the Greek way of life was based on the principle that every faculty in man should be allowed to develop freely in accordance with its nature. In modern society with its innumerable social and religious taboos, such free and natural development was impossible. Nowhere was the modern social code so destructive of the proper growth of mind and body as in the restrictions which it put on the sexual relations between man and woman.

> In der heroischen Zeit, da Götter and Göttinnen liebten,
>   Folgte Begierde dem Blick, folgte Genuss der Begier.
> Glaubst du es habe sich lange die Göttin der Liebe besonnen,
>   Als im Idäischen Hain einst ihr Anchises gefiel?
> Hätte Luna gesäumt, den schönen Schläfer zu küssen,
>   O, so hätt' ihn geschwind, neidend, Aurora geweckt.
> Hero erblickte Leander am lauten Fest, und behende,
>   Stürzte der Liebende sich heiss in die nächtliche Flut.
> Rhea Sylvia wandelt, die fürstliche Jungfrau, der Tiber
>   Wasser zu schöpfen, hinab, und sie ergreifet ein Gott.[1]

This was the teaching and example of the ancient world in such matters, and Goethe was determined to follow it. Whether or not there was in fact a Roman "Faustina", with whom he had had a semi-permanent relationship, there is no doubt that he took steps in Rome to satisfy the physical needs of his sexual nature, and so to keep his body in a "delightful equilibrium".[2] It is clear that he attributed his "physical-moral troubles" of the last years before the Italian journey partly to the unnatural state of celibacy in which he had lived.[3] On his return to

---

[1] *Römische Elegien*, III (WA. I, p. 236; WA. IV, 8, p. 347; also *ibid.* p. 314): "In the heroic age, when gods and goddesses loved, desire arose at first sight, enjoyment came hard on desire. Do you suppose the goddess of love deliberated long, when once in the grove of Ida Anchises took her fancy? Had Luna been slow to kiss the fair sleeper, swiftly Aurora would have waked him in envy. Hero caught sight of Leander at the busy festival, and straight the lover plunged into the midnight flood. Rhea Sylvia, the royal maiden, goes down to the Tiber to draw water, and a god seizes her."

[2] "Ein köstliches Gleichgewicht."

[3] Cf. WA. IV, 8, p. 327, lines 17 foll.

Weimar he lost little time in ensuring that he should not make
the same mistake again. As Mars took Rhea Sylvia on her way
to draw water at the Tiber, so Goethe took Christiane and
made her his mistress. It was a relationship in the Italian style,[1]
founded not on a sentimental community of ideas or outlook
(Christiane was illiterate and utterly incapable of sharing
Goethe's intellectual life), but on the simpler, deeper need of
man and woman, and on the common joys and sorrows of
making and rearing a family.

> Warum treibt sich das Volk so, und schreit? Es will sich
> ernähren,
>   Kinder zeugen, und die nähren, so gut es vermag.
> Merke dir, Reisender, das, und thue zu Hause desgleichen.
> Weiter bringt es kein Mensch, stell er sich, wie er auch will.[2]

This was the fundament of life, an existence based on the
primary instincts. The common people lived so; the Greeks
had lived so; the modern disciple of the Greeks must live so
too.

The return to "Nature" in sex matters carried Goethe even
further than this. He loved Christiane and regarded her as his
wife, but this did not prevent him, while in Venice, from
seeking sexual satisfaction where he could find it. He was
following a natural law, which was accepted as valid by the
Greeks, that a certain degree of promiscuity is natural to the
male. All the Achaean heroes at Troy had their mistresses; and
Odysseus, though faithful in mind to Penelope through all his
ten years' wanderings, slept with Circe and Calypso and thought
no wrong. A similar fundamental faithfulness, that is not
disturbed by occasional promiscuity when circumstances
demand, is one of the themes running through the Venetian
Epigrams.[3] For a pagan, promiscuity needed no other justifica-

---

[1] Cf. WA. IV, 8, p. 314: "Was das Herz betrifft, so gehört es gar nicht in
die Terminologie der hiesigen Liebeskanzley."

[2] *Venezianische Epigramme*, x (WA. I, p. 310): "Why does the common
folk jostle and shout so? They want to feed themselves, get children and
feed them, as well as they may. Note that, traveller, and do the same at
home. No man can do more, try how he will."

[3] In Nos. 3, 13, 28, he longs for Christiane; 36–45 (Bettine), his eye begins
to rove; 49, he remembers Christiane; 68–72 and 85, he goes to the brothel;
90, 91, 94, 96, 98, 100, 101, 102, but is fundamentally true to his wife and
their son.

tion than the example of Zeus. In the myths of the loves of Zeus, that shock modern sentiment, the Greeks had given religious sanction to a practice that springs from the nature of man. In Goethe's opinion modern sentiment was unnatural and therefore wrong. He was not ashamed to follow the Greeks.

Goethe took Christiane in order to maintain the "köstliches Gleichgewicht" that he had established in Rome; but he soon found, what he had probably expected to find, that physical and spiritual are brothers not enemies. Goethe's love for Christiane was a very different thing from his soul-matings with Lotte Buff and Frau von Stein. It was fundamentally physical, while these had been purely spiritual. But for a while at least it was for him a spiritual experience of great purity and intensity. Here too the Greeks showed him the way. Their holiest mysteries had taught the secrets of love-making.[1] Physical delights were hallowed by them as the command and teaching of a god. The discovery of what love in this sense meant, filled him with awe and wonder, and a deep joy. With his eyes he saw the very human body of his little German flower-girl; his spirit saw and worshipped the great goddess, Kupris-Aphrodite.

The success of his experiment in pagan love enabled him for a moment to feel himself in harmony with life, as the Greeks had done. From the strength of this serenity he was able to give his experience poetic form in the Greek manner.

Lebe glücklich, und so lebe die Vorzeit in dir.

He was happy, and for a brief space antiquity lived again in his poetry. He found the door to the "school of the Greeks" still open; the years had not closed it.[2] The *Römische Elegien* ("Erotica" Goethe first called them) were written between October 1788 and April 1790.[3] The Roman elegists, especially

---

[1] *Römische Elegien*, XII: WA. I, p. 247. Goethe sought guidance also in the *Priapea*, a collection of Latin *carmina* in honour of Priapus. See WA. 53, pp. 197 foll., 492.   [2] Elegy XIII: WA. I, p. 247.

[3] Goethe was certainly misstating the facts when he told Göschen (4 July 1791; WA. IV, 9, p. 277) that he had written the elegies in Rome. Even if some of the elegies were begun in Rome, the greater part of the work was certainly done in Weimar (cf. Hans v. Arnim, *Entstehung und Anordnung der Römischen Elegien. Deutsche Revue*, XLVII, 2, p. 135).

Propertius and Tibullus, provided the model for their form as well as for much of their content. But on a deeper plane their inspiration lay in Homer. In them for the first time Goethe was able to practise the style of composition that he had learnt in Sicily from his reading of the *Odyssey*. Their central theme is the love of the poet for his "Liebchen". Goethe was no novice in this branch of poetry. Friederike, Lili, Charlotte von Stein, had all inspired him. Around each name there clings a group of Goethe's love-poems. Each group is different in style and mood, but all have this in common, that they are lyrics, direct expressions of the emotion aroused in the poet by his love. From none can one learn much of the circumstances of that love, still less of the character or appearance of the beloved.[1] In the *Römische Elegien* the poet's approach is entirely different. Several whole elegies and large parts of many others are devoted to a close description of his relations with his girl in their various aspects. The end of Elegy II explains the business basis of the liaison. In Elegy III he dispels her fears that he may despise her for having yielded to him so quickly. The fourth Elegy hints at the secret rites that lovers know, and at the end contains a description of the beloved as she first appeared to him. So each Elegy adds some touch to the picture of the two lovers, or sheds some light on the progress of their love. These passages of objective description are treated with the greatest simplicity, but with an "indescribable clarity and inner understanding",[2] which makes them great and moving just as Homer's description is great and moving. But this is not their only beauty. They are the essential element in the whole series of elegies. Without them the other themes—the Roman background, the conflict with society, the ancient gods and goddesses—could never have been brought together to give each its shade of deeper significance to the whole. At first Goethe intended to write just "Erotica", descriptions of his love. Then because this love had helped him to recover the antique poise in living, he painted his Erotica on a Roman background, to symbolise this return to antiquity.[3] The strictures of society

---

[1] Those to Lili are the most objective, especially "Lili's Park", which is not really a lyric at all. But still it would not be possible to reconstruct the story of Goethe's relationship to Lili from these poems alone.

[2] Cf. above, p. 161.   [3] Cf. v. Arnim's article and Elegy VII.

were woven in, so that the happy love of man and woman
might appear as a green island, in the sea of human pettiness;
and through the whole there walk the radiant figures of the
gods, who raise the poet's common human experience to ideal
significance, because like him they did not disdain to love. The
simple experience which inspired the *Römische Elegien* worked
like a stone dropped into a pool; from it spread rings of significance that lapped at last on the obscurest problems of existence.
This was "style" as Goethe understood it after finding Greece
in Italy: a faithful reproduction of Nature in a manner that
rested on "the knowledge of the nature of things".[1]

For the execution of his intentions in detail Goethe also
practised imitation of Greek and Latin models on a large scale.
From his return to Italy until the end of the century the majority
of his poetical works were written in classical metres,[2] and
resembled classical models in their outward form. But this
was not all. He was not ashamed to borrow innumerable
traits, situations, metaphors and turns of phrase from classical
authors. This was indeed nothing new: *Iphigenie*, even in its
earlier form, was full, as we have seen, of such borrowings;
and even in the days of *Sturm und Drang* the Greek authors
sometimes lent him material.[3] But now this borrowing was an
essential part of his poetic technique, and was made into a
principle of composition. This principle is laid down in a letter
to Meyer, written while Goethe was at work on the *Römische
Elegien.*[4] Meyer, who had sent Goethe a sketch for a picture
representing Oedipus guessing the riddle of the sphinx,[5] had
excused himself for making Oedipus's attitude resemble a
figure of Pylades on an antique vase. Goethe replied[6]: "It

---

[1] See *Einfache Nachahmung, Manier, Stil*: WA. 47, p. 80; and cf. Elegy XIII,
line 24: WA. 1, p. 249.

[2] See Appendix below.   [3] See above, pp. 61–62.

[4] April 27, 1789 (WA. IV, 9, p. 110); cf. *ibid.* p. 26, line 22; also WA. 48,
pp. 43, 64; WA. 49, 2, p. 19, line 22, and WA. 33, p. 254.

[5] Reproduced in *Schr. der G-G.* XXXVIII, No. 2.

[6] WA. IV, 9, p. 110: "Es hat gar nichts zu bedeuten, dass Ihr Oedipus dem
Pylades auf der Vase einigermassen gleicht. In dem Kreise, in welchem Sie
arbeiten, liegen die Nüancen gar nah beisammen. Die menschliche Figur ist
von den Alten so durchgearbeitet, dass wir schwerlich eine ganz neue Stellung
hervorbringen werden, ohne aus den Grenzen des guten Geschmacks zu
schreiten. Es kommt nur darauf an dass sie das ausdrucke, was wir gedacht
haben, und dass wir sie *zu unsrer Absicht wieder* hervorbringen können."

does not matter, that your Oedipus is somewhat like the Pylades on the vase. In the field in which you work, the nuances are so very slight. The human figure has been so thoroughly worked over by the ancients, that we can hardly expect to produce an entirely new attitude without transgressing the limits of good taste. The important thing is that it should express what we have thought, and that we should be able to reproduce it *for our own purpose*." Goethe was thinking of his own problems as well as Meyer's when he wrote this judgment. He had accepted the whole of ancient literature and art as an indispensable source from which to draw the means of sensual expression for his ideas. A certain amount of adaptation to the individual context was all that these borrowed traits needed.

In the manner of this adaptation lay Goethe's opportunity to exercise his genius. The *Römische Elegien* offer innumerable examples,[1] amongst which the myth of Fama and Amor, in the nineteenth Elegy, presents the best occasion for a study of Goethe's methods. This myth of the eternal conflict between reputation and love occurs nowhere in ancient literature or mythology. It was invented by Goethe to give poetic expression to the trouble which the gossips of Weimar were causing him. But each individual *motiv* in the execution of the idea is taken from some writer or work of art of antiquity. Bronner has proved direct use of material from the Latin elegists, Ovid, the Greek Anthology, an antique gem, the *Odyssey* and "Anacreon".[2] The result of this wholesale plagiarism is a poem of great originality, true in its conception and vital in its expression. The same method of direct imitation, with a larger or smaller element of adaptation, is easy to detect in all the other "classicising" works of this period. The *Venezianische Epigramme* take their material chiefly from the Latin elegists and Martial.[3] In *Amyntas* and *Der neue Pausias* Goethe made free use of Theocritus, the Anthology and other Greek and Latin authors.[4] The *Achilleis* is full of reminiscences of Homer, Hesiod and the tragedians. The *Helena* of 1800

---

[1] Cf. *Goethes römische Elegien und ihre Quellen*, by F. Bronner, in *Neue Jahrbücher für Philologie*, 1893; also *Die Göttin der Gelegenheit*, by Leitzmann, in *Euphorion*, XVIII, p. 158.

[2] P. 453.   [3] Ernst Maass, *Jrb. der G-G.* XII, pp. 68 foll.

[4] Cf. JA. I, pp. 354, 355.

borrows freely from the tragedians. Only *Hermann und Dorothea* carries its sources of material within itself.

The *Römische Elegien*, and in a lower degree, the *Venezianische Epigramme*, show Goethe's new style of composition "im Sinne der Alten". *Tasso*, on the other hand, composed for the most part during the first months of Goethe's work on the *Römische Elegien*, owes almost nothing to the new principle of "Homeric style". Apart from the use of a few Greek turns of speech[1] (a habit that had by now become subconscious with Goethe), there is nothing in *Tasso* to remind one of the Greek tragedians or of Homer. Its greatness lies in the combined power and subtlety with which it portrays the psychological condition of an abnormally subjective man, who through the fault of his nature falls into a state of morbid distrust of the world around him. It is a state as far removed as possible from that of the Greek man, living in perfect harmony with Nature; and the means suitable for its portrayal were not any that the Greeks had known, but rather those that Goethe had perfected in *Iphigenie* for exploring emotional conditions into their finest ramifications. In style and mood *Tasso* is nearer to *Iphigenie* than to any other of the great works that Goethe produced during the fifteen years after his return from Rome. The lofty "*Humanität*" that inspires all the characters was Goethe's pre-Italian ideal, which after Italy he tended to despise. The conflict between "Erlaubt ist, was gefällt" and "Erlaubt ist, was sich ziemt"[2] was the chief problem of his first ten years in Weimar, and the essence of his relationship with Frau von Stein. In Italy he found the synthesis, and so the conflict ceased to interest him. *Tasso* is a relic of the troubled years before the Italian journey. That is precisely its interest to us. It reminds us that Goethe's genius was always more powerful than any particular obsession that might for a time have a hold on his intellect. After Rome Hellenism was an obsession with Goethe. It was an ideal from which, with German concentration, his intellect was busy drawing "last consequences", and demanding that he should put these into practice in art and in life. If Goethe's intellect had not been more than balanced by an

---

[1] Cf. H. Morsch, *Goethe und die griechischen Bühnendichter*, p. 35.

[2] Lines 994–1006: "What is pleasant, is allowed" and "What is proper, is allowed".

emotional life of great power and depth, this obsession might have worked negatively, so as to make him reject any productive urge that could not be made to çonform to the rules of the obsession. The need to give the Tasso-problem its final expression was imperious after Goethe's return from Italy. It was a subject that could not be treated "in the manner of the ancients"; and so in spite of his obsession, Goethe treated it as it had to be treated, in the manner that suited it.

The first eighteen months after Goethe's return to Weimar saw *Tasso* finished and the greater part of the work on the *Römische Elegien* completed. In the spring of 1790 the *Venezianische Epigramme* came as a pendant to the two great works of this productive period. After the Epigrams, which already show his genius flagging, there lies a period of three years in which Goethe could produce nothing worthier of immortality than *der Bürgergeneral* and *der Gross-Kophta*. The only literary work of this period that has any connexion with Goethe's Hellenism is the unfinished allegorical story, *Die Reise der Söhne Megaprazons*. The political problems of the day form the subject of the allegory; the setting is taken in part from Rabelais; the local colour, in so far as there is any, is modern;[1] but the names of the six brothers are Greek. This mixture of Greek and modern throws light on Goethe's attitude to the Greek tradition. The sons represent human characters in ideal expression. It was fitting therefore to give them Greek names— Epistemon the understanding eldest brother; Panurg the tireless worker; Eutyches the carefree youngest—since the Greeks had first evolved, and best understood, the representation of ideal characters. The Greek names also helped to preserve for the individualised ideas their timeless significance. But it was not necessary to place the whole story in an ancient Greek setting, with Greek costume and historical background. The significance of Greece for the modern world was in Goethe's view quite independent of the outward circumstances of Greek life.

The unproductive period, 1790–1793, was for Goethe a period of generally lessened interest in Greek things. On 5 November 1789 he wrote to Karl August: "I am going

[1] WA. 18, p. 371.

ahead eagerly with Greek."[1] From then until November 1793, when he turned once again to Homer, there is evidence on only one occasion of Greek reading: in the last days of January 1793, he read the *Symposium, Phaedrus* and *Apology* of Plato with great delight.[2] His interest in Greek art was kept alive by his correspondence with Meyer; and, from November 1791 onwards, by Meyer's presence in Weimar. But his researches, except those connected with the portrayal of ideal characters in sculpture,[3] were desultory and unproductive. The most important event in this period for the development of his knowledge and understanding of Greek art was his acquisition on loan of the gem collection of Princess Gallitzin. The collection arrived in Weimar in January 1793,[4] and remained in Goethe's hands until February 1797.[5] The possession of this fine collection enabled Goethe to acquire a comprehensive and thorough knowledge of a branch of ancient art which he had previously been able to study only for fleeting moments, as the chance of his travels brought him in contact with this collection or that. He was never tired of expressing his thanks for the loan both privately and publicly.[6]

In January 1793, Goethe's genius struggled clear of the deadening influences which had reduced it to impotence for three years, and produced in less than three months the four thousand hexameters of *Reinecke Fuchs*. According to Goethe's own account in the *Campagne in Frankreich*,[7] he chose the hexameter for his re-working of this medieval epic, because he wished to give himself practice in writing this metre according to the stricter rules which Voss was beginning to preach and to practise.[8] In fact the reason for his choice lay deeper. In its

[1] "Das Griechische wird eifrig betrieben": WA. IV, 9, p. 161. Theocritus and the other Greek idyllic poets were probably his chief study. Cf. WA. III, 2, p. 323.

[2] WA. IV, 10, p. 47. The reference in a letter to Jacobi of March 1790 (*Ibid.* 9, p. 184) to "studying the ancients and following their example", probably alludes to Goethe's study of the *Priapea*. Cf. WA. 53, pp. 491–2.

[3] See above, p. 176.   [4] Cf. WA. III, 2, p. 30.

[5] WA. IV, 12, p. 32.

[6] *Ibid.* 12, pp. 8, 32; 33, pp. 253 foll., 259; 48, p. 133; 49, 2, p. 102. For further occupation with ancient art in this period (1790–1793) see *Schr. der G-G.* XXXII (Goethe-Meyer Briefwechsel), pp. 60, 65, 67, 74, 76; also WA. IV, 9, p. 218, 10, pp. 37, 54, 73.

[7] WA. 33, p. 266.   [8] See Appendix below.

naiv description of the world as it is, without "sentimental" commentary from the poet, *Reinecke Fuchs* is a subject of the Homeric type.[1] The world it describes is indeed not an ideal world, as Homer's is; but Goethe could not have chosen an ideal subject at that moment, embittered as he was by the violence of the French Revolution and by his own loneliness among friends who could not understand him. The world of *Reinecke Fuchs* was as near as he could now come to the world of Homer. By his choice of the Homeric metre Goethe indicated clearly that he wished to acknowledge Homer as godfather to his Low-German Odysseus. It is idle to look for further imitation of Homer in *Reinecke Fuchs*, for Goethe's poem is merely a versification of Gottsched's prose version of the old Low German epic. The chased mirror in the tenth Book, for instance, with its carved scenes that appear to move and live like the scenes on the Shield of Achilles, is not a reminiscence or imitation of the *Iliad*. Goethe found the whole description in Gottsched. The hexameter produced its effect at least on Goethe's contemporaries. Schiller told Körner that he was delighted by Goethe's *Reinecke Fuchs*, "especially on account of the Homeric tone, that is observed in it without affectation".[2]

The summer of 1793 passed without any fresh contact with Greek things. On 18 November Goethe wrote to Jacobi: "In order to have some limitless occupation I have betaken myself to Homer. So I hope, I shall never be hard up again in all my life."[3] This was in fact the starting-point of a study of Homer, which continued with unrelenting intensity for more than five years and finally made the Homeric world as much a part of Goethe's life as was the air he breathed. It is conceivable, though not likely, that Goethe had in mind to translate the whole of Homer, when he wrote to Jacobi. A fragment of four lines from the *Odyssey* (Book VII, 81-5) has survived, which is probably to be dated shortly after Goethe's return from the siege of Mainz.[4] Other longer and more

[1] Cf. WA. 35, p. 22.   [2] 12 June 1794 (Jonas, III, p. 453).

[3] WA. IV, 10, p. 127: "Um etwas Unendliches zu unternehmen habe ich mich an den Homer gemacht. Da hoffe ich nun in meinem übrigen Leben nicht zu darben."

[4] Late August 1793. See WA. V, 2, pp. 203.

finished translations of various passages from the *Iliad* and *Odyssey* followed, probably in the next two years.[1] None was published in Goethe's lifetime.

In the following summer (1794) Goethe's interest in Homer was powerfully stimulated by the presence in Weimar of the scholar-poet and translator, J. H. Voss. In the first days of June Voss read aloud from his translation of the *Odyssey* to Goethe, Herder, Wieland, Knebel and Böttiger—as notable a constellation of minds as ever listened at one time to the words of the father of poetry. There was discussion too of Homer's geography (a question into which Goethe later enquired more deeply);[2] and Böttiger was bold enough to propound those ideas that were soon to cause revolution and civil war in the learned and literary worlds: F. A. Wolf's contentions as to the origin of the Homeric poems.[3] They found little approval in that company, except perhaps from Herder.[4] In July Voss sent Goethe his recently published translation of Homer.[5] The problems of Homeric translation came therewith into the forefront of Goethe's interest. In November and perhaps throughout the winter, 1794–1795, he read aloud from Voss's *Iliad* to the *Freitagsgesellschaft*,[6] and these readings were often followed by discussion of the merits and faults of Voss's rendering.[7] It is natural to suppose that most of Goethe's translations from Homer were made at this time, partly with the intention of improving on Voss. Suphan is doubtless right that Goethe's rendering of Homer's description of the palace and gardens of Alcinous is truer in essentials than Voss's attempt.[8] But one passage throws light on a curious blindness in Goethe towards one aspect of the Homeric genius. Where Homer has:

---

[1] WA. 5, 2, pp. 382–7, and 4, p. 326. Also G-J. XXII, pp. 3–16. The passages are: *Il.* VI, 1–6, XII, 442–52, XIII, 95–110, XIV, 329–51; *Od.* VII, 78–132, VIII, 267–326 and 339–53. In the summer of 1795 Goethe translated the first half of the Homeric Hymn to Apollo (WA. 4, p. 321). The translation was published in the *Horen*, 1795, 9. Stück (cf. WA. IV, 10, p. 288).

[2] Bied. I, p. 217.　　　　　　　　　　[3] *Ibid.* pp. 199 foll.

[4] Cf. Bied. v, p. 37.　　　　　　　　　[5] G-J. v, p. 40.

[6] A circle of the intellectual *élite* of Weimar, that met on Fridays about once a month from September 1791 until some time in 1796, usually at the palace of the Duchess Amalia.

[7] Bied. I, pp. 215, 217.　　　　　　　　[8] G-J. XXII, pp. 6 foll.

χρύσειοι δ' ἑκάτερθε καὶ ἀργύρεοι κύνες ἦσαν,
οὓς "Ηφαιστος ἔτευξεν ἰδυίῃσι πραπίδεσσι
δῶμα φυλασσέμεναι μεγαλήτορος 'Αλκινόοιο
ἀθανάτους ὄντας καὶ ἀγήρως ἤματα πάντα.[1]

Goethe translates:

> Golden und silberne Hunde, zu beiden Seiten, bestellte
> Vor Alcinous Haus unsterbliche Wächter Hephaistos.[2]

Homer's four lines have shrunk to two, and in the process all
the naïve love of the old poet for rather obvious but significant
detail has gone. It is not merely that Alcinous has lost his conventional "great-hearted". There is no mention of Hephaestus's
"cunning mind", which to Homer was a thing of awe whenever he thought of it, and deserved to be mentioned, however
obvious an attribute it was of the craftsman god. Saddest of
all, Homer's ἀθανάτους ὄντας καὶ ἀγήρως ἤματα πάντα
has dwindled to the single adjective "unsterbliche". Here was
to Homer the greatest marvel of all. The dogs were immortal,
and not only immortal, but ageless! and that for all their days!
Of all this Goethe kept nothing but the one idea "immortal",
which he stuck in, unemphasised, almost unnoticed. A lack of
such completely naïve touches is one of the un-Homeric
features of Goethe's *Achilleis*.[3]

The renewal of interest in Homer was accompanied by
fresh efforts to solve some of the problems of Greek art. In
August 1794 Goethe was in Dresden, where Meyer had been
since May. Together they continued their researches into the
portrayal of ideal characters in Greek sculpture and into the
characteristics of the different periods of Greek art.[4]

[1] "And on each side were gold and silver dogs, which Hephaestus made
with cunning mind to guard the house of great-hearted Alcinous; immortal
were they and ageless all their days": *Od.* VII, 91–4.
[2] "Golden and silver dogs on either side did Hephaestus set as immortal
guards before Alcinous's house."
[3] See below, p. 238.
[4] *Schr. der G-G.* XXXII, pp. 93, 94, 98, 101, 106, 111, 116, 133, 322.

B. SCHILLER

The summer of 1794 is a landmark in Goethe's life. It brought him Schiller's friendship. To Schiller is usually given all the credit for the reawakening of Goethe's genius; but in fact the process had begun with *Reinecke Fuchs*, and was continuing in the return to Homer, and still more notably in the work on *Wilhelm Meister*. Goethe had taken this up again in March 1793, and had found the courage to bind himself to finish it, before the "Bund mit Schiller" had been formally sealed by the exchange of letters of 23 and 27 August 1794. Nevertheless Schiller's friendship completed the process of emancipation, and enabled Goethe to enter on a period of productivity hardly less remarkable than the hectic years of *Sturm und Drang*.

With extraordinary speed and sureness Schiller broke down the many fences of distrust that guarded Goethe's heart. Goethe gave him passage, because he found in the younger man understanding for his new life-purpose, such as no one else had been able to show him since his return from Italy. Not the smallest part of Goethe's delight was due to Schiller's clear realisation and approval of the position and function of the Greek ideal in that purpose. On 23 August 1794, when the *rapprochement* between the two proud men of genius had been in progress little more than two months and was still a far from hardy shoot, Schiller took a step that a lesser man would not have dared to take, or, had he dared, would not have carried out successfully. He wrote to Goethe and analysed to him his own genius and the nature of the task which he had set himself to accomplish. "For long," he wrote, "although at a considerable distance, I have watched the progress of your spirit, and have with ever renewed admiration noted the road that you have set for yourself. You are seeking law in Nature, but you seek it by the hardest path, that any weaker mind would avoid. You take the whole of Nature together, in order to get light on the individual; you seek the explanation of the individual in the sum of Nature's manifestations. Beginning from the simplest organism, you mount step by step to the more complex, so that at the last you may construct the most complex of all, man, organically out of the materials of the whole temple of Nature. By re-creating as it were in Nature, you seek to probe the secret technique of man's creation. A great and truly heroic idea! that displays sufficiently, how well your spirit holds the varied totality of its conceptions in a proper unity. You can never have hoped that your life would suffice for the accomplishment of such a purpose; but only to set out on such a path, is worth more than to complete any other. You have chosen, like Achilles in the *Iliad*, between Phthia and immortality. If you had been born a Greek, or even an Italian, and had been surrounded from the cradle by an ideal Nature and an idealising art, your way would have been enormously shortened, perhaps made quite unnecessary. With your first perception of things you would then have absorbed the form of the ideal, and with your first experiences the great style would have developed in you. Now that you have been born a German, now that your Grecian spirit has been thrown into this northern world, you had but the two alternatives, either to become a northern artist, or to provide your imagination by means of your intellect with the material which the real world could not give it, and so to produce your Greece as it were from within, by an intellectual process. In that period of your life when the spirit is creating its inner world out of the outer world, you were surrounded by imperfect forms, and so had already been imbued with a lawless, northern world; but your victorious genius, mightier than the material world, discovered this imperfection from within, and was confirmed in its view by evidence from without, through acquaintance with the Greek world. You then had to correct the older, worser world, that had been forced upon your imagination, in accordance with the pattern that your creative spirit made for itself. That can be accomplished only with the help of guiding principles. But this logical tendency, which the spirit cannot avoid in contemplation, is not easily compatible with the aesthetic function, through which it creates. You had therefore one more labour: as you previously passed from perception to abstraction, so now you had to turn logical conceptions back into intuition, and change thought into feeling, since genius can bring forth only with the help of the latter."[1] In these words Schiller gave back to Goethe his lost confidence in the rightness of his struggle to recapture Greek standards in life and in art, and so achieve the highest form of existence of which man is capable.

[1] Jonas, III, pp. 472-4: "Lange schon habe ich, obgleich aus ziemlicher Ferne, dem Gang Ihres Geistes zugesehn, und den Weg, den Sie Sich vorgezeichnet haben, mit immer erneuerter Bewunderung bemerkt. Sie suchen das Notwendige der Natur, aber Sie suchen es auf dem schwersten Weg, vor welchem jede schwächere Kraft sich wohl hüten wird. Sie nehmen die ganze Natur zusammen, um über das Einzelne Licht zu bekommen; in der Allheit ihrer Erscheinungsarten suchen Sie den Erklärungsgrund für das Individuum auf. Von der einfachen Organisation steigen Sie, Schritt vor Schritt, zu den mehr verwickelten hinauf, um endlich die verwickeltste von allen, den Menschen, genetisch aus den Materialien des ganzen Naturgebäudes zu erbauen. Dadurch dass Sie in der Natur gleichsam nacherschaffen, suchen Sie in seine verborgene Technik einzudringen. Eine grosse und wahrhaft heldenmässige Idee, die zur Genüge zeigt, wie sehr Ihr Geist das reiche Ganze seiner Vorstellungen in einer schönen Einheit zusammenhält. Sie können niemals gehofft haben, dass Ihr Leben zu einem solchen Ziele zureichen werde, aber einen solchen Weg auch nur einzuschlagen, ist mehr wert, als jeden anderen zu endigen, — und Sie haben gewählt wie Achill in der Ilias, zwischen Phthia und der Unsterblichkeit. Wären Sie als ein Grieche, ja nur als ein Italiener geboren worden, und hätte schon von der Wiege an eine auserlesene Natur und eine idealisirende Kunst Sie umgeben, so wäre Ihr Weg unendlich verkürzt, vielleicht ganz überflüssig gemacht worden. Schon in die erste Anschauung der Dinge hätten Sie dann die Form des Notwendigen aufgenommen, und mit Ihren ersten Erfahrungen hätte sich der grosse Stil in Ihnen entwickelt. Nun, da Sie ein Deutscher geboren sind, da Ihr griechischer Geist in diese nordische Schöpfung geworfen wurde, so blieb Ihnen keine andere Wahl, als entweder selbst zum nordischen Künstler zu werden, oder Ihrer Imagination das, was ihr die Wirklichkeit vorenthielt, durch Nachhilfe der Denkkraft zu ersetzen, und so gleichsam von innen heraus und auf einem rationalen Wege ein Griechenland zu gebären. In derjenigen Lebensepoche, wo die Seele sich aus der äusseren Welt ihre innere bildet, von mangelhaften Gestalten umringt, hatten Sie schon eine wilde und nordische Natur in sich aufgenommen, als Ihr siegendes, seinem Material überlegenes Genie diesen Mangel von innen entdeckte, und von aussen her durch die Bekanntschaft mit der griechischen Natur davon vergewissert wurde. Jetzt mussten Sie die alte, Ihrer Einbildungskraft schon aufgedrungene schlechtere Natur nach dem besseren Muster, das Ihr bildender Geist sich erschuf, corrigieren, und das kann nun freilich nicht anders als nach leitenden Begriffen von Statten gehen. Aber diese logische Richtung, welche der Geist bei der Reflexion zu nehmen genötigt ist, verträgt sich nicht wohl mit der ästhetischen, durch welche allein er bildet. Sie hatten also eine Arbeit mehr, denn so wie Sie von der Anschauung zu der Abstraktion übergingen, so mussten Sie nun rückwärts Begriffe wieder in Intuitionen umsetzen, und Gedanken in Gefühle verwandeln, weil nur durch diese das Genie hervorbringen kann."

The fundamental importance of Hellenism became ever clearer as the two friends revealed to each other more of their problems and beliefs. Schiller had for some time been devoting his best energies to a philosophical enquiry into the nature of beauty and its importance for man. The first results of this enquiry were published in June 1793, in the essay *Ueber Anmut und Würde*. Reduced to the simplest language, Schiller's contention in this essay is that a complete victory for man's moral nature in the age-old conflict between duty and inclination, spirit and matter, "*Sittlichkeit*" and "*Sinnlichkeit*", is not desirable because it is not "beautiful". For him the highest form of human existence is reached when man can stand above the moral conflict because he desires only what his moral instinct approves.[1] To despise the world of sense is as much an imperfection in man as to become subjugated by the material element in life. Harmony and co-operation between the two instincts are necessary before "the ideal of perfect humanity" can be attained.[2] Of course such a condition of harmony presupposes complete control of the sensual instincts by the will. But this alone is not enough; it gives man only dignity.[3] As long as any trace of conflict or effort in suppressing the sensual instincts is visible, perfection is not achieved, because beauty[3] is lacking. The Greeks understood this highest morality, that is above morality, and gave it expression at least in their art. Schiller cites the Niobe and the Apollo Belvedere.[4]

This was the point at which Schiller had arrived when he and Goethe came together in the summer of 1794. By a very different road he had reached the same position as Goethe. To their surprise they found themselves side by side on the same lofty pinnacle, looking down on a misunderstanding world. It was the miracle that Goethe needed to restore his faith in himself and God.

Schiller was already engaged on a fuller exposition of his morality of beauty. Since June 1794 he had been at work on those letters which later became the *Briefe über die ästhetische Erziehung des Menschen*, in which he intended fully to define and establish the nature of beauty and its dominant position

---

[1] Schiller, *Werke*, xiv, pp. 33–43, especially pp. 36 and 42, 43.
[2] *Ibid.* p. 54.
[3] "Würde" and "Anmut".   [4] *Werke*, xiv, p. 57.

in the nature of the proper man. Before he had advanced far, his contact with Goethe had begun to enrich and deepen his ideas. Joachim Ulrich has attempted with great skill to establish the exact extent of Goethe's influence on the *Aesthetische Briefe*.[1] He attributes, no doubt rightly, the contrasted pictures of Greek and modern society in the Sixth Letter[2] to his influence. The essence of this contrast is that the Greeks were complete men, whereas we are cogs in the machine of the community. Each individual Greek was a worthy representative of the species. With us the individual represents only one aspect of the idea of the species. Thousands of individuals must be taken together in order to get a true conception of that idea. Until each individual is once again complete, with all his powers fully developed and in use, society will not recover from its ills. In the later letters Schiller points the road that is to lead mankind upwards to the new "completeness".[3] His solution is the morality of beauty, by which the conflict of spirit and matter is overcome. Ulrich's contention that Goethe is responsible for the whole conception of a third, harmonising instinct (the "*Spieltrieb*", play-instinct), is perhaps misleading. Already in *Ueber Anmut und Würde* Schiller had used the term "*Spiel*" to denote that condition of moral freedom which results when man is able to rise above the conflict of duty and desire.[4] But it may be true that Goethe's encouragement induced Schiller to give man's capacity for harmony the rank of an "instinct" (*Trieb*), to make it, that is to say, as fundamental an element in man's nature as his "*Formtrieb*" (moral instinct) and his "*Stofftrieb*" (material instinct). Once again in the *Aesthetische Briefe* the illustration of the morality of beauty is taken from Greek art. The Greeks embodied their ideal of life in their gods. "They released the blessed ones from the bonds of every object, every duty, every care, and made idleness and indifference the envied lot of godhead, applying merely human names to the freest and loftiest existence."[5] The Ludovisi Juno (Goethe's favourite antique) is cited as the perfect expression of the highest moral state, above conflict, above desire, above moral effort of any sort.

[1] *Jrb. der G–G.* xx, pp. 164–212.
[3] "Ganzheit."
[5] *Ibid.* pp. 175 foll.

[2] *Werke*, xiv, pp. 132–4.
[4] *Ibid.* p. 36.

Schiller's next philosophical essay, *Ueber naive und senti-mentalische Dichtung*,[1] shows even clearer traces of Goethe's influence. For here it is not merely the Greek gods, in their representation in art, who are cited as illustrations of perfect humanity. The Greeks themselves are given the credit of having achieved perfection in real life. Schiller contrasts the modern way of life with that of the Greeks. Why, he asks, do we moderns feel a sentimental delight in contemplation of inconscient Nature, in brooks and trees, in sunsets and bird-song? And why was this emotion unknown to the Greeks? It is because we have exiled ourselves from Nature by our artificial manner of life. We long to return, but we cannot. Our society is an artificial patchwork;[2] our religion the product of over-subtle reasoning: we feel that our humanity is a failure and are only too glad to escape from "a form that has failed so utterly" to the naïve rightness of Nature.[3] The Greeks on the other hand were still part of Nature. They felt no need to escape from a humanity divided within itself. For they were not divided. They were whole. "United in himself and happy to feel himself a man, he was content to regard humanity as the highest and to endeavour to raise the rest of Nature to this level."[4]

This is in all essentials the picture of the Greeks which Goethe won for himself in Sicily. It was part of Goethe's belief, that the Greeks really had been perfect men (just as he hoped to find the "*Urpflanze*" growing in Sicily), not merely that they had been able to express the ideal in their art. This passage in *Ueber naive und sentimentalische Dichtung* can be taken as being a very exact expression of Goethe's own view of the Greek ideal and its relation to modern man. There is no relevant utterance of this date from Goethe himself. For Goethe the Greek way of life was at this time too living a necessity for him to be able to define it in any but poetically allusive terms. Ten years later, when he had at last realised that it was unattainable, he wrote:[5] "Man is capable of much through proper use of isolated

---

[1] *Werke*, xv, pp. 1–102. Begun in 1794, but mostly written in the latter half of 1795.   [2] "Machwerk der Kunst."
[3] "Eine so mislungene Form": *Ibid.* pp. 18–21.
[4] *Ibid.* pp. 18–21.
[5] WA. 46, pp. 21–3: *Winckelmann und sein Jahrhundert*, "Antikes".

abilities; he can produce extraordinary results if he combines several gifts; but the unique, the utterly unexpected, he achieves only when all his qualities unite in him in equal force. This last was the fortunate lot of the ancients, especially of the Greeks in their best period. We moderns are forced by Fate to content ourselves with the first two."[1] The highest creation of Nature is man, when he "works as a whole, when he feels himself in the world as in a great, fair, worthy and valuable whole".[2] Modern man attempts the unlimited and, failing, must be content to confine himself to some specialised sphere of activity; the ancients were content to occupy themselves within "the delightful boundaries of the lovely world. Here they had been set; this was their appointed place; here they found room for their energy, material and nourishment for their emotional life."[3] "Feeling and thought were not yet split in pieces, that scarce remediable cleavage in the healthy nature of man had not yet taken place."[4]

How consistently Goethe held to the essence of his Greek creed can be seen when these passages from *Winckelmann und sein Jahrhundert* (1805) are compared with the words in which he described his emotion at sight of the antique stelae in Verona, nearly twenty years before.[5] There the "scarce remediable cleavage" of modern life is symbolised in the knight in armour who casts his eyes to Heaven and awaits the mystical bliss of a resurrection in a better world. The ancients on the other hand, even in their thoughts of death, stayed within the "pleasant boundaries of the lovely world". "There one sees a man, who stands with

---

[1] "Der Mensch vermag gar manches durch zweckmässigen Gebrauch einzelner Kräfte, er vermag das Ausserordentliche durch Verbindung mehrerer Fähigkeiten; aber das Einzige, ganz Unerwartete leistet er nur, wenn sich die sämmtlichen Eigenschaften gleichmässig in ihm vereinigen. Das letzte war das glückliche Los der Alten, besonders der Griechen in ihrer besten Zeit; auf die beiden ersten sind wir Neueren vom Schicksal angewiesen."

[2] "Als ein Ganzes wirkt, wenn er sich in der Welt als in einem grossen, schönen, würdigen und werten Ganzen fühlt."

[3] "Innerhalb der lieblichen Grenzen der schönen Welt. Hieher waren sie gesetzt, hiezu berufen, hier fand ihre Tätigkeit Raum, ihre Leidenschaft Gegenstand und Nahrung."

[4] "Noch fand sich das Gefühl, die Betrachtung nicht zerstückelt, noch war jene kaum heilbare Trennung in der gesunden Menschenkraft nicht vorgegangen."

[5] WA. III, I, pp. 199 foll.

his women-folk and looks out of a niche as though out of a window. There stand father and mother, their son between them, and look at each other with indescribable naturalness. There a couple take each other's hands."[1] In Verona, if not earlier, the sickness of the modern world and the soundness of the ancient were revealed to Goethe. What he saw and learnt in Rome and Sicily confirmed that revelation and enriched it. The necessity for "*Ganzheit*", wholeness, as the complement to antique contentment in the world, came to him in Italy also.[2] In both its senses—both as freedom from the moral conflict and as the ability to develop the human personality in well-balanced universality—Goethe took "wholeness" as his creed during the fifteen years after his return from Italy. In preparatory work for an unwritten essay of 1798 or 1799 he wrote: "The highest idea of man can be attained only through manysidedness, liberality. The Greek was capable of this in his day. The European is still capable of it."[3] It is far truer to say of him than of Winckelmann that his life was "whole and rounded, entirely in the antique manner".[4] Winckelmann was only a scholar of genius. The gift that made him great was confined in its working to a very limited sphere of human activity. But Goethe was a universal genius such as even Greece had not known, except perhaps (who can say?) in Homer. The unfailing energy which is the basic element of genius, found in his case an outlet not only in his poetic gift (which was itself of an extraordinarily universal character); in the realm of the spirit he was not content to accept the condition of an amateur in any branch of natural science or art. In politics, so essential a part of the life of every Greek,[5] he was

---

[1] See above, p. 126.

[2] WA. IV, 8, pp. 231–2, 324. Cf. Korff, *Geist der Goethezeit*, II, p. 321. Herder's clear picture of the Greeks in his *Ideen* (*Werke*, XIV, pp. 92–150), with its emphasis on their many-sided culture (pp. 92, 98, 129) and on the perfect flowering of their culture (pp. 143, 121), no doubt gave Goethe valuable support in clarifying his own conception of the Greeks. Goethe read this part of the *Ideen* in Italy (WA. 32, pp. 105, 110, 112, 113, and IV, 8, p. 233).

[3] WA. 47, p. 292: "Der höchste Begriff vom Menschen kann nur durch Vielseitigkeit, Liberalität erlangt werden.—Dessen war zu seiner Zeit der Grieche fähig.—Der Europäer ist es noch."

[4] WA. 46, 24: "Ganz und abgeschlossen, völlig im Antiken Sinne."

[5] Cf. WA. 46, p. 23, line 3.

conversant with realities through long practice as a minister of
state. It is not fanciful to suppose that his interest in military
life during the years 1792 and 1793 was dictated partly by the
reflexion that every Greek was a soldier, and that this experience
too was necessary to the achievement of "wholeness".

With all the consequence of a German mind he strove to
live as he conceived a Greek would have lived. By a conscious
effort he was trying to win that harmony in Nature to which
the Greek had been born. The Greek had needed only to
follow his instincts, and his life was beautiful. But for the
modern man, who started from a condition of *"Kultur"*
(artificially spoilt life), it was not enough to follow instinct.
This had been the belief of *Sturm und Drang*, and both
Goethe and Schiller had passed beyond that stage. As Korff puts
it,[1] their motto was no longer: "Back to Nature!", but "On
to the second Nature!". This "second Nature" had to be
attained deliberately. Once attained, instinct could be allowed
free play. Moral beauty would exist without effort.

From his comparison of modern and ancient man in *Ueber
naive und sentimentalische Dichtung*, Schiller proceeded to the
real object of his essay, the definition of the two styles of poetic
production, the *naiv*[2] and the "sentimental", which were
illustrated respectively by ancient and modern poetry.[3] The
distinction rests on the difference in outlook between the Greek
and the modern. As the Greek was still part of Nature, content
to seek the satisfaction of all his desires within the world, so his
poetry was the "completest possible imitation of the real
world". For the *"Kulturmensch"* on the other hand, who
cannot regard the world around him or within him as an ideal,
the object must be "the raising of real life to the ideal, in other
words, the representation of the ideal".[4] The *naiv* poet is
content to describe, without intruding his personality on the
listener; the "sentimental" poet cannot refrain from reflexion
and comment, even if for a time he may describe objectively,

---

[1] *Op. cit.* II, p. 306.
[2] I shall spell this word in the German way, whenever it is used in the
special sense given it by Schiller.
[3] With notable exceptions: Horace is the king of "sentimental" poets,
Shakespeare a great *naiv* poet.
[4] *Werke*, xv, p. 28.

for the badness of the world in which he lives makes him burn to preach the ideal at every opportunity.[1] This distinction reminds us irresistibly of Goethe's definition of the difference between ancient and modern poetry as it appears in the *Italienische Reise*: "They portrayed reality, we the effect. They described terrible things, we describe terribly; they pleasant things, we pleasantly, and so on."[2] There is no means of telling whether Goethe actually wrote these words in Naples. Perhaps they were written nearly thirty years later, when he was preparing this part of the *Italienische Reise* for publication. But there can be little doubt that he had already formulated the distinction to himself in this manner before he left Italy. The definition of *naiv* poetry in *Ueber naive und sentimentalische Dichtung* was nothing new to him, and added nothing to his understanding of the Greeks. It was more probably Goethe's exposition of his conception of Greek literary style, which inspired Schiller to defend modern poetry as a fundamentally different, but equally valuable, species.[3] There is evidence that it was a new idea for Goethe to look on modern poetry in this light. It helped to reconcile him with the "sentimental" traits in his own genius.[4] In fact he probably granted Schiller's contention that, in theory at least, "the ideal of beautiful humanity can only arise out of the close combination" of the *naiv* and the "sentimental" character.[5]

The fruits of Schiller's enlivening effect on Goethe's genius were not ripe for gathering until the early part of 1796; but already in the previous year there were diffident buddings of new conceptions. One of these perhaps stands in a closer relationship to Schiller's ideas than is generally realised. This was *Die Befreiung des Prometheus*, with which Goethe was occupied in April 1795.[6] The fragments of this drama that remain,[7] twenty-three lines in all, were probably not written at this time,[8] but the plan at least in its broad outline must have been

[1] *Ibid.* pp. 24 foll. [2] WA. 31, p. 239; see above, p. 163.
[3] Schiller was already considering an essay "Ueber das Naive" in October 1793 (Letter to Körner, 4 Oct. 1793: Jonas, III, p. 360).
[4] Letter to Schiller, 29 Nov. 1795 (WA. IV, 10, p. 339). Cf. Schiller to Humboldt, 9 Jan. 1796 (Jonas, IV, p. 389).
[5] *Werke*, xv, p. 88.
[6] Schiller's letter to Körner, 10 April (Jonas, IV, p. 163).
[7] WA. 11, p. 333. [8] See below, p. 224.

clear in Goethe's mind. Nothing is known of the plan except what can be reconstructed with more or less of certainty from the fragments. We know however from Schiller's letter to Körner that the subject of the play was "the liberation of Prometheus". The best-known account of the liberation is that given by Hesiod,[1] who states that Hercules at Zeus's bidding slew the eagle which daily devoured Prometheus's liver, and "freed the son of Iapetus from his affliction". It is reasonable to assume with Düntzer[2] that this myth was to be the basis of Goethe's plan, although no allusion to it can be made out from the fragments. Why should Goethe have chosen to dramatise this myth at this moment? He was probably reading or at least discussing Aeschylus, and perhaps the *Prometheus Vinctus*, with Humboldt and Schiller just at that time.[3] But he would not have undertaken to write the last play of Aeschylus's trilogy, unless the Greek myth had seemed to him suitable to the expression of some idea that was mightily exercising his spirit. In April 1795 Schiller was at work on the *Aesthetische Briefe*; and Goethe was still full of the wonder and joy that had come over him when he found his own deeply held convictions confirmed and marvellously clarified by Schiller's closely reasoned conclusions. It was inevitable that he should wish to re-express his faith in natural morality in his own way, in poetry. The old tale of Hesiod seemed to give him the right symbols. Prometheus should be civilised man, a role for which he was better fitted than any of the ancient gods and heroes; the eagle was the "scarce remediable cleavage", the rending inner conflict of duty and desire, the enfeebling falsity of civilisation, the destructive Christian doctrine of sin; Hercules, the liberator, must then have spoken with the voice of "aesthetic man"; and when the eagle was laid low, Prometheus would arise whole and free, as man was whole and free, when he had overcome the moral conflict.

So once again Goethe turned to the most ancient myths

---

[1] *Theogony*, lines 526 foll.   [2] *Zur Goetheforschung*, p. 22.
[3] Cf. *G-J.* IX, p. 78. The longest fragments refer to Zeus's desire to mate with Thetis, a step from which Prometheus warned Zeus to desist (*G-J.* IX, p. 81; *Achilleis*, lines 174-9, and Carl Robert, *Vierteljahrschrift für Literaturgeschichte*, I, p. 594). This was a part of the preliminary bargaining which led up to the liberation of Prometheus.

of Greece to find the poetical garment of his thoughts. This was nothing new. But in another way *Die Befreiung des Prometheus* marks a stage on Goethe's Hellenic road. Schiller says it was to be "in ancient Greek style"; and the extant lines represent two fragments of chorus, and two lines in iambic trimeters, the six-footed iambic line peculiar to Greek tragedy. The fragments date from 1797,[1] but the play was probably conceived from the first in Greek form, that is to say, with chorus and perhaps with the dialogue in trimeters instead of five-footed iambics. Never before had Goethe contemplated using the outward forms of Greek tragedy. *Nausikaa*, his most recent plan for a drama with Greek subject, was to have had no chorus and to have been written in blank verse. In 1795 and still in 1797 the execution of his intention was beyond his powers technically. The Greek metres were too foreign to him: in April 1797 he sent Wilhelm von Humboldt the rough draft of a dialogue between Prometheus and the daughters of Oceanus, and asked him to find a metre suitable to it. Further intense study of the Greek tragedians and of the Greek tragic metres was necessary, before Goethe could produce the 190 trimeters of the first version of *Helena*.[2] Nevertheless, by 1795 he had arrived at the conclusion that the Greek tragic form was necessary to the expression of at least a certain type of dramatic idea.

Strengthened by Schiller's tribute to him as the outstanding *naiv* poet of modern times, Goethe turned his energies in 1796 to the production of works of *naiv* art. For a time he considered the possibility of treating the legend of Hero and Leander poetically, whether as epic, as elegy or as drama is not known.[3]

[1] Cf. *G-J.* IX, pp. 77 foll.; x, p. 213; Hermann Henkel, *Studien zur vergleichenden Literaturgeschichte*, 1907, pp. 362 foll.; Düntzer, *Zur Goetheforschung*, 1891, pp. 9 foll. Hermann Henkel dates the fragments 1800, but I find his grounds inadequate. There is no reason why Goethe should not have attempted trimeters in 1797. From May to December of that year he borrowed Tobler's translations of Aeschylus from the library, many of which are in trimeters (*Goethe als Benutzer der Weimarer Bibliothek*, p. 14).

[2] September 1800 (WA. 15, 2, pp. 72 foll.); see below, p. 243.

[3] All that is known of this idea of Goethe's is contained in three references: in Schiller's correspondence with Körner; in a letter of W. Humboldt to his wife, 29 May 1796; and one in a letter of Körner to Goethe. *Schillers Briefe*, IV, p. 451; Bied. I, p. 254; *G-J.* VIII, p. 54. Also *Schiller-Körner Briefwechsel*, III, p. 241.

It may be assumed that the poem was to be a development of those two lines in the third Roman Elegy:

> Hero erblickte Leandern am lauten Fest, und behende
> Stürzte der Liebende sich heiss in die nächtliche Flut.

A sudden blazing up of love; no thought between the lovers but of instant fulfilment; a tragic ending—it was a subject out of which the *naiv* style could well produce something significant. But Goethe gave up the idea, and turned instead to the idyll *Alexis und Dora*, which was written in May 1796.[1] Here too Goethe's object was to portray (*dar-stellen*) the flowering of love between man and woman in a state of unspoilt "Greek" nature.[2] To this "*Darstellung*" belonged not only a description of events but also a portrayal of the emotions experienced by the lovers. Jealousy is by nature one of these emotions and could not be omitted.[3] So too the whole introduction (to line 39), which seems at first reading in the highest degree "sentimental", does not conflict with the nature of *naiv* poetry. The poet stands outside these emotions. He merely "stellt sie dar".

It may be objected that in one respect *Alexis und Dora* is not a purely *naiv* poem. Goethe was preaching an ideal in it, the ideal of the natural morality that follows instincts, in the confident assurance that they are commands of the gods.[4] He does not preach in his own person. He does not interrupt the course of the description to point the moral directly. But the whole poem is a condemnation of the northern-modern world in which Goethe was forced to live. The truly *naiv* Greek poet would have had no other object in writing the poem but the "*Darstellung*" itself for its own sake. The objection is valid. It touches the deepest problem of Goethe's Hellenism. He knew that it was impossible for him to create as a Greek, because he did not live in the Greek world. However free of "sentimentality" he made his poetry, it would still not be *naiv* as Greek poetry is *naiv*. For its *naiv* qualities would be con-

---

[1] WA. I, p. 265. Cf. Gräf, *Lyrik*, I, p. 209 and WA. III, 2, p. 44.
[2] Cf. Korff, *op. cit.* II, p. 331. The local colour is Greek (line 39, "zum Tempel"). Cf. also letter to Schiller, 7 July 1796 (WA. IV, 11, p. 120).
[3] Letter to Schiller, 22 June 1796 (*Ibid.* p. 106).
[4] Lines 110 foll.

sciously achieved. It would be the product of "second Nature", not of the unconscious Nature in which the Greeks lived and worked. Goethe was well aware that in this sense he could never achieve perfect Hellenism, but this did not trouble him. His motto was not: "Back to Hellas!" but "On to the second Hellas!" When he had won to this "second Hellas", he might hope that he would produce poetry as eternally valuable as that of the Greeks.[1]

His success with the *naiv* style in *Alexis und Dora* encouraged Goethe to undertake a much larger work that had been ripening in his mind for some time. *Hermann und Dorothea* was begun on 11 September 1796. In the following nine days six of the nine books were written down, essentially in the form in which they were published. Schiller watched dumbfounded as the hexameters poured out, a hundred and fifty a day.[2] This effortless production showed that Goethe had accomplished what Schiller had foretold[3] would be the hardest part of his great task, the turning of his consciously won Hellenism into the intuitive energy from which alone artistic production could spring. The poem was not finished at this first rush. Goethe let it slumber through the winter, and then finished it (all but a hundred hexameters) in the first two weeks of March 1797. At first he spoke of it as the "great idyll"[4], but already by 28 September 1796 it was to him "the epic poem".[5] From the first indeed Homer was its godfather. In the previous summer Goethe's interest in Homer had been powerfully quickened by the "Homeric controversy", which broke out early in the year on the appearance of F. A. Wolf's famous *Prolegomena*, and by his meeting in May with Wolf himself. In the Elegy *Hermann und Dorothea*[6] Goethe gives us to understand that in writing his German epic he felt himself to be the last of the Homeridae, those gifted singers who developed the Homeric poems from their original kernel to

---

[1] A keen-sighted observer (the Marquis de Custine) remarked of Goethe in 1814: "On pourrait le croire naïf: il est pourtant à une distance immense de la naïveté; en lui tout est volonté et conscience de la volonté" (*Jrb. der G-G.* 1938, p. 301).
[2] Letter to Körner, 28 Oct. 1796 (Jonas, v, p. 97).
[3] Letter to Goethe, 23 Aug. 1794.
[4] *Tagebuch*, 9 Sept. 1796 (WA. III, p. 47). [5] WA. IV, II, p. 48.
[6] Written November 1796 (WA. I, p. 293).

the extent and form which they now possess. *Hermann und Dorothea* does in fact remind us irresistibly of the *Odyssey* in a variety of ways. It will be worth while to establish exactly the extent and nature of Goethe's imitation of Homer in this greatest of all his Hellenising poems.

The un-Homeric elements in *Hermann und Dorothea* are not hard to define. In the first place the scene is laid in Germany; the time is the immediate present. The social and political questions that play so large a part in the poem are those which the French Revolution had raised, and which were burning in the mind of every German. The characters are typical men and women from a prosperous small country town of the time. Their emotions and actions fill us with no sense of strangeness, as of people from a different state of culture from our own. The complete Germanity of the setting was the reason for the delight with which Goethe's countrymen greeted the poem when it appeared.

In such a modern setting gods and goddesses in Homeric style were of course unthinkable. But Goethe was right in feeling that by their absence the poem lost an epic trait of great importance. The hovering fear of the French Revolution and foreign invasion, "chance" that brings the lovers together for the second time,[1] are poor substitutes for the "physical-poetical power" of the ancient gods.[2] In this matter Goethe deserted Homer by necessity, not choice.

The subject itself is not "epic" in the manner of the *Iliad* and *Odyssey*. It lacks their complexity. It is a single theme which develops and moves to its conclusion without a pause, more in the manner of the drama than the epic.[3] Its *milieu* is idyllic rather than epic, for which reason Goethe first spoke of it as the "great idyll". In the *Iliad* we are in the centre of great events. Kings and heroes struggle together and are killed; the tide of battle ebbs and flows; the gods themselves mingle in the conflict, and give it more than human significance. The central figure of the *Odyssey* is a king and hero, a unique figure in the history of his age. He moves among gods and giants and princes. His wanderings take him beyond the verge

---

[1] Victor Hehn, *Goethe's Hermann und Dorothea*, 1893, p. 77.
[2] Letter to Schiller, 23 Dec. 1797 (WA. IV, 12, p. 384).
[3] Cf. the same letter to Schiller.

of earth, and culminate in a mighty slaying. Schiller's *Frederi-
ciade*, the epic that he never wrote, would in this way have been
more Homeric than *Hermann und Dorothea*. Goethe's "epic"
world is an island of peaceful human life, upon whose shores
waves from the ocean of great events, stirred by a distant
storm, lap with more than customary insistence.

The interest of the poem lies rather within the hearts of the
characters than in their actions. This too Goethe recognised as
an un-epic trait.[1] It justified, in his view, the scarcity of similes,
of which a bare six can be counted in the nine books.

Despite all these points of difference, *Hermann und Dorothea*
reminds us of Homer in many ways. It is Homeric; and
Goethe meant it to be. Goethe had discovered the secret of
Homer's art in Sicily. It was based on his power to reproduce
the world around him in words with a "terrifying clarity and
inner understanding". Since the Greek world was an almost
perfect expression of Nature's intentions, Homer needed only
to be *naiv*, and his poetry could not help being ideal; that is, it
would express perfectly those ideas or intentions which Nature
did not always succeed in bringing to faultless manifestation.[2]
In *Hermann und Dorothea* Goethe set out to compose in the
same way. This was the most fundamental manner in which
he imitated Homer in this poem. But his problem was not so
simple as Homer's; for in Goethe's opinion the German world
of his own day was in no way a perfect expression of Nature's
intentions, as Homer's had been. If the *naiv* style was to produce
something ideal, a most careful selection must be made of the
aspects of the world which were to be described. Homer had
painted men of all kinds and degrees from kings to swineherds,
and all had been in their different ways representatives of ideal
humanity. But whole classes of men were useless to Goethe,
kings and nobles most of all, since among them the disease of
artificiality had most completely undermined the healthy
nature of man. Wherever civilisation had produced the "scarce
remediable cleavage", as amongst the well-to-do dwellers in
great cities and all the "cultured" who wept with Pamela
and Werther, there was no material for the *naiv* poet. So
Goethe sought his "natural men" in one of the classes of society

[1] WA. IV, 12, p. 384; and cf. WA. 41, 2, p. 221.
[2] For a fuller discussion of this point, see above, p. 163.

where they were still to be found: among the prosperous citizens of a small country town.[1] The men and women in *Hermann und Dorothea* have the same outlook on life as Homer's characters. Their existence is still inextricably bound to that of inconscient Nature: they plough and sow the earth; they care for their own horses; they watch the weather; their labours and their joys are physical.[2] Yet they are not rude peasants. They are well enough off to be free from deadening drudgery or the fear of want, but not so wealthy as to entertain any sentimental notions about the beauty of being poor.[3]

So their closeness to Nature develops in them a natural fineness of feeling, an instinctive goodness, that holds them nearer to God than all the theorisings of cultured man can do. Hermann, like Schiller's ideal, desires only what is fitting for him.[4] Even the Parson, the representative of that religion which, in Goethe's view, had done so much to destroy man's inner unity, is filled with a natural and healthy wisdom that is based on his knowledge of men, and untroubled by the demands of impossible ideals. It is he who defends man's instincts as guides, since they often lead us aright, where conscious reasoning would fail.[5] Perhaps he is intended as the representative of "second Nature" amongst the completely *naiv* countrymen. He is an educated man, and knows not only the Bible but also "the best worldly writings". Homeric, but also true to Nature, is the directness with which the characters express their feelings. No false politeness restrains them, even when they are displeased: "Keinesweges denk' ich wie euch und tadle die Rede", says Hermann to the apothecary.[6] So Odysseus, when Euryalus has displeased him, exclaims: "Stranger, thou hast not spoken well. Thou seemest a man of little wit."[7] Yet Goethe's men, like Homer's, are far more than courteous. They are thoughtful of their fellows in small

---

[1] Gesang v, lines 31–6.
[2] Victor Hehn, *op. cit.* p. 104; cf. *Ueber epische und dramatische Dichtung*: WA. 41, 2, p. 221.
[3] Gesang II, lines 164–85. 　　　　[4] Gesang v, line 65.
[5] Gesang I, lines 84 foll.; cf. v, lines 10 foll.
[6] Gesang II, line 98; cf. II, line 246: "In no wise do I think as you do, and I censure your words."
[7] *Od.* VIII, 166.

things, and generous to help, when help is needed. Their joy in Nature is not a sentimental, but a real one.

> Immer noch wandelte sie auf eigenem Boden und freute
> Sich der eigenen Saat und des herrlich nickenden Kornes,
> Das mit goldener Kraft sich im ganzen Felde bewegte.[1]

The great pear tree, under which the mother finds Hermann is not praised for its beauty, the colour of its foliage, the grace of its stem and branches. It is noteworthy because it is a landmark in the neighbourhood, because of its fruit, and because of its wide shade, in which man and beast seek relief from the heat of noon.[2]

Goethe had hoped to bring from Sicily "shadow pictures of this blest abode" from which he could reproduce the ideal, even when he was back among the Cimmerian mists.[3] Now was the time to use these pictures, to give the German landscape, the German weather, all the externals of German life, something of the Sicilian quality. Here again selection was necessary. The scene is laid in the Rhineland, where Germany is at her most smiling, and every prospect is framed by a distant range of mountains.[4] The moment selected is high summer, just at harvest time, when the corn is ripe and the grapes are swelling and darkening:

> Solch ein Wetter ist selten zu solcher Ernte gekommen,
> Und wir bringen die Frucht herein, wie das Heu schon herein ist,
> Trocken; der Himmel ist hell, es ist kein Wölkchen zu sehen,
> Und von Morgen wehet der Wind mit lieblicher Kühlung.[5]

And when the sky is darkened and rain comes, it does not drizzle down half-heartedly in the northern manner out of a clinging pall of mist, but comes in storm with the life-giving power of Jupiter Pluvius; and the sun will shine again after it has passed.

---

[1] Gesang IV, lines 49–51: "Still she was walking over her own land, and rejoiced at sight of her own crops and the gloriously bending corn, that swayed in golden strength over the whole field."

[2] Gesang IV, lines 53–8; cf. IV, lines 77–80.

[3] WA. 31, p. 91. [4] Gesang IV, line 62.

[5] Gesang I, lines 45–48: "Such weather has seldom come with such a harvest. We bring in the corn, as we did the hay, dry. The sky is clear, there is no cloud to see; from morning on the breeze blows with delicious coolness."

In order to create his ideal world in the *naiv* style, Goethe adopted certain of Homer's mannerisms. Most noticeable of these is the tendency to idealise the material world; Steckner[1] calls it the "optimistische Sehweise".

> Hermann eilte zum Stalle sogleich, wo die *mutigen* Hengste
> Ruhig standen und *rasch* den *reinen* Hafer verzehrten
> Und das *trockene* Heu, auf der *besten* Wiese gehauen.[2]

So in the rest of this description: the bits are bright, the buckles beautifully silvered, the reins long and rather broad; the groom is willing; the carriage moves easily, the traces are polished and the seats roomy. Like the *Iliad* and *Odyssey*, *Hermann und Dorothea* is larded with such passages of idealising description.[3] They give an impression of a world in which man's material surroundings are finely devised, perfectly executed, and always in faultless condition. Goethe paints the opposite of this happy state in the condition of the refugees;[4] but these are men and women reduced to extremities by misfortune, like Odysseus at his landing on Scheria. The normal state of human existence which Goethe portrays, is naïvely ideal like that of the Phaeacians or of the princes whom Telemachus visited on his search for Odysseus.

Hermann und Dorothea owes its Homeric character in part also to the poet's leisurely delight in description for its own sake. There is no anxious hastening on with the story. Each moment is an end in itself; and every detail that can make the moment more present to the listener is worthy of inclusion. This quality of "epic breadth"[5] is to be observed throughout the poem. One example will illustrate it as well as another. Goethe requires five hexameters to tell us that the parson and the apothecary sat down beside the landlord and his wife and that the apothecary spoke:

> Freundlich kamen heran die beiden und grüssten das Ehpaar,
> Setzten sich auf die Bänke, die hölzernen, unter dem Torweg,

---

[1] *Der epische Stil von Hermann und Dorothea*, by Hans Steckner, Leipzig, 1927, p. 196: "Optimistic manner of seeing."

[2] "Hermann hurried at once to the stables, where the spirited stallions stood quietly and ate with speed the pure oats and the dry hay cut from the best meadow" (Gesang v, lines 132–4).

[3] Gesänge I, lines 166–71; II, lines 22–6; III, lines 81–3; v, lines 169–76.

[4] Gesang I, lines 102–50.   [5] Steckner, *op. cit.* p. 188.

Staub von den Füssen schüttelnd und Luft mit dem Tuche sich
fächelnd.
Da begann denn zuerst, nach wechselseitigen Grüssen
Der Apotheker zu sprechen und sagte, beinahe verdriesslich.[1]

So Homer (to take but one instance out of hundreds) is not
content to say merely that Agamemnon cut the throats of the
lambs for sacrifice. He adds that they lay on the ground
"gasping and failing of breath; for the bronze had robbed them
of their strength".[2] In his later theorising Goethe defined the
basic law of epic poetry as being this freedom from all desire to
arrive at an objective, this perfect contentment in the moment.[3]
In the design of the true epic poem this law produced the subsidiary law of "retarding motives",[4] the importance of which
Goethe had not realised when he wrote *Hermann und Dorothea*;[5]
in the style, it produced this "epic breadth", which Goethe
had perceived in Homer, in time to reproduce it in *Hermann
und Dorothea*.

From the enumeration and discussion of these points of
contact between *Hermann und Dorothea* and Homer, we begin
to see in what way Goethe "imitated" Homer in this poem.
It is not a mechanical copying but an imitation from the idea
outwards, a re-creation of epic poetry from a vision of its
essential nature, derived from the study of Homer. The men
and women, as we have seen, are not Homeric characters; they
lack especially the heroic quality.[6] Goethe created his characters,
as Homer had done, from the vision of man, which he had
acquired partly by his own observations but largely by his
study of Homer. So too the natural setting is not Homeric
but German. Yet the German countryside is treated so that it
becomes "*Urlandschaft*". This too was a vision which Goethe

---

[1] Gesang I, lines 65–9: "In friendly fashion the two came up and greeted
man and wife, and sat down on the wooden seats under the doorway,
shaking the dust from their feet and fanning themselves with their hand-
kerchieves. Then after greetings on both sides the apothecary began first to
speak and said, almost in anger."
[2] *Il.* III, 294.
[3] Letter to Schiller, 22 April 1797 (WA. IV, 12, p. 93).
[4] *Ibid.* p. 91; WA. 41, 2, p. 221; *Ueber epische und dramatische Dichtung*,
1797.
[5] WA. IV, 12, pp. 383–4.
[6] In spite of Dorothea's "Heldentat" (Gesang VI, lines 108–18).

owed to his reading of Homer. The tendency to "idealising description" is a direct imitation of the Homeric style; but Goethe would not have chosen to imitate Homer in this, if he had not seen that the idea of epic poetry could be realised only if it had to deal with an ideal material world. Here too he was working in obedience rather to his conception of epic poetry than to blind reverence for Homeric practice. The Homeric poems were in short not his direct models. The idea of epic poetry was revealed in them with extraordinary clarity. But the idea is always more than any single manifestation. *Iliad* and *Odyssey* are not a complete or perfect expression of the idea. So in April 1797 Goethe wrote to Schiller. "The fact that those great poems...could not be brought to perfect and complete unity [of plan]...does not prove that a poem of this kind can and should in no circumstances be perfect and complete."[1] The modern Homerid must therefore not copy Homer, but must rise through study of Homer and by the power of his genius to perception of the idea that lies behind and above the great models, and re-create epic poetry from that perception. After he had finished *Hermann und Dorothea*, Goethe attempted to define the ideas of both epic and dramatic poetry in the short essay: *Ueber epische und dramatische Dichtung*.[2]

It may be said that Goethe's choice of the hexameter for the treatment of so German a narrative is an obvious example of sterile imitation of Homeric form. Goethe would have denied this vigorously. For him the hexameter was the only possible metre for the poetic treatment of an epic subject.[3] Its steady but varied flow, and the length of its swing from one wave-crest to the next, favour the effortless unfolding of a narrative and the essential absorption in the moment, as no other metre could do. It is significant that Goethe first conceived *die Jagd*

---

[1] WA. IV, 12, p. 105: "Denn daraus dass jene grossen Gedichte erst nach und nach entstanden sind, und zu keiner vollständigen und vollkommenen Einheit haben gebracht werden können (obgleich beide vielleicht weit vollkommner organisiert sind als man denkt), folgt noch nicht: dass ein solches Gedicht auf keine Weise vollständig, vollkommen und Eins werden könne noch solle."

[2] WA. 41, 2, pp. 220–4. Cf. Schiller to Goethe, 5 May 1797 (Jonas, v pp. 187 foll.).

[3] Steckner, *op. cit.* p. 77. Cf. Schiller to Humboldt, 21 March 1796 (Jonas, IV, p. 434).

as an epic poem in hexameters; only when he began to realise that it was not a truly epic subject, did he think of casting it in the romantic form of rhymed strophes.[1] The hexameter was as much a part of the idea of epic poetry as the technique of *naiv* description and the figure of the "*Urmensch*". If the Greeks had not evolved it, it would have been necessary for later poets to do so. As Goethe was here too not imitating but re-creating, he was not so much concerned with metrical correctness as with the achievement of a general effect similar to that of Homer's hexameters. The hexameters of *Hermann und Dorothea* are more correct, according to the rules of the contemporary prosodists, than those of *Reinecke Fuchs*; but in comparison with those of the *Achilleis*, they are full of mistakes.[2] They represent perhaps a happy blending of freedom with observance of rules derived from classical models.[3]

There are of course certain imitations and borrowings from Homer which are merely imitations, and cannot be explained as aspects of "re-creation from the idea". There are compound adjectives as "wohlgezimmert", which are translations of Homeric adjectives; and others ("wohlumzäumt", "allverderblich"), which Goethe coined on the Homeric model. Some Homeric phrases he adopted literally: "geflügelte Worte" for ἔπεα πτεροεντα; "süsses Verlangen ergriff sie" from καί με γλυκὺς ἵμερος αἱρεῖ. "Die rasche Kraft der Pferde" is a circumlocution formed on the analogy of such expressions as "μένος 'Αλκινοοῖο". It amused Goethe to enrich the German language with these Homerisms; and at the same time by their naïvely visual quality they helped the epic tone of the poem.

But Goethe was not dependent on such superficial imitation for the achievement of his great object, the re-birth of Homeric art in the modern world. He deliberately avoided some of the most characteristic of Homer's mannerisms. The conventional epithet is for instance most sparingly used, except in the case of the mother, who is usually "die gute Mutter" or "die gute verständige Mutter". The verbatim repetition of a whole

---

[1] Letters to Schiller, 22 and 27 June 1797 (WA. IV, 12, pp. 168, 170), and Gräf, *Epos*, I, 212 foll. Cf. Bied. I, p. 255, and Eckermann, 15 Jan. 1827.

[2] Andreas Heusler, *Deutscher und antiker Vers*, Strassburg, 1917, pp. 36, 95, 101, 102, 107, 112, 115. See also Appendix B, p. 298.

[3] Steckner, *op. cit.* pp. 79, 82.

passage, so common in Homer, occurs only once in *Hermann und Dorothea*, in the minute description of Dorothea's costume.[1] The emphasis thus laid on this passage reveals Goethe's attitude to such superficial copying. He is amused, as Hehn has pointed out,[2] by the slight disproportion which arises between the modern material and the unassimilated antique form. Stomacher, bodice and frilled shirt stand out quaintly in a passage of *naiv* description in the Homeric style.

Direct reminiscences of Homeric situations are very rare in *Hermann und Dorothea*. The harnessing of the horses[3] suggests the similar scene in the *Odyssey*;[4] but the correspondence is not remarkably close. Goethe's description would not have fallen out very differently, if there had been no Homeric model; for when two people give *naiv* accounts of the same series of actions, their accounts are naturally alike. On the other hand Hermann's relation of his own prowess as a boy, when he chastised his ill-bred companions for laughing at his father and they "howled with bloody noses",[5] is undoubtedly a reminiscence of that moving passage in the *Odyssey*,[6] in which the shade of Achilles complains of his lot, because he cannot return to earth to protect his aged father from ill-treatment at the hands of insolent men. Again Goethe laughs at himself for such superficial imitation. With delicate humour the German country lad is compared to the man-slaying hero of the Achaeans, the bloody noses of his small schoolfellows to the revenge that Achilles would have taken on his enemies, if he had had "such strength as once was mine, when I slew the best of the host in defence of the Argives".

The absence of reminiscences in *Hermann und Dorothea* is remarkable, when one considers the importance which Goethe attached to this form of borrowing from ancient sources at the time of his work on the *Römische Elegien*.[7] Moreover the later works of his Hellenistic period, the *Achilleis* and *Helena*, are again full of reminiscences. For a brief moment Goethe was raised above the necessity of such laborious gleaning. In the

---

[1] Gesang v, lines 168–76 and vi, lines 137–45.
[2] Hehn, *op. cit.* pp. 125, 127.   [3] Gesang v, lines 132–43.
[4] *Od.* vi, 71 foll.; cf. *Il.* v, 722–32.
[5] Gesang iv, lines 155–62.   [6] *Od.* xi, 501–3.
[7] See above, p. 184.

great upsurge of energy which came with Schiller's friendship, Goethe's genius achieved the end towards which it had been struggling, and mated at last with the spirit of ancient Greece. No matter then how modern or how German his material, the flame of Hellas would pass through it all and purify it; the ore would be gold and he could mould it to the eternal forms. *Hermann und Dorothea* is the crown of Goethe's Hellenism. It is the justification for the battle that he had fought for twenty years, to tame his northern genius and teach it Greek ways. Could he have been content with this victory, could he have realised that this was all that Hellenism could give him, that in achieving this blending of his own genius with the spirit of Greece he had accomplished his task, could he in fact have stood still for a while and bid the moment stay; he might have produced in the next few years other works as great as *Hermann und Dorothea*; and he would have spared himself fruitless toil and final disappointment. But his spirit could never rest. In the moment of achievement the thing achieved became worthless to him, and he saw a new goal before him. *Hermann und Dorothea* was hardly done when he started on a still more intense pursuit of the Greek ideal. To write as a German under the guidance of the Greek ideal, no longer satisfied him. He would write now as a Greek; he would continue the *Iliad*; he would add jewels to the broken necklace of Greek tragedy. The possible had been granted him. Now, still Faust at heart for all his Hellenism, he would accomplish the impossible.

C. CRISIS AND FAILURE

In the summer and autumn of 1797 Goethe set to work to codify his beliefs on the nature and proper practice of the plastic arts. His aesthetic ideas had attained their final form in Italy; but the essays which he published in the *Teutscher Merkur* on his return to Weimar[1] are in no way an exhaustive exposition of these ideas. During the following years he com-

---

[1] *Zur Theorie der bildenden Kunst*, WA. 47, pp. 60–76; *Einfache Nachahmung der Natur, Manier, Stil*, ibid. pp. 77–83; *Ueber die bildende Nachahmung des Schönen von C. P. Moritz*, ibid. pp. 84–90; *Ueber Christus und die zwölf Apostel*, ibid. pp. 227–34; *Von Arabesken*, ibid. 235–41; *Frauenrollen auf dem römischen Theater durch Männer gespielt*, ibid. pp. 269–74.

municated his aesthetic theories only to Meyer. Their correspondence contains many important utterances on the subject.
But it was not until Schiller's friendship gave him courage again
to work for the good and the true, that Goethe roused himself
to write down and to publish his ideas on art. Even these
essays, which appeared in, or were intended for, the *Propyläen*,
do not form a logically developed theory of art in its nature
and application. Goethe's fundamental conception of the
function of art in the world could not be discussed in the ante-
chamber of the temple.[1] Nevertheless a fairly complete picture
of his beliefs can be put together from these essays and fragments. In particular the position of Greek art in the whole
structure is clear enough.

"Re-creation from the idea" was here, as in literature, the
basic conception in Goethe's theory and practice. Mechanical
imitation of the visible world was not art in its highest sense;
nor yet could this high title be claimed by "*Manier*", a system
of conventional formulas that represented nothing but the
artist's individual manner of seeing and expressing the world.[2]
The artist who would deserve the name, must know how to
see through the confusion of phenomena to the ideas or intentions that strive unsuccessfully to find expression in the
world and so "rivalling Nature, to bring forth something
spiritually organic".[3] This highest art, which "seizes the object
on that plane where it is stripped of all that is common and
individual",[4] was understood and practised by the Greeks as
by no other race.[5]

The stupendous task of re-expressing Nature's intentions in
sculpture or painting was fulfilled by the Greeks with extraordinary ease. This was due only in small part to the excellence
of their technical methods, though this excellence was assumed
by Goethe not only in sculpture but also in painting. Both
Goethe and Meyer at this time denied that the Greeks had
understood less about painting than the moderns;[6] their under-

---

[1] Cf. WA. 47, p. 5.   [2] *Ibid.* pp. 77-79, 82, 83.
[3] "Etwas geistig Organisches": *Ibid.* p. 12 in *Einleitung in die Propyläen*.
[4] "Man fasst ihn auf der Höhe, wo er von allem Gemeinen und Indivi-
duellen entkleidet [ist]."
[5] *Ueber die Gegenstände der bildenden Kunst, Ibid.* pp. 91, 92.
[6] *Schr. der G-G.* XXXII, p. 175; WA. II, 3, p. 120. By 1803 Goethe had
modified his claims for Greek painting (*Polygnot,* WA. 48, pp. 100, 102),

standing of the mysteries of colour-harmony was believed by Goethe to be greater than that of any modern painter or scientist.[1]

Their success in expressing the ideal was due to the instinctive rightness with which they chose their subjects. In the first place they knew exactly what could, and what could not, be expressed in paint or marble. They avoided the fault so often made by modern artists of trying to express moral ideas in a sensual medium. Only certain moral ideas are suitable to representation by the plastic arts, namely those "which are most closely related to the sensual world and permit of expression through form and attitude".[2] The Greeks knew that a work of plastic art must express everything in and by itself.[3] The supreme example of such a self-expressing work of art was the Laocoön.

Goethe believed, as we have seen,[4] that the statues of the gods were the greatest contribution of the Greek genius to art and to the human race. They were a revelation, for those who had eyes to see, of the ultimate nature of the world and of man in it. When the brothers Riepenhausen dared to suggest that Greek art was incapable of symbolising such profound truths, which had become the property of art only with the revelation of the Christian religion, Goethe's ire was roused and he thundered against the "neo-catholic sentimentality" and "das klosterbrudrisirende, sternbaldisirende Unwesen".[5] Nevertheless he never expounded his doctrine of ideal characters in public. In the *Propyläen* essays there is hardly a hint of this inner teaching. It was the mystical basis of Goethe's aesthetic creed, and it was not communicable to all and sundry. The statues of the gods are not often cited by Goethe in these essays.

though in 1808 he still resented the commonly repeated assertion that in painting the Greeks had not been the equals of the moderns (Bied. II, p. 12).
   [1] *Schr. der G-G.* XXXII, pp. 175, 195, 208, 217, 270; WA. II, 3, pp. 61, 108–23, especially pp. 116, 120.
   [2] *Schr. der G-G.* XXXII, p. 37. Cf. *Einleitung in die Propyläen*, WA. 47, p. 18.
   [3] *Schr. der G-G.* XXXII, p. 28: "Man sollte sich nicht etwas *bei* dem Bilde denken."   [4] See above, pp. 177–8.
   [5] WA. 48, p. 122: *Herzensergiessungen eines kunstliebenden Klosterbruders* by Wackenroder and Tieck's *Franz Sternbald* were the two works in which the standard of Romantic medievalism in art was raised against Classicism.

Their pre-excellence is assumed; they are "the first and favourite subjects of sculpture";[1] but no analysis of their greatness is given.

In the less lofty subjects of human action and suffering the Greek genius showed itself no less supreme; and Goethe was eager to point out the reasons for this excellence. His ideas found their most consequent expression in the essay *Ueber Laokoon*[2] and in his reconstruction of the wall-paintings of the fifth-century Athenian painter, Polygnotus.[3] In both these works Goethe admired above all the profundity of the conception and the wisdom with which the central theme was set off by balancing or contrasting secondary motives. In the paintings by Polygnotus Goethe admitted that the technique must have been so crude that the composition can have had no unity of visible form but only of thought and feeling.[4] Nevertheless the idea itself was so powerful in its simplicity, yet so rich in effective motives, that Goethe recommended it and similar "simple-lofty and profound-naïve" subjects with eager insistence to the artists of his day. We need quote only a short passage, from his comments on the central painting, the "Glorification of Helen", to illustrate what it was that Goethe most admired in Greek works of art of this kind. The moment chosen by the artist is after the sack of Troy, when the Greeks are about to sail home with their booty. The captured Trojan women are shown, herded together, bewailing their lot. Wounded Trojans, the last remnant of that glorious army that for ten years successfully resisted the Greek attack, are also shown in captivity. "And all this suffering of body and spirit, for whose sake is it endured? For a woman's sake, the symbol of the highest beauty. There she sits, a queen again, waited on and surrounded by her maids, admired by a former lover and suitor, greeted with awe by a herald....Among the crowd of captives she sits as a queen, in whose power it lies to loose and to bind. Every sin against her majesty brings the bitterest consequences; her sin is wiped out by her presence....Up to this moment the

---

[1] WA. 47, p. 105.
[2] Published in the *Propyläen*, Stück 1, 1798: WA. 47, pp. 101-17.
[3] *Polygnots Gemälde in der Lesche zu Delphi.* 1803, published in the *Jena Allgemeine Litteratur-Zeitung*: WA. 48, pp. 83-122.
[4] *Ibid.* p. 104.

object of a destructive war, she now appears as the fairest prize of victory; raised upon heaps of dead and of captives, she sits enthroned at the summit of her power. All is forgiven and forgotten; for she is there again."[1] Every subsidiary figure was designed by position and association to impress on the onlooker this central idea.

The Laocoön group shows the same grandeur of conception and the same faultless planning of the means of execution. These qualities, together with the technical mastery of the material, made it in Goethe's view a perfect work, from which one could deduce all the laws of art.[2] It is not necessary for my purpose to discuss the whole of Goethe's analysis of the group. That has often been done before; and it would throw little light on Goethe's conception of the Greeks, except to emphasise the fact that he held them to have been all-wise and all-competent in matters of art. Two points alone need be stressed.

The first conception of the Laocoön group was great in Goethe's eyes, because the artists had stripped the subject of all its local and secondary associations such as Laocoön's priesthood, his Trojan nationality, and all the special circumstances of the fable, and so permitted the purely human aspect of the situation to receive all the emphasis of their art. Laocoön "is nothing of all that the myth makes him to be. It is a father with two sons in danger of succumbing to two dangerous beasts."[3] Two aspects of the Greek genius were illustrated by this: its instinct for seizing the ideal essence of a subject, before it has become confused and obscured by the world;[4] and its insistence on man as the sole subject for artistic representation, and as the adequate measure of all things.

In the essay *Ueber Laokoon* Goethe touched for the first time on a point which is of fundamental importance for a proper understanding of his view of the Greeks. The artist's genius, he wrote, "shows itself in its highest energy and dignity, when it...knows how to *moderate and restrain the passionate outbursts of man's nature* in its artistic representation."[5] We are carried back by these words to that old controversy begun by Winckelmann and pursued by Lessing, in which Goethe as a lad of

---

[1] *Ibid.* pp. 107–9; cf. p. 105.   [2] WA. 47, p. 103.
[3] *Ibid.* p. 106.
[4] *Ibid.* p. 91, quoted above, p. 216.   [5] *Ibid.* p. 116.

twenty had thought of taking part: the controversy over the reason for Laocoön's half-closed mouth. Since that lost essay and the remarks in the *Ephemerides*,[1] Goethe had shown little interest in the subject. Now his attention had been brought back to the whole question by an essay published in the *Horen*[2] and written by the antiquarian, Aloys Ludwig Hirt, whom Goethe had known in Rome. In this essay, the subject of which was also the Laocoön group, Hirt roundly denied that the expression on Laocoön's face was toned down (*gemildert*) at all; Laocoön did not scream, because he could not scream; and he could not scream, because he was in the last agony, about to succumb to the poison of the snake's bite.[3] The moment chosen was in fact the most terrible of the whole gruesome tale. From this Hirt proceeded to deny that beauty, as Lessing had held, or "noble simplicity and quiet greatness", in Winckelmann's phrase, was the basic principle in Greek art. "Individuality of meaning, and character"[4] was its peculiarity.[5] The thought or meaning peculiar to, or characteristic of, the subject to be treated, had to be expressed as clearly and fully as possible. So if the artist chose to portray the destruction of a father and his two sons by monstrous snakes, a subject in the highest degree tragic and horrible, his object must be to convey the tragedy and horror of it to the onlooker with the greatest possible force and clarity.

Goethe was impressed by Hirt and by his essay. He and Schiller agreed that character and individual meaning ought to be stressed as qualities of Greek art, as the tendency at the time was to regard Greek art as only ideal.[6] But he held Hirt's point of view to be one-sided; and as he developed his own views, while at work on his Laocoön essay, he came more and more to feel the danger of Hirt's theories. He replied to them not only in *Ueber Laokoon* but also in *der Sammler und die Seinigen*, where Hirt appears, somewhat unsympathetically sketched, as the "*Charakteristiker*". In Goethe's view Hirt applied the principle of ideal characters too pedantically, so

---

[1] See above, p. 47.
[2] 1797, Stück 10, pp. 1–25.
[3] Pp. 7 foll.
[4] "Individuellheit der Bedeutung, Karakteristik."
[5] Pp. 11, 12.
[6] *Goethe-Schiller Briefwechsel*, 1 to 8 July 1797; especially Schiller to Goethe, 7 July, and Goethe's reply.

that with certain subjects, particularly terrible subjects like the
Laocoön, he was forced to attribute to great works of art a
purpose and meaning which was incompatible with the highest
function of art. If the Laocoön group really were as Hirt held
it to be, "it would deserve to be instantly broken in pieces".[1]
Goethe demanded that terrible subjects such as the stories of
Laocoön and of Niobe should be treated so that they should
make a pleasant impression on the eye and mind. This was
achieved by the Greeks by careful consideration of principles
of symmetry, balance, contrast of masses and so on, by all in
fact that could give the work beauty or "*Anmut*" of appearance.
He held the Laocoön group to be "a model of symmetry and
variety, repose and movement, contrasts and gradations, which
together impress themselves on the onlooker, some through
his senses and some through his mind, and so alongside the
high emotional content of the representation arouse a sensation
of pleasure, and moderate the storm of suffering and passion
through beauty both sensual and spiritual".[2] The spiritual
means adopted to moderate the impression of terror that such
a subject could produce, were illustrated in the Laocoön group
by the condition of the two sons. "In order to moderate the
violent impression of terror (aroused by the sufferings of the
father), it inspires pity for the condition of the younger son,
and anxiety for the elder, while yet leaving some hope for his
survival."[3] It was the business of art to please and uplift even
in representations of terrible subjects. This the Greeks had
known and had proved not only in their sculpture but also in
their tragedies. The subjects chosen by the tragedians were
often intolerable and loathsome. But the tragedies themselves
are not loathsome nor even terrible. "Of course if one sees
in poetry only the material out of which the poem is formed,
if one speaks of the work of art as though one had experienced
what it portrayed, in real life instead of through its medium, then

---

[1] *Sammler*, WA. 47, p. 167.
[2] *Laokoon, Ibid.* p. 105. Cf. *ibid.* pp. 162 foll.: "Ein Muster von
Symmetrie und Mannigfaltigkeit, von Ruhe und Bewegung, Gegensätzen
und Stufengängen, die sich zusammen teils sinnlich teils geistig, dem
Beschauer darbieten, bei dem hohen Pathos der Vorstellung eine angenehme
Empfindung erregen, und den Sturm der Leiden und Leidenschaft durch
Anmut und Schönheit mildern."
[3] *Ibid.* p. 115.

even the tragedies of Sophocles can be made out to be loathsome and horrible." But they are not, for the treatment of the
material makes everything not merely tolerable but beautiful.[1]
Goethe does not defend more fully the necessity for this
"law of moderating beauty".[2] The fact that it prevents a
work of art from arousing "unpleasant sensations" in the
onlooker, is apparently sufficient justification. This may hardly
seem the case to us, for some degree of sincerity must be
sacrificed to it in such subjects as the Laocoön. But Goethe
was afraid of such "unpleasant sensations", still more of any
art whose object it was to produce them. The acute susceptibility that was the basis of his genius in the days of *Sturm und
Drang*, had not grown less with the years, though it had
perhaps been driven deeper underground. It was there still,
ready to respond to any sudden stimulus and to break through
in all its old terrifying force. Men like Hirt knew nothing of
such dangers. But the Greeks had known. They had felt the
cruelty of life with souls sensitive by nature to pain no less
than to joy. They had not tried to shut their eyes to suffering.
They had used it, as all great artists must, as material for their
art; but they had created out of it, not something that made the
world more horrible to live in, but something that enriched
man's life and strengthened him to endure and to enjoy, by
showing that new life, new beauty, new greatness could grow
even out of pain and death. The ancient artist who adorned a
sarcophagus with the destruction of Niobe's children achieved
thereby the "greatest audacity of art".[3] "Art adorns no longer
with flowers and fruits, but with corpses of men, with the greatest
catastrophe that can overtake a father and mother, the sight of
a blooming family reft at one stroke from before their eyes."[4]

---

[1] WA. 47, pp. 167, 168: "Freilich, wenn man in der Poesie nur den Stoff
erblickt, der dem Gedichteten zum Grund liegt, wenn man vom Kunstwerke
spricht, als hätte man, an seiner Statt, die Begebenheiten in der Natur erfahren,
dann lassen sich wohl sogar Sophokleische Tragödien als ekelhaft und
abscheulich darstellen."   [2] "Milderndes Schönheitsprinzip."
[3] "Die höchste Schwelgerei der Kunst."
[4] *Ibid.* p. 163: "Sie verziert nicht mehr mit Blumen und Früchten,
sie verziert mit menschlichen Leichnamen, mit dem grössten Elend, das
einem Vater, das einer Mutter begegnen kann, eine blühende Familie auf
einmal vor sich hingerafft zu sehen."

Hermann und Dorothea was barely finished in the spring of 1797, when Goethe plunged with redoubled vigour into the study of Greek literature. This new effort continued with remarkable steadiness for three years. It was Goethe's final struggle to win entry into ancient Hellas. When it failed, there crept over him slowly the realisation that he had won all that he could from the Greek example, and that further striving in that direction was useless.

The reading that he undertook was varied. The most persistent study was devoted to Homer and the tragedians; but Aristophanes, long neglected, was twice read;[1] for the first time in his life Goethe read Herodotus and Thucydides with understanding;[2] Plutarch's *Lives* occupied him at different times;[3] and Hesiod was consulted for the work on the *Achilleis*.[4] He found it worth while, or at least entertaining, to turn over the lumber in the dark corners of ancient literature: *The Battle of Frogs and Mice* he read in March 1797,[5] and in the summer of 1798 he begged Friedrich Schlegel to send him all that was known of another of the burlesque, pseudo-Homeric epics, the *Margites*.[6] Even the dusty compilations of Athenaeus attracted him.[7] Works on ancient geography and topography,[8] treatises on the trade and handicrafts of the ancient world[9] helped to make those times and places real to him.

By far the greatest part of his reading was devoted to Homer and to the tragedians. It was Aeschylus to whom he first turned after finishing *Hermann und Dorothea*. Humboldt's translation of the *Agamemnon* led him on,[10] and in April and May 1797 he read at least the *Choephori* and *Supplices*.[11] From

---

[1] *Tagebuch*, 11 Jan. 1798 (WA. III, 2, p. 196): Aristophanes Ritter, *Uebersetzung von Wieland*; von Keudell, *op. cit.* p. 34 : *Aristophanis Comoediae*, 12 Dec. 1799–7 Jan. 1800.

[2] Letter to Schiller, 16 Dec. 1797 (WA. IV, 12, p. 378).

[3] WA. III, 2, pp. 217, 284.

[4] *Tagebuch*, 22 and 25 March 1799 (*Ibid.* p. 238).

[5] *Ibid.* p. 58.

[6] WA. IV, 13, p. 208. Cf. Gräf, *Epos*, I, p. 206.

[7] *Tagebuch*, 13 Sept. 1799 (WA. III, 2, p. 258).

[8] *Ibid.* p. 204 (de Chevalier, Wood), p. 215 (Lenz), p. 313 (Guilletière); Keudell, *op. cit.* p. 24 (Le Roy), p. 40 (Anacharsis, Pausanias).

[9] WA. III, 2, pp. 69, 70 (Heeren).

[10] *Tagebuch*, 23, 27, 29 March 1797 (*Ibid.* p. 62).

[11] *Tagebuch*, 27 April and 20, 21 May (*Ibid.* pp. 66, 68).

May to December he had Tobler's translations of Aeschylus from the library.[1] In the spring of both 1798 and 1799 Euripides was read with some intensity. The references to reading of Sophocles are rarer; but there can be no doubt that, in all the discussions with Schiller about the nature of tragedy, Sophocles was most often referred to, as being the most canonical of the three tragedians.[2]

Homer was seldom far from Goethe's elbow in the two years following *Hermann und Dorothea*. The newly-raised "Homeric question", the theoretical discussions with Schiller, and finally the preparatory work for the *Achilleis*, all combined to keep Homer in the van of Goethe's thoughts.[3] Especially in the spring of 1798 the best part of Goethe's energies was devoted for a time to making a digest of the *Iliad*,[4] which gave him at last a clear view over the whole of the complicated action. But when the *Achilleis* had been given up, he laid his Homer aside for a while.

All this intensive reading of Greek authors was accompanied by the renewed contemplation of ancient art which his aesthetic essays necessitated; by fresh study of Winckelmann from August 1798 onwards;[5] and by continuous discussion of Greek subjects with Schiller and Meyer, with the Schlegels, with Böttiger, and with distinguished classicists such as Humboldt, Wolf, Hirt or Hermann, who visited Weimar, or whom Goethe met while travelling. During these three years Goethe lived and breathed and had his being in Greece.

Of the poetical works which he planned or carried out in this time many were Greek in subject and form, while others were more or less antique either in form or in subject. During the spring and early summer of 1797, Goethe probably wrote all that was ever written of his *Befreiung des Prometheus*.[6] In

---

[1] Keudell, *op. cit.* p. 14.

[2] Cf. letter to Schiller, 23 Dec. 1797 (WA. IV, 12, p. 381).

[3] 1797, 19, 20 April (WA. III, 2, p. 65; WA. IV, 12, p. 90); 28 April (WA. III, 2, p. 66; WA. IV, 12, p. 105); 6 May (*Ibid.* p. 118); 21 May (WA. III, 2, p. 68); 1798, 29, 31 March, 1, 2, 3, 5 April, 11–17, 21, 22–27 May (*Ibid.* pp. 203, 204, 207, 208, 209; WA. IV, 13, p. 140); 1799, 17 Feb. to 5 April (*Achilleis*); 1800, 13 Feb. (WA. III, 2, p. 283).

[4] *Tagebuch*, 29 March to 21 May 1798 (*Ibid.* pp. 203, 207). The digest is printed WA. 41, 1, pp. 266–327.

[5] Keudell, *op. cit.* p. 24; WA. III, 2, p. 258.   [6] See above, p. 201.

May he conceived the idea of writing the third play of Aeschylus's *Supplices* trilogy, to be called *die Danaïden*. Some part of the plan was perhaps written down, but no shred survives. It was to be a true sequel to Aeschylus's play in that the chorus was to play a leading role.[1] A new idea for an epic poem, to be called *die Jagd*, came to him in March 1797,[2] and occupied his mind for the following months. The scene was to be modern, but as at first conceived, the poem was to be in hexameters.[3] So too his epic treatment of the legend of William Tell, conceived in Switzerland in October 1797, was to have been written in hexameters.[4] *Die Braut von Korinth*, on the other hand, employed the modern ballad form; but its story was laid in the last days of the ancient world, and its moral was a vindication of the pagan life that had been destroyed by the coming of the new religion. *Der neue Pausias*, *Euphrosyne* and *Amyntas*, all written in 1797, with their elegiac metre and allusions to classical themes,[5] bear further evidence to Goethe's complete absorption in the ancient world. But already his genius was knocking to be free. Faust had reappeared and, to Goethe's bewilderment, was demanding an increasing share of his time and energies.[6]

On closer examination of the nature of epic poetry, *Hermann und Dorothea* had been seen by Goethe to be not truly an epic.[7] Despite its excellence, of which Goethe was well aware, it could not therefore be the highest that could be attained. It could not be that re-expression of the epic idea, for which Goethe was striving. *Die Jagd* had proved even less satisfactory as an epic subject. *Wilhelm Tell* too was given up. In the *Tag- und Jahres-Hefte*[8] Goethe gave as the reason for this, that there

---

[1] *Ibid.* p. 68. Cf. Gräf, *Drama*, I, 193–5.
[2] *Tagebuch*, 23 March (WA. III, 2, p. 62).
[3] Eckermann, 15 Jan. 1827. Cf. also Schiller's letter to Goethe, 26 June 1797.
[4] *Tag- und Jahres-Hefte*, WA. 35, p. 183.
[5] WA. I, pp. 272, 281, 288. Cf. JA. I, pp. 354, 355.
[6] Letters to Schiller, 22, 27 June, I, 5 July, 6 Dec. 1797 (WA. IV, 12, pp. 167, 169, 179, 181, 372). Letter to Charlotte Schiller, 14 April 1798 (*Ibid.* 13, p. 116; WA. III, 2, p. 205).
[7] Letter to Schiller, 23 Dec. 1797 (WA. IV, 12, pp. 383–4).
[8] WA. 35, p. 185.

were no accepted rules for the composition of German hexameters; but this explanation is obviously inadequate, since this
lack of an accepted prosody did not deter him from pushing
ahead vigorously with his plans for the *Achilleis*, nor at last
from beginning on its execution. More probably *Tell* was
pushed aside by the idea of the *Achilleis*. They appear together
as equally actual on 23 March 1798.[1] Then followed Goethe's
intensive study of the *Iliad*; at the same time the plot of the
Achilleis was first sketched in detail. Goethe was inflamed with
the idea of finally kicking the modern world away from
beneath him and rising on Hellenic wings into the pure ether
of poetry. As long as this idea seemed in any way possible of
realisation, a modern subject such as *Tell* could not interest
him. Only when for a moment the *Achilleis* seemed beyond
his powers, did he think again of *Tell*.[2]

The idea of the *Achilleis* came to Goethe towards the end of
December 1797.[3] At first he was uncertain whether to treat
it as a tragedy or as an epic. By March 1798, when he first
began serious work on it, the *Achilleis* had taken clear shape
in his mind as an epic poem.[4] On 31 March the plan for the
whole poem was written down in some detail, and a provisional
division of the material into eight books made.[5] After a
momentary interruption in the middle of April, caused by
Faust's unbidden intrusion,[6] the work of preparation was resumed with redoubled energy in May.[7] Goethe was ready to
begin composition;[8] but at the last moment he laid down his
pen, and for ten months hardly thought of the *Achilleis*.[9] On
17 February 1799 he discussed the subject again with Schiller.
On 9 March he turned his attention to it more seriously, revised his plan, and next day started to compose.[10] Throughout

---

[1] Letter to Meyer (WA. IV, 13, p. 102).
[2] Letters to Schiller, 30 June and 21 July 1798 (*Ibid.* 13, pp. 199, 222).
[3] Letters to Schiller, 23 and 27 Dec. (*Ibid.* 12, pp. 385, 387).
[4] Letter to Meyer, 23 March (*Ibid.* 13, p. 102).
[5] WA. 50, pp. 435–9.
[6] WA. III, 2, p. 205, and letter to Charlotte Schiller, 14 April 1798 (WA.
IV, 13, p. 116).
[7] Gräf, *Epos*, I, pp. 9 foll.
[8] Letters to Schiller, 16 and 19 May (WA. IV, 13, pp. 149, 151).
[9] Cf. *Tagebuch*, 19 July (WA. III, 2, p. 215), and letter to Humboldt,
16 July (Gräf, *Epos*, I, p. 160).
[10] WA. IV, 14, p. 34; III, 2, p. 236.

March the work continued steadily, though with none of the ease of production of *Hermann und Dorothea*. On 2 April he sent the first canto, nearly finished, to Schiller, and announced his intention of pausing to review the ground. That pause was never broken. No more of the *Achilleis* was ever written, though Goethe continued for a few weeks longer to plan and to revise his plans.[1]

In his work on the *Achilleis* Goethe was brought face to face with the basic problem of his attempt to recapture Greece; and this time the issue could not be evaded. Was it enough to continue, as in *Hermann und Dorothea*, to treat essentially modern subjects in a Greek manner? or might he dare to re-create Greek literature itself, to write not "as a modern for moderns", but as though he had himself been born in Hellas in the days of the rhapsodists or of the bloom of Athens? When he first perceived that there was room and material for an epic between the *Iliad* and the *Odyssey*, he seems still not to have realised that the second course might be possible. He asked Schiller whether it would be wise to treat an essentially tragic subject, such as the death of Achilles, as an epic. "Much may be said on both sides. As far as the effect is concerned, a modern writing for moderns would be better off in spite of everything, since it is almost impossible to win the approval of our age without a sentimental interest."[2] From the first Goethe realised that the idea which the *Achilleis* was to symbolise was in many ways purely modern and incompatible with a Homeric mentality. Yet he decided to treat it epically and to bring it as near as could be to Homer in its outward form; this was the object of his close study of the *Iliad*, which he began at the end of March 1798. It was evidently his hope to produce something which should combine the merits of the Homeric style with the interest of a modern subject, and so to achieve Schiller's poetic ideal—the blend of *naiv* and "sentimental" poetry.[3]

[1] WA. III, 2, pp. 241, 247, 249.

[2] Letter to Schiller, 27 Dec. 1797 (WA. IV, 12, p. 387): "Was den Effect betrifft, so würde ein Neuer der für Neue arbeitet, immer dabei im Vorteil sein, weil man ohne pathologisches Interesse wohl schwerlich sich den Beifall der Zeit erwerben wird." [3] See above, p. 201.

On 12 May, however, Goethe wrote Schiller a letter which perturbed the watchful friend. "If I am to produce a poem which is at all worthy to come after the *Iliad*, I must follow the ancients even in those things for which they are criticised; I must even assimilate what is objectionable to me personally."[1] Schiller wrote back: "Of course you will not purposely imitate those elements in Homer which displease you; but if any such get into your work, they will be proofs of the completeness with which you have entered into the Homeric spirit and of the genuineness of your mood."[2] If Schiller could have seen a letter which Goethe wrote to Knebel three days later, he would have realised that his friend in Weimar was going through some serious crisis. Goethe spoke there of his new enterprise, which might indeed be overbold. "Yet even clearly to realise that some lofty model is beyond our reach, gives ineffable delight." And he stressed the necessity for any man of culture to make up his mind about these old masterpieces.[3] Next day, 16 May, Goethe wrote again to Schiller. After saying that his reading of the *Iliad* had hounded him through a recurring circle of emotions, from rapture through hope and understanding to despair, he went on to lay stress on certain aspects of his problem: the organic completeness of the *Iliad*, that made any addition to it impossible; the fact that the *Achilleis* was not merely a tragic, but also a "sentimental" subject; and the fact that its interest was personal and private, whereas the *Iliad*'s was universal. He asked Schiller to decide for him whether under these circumstances he should undertake the execution of the poem.[4] None of the points which Goethe mentioned would have hindered the accomplishment of his first intention, to mate the "sentimental" with the *naiv* and produce an

---

[1] WA. IV, 13, p. 141: "Soll mir ein Gedicht gelingen, das sich an die Ilias einigermassen anschliesst, so muss ich den Alten auch darinne folgen, worin sie getadelt werden, ja ich muss mir zu eigen machen was mir selbst nicht behagt."

[2] Jonas, v, p. 382.

[3] WA. IV, 13, pp. 145 foll.: "Und selbst die klare Einsicht von Unerreichbarkeit eines hohen Vorbildes gewährt schon einen unaussprechlichen Genuss. Ja es ist jetzo gewissermassen einem jeden der sich mit ästhetischen Gegenständen beschäftigt die höchste Angelegenheit sich über diese alten Meisterstücke, wenigstens mit sich selbst, in Einigkeit zu setzen."

[4] WA. IV, 13, pp. 148 foll.

antique-modern poem of essentially the same type as *Hermann und Dorothea*. But if Goethe were hoping to re-create Homeric poetry in its purest nature, then all these circumstances were stumbling-blocks in his way. Schiller saw all too well how his friend's mind was working, and wrote: "Since it is certainly true that no other *Iliad* is possible after the *Iliad*, even if there were another Homer and another Greece, I believe I can wish you nothing better than that you should compare your *Achilleis*, as it now exists in your imagination, only with itself, and should seek only the right mood and atmosphere from Homer, without really comparing your work with his." Schiller went on to encourage Goethe to have faith in his own genius, and added: "It is certainly a virtue rather than a fault of the subject that it meets the demands of our age halfway, for it is a thankless, nay an impossible task for a poet to leave his native soil entirely and really to set himself against his age. It is your fair calling, to be citizen of both poetic worlds, and because of this great advantage you will not belong exclusively to either."[1] Goethe replied that Schiller's words had comforted and encouraged him;[2] but in fact they had given the death-blow to his hopes of making Homer live again. The *Achilleis* was put away and not taken up again until the following spring, when, as we shall see, Goethe tried to carry it out according to his original plan, as a modern work in Homeric dress.

Throughout these letters, in which Goethe told Schiller of his doubts and hopes, there recurs the question of the authorship of the Homeric poems. The problem which Wolf's *Prolegomena* had raised three years before was evidently of great importance to Goethe in deciding how to handle the *Achilleis*. His attitude to the Homeric controversy in fact gives the clue to some of his more hidden thoughts in the crisis that the *Achilleis* brought about. When the *Prolegomena* came out in May 1795, Goethe's first reaction was one of disapproval.[3]

[1] 18 May 1798 (Jonas, v, pp. 384 foll.).   [2] WA. IV, 13, p. 151.
[3] Letter to Schiller, 17 May (*Ibid.* 10, p. 260). Goethe speaks here of Wolf's *Vorrede zur Ilias*, but probably means the *Prolegomena*. Wolf had actually published a *Vorrede zur Ilias* in 1785, but it is hard to see why Goethe should have been reading this work just at the moment when the far more important *Prolegomena* had appeared.

But a few weeks later he met Wolf, and was filled at once with respect and admiration for his mind and personality.[1] The result was a change in his attitude to Wolf's theories. He came to accept Wolf's basic contention, that Homer, even if there had once been such a person, could not have been the sole, nor even the chief, author of the *Iliad* and *Odyssey*; but that these poems were the result of a long process of development in which innumerable poets and editors over a period of many centuries had all played a part.[2] Goethe gave up the idea of a personal Homer without difficulty; but he strongly opposed any tendency to tear the poems in pieces and show that they had no artistic unity.[3] The more he studied the *Iliad*, the more clearly he saw that it had poetic unity in the highest sense, so that "it is impossible either to add to it or take away from it".[4]

Goethe conceived the origin and growth of the Homeric poems thus: nameless bards (ἀοιδοί) had made up and sung innumerable ballads of the deeds of the Trojan heroes; these had been handed on and added to by the rhapsodists; in time this vast but formless "ocean of poetry" had tended insensibly, without the aid of any great poetic genius, to coalesce around two major themes, the wrath of Achilles, and the return of Odysseus; what could not be related to these, dropped out of use and was forgotten; later ages continued to work at these at first loosely organised complexes, the tendency being rather to cut out what was irrelevant than to add new material; this process continued down to the days of the grammarians of Alexandria.[5] The Homeric poems could therefore be regarded as an anonymous product of the whole Greek race. At the same time this unconscious process had created poems that had every appearance of being the most finished products of conscious art. Here was a mystery before which Goethe's

---

[1] WA. IV, 10, pp. 415, 420; and Humboldt's letter to Wolf, 3 June 1795.
[2] For a very satisfactory résumé of the *Prolegomena* see Richard Volkmann's *Geschichte und Kritik der Wolfschen Prolegomena*, Leipzig, 1874. For Goethe's references to the Homeric question up till March 1798 see Bied. I, p. 229; WA. I, p. 293; WA. IV, 11, pp. 278, 296; 12, pp. 90, 105; WA. III, 2, p. 68.
[3] Letter to Schiller, 28 April 1797 (WA. IV, 12, p. 105).
[4] Letters to Schiller, 28 April and 16 May 1798 (*Ibid.* 13, pp. 126, 148).
[5] See especially letter to Schiller, 2 May 1798 (*Ibid.* 13, pp. 134 foll.). Also letter to Schiller, 19 April 1797 (*Ibid.* 12, p. 90).

mind stood still in wonder. Then as he gazed on it, a thought, a hope, rose up in him. These poems were such perfect representatives of epic poetry,[1] because the individuality of every poet who had worked on them had been obliterated by the work of all the rest. The element of caprice (*das Willkürliche*) which the individuality of even the greatest artist introduces into his work, was wholly absent from the *Iliad* and *Odyssey*. Of these poems too one could say: "Alles Zufällige fällt zusammen, da ist Notwendigkeit, da ist Gott".[2] Might it not be possible for him also to sink his individuality in the mighty tradition of the Greek epic, to let the idea of epic poetry merely blow through him as it had blown through those scores of nameless singers? This was his struggle in those days of May: first to identify himself so completely with the Homeric world, that in studying it he would be raised above the limits of a subjective judgment;[3] to suppress every objection that his individual nature might make to what he saw;[4] then having attained this state of super-personal receptiveness, to let his *Achilleis* grow of itself, as the seed sown broadcast on the well-tilled earth grows through the will of God.[5] The idea was bold beyond hope of fulfilment, for to accomplish it, Goethe would have to be bard, rhapsodist and grammarian in one; the process that before had taken centuries to work out, would have to be completed in a few months. For four days perhaps Goethe was held in the power of this vision. In those four days he saw at least how his dream of Hellas re-born might be fulfilled. They were the culminating point of his Hellenism. On 15 May, in his letter to Knebel, he still wrote as a man who hopes with bated breath for a victory he dare not expect. On the next day he had given up the fight and admitted defeat. No man alive, nor any that ever should be born, he wrote to Schiller, was capable of judging the *Iliad*. For his part he found himself forced back every moment on a subjective judgment.[6]

It may be assumed that Goethe would have radically altered

---

[1] Bied. I, p. 267 (No. 546).   [2] See above, p. 172.
[3] Letter to Schiller, 12 May (WA. IV, 13, p. 141, line 6): "Dass ich alles Subjective und Pathologische aus meiner Untersuchung entferne."
[4] *Ibid.* line 10: "Ich muss mir zu eigen machen, was mir selbst nicht behagt."
[5] *Ibid.* p. 140, line 21; p. 131, line 4.
[6] Letter to Schiller, 16 May 1798 (*Ibid.* p. 148).

his plan for the *Achilleis*, if he had attempted seriously to compose as "Homer". He indicated as much when he wrote to Schiller on 12 May, that he was "looking round for the best seed" to sow in the well-prepared soil.[1] He would have had to find a subject that had no special connexion with his own life. The *Achilleis*, as he had planned it, was based on a personal experience of his own.[2] This personal aspect of his subject would have been fatal to the achievement of his object, the complete subordination of his poetic individuality to the spirit of Homeric poetry. Yet of all poets Goethe was the least capable of separating his poetry from his life. He was demanding of his genius a thing that by its nature it could not do. In this dilemma Goethe was forced at last to realise that he could not get nearer to Greece than he had done in *Hermann und Dorothea*, for he could not escape from himself and still remain a poet. From this moment on, Goethe's Hellenism was on the wane. Its decline was gradual, for Goethe was loath to part with the joys and hopes that it had brought him. But it was certain now that his obsession with Greek things would prove to be only a stage in the development of his spirit, a preparation for higher things, not the end and object of his days on earth.

Despite the conflict which it had provoked, the *Achilleis* was not laid aside for good. Goethe could not give up the hope of making something out of it, even if it could not be the second *Iliad* of which he had dreamed. In March 1799 he took it up again, and composed six hundred and fifty lines, nearly the whole of the first canto.[3] The plan which he had made a year earlier, before the May crisis, formed in all essentials the basis for the work of composition. This plan contained certain elements which, as Goethe himself realised, were modern and un-Homeric. The fact that it was, by his and Schiller's definition, a tragic rather than an epic subject, is not of great importance, for this merely meant that the subject was un-Homeric, not necessarily un-Greek. But Goethe also admitted that the subject was "sentimental",[4] and therefore really modern not antique.

What was this "sentimental" element in the idea of the *Achilleis*? In 1807 Goethe summed up the intended action of

---

[1] WA. IV, 13, p. 141.
[2] See below, p. 234.
[3] WA. 50, pp. 271–94.
[4] Letter to Schiller, 16 May 1798.

the poem in these words: "Achilles knows that he must die; but he falls in love with Polyxena, and clean forgets his fate, in accordance with his crazy nature."[1] The two written plans of the *Achilleis* that have survived confirm this summary, and permit us to fill in most of the details. The action opens during the twelve days' truce that followed the return of Hector's body to the Trojans. Achilles knows that he is fated soon to die, and is passively resigned to his fate. He is occupied in constructing the great barrow that is to cover his ashes and those of Patroclus, when he is dead. In the course of negotiations for peace, the Trojans send Polyxena and Cassandra to the Greek camp, as possible substitutes for Helen in Menelaus's favour. Achilles sees Polyxena and falls in love with her. He determines to marry her, and make peace between the Greeks and Trojans. The wedding is to take place in the Thymbraean temple outside the walls. When all are assembled, Achilles is killed, partly through the treachery of Odysseus and Diomede, who oppose his plans for peace, partly perhaps through direct divine intervention.[2]

The "sentimental" or pathological element in this plot was undoubtedly the mood of life-weary resignation to his fate which holds Achilles at the opening. The first canto is chiefly taken up with the depiction of this state of mind. Achilles is discovered moodily watching the last flames that play over the pyre of the man who slew his friend.[3] When he rouses himself, it is to speak of his own coming death, and to superintend the erection of his own burial-mound.[4] In the scene in Olympus which follows, we learn from Thetis that her son has forgotten her, and thinks only with longing of the friend who has gone before him to the shades and whom he is eager to follow.[5] In the long scene which occupies the last two hundred and fifty lines of the canto, Athena, in the guise of Antilochus, attempts to rouse Achilles from his lethargy by reminding him of the deathless fame that will be his, because he chose a short and glorious life rather than a long and easy one. Her comfort is

---

[1] Riemer, *Mitteilungen*, II, p. 523; Gräf, *Epos*, I, p. 27: "Achill weiss, dass er sterben muss, verliebt sich aber in Polyxena und vergisst sein Schicksal rein darüber, nach der Tollheit seiner Natur."
[2] Cf. Morris, *Goethestudien*, II, p. 153.   [3] Lines 7–12.
[4] Lines 18–51.   [5] Lines 160–3.

a purely sentimental one. It does nothing to overcome Achilles's unnatural longing for death; it rather confirms him in resignation to his fate. At the close of their conversation Achilles admits that he feels neither hunger nor thirst nor any other earthly desire.[1] This mood of other-worldly asceticism is utterly different from Achilles's vow in the *Iliad*,[2] not to eat or drink till he has avenged Patroclus. Homer's Achilles took that vow of abstinence because he had before him a task that demanded the greatest possible concentration of effort for its speedy accomplishment. Goethe's Achilles has nothing more to live for; the world is empty, and its joys are barren. This mood is the quintessence of all that Goethe most hated and feared in the Christian attitude to life. How extraordinary that he should make the greatest of the Greek heroes succumb to the disease![3] This motive of Achilles's life-weariness was invented by Goethe. Almost every other motive in the poem can be traced to some source, if not in the *Iliad*, then in Hesiod, in the tragedians, or in one of the late re-workings of the heroic sagas such as Dictys Cretensis, Philostratus' *Heroikos*, the *Posthomerica* of Quintus Smyrnaeus, or Statius's *Achilleis*.[4] Not one of these, nor yet Thomas Corneille in his *Mort d'Achille*, gives the least hint of any flagging of Achilles's warlike ardour after the death of Hector. Why did Goethe invent a mood which so completely destroys the ideal character of Achilles as Homer portrayed it?

Achilles in Goethe's plan is a man who has lost all interest in life, and who then perceives something which fills him with a passionate desire, so that he forgets all fears, all doubts and cares in the pursuit of the desired object. This was an experience that Goethe had had on more than one occasion. He was, despite the inexhaustible fruitfulness of his mind, prone at all times to a deadly ennui; and at certain periods this mood had become the dominant one in his life. A few years before the *Achilleis*, he had been rescued from such a period by Schiller's friendship. Before that, Italy and the beauty he found there had been his "Polyxena", that drove away the hopelessness of

---

[1] Line 621.   [2] *Il.* XIX, 209-14.
[3] For further evidence of life-weariness in the plan for the *Achilleis* see WA. 50, p. 439, line 23-p. 440, line 12; p. 445, lines 6, 14.
[4] Cf. A. Fries, *Goethes Achilleis*, pp. 11-14.

those last years in Weimar, and set before him an object for which he could strive with all the reckless ardour of his mighty spirit. Perhaps even earlier he had had the same experience, in Strassburg, when Herder showed him the way to set his genius free, after three years of frustration had nearly broken him in mind and body. Achilles's ennui and his sudden cure symbolised a personal experience of Goethe's, as surely as *Iphigenie* had done, and the *Achilleis* is an "*Erlebnisdichtung*"[1] no less than *Werther* or *Tasso*.

It may be objected that in this experience of Goethe's there is nothing with which Achilles's death can be made to correspond; that Goethe did not bring on himself any catastrophe through his sudden return to life and energy; that after all the death of Achilles is the central theme of the *Achilleis*, and unless this is in some way connected with an experience in Goethe's life, the *Achilleis* cannot justly be called an "*Erlebnisdichtung*". Let us consider the circumstances of Achilles's death. He is killed just as he is about to take possession of the object of his desire; his death is brought about by the foolhardiness with which he has pursued this object, blinded to the dangers of his course by his "crazy nature". Thus analysed his death is seen to have a remarkable resemblance to a more famous scene in Goethe's poetry, Faust's premature attempt to seize the apparition of Helen;[2] and this again is identical with that scene in the *Märchen*,[3] in which the youth, in an access of heroic madness, tries to seize the "beautiful Lily", and is turned to stone by her touch. The *Märchen* was written hardly more than two years before the *Achilleis* was first conceived. What Goethe meant by this thrice repeated symbol, need not be discussed here.[4] Perhaps he meant nothing; but it is probable that he wished it to express some spiritual experience, perhaps of a kind that only exceptionally receptive spirits can know.

Be that as it may, the theme of Achilles's life-weariness and recovery undoubtedly represents an experience of Goethe's;

---

[1] A poem founded on, and giving poetic significance to, some personal experience of the poet.
[2] *Faust*, II, Act I, lines 6544–65; WA. 15, I, p. 88.
[3] WA. 18, p. 253.
[4] Cf. Rudolf Steiner, *Goethes geheime Offenbarung*, Dornach, 1932, pp. 48 foll., and *Goethes Faust als Bild seiner esoterischen Anschauung*, Berlin, 1902, p. 20.

and this was an emotional experience peculiarly modern and "sentimental" in its nature. It is unreasonable therefore to be surprised at finding un-Homeric elements in the *Achilleis*. As first planned and as finally executed, it was intended to be a blending of modern thought and sentiment with the Homeric style and manner of presentation. Goethe certainly knew that the long discussion between Athene and Achilles was un-Homeric, in that it was concerned with problems not of action but of the mind. Morris points out,[1] rightly enough, that Homer would never have made a consciously artistic triad out of three similar events, one past, one present, one future,[2] in order to produce a sentimental effect. Such touches lay in the sentimental nature of the subject. They had to fit themselves to the hexameter and the rest of the Homeric style as best they could. Such an expression as "der Flammen schreckliches Spiel"[3] is in the highest degree "sentimental" and destructive of the *naiv* quality of the style. It may be doubted whether un-Homeric traits of this sort were intentional on Goethe's part. They were more probably unnoticed lapses from the high standard of *Naivetät* which he set himself to achieve in the style.

For in everything that went to clothe the central idea, Goethe was determined to reproduce Homer as closely as possible. He took infinitely more care than with *Hermann und Dorothea*, to make his hexameters approximate to the ancient practice, in accordance with the system favoured by Voss and Humboldt; and this correctness he achieved by himself, without submitting what he had written to the experts.[4] He took enormous pains to make the local colour truly Homeric throughout the poem. For this he read what he could find in the Jena and Weimar libraries,[5] particularly topographical descriptions of the plain of Troy.[6] In the second written plan to the *Achilleis* he made a note: to find out whether the Thymbraean temple, in which the catastrophe was to take place, was not perhaps of more recent date than Homeric times.[7]

---

[1] *Goethestudien*, II, p. 166.   [2] Lines 18–25.
[3] Line 9: "The dreadful play of the flames."
[4] Heusler, *op. cit.* pp. 112, 115. Cf. Appendix B, p. 298 fol.
[5] WA. III, 2, pp. 203–4. Cf. Gräf, *Epos*, I, p. 5.
[6] WA. III, 2, p. 204, line 13 and p. 215, line 13.   [7] WA. 50, p. 441.

So important to him was it to make a realistically Homeric setting for his modern hero. He read every available ancient source that related any part of the cycle of Trojan legends; and from these he constructed his plot. There are in fact few themes or incidents in all the complicated action of the eight cantos, which were not at least suggested by something which Goethe read in one or other of these sources. Aeneas's role as leader of a party opposed to Priam's dynasty is hinted at in the *Iliad*;[1] Agamemnon's interest in Cassandra, a very subordinate theme in the whole plot, derives from Aeschylus's *Agamemnon*; Chrysaor's presence in the Thymbraean temple was suggested to Goethe by a half-understood passage in Hesiod;[2] the plot of Odysseus and Diomede to take Achilles's life is taken from Dictys;[3] Achilles's recollections of his first love, Deïdameia, would have been derived chiefly from Statius's *Achilleis*.[4] The list of these borrowings could be lengthened indefinitely.[5] It is the old technique of "reminiscences", which Goethe had employed deliberately in the *Römische Elegien*, but had been able to discard in *Hermann und Dorothea*.[6] His fresh study of ancient literature in 1797 and 1798 had brought him back to the view that a *naiv* style could most easily be achieved by a free use of the material provided in the *naiv* writers of antiquity.

The effect of all this archaeological paraphernalia in combination with the sentimental subject is not happy, at least in so far as it can be judged from the completed first canto. For all the accuracy of the Homeric setting, for all the references to the topography of the plain of Troy,[7] for all Goethe's intimate understanding of the personal and political relationships on both sides, Achilles reminds us, as Fries says,[8] of Hamlet rather than of Homer's hero. Despite all his efforts Goethe had not recaptured the *naïveté* of the Homeric mentality. In the *Iliad*, when Andromache says farewell to Hector at the Scaean gate, she tells her man that she will have no comfort left in life if he is killed, for she has neither father nor mother alive; then she

---

[1] *Il.* XIII, 460, and XX, 180 foll., 307.

[2] *Theogony*, 280–6. Cf. Morris, *Goethestudien*, II, pp. 151, 153.

[3] IV, 10.   [4] Fries, *op. cit.* p. 14.

[5] Most of them are excellently set out in Morris, *Goethestudien*, II, pp. 129–73.   [6] See above, pp. 184 and 214.

[7] Letter to Schiller, 18 March 1799 (WA. IV, 14, p. 47).

[8] Lines 400–10.

goes on to tell him exactly how her father was slain by Achilles, how Achilles did not despoil him but burnt him in his armour "richly dight, and heaped over him a barrow; and all about were elm-trees planted by nymphs of the mountain, daughters of Zeus that beareth the aegis".[1] Hector certainly knew all this before, but such a common-sense consideration does not prevent Homer from telling his hearers about the death of Andromache's father, since the flow of the narrative has brought him to the subject. In the *Achilleis* there is none of this simple absorption in the moment. The whole moves forward logically step by step; there is not a word in the whole canto that is not relevant to the poet's main purpose. This lack of *naïveté* in the *Achilleis* reminds us of the same failing in Goethe's translations from the *Odyssey*.[2]

Goethe himself had grave doubts whether his attempted union of ancient and modern "was good for anything".[3] There are moments indeed when the Homeric form is not belied by the content, and it is possible to imagine that one is reading a wonderfully poetical translation of Homer. Especially is this the case with the whole scene in "Zeus Kronion's holy house",[4] where the gods assemble to discuss anew the fate of Achilles and of Troy. The scene is founded on the descriptions in the *Iliad*[5] of the gods in assembly; but it is far more than a mere re-working of the themes that recur in those descriptions. It is a re-creation of the Greek heaven from Goethe's own belief in its fundamental truth. The figures of the gods are clear-seen and alive with all the attributes of power, with all the passion and the beauty that they show in Homer.

> Also sprach er und schwieg; da riss die göttliche Here
> Schnell vom Sitze sich auf und stand, wie ein Berg in dem Meer steht,
> Dessen erhabene Gipfel des Aethers Wetter umleuchten.
> Zürnend sprach sie und hoch, die Einzige, würdigen Wesens.[6]

---

[1] *Il.* VI, 410-20.   [2] See above, p. 191.
[3] WA. IV, 14, p. 47.   [4] Lines 67-397.
[5] Especially I, 490-611; IV, 1-72; VIII, 1-40; also XV, 85-167; XX, 1-30; XXIV, 30-76.
[6] Lines 264-7: "Thus he spoke and ended. Thereon the goddess Hera sprang up from her seat and stood as a mountain stands in the sea, around whose lofty peaks the storms of Aether flash. With voice of anger she spoke, the matchless one of awful presence."

No merely literary or aesthetic appreciation of Homer's picture of the gods would have enabled Goethe to make them live again, as they live in such passages as these. The gods were as real to him as they had been to Homer. Since this knowledge of them was derived as much from Greek sculpture as from Homer, he sometimes used this knowledge in the *Achilleis* to give their figures a plastic quality that is not found in Homer. Homer would never have described Aphrodite in these words:

> Spät kam Aphrodite herbei, die äugelnde Göttin...
> ...Reizend ermattet, als hätte die Nacht ihr zur Ruhe
> Nicht genüget, so senkte sie sich in die Arme des Thrones.[1]

This is the Medici Venus in movement. For the most part, however, Goethe was content to indicate the ideal characters of the gods as Homer had done, by description of their actions and their emotions, not of their appearance.

> Ares schreitet mächtig heran, behende, der Krieger,
> Keinem freundlich, und nur bezähmt ihn Kypris, die holde.[2]

It is above all in the words which they address to one another, that we recognise them as Homer's gods. We see them, in human form, as powers, allied or opposed one to another, each pitiless in pursuit of his will, confident in his might, yet all subordinate to Zeus, who needs only to hint at his own supreme power to silence opposition.

D. *HELENA*

The idea of re-creating Greek literature through suppression of his own individuality had proved impracticable. The objective representation of a strange world was impossible for him: this was the lesson of the May crisis. There remained one possibility, if he was to make something of pure Greek gold: the recreation of Greece must be a subordinate theme in a greater poem of subjective self-expression. Thus with strange

---

[1] Lines 131-4: "Last came Aphrodite, goddess of the wanton glance; with weary grace, as though the night had not sufficed her for repose, she sank into the arms of her throne."

[2] Lines 129, 130: "Ares strides onward, mighty, swift, the warrior, friendly to none, whom only lovely Cypris tames."

inevitability Goethe's longing for a higher and purer style in life and art, that led him to despise the northern world around him, was driven to take refuge with that most northern, least Grecian symbol of himself: with Faust. In the *Helena* of 1800 Goethe recaptured the authentic tones of Greek tragedy. He achieved this because he was content to treat Greece merely as one of Faust's experiences.

It was no new idea for him, that Faust and Helen should meet and mate. Back in the days of *Sturm und Drang*, when the legend of Faust first excited his poetic imagination, he had determined to use and develop in his own way the tradition of the *Faustbücher*, that Mephistopheles had procured Helen by his magic arts for Faust's enjoyment. The Helena episode, as Goethe completed it in 1826, was planned in its essential elements fifty years before.[1] When Goethe was working on *Dichtung und Wahrheit* in 1824, still believing he would never finish *Faust*, he wrote a summary of the plot of the Second Part, for insertion in the eighteenth book of his autobiography. This summary purported to represent the plan as he first conceived it, and as he related it or even read parts of it to friends during his last months in Frankfurt in 1775.[2] According to this sketch it was Goethe's intention that Faust should call up the apparition of Helen to entertain the imperial court. Having seen her he falls in love with her and demands that Mephistopheles should produce her and give her into his arms. There are difficulties: Helen belongs to Orcus and can be at best lured out by magic arts, but not held fast. Faust insists, and Mephistopheles undertakes the task. Faust shows his boundless longing for the highest beauty, now at last seen and recognised. Helen, to whom corporeal existence has been given back through a magic ring, is brought to a castle in Germany. She believes she is coming from Troy and is arriving in Sparta. She finds everything deserted and longs for company, particularly for that of men, which she has never been able to do without. Faust appears, and as a German knight contrasts most strangely with the antique hero-form. She is shocked by him; but gradually gets used to him. They mate and have a son, who from the

---

[1] Cf. Letters to Boisserée and Humboldt, 22 Oct. 1826 (WA. IV, 41, pp. 202, 209).

[2] WA. 15, 2, pp. 173–7, Paralipomenon 63.

moment of his birth, dances, sings and hews the air as though in combat. Transgressing the magic bounds of the castle, this son is killed. In her lamentations Helen pulls the magic ring from her finger and vanishes, leaving only her raiment in Faust's arms. At Mephisto's suggestion Faust turns his energies to the acquisition of wealth through war.

It is impossible to say how closely this summary corresponds to Goethe's conception of 1775.[1] At least the skeleton of the plan may be assumed to have been clear to Goethe even then: Helen was to be brought to Faust in Germany; they were to live together and produce a son; Helen was to return to Orcus at the son's death. No written fragments of this early *Helena* have survived, if any such ever existed.

For the next twelve years after 1775 *Faust* was laid aside. In Rome Goethe wrote some more scenes and re-made the plan, but whether of the whole or only of the First Part is uncertain.[2] Perhaps the Helena episode was included in this re-planning, but there is no scrap of evidence to indicate how Goethe conceived it at this period.

Nine years later, in June 1797, Goethe returned to work on *Faust* in earnest.[3] On the 23rd he made a detailed plan,[4] but of this too it cannot be said whether it applied only to the First Part or to the whole poem. Very probably at this time,[5] or perhaps two years later, in July 1799,[6] Goethe jotted down the half-intelligible notes which have become famous in Goethe-scholarship as "Paralipomenon 1".[7] For the most part they concern the First Part only, but the last three lines indicate in broad outline the ideas which underlay Goethe's conception of the Second Part, no line of which had yet been written. The First Part was to symbolise: "Lebensgenuss der Person

---

[1] J. Niejahr (*Euphorion*, I, p. 81) and W. Büchner (*Jrb. der G-G.* IX, p. 34) believe it to be essentially reliable. Valentin (*Die klassische Walpurgisnacht*, 1901, p. 19) thinks it represents the stage at which *Faust* had arrived in 1816.

[2] WA. 32, p. 288. Cf. Gräf, *Drama*, II, pp. 41 foll.

[3] Letter to Schiller, 22 June (WA. IV, 12, p. 167).

[4] WA. III, 2, p. 74.

[5] Cf. Eduard Castle, *Chronik des Wiener Goethe-Vereins*, XXV, p. 70, and Meissinger, *Helena*, p. 67.

[6] Cf. Gräf, *Drama*, II, p. 83.

[7] WA. 14, p. 287. Cf. also Gräf, *Drama*, II, pp. 83, 84 and *G-J.* XVII, p. 209.

(von aussen gesehen—in der Dumpfheit—Leidenschaft)"; the Second Part in contrast: "Tatengenuss (nach aussen—und Genuss mit Bewusstsein—Schönheit)."[1] When he wrote these words, the new and deeper meaning that was to be laid into *Helena* was already clear to him.

From this moment on Goethe was getting ready to begin the composition of *Helena*. A rough sketch of the action, with a few lines of dialogue,[2] has survived, and dates certainly from the period between June 1797 and May 1800.[3] It reveals a conception fundamentally different in many respects from the *Helena* of September 1800. Helen and her maids are discovered in Germany, in the Rhine valley. Helen speaks with an "Egyptian woman"[4] (Mephisto in disguise), who tells her, in impudent *Knittelvers*, of the strange world to which she has been brought. Helen speaks in trimeters.[5] Thus there was to be no pure re-creation of Greek tragedy, no return to the soil of Sparta and the air of Athens, but from the beginning antique and modern styles were to be mingled and contrasted. This fact suggests that the plan dates from before Goethe's failure with the *Achilleis*, probably from before the crisis of May 1798. Goethe read several plays of Euripides in March 1798.[6] On 9 April of that year "Faust and Company" interrupted the work on the *Achilleis*.[7] Perhaps Paralipomenon 84 dates from some time during these weeks.

Early in May 1800 Goethe was in Leipzig, where he met Hermann, the young but already distinguished Greek scholar.[8] The two men discussed Aeschylus and Euripides, and Goethe sought instruction and advice on Greek metres and prosody. At about the same time, perhaps a few weeks later, Goethe wrote the stanzas *Abschied*, intended as epilogue to the nearly completed First Part of *Faust*.[9] In them he speaks of his relief

---

[1] "Personal enjoyment of life (seen from outside—blindly—passion)." "Joy in deeds (outwards—and conscious enjoyment—beauty)."

[2] Paralipomenon 84: WA. 15, 2, p. 184.

[3] One other fragment (Paralipomenon 52, WA. 14, p. 311) may be placed with some confidence in this period. Cf. Morris, *Goethestudien*, I, p. 169.

[4] =a gipsy? Cf. line 15, "Kartenschlagen, Händedeutung".

[5] Cf. Morris, *Goethestudien*, I, p. 179.   [6] WA. III, 2, p. 203.

[7] *Ibid.* p. 205 and IV, 13, p. 116.   [8] WA. III, 2, p. 293.

[9] Cf. Gräf, *Drama*, II, pp. 88–90.

at being rid of the necessity to depict "the stress of human passion" and "the power of the dark"[1] (compare Paralipomenon 1, Lebensgenuss der Person—in der Dumpfheit—Leidenschaft),[2] and announces with joy his intention of turning his eyes to the East, and of continuing, in company with his trusted friends, on the "road to clarity", in steadfast admiration of antiquity (compare: Genuss mit Bewusstsein—Schönheit). It can hardly be doubted that in these lines Goethe expressed his intention of moving the action of *Faust* at once to Greece, that the mists of passion and magic might be drunk up, for an hour at least, by the sun of Hellas. He had in fact decided to begin his *Helena* as a Greek tragedy. A plan for this earliest form of the purely Greek *Helena* has survived.[3] It shows us Helen arriving in Sparta from the ship. The chorus was to sing of Helen's ancestry and the beauty of the children of Leda. Mephistopheles was to appear no longer as an Egyptian woman or gipsy, but as Phorkyas. Only one important *motiv* of the written *Helena* fragment is lacking: that of the threatened sacrifice with Helen as the victim. Apparently Goethe still thought of Faust's castle, to which Helen is transported, as being in Germany (not, as in the final *Helena*, in Mistra, a little way up the hill from Sparta); for the chorus are vaguely aware of a "great removal in time *and space*".

Throughout the summer of 1800 the *Helena* grew clearer and clearer in his mind.[4] At last on 12 September Goethe began to write. Composition continued steadily. A week later he read at least Helen's opening monologue to Schiller.[5] After 26 September there is no further mention of progress in the diary or in letters. Probably therefore the 265 lines of the *Helena* fragment[6] were all written in those two weeks in the middle of September 1800. Along with the composition of the opening scene, Goethe worked at the plan for the whole act, and established the chief themes to his own satisfaction.[7]

---

[1] "Den Drang menschlichen Gewühles" and "die Macht der Dunkelheit".

[2] See above, p. 241.

[3] Paralipomenon 162: WA. 15, 2, p. 227. Cf. Niejahr (*Euphorion*, I, p. 86).

[4] Gräf, *Drama*, II, p. 93.

[5] Schiller's letter of 23 Sept. (Jonas, VI, p. 202).

[6] Printed together, WA. 15, 2, pp. 72–81.   [7] WA. IV, 15, p. 111.

In the middle of November he read La Guilletière's *Lacédémone ancienne et nouvelle*,[1] a rambling and uninspired account of a visit to Sparta by a French gentleman of the later seventeenth century. The day after his reading, Goethe wrote to Schiller that he had come on some good ideas for *Helena*. It is natural to suppose that La Guilletière had suggested them. It may well be that the description of the medieval castle, built on its sugar-loaf hill and dominating the site of the ancient town[2] (La Guilletière did not realise that ancient Sparta lay three miles away from the Mistra of his day), first gave Goethe the idea of bringing Faust to Lacedaemon instead of transporting Helen to Germany. Other material that Goethe may have used is hard to find in La Guilletière, unless it be that the swans "d'une beauté et d'une blancheure extraordinaire", that floated on the stream of Eurotas,[3] suggested that theme which in its final form appeared as Faust's dream of Leda in Wagner's laboratory and the *Klassische Walpurgisnacht*. It is not impossible that the seed lay dormant for more than a quarter of a century.

As far as is known Goethe did not add a line to the *Helena* between September 1800 and March 1825. But up till 1805 the further course of the action occasionally occupied his mind.[4] There is indirect evidence that this was especially the case in 1803. In the spring of that year he took advantage of Voss's presence in Jena to practise with him the composition of trimeters and choric metres.[5] This suggests that he was still hoping to continue the *Helena* when the mood should be right. Then in September his thoughts must have been brought back powerfully to his Faustian heroine, for he read Pausanias's description of Polygnotus's frescoes at Delphi,[6] of which the central panel represented the "Glorification of Helen".[7] The conception of Lynceus's ecstasy at sight of Helen[8] and of his pardon at her hands may have been suggested by this picture.[9]

[1] WA. III, 2, p. 313.
[2] *Op. cit.* II, p. 387. La Guilletière knew nothing of the Frankish knights who occupied the Morea in the thirteenth century. Cf. II, pp. 366 foll.
[3] *Op. cit.* I, p. 97.   [4] WA. 15, 2, p. 214.
[5] WA. III, 3, pp. 71, 73 (19, 21 April, 9 May); Bied. I, p. 327 (15 May). Cf. Schiller's letters: Jonas, VII, p. 41.   [6] WA. III, 3, p. 81.
[7] See above, p. 218.   [8] *Faust*, lines 9192–257.
[9] WA. 48, pp. 107, 108. Cf. Szanto, *Zur Helena in Faust. Ausgewählte Abhandlungen*, Tübingen, 1906, p. 362.

Few will deny that the *Helena* fragment of 1800 is, as Mr Fairley says,[1] "no copy of the Greek spirit, but the complete evocation of it by one who has made himself a Greek and has only to speak with his proper voice, falsifying nothing, abating nothing, to make all Hellas live again as it lived of old". Yet opinions may differ as to the nature of Greek tragedy, and it is beyond my competence and no part of my purpose to decide whether Goethe's *Helena*, if translated into Attic Greek, could pass for a fragment of a lost tragedy of the Athenian stage. I can only try to demonstrate that Goethe intended to re-create Greek tragedy in this fragment, and believed that he had succeeded.

The fact that in the form of the play—in the choice of iambic trimeters for the dialogue, in the importance of the role played by the chorus, and so on—Goethe closely copied Greek practice, is of little importance. In such matters the *Achilleis* too was to have been an exact imitation of Homer, yet taken as a whole it was to have represented a blending of ancient and modern. The stage setting of the *Helena* fragment was conceived as antique rather than modern. There is a main stage in front, used by Helen and the chorus, then steps leading up to the palace, with the main door in the centre of the back of the stage. Behind this door terrible things occur or are discovered; through it dramatic or imposing entries are made, rendered more impressive by the height of the palace level above the main stage. There is no doubt that Goethe's close reproduction of the Athenian stage-setting adds powerfully to the Attic atmosphere of the *Helena*. Yet here too he would have followed Greek practice, even if he had been making an antique-modern poem on the lines of the *Achilleis*.

Again the "reminiscences", out of which the plot of the *Helena* fragment is constructed, prove perhaps no more than that Goethe was aiming at a *naiv* style, as in the *Achilleis*. Yet they produce a different effect in the *Helena*. When Helen comes out of the palace in terrible agitation and tells of the monstrous woman

In hagrer Grösse, hohlen, blutigtrüben Blicks,[2]

[1] *Goethe as Revealed in his Poetry*, Dent, 1932, p. 114.
[2] "Vast and emaciated, with hollow, blood-shot eye."

who barred her passage to the inner chamber, we are reminded, certainly, of the discovery of the Furies in the temple of Apollo;[1] but we are not conscious of a conflict of atmosphere between this imitation and the subject matter of the poem, as we are in similar cases in the *Achilleis*: the terror and loathing aroused by Phorkyas is an essential part of the plot, whereas the "reminiscences" from the *Iliad* in the *Achilleis* could only give Homeric colour to a modern conception.

The most pregnant of all the "reminiscences"[2] in the *Helena* is that which Goethe took from the *Troades* of Euripides,[3] the unusual version of the myth, unknown to Homer: that Menelaus took Helen back to Greece only to slay her in revenge for her unfaithfulness and for the sorrows she had brought upon the Greeks. The addition of this theme to the original plan[4] secured for Goethe the success of his attempt to re-create Greek tragedy. Fear and uncertainty (for Helen does not know, she only suspects, that she is doomed) permeate the whole fragment; Helen and the chorus are aware of danger, they sense a hostile Fate, and are pitifully conscious of their own helplessness. In this atmosphere of strain the discovery of Phorkyas adds a new and uncanny element to their fears. The vehemence of the chorus's attack on her is explained psychologically by the nervous tension which the fear of death has brought about. In all this Goethe had re-created the mental background of the Greek tragedies, that overwrought condition of the spirit, in which the threat or the memory of violence gives birth to fear and hatred, which in their turn beget more violence, more injustice and more hatred. It was that unlovely aspect of the Greek spirit, which in *Iphigenie* Goethe had tried to ban by the forceful assertion of a humane morality. Now he had other methods of dealing with this black streak in the human spirit, methods which he had learnt from the Greeks. The picture of an unhappy woman sent to

---

[1] *Eumenides*, 34 foll.

[2] Line 876. Cf. also line 29: *Orestes*, 54 foll.; lines 90 foll.: *Eumen.* 34; "Weihe und Säuberung", Paralipomenon 162: *Eumen.* 63; lines 145 foll.: *Troades*, passim; lines 182–8: *Prom. Vinctus*, 793 foll.; line 217: *Ag.* 750, *Trachin.* 1. See also JA. XIV, pp. 358 foll.

[3] Lines 876–9, 1055.

[4] Niejahr (*Euphorion*, I, p. 92) suggests that the *Opfermotiv* occurred to Goethe after he had already written twenty lines of Helen's opening speech.

make all ready for a sacrifice in which she is to fall a bloody victim at her husband's hands, is a "shocking subject" of the Sophoclean type.[1] But the very threat of horror makes the figure of Helen rise in heroic stature before our eyes. In the first plan, which lacked the motive of the sacrifice, Helen was merely a beautiful woman who yielded to the procurer's arts, which Mephisto practised.[2] In the fragment she is a heroine, worthy to stand beside Electra and Antigone. To this moral beauty is added the sensual beauty of the poetry, which in the dialogue and in the choral lyric shows Goethe at his greatest. With the assurance of the master Goethe firmly seized and plucked the nettle of Greek inhumanity, and treated it as the Greeks themselves had done, making new life and beauty out of a tale of death and terror.

The plot of the *Helena* fragment, taken by itself without reference to *Faust*, has not the remotest connexion with any experience in Goethe's life. It is a "*naiv*-significant" subject such as Sophocles or Euripides might have chosen as the theme for a tragedy. There is in fact no strain of modernity in the Helena fragment. It is as close a re-creation of Greek tragedy as Goethe knew how to make it.

As soon as he began to compose the rolling iambic lines, he knew that at last he had accomplished what for so long had seemed impossible. Greek art itself, not merely its modern substitute, was rising again at the touch of his genius. For a moment, he was tempted to cut his Helen free from Faust, and finish the *Helena* as he had begun it, as a complete Greek tragedy.[3] Almost it seemed that he had despaired too soon, and that he was after all to be allowed to enter the temple and to be admitted to the company of the immortal Greeks. But after a moment of such hopes he remembered that this success had been granted him only on condition that Helen's fate was subordinated to that of Faust. Though with all his soul he hated the thought of carrying off his Grecian heroine to the barbarous medieval world of knights and sorcerers, he knew that he must do it. Helen and Faust had got to meet, and to

---

[1] "Abscheulicher Gegenstand." Cf. WA. 47, pp. 167, 168; and see above, p. 221.

[2] Paralipomenon 162: WA. 15, 2, p. 227: "Kuppeley."

[3] Letter to Schiller, 12 Sept. 1800 (WA. IV, 15, p. 102).

meet as equals and as representatives of their contrasted worlds. Faust could not become a Hellene. Goethe knew (the *Achilleis* had taught him), that he was, beyond hope of release, a modern and a German. More than this, he knew already in his heart, that Faust, the modern, northern man, was, in his way, as valuable a creature of God as Helen, the symbol of Greek life; that, as Petsch puts it, "he faces Helen as an equal in power and in rights".[1] Goethe had therefore already determined to bring Helen to Germany and introduce her into Faust's modern world.[2] But, despite Schiller's encouragement, who feared as in May 1798 that his friend was about to launch out on a hopeless adventure,[3] Goethe could not bring himself to turn his *Helena* into a "grotesque farce",[4] by passing from the antique to the romantic section. The abuse which the chorus hurls at Phorkyas:

> Ausgeburt du des Zufalls,
> Du, verworrener,
> Du erschöpfter Kraft
> Leidige hohle Brut,[5]

and their complaint that they, "happily formed by the gods", are forced against their will to look on such ugliness, reveal Goethe's own feelings about modern civilisation. He loathed some aspects of it, and like the chorus he was powerless to alter or to escape from them. Faust's appearance would have shown the good in modern life, which Helen and the chorus would in time have come to accept.[6] But it is significant that in 1800 Goethe could not portray this good side of the modern world; he got no further than venting his spleen on what was evil in it, in these three strophes of the *Helena*.[7] The modern section of the *Helena* remained no more than a plan for a quarter of a century. In 1800 Goethe was still so deep in Hellenism, that as a poet he could not move freely outside it,[8]

---

[1] *Germanisch-Romanische Monatsschrift*, XII, p. 206: "Gleichberechtigtes Kraftzentrum der Helena gegenüber."
[2] Paralipomenon 162: WA. 15, 2, p. 227; WA. IV, 15, pp. 102, 108; Schiller's letter to Goethe, 13 Sept. 1800 (Jonas, VI, p. 198).
[3] Jonas, VI, p. 198.   [4] "Fratze."
[5] "Thou, child of Chance, thou, wretched, empty offspring of power confused, exhausted."
[6] Paralipomenon 162.   [7] WA. 15, 2, p. 79, lines 198–216.
[8] Cf. Niejahr (*Euphorion*, I, p. 84).

though as a man he might realise that for him Greece was not the end, but only a stage on the road. Above all he had no interest in any other world than the Greek, least of all in the Middle Ages. He utterly lacked material for the modern half of the *Helena*. The broadening of interest that came to Goethe after 1805, especially his realisation of the value of medieval German art, had to take place before Goethe could complete the *Helena*. As he wrote to Humboldt in 1826,[1] "the piece could be finished only in the fulness of time".

All that Goethe could accomplish in 1800 was to portray objectively what Faust experienced, not the moment of his experiencing nor the effect upon him of the experience. Both these further steps were planned in September 1800 but were not carried out until a quarter of a century later. It is plain, however, that already in 1800 Goethe attached extraordinary importance to the meaning which they were to convey. On 23 September he wrote to Schiller that the chief moments of the plan (of the *Helena*) were in order: "I see already that from this hill-top I shall get at last a proper view over the whole [of the Second Part of *Faust*]."[2] Schiller agreed that the other themes to be treated in the Second Part must all depend for their inner meaning on the *Helena* act.[3] In Paralipomenon 1 Goethe had defined the two themes of the Second Part as "*Tatengenuss*" and "*Schöpfungsgenuss*", joy in doing and in creating. So by attaining to knowledge of Beauty, symbolised in his mating with Helen, Faust was to rise from his old state of blind desire (*Dumpfheit, Leidenschaft*) to a state in which activity and creation could alone satisfy him. He was to undergo in fact an "aesthetic education" by which alone, as Schiller taught, man could attain to the free use of all his powers. The *Helena* was to be the poetic expression of the philosophy of life which Goethe had won for himself in Italy through understanding of ideal beauty, and which Schiller had clarified in philosophical terms in the *Aesthetische Briefe*.[4] Inevitably Goethe chose the Greek world to represent ideal beauty. It was through study of Greek sculpture and Homer and the Greek way of life, that he had himself been granted the

[1] WA. IV, 41, p. 202. [2] *Ibid.* 15, p. 112.
[3] 23 Sept. (Jonas, VI, p. 202).
[4] See above, pp. 195 foll. Cf. Meissinger, *op. cit.* pp. 74 foll.

visions which revealed to him the inner nature of beauty and
of the aesthetic existence. This state of being, for Goethe the
highest form of life that man could achieve, was unattainable
for modern man without the example of Greece. And this
highest existence was not merely a passive condition of perfection; it brought with it activity and that highest form of
activity, creation. The Second Part of *Faust* was to show how
Goethe owed all this to the Greek spirit:[1] his attainment of the
aesthetic life, with its inner harmony of spirit and its balanced
use of all faculties, had given him "*Tatengenuss*", delight in
activity as an end in itself, and finally "*Schöpfungsgenuss*", joy
in the process of creation. It is true that Goethe had known
both these joys before he attained to new knowledge in Italy;
but Paralipomenon 1 reminds us of the difference of which
Goethe was aware, between his pre-Italian and his post-Italian
creation. Since Italy he had "*Genuss mit Bewusstsein*", he knew
and understood the processes by which his genius brought forth.
Homer and the Greek sculptors had shown him how the artist
creates in accordance with the laws of Nature. This process of
creation was to be portrayed in the epilogue to the Second Part.[2]
So the Second Part, as planned in 1800, was to have shown the
aesthetic life as a passive condition and as activity; and the
whole was to derive from, and depend on, Faust's meeting
with Helen, Goethe's experience of Greece. Goethe knew no
other way than this of demonstrating the superlative importance
of Greece to himself and to any man who wished to live the
best and fullest life.

The years that followed the composition of the *Helena* fragment were almost empty of Greek studies. Apart from
occasional occupation with antique gems and coins,[3] the only
important addition to Goethe's knowledge of Greek art during
these years came from his study of Pausanias's description of

---

[1] Cf. Scherer, *Goethe-Aufsätze*, p. 343.

[2] Paralipomenon 1: "Schöpfungsgenuss von innen. Epilog im Chaos
auf dem Weg zur Hölle."

[3] *Mionnets Pastensammlung*, WA. IV, 15, p. 229; 16, pp. 24, 146, 163,
173; WA. III, 3, pp. 69, 95, 97; cf. *Jrb. der G-G.* VII, pp. 213 foll.; *Köhlers
Münzbelustigung*, WA. III, 3, pp. 78, 79, 80, 87, 88, 91 (August–December
1803); *Ibid.* p. 102 (2 April 1804); Bied. I, p. 381 (January 1805). See also
WA. IV, 16, pp. 169, 180.

the frescoes by Polygnotus at Delphi.[1] There was none of that intensive reading of Greek literature that had been so remarkable a feature of the three years leading up to the *Helena*.[2] In those three years Goethe had made his final effort to achieve the mentality of a Greek; in his work on the *Achilleis* and the *Helena* he had found out the extent and the limits of what was attainable. Further soaking in the relics of the Greek genius had no purpose for him. He had, as Fairley puts it,[3] "mastered the Homeric sensibility" (and also that of the tragedians), he had "adjusted his sense-perception to theirs", had "let their rhythm, their idiosyncrasy, their consciousness pass into him"; "and having done this he moves on slowly to new experiences". From the moment of his success in the *Helena*, the driving power went out of his Hellenism. His long struggle to be absorbed by Greece ended instead in his absorbing Greece and passing on, enriched and strengthened, yet essentially the same all-mastering personality as before.

It is doubtful whether he immediately understood that Greece had served its purpose for him, and that he had now merely to look back on it, as he looked back on those other worlds he had from time to time added to his range of experience. For several years at any rate no other world took its place. Goethe continued to write and speak of Greece as of a phenomenon far transcending all other earthly phenomena. It was for him still the absolute, unattainable perhaps, but still the only goal worth seeking. So, while his spirit, in the forceful darkness of the subconscious, was already moving away from Greece to a broader appreciation of life in all its forms, his conscious mind still lagged, and strove for the same ends that had occupied it for the last thirteen years. He continued especially that educative campaign in favour of Greek standards in art, which he had launched in the *Propyläen*. His chief

---

[1] The significance of Goethe's explanatory essay has been discussed above, p. 218.

[2] Keudell, *op. cit.*, gives 1801, Xenophon, January–February; Statius, *Achilleis*, October; Plato, October; *Philosophia vetus et nova*, and Aristotle, November. Other Greek reading: *G-J.* XIII, p. 132; *Iliad*, January 1804; late summer and autumn, 1804, several Greek tragedies, especially Sophocles, with the younger Voss (Bied. I, pp. 373, 375, 377, 405); November 1804, *Timaeus* (WA. IV, 17, p. 219).

[3] *Op. cit.* p. 163.

vehicle of education was the yearly prize competition on set subjects, in which all German artists were invited to take part. This annual event began in 1799 under the auspices of the *Propyläen*, and continued after the collapse of that periodical in 1801, until 1805. Its object was to combat the prevailing tendency to "historical, sentimental-unsignificant, and un-inspired-naturalistic" subjects, by setting subjects which gave opportunity for the practice of the proper sensual-symbolical function of art.[1] All but one of the subjects set was derived from Homer or from Greek mythology and legend. In his announcement of the first competition in 1799, Goethe re-commended Homer as "the richest source from which artists have always taken material for their works of art".[2] And in the announcement of the subject for 1801, he repeated his recommendation on the same ground.[3] This advice was repeated in 1803, and the tragedians were commended to the artist's attention as interpreters of the body of traditional myths.[4] How utterly Goethe regarded Greece as the foundation of all true art is shown especially by that first statement, that "Homer has always been the richest source of material for artists". The Christian tradition is simply ignored. Christ and his Mother and all the Saints might never have been subjects of painting or sculpture, for all Goethe appeared to know, or at least to care. The excellence of art in Stuttgart and Cassel Goethe attributed to the presence there of antiques, which artists could copy; the sentimental-theatrical tendency notice-able in Saxony was due to the absence of antiques. Goethe suggested that some should be acquired and exhibited for a moderate entrance fee. "The capital outlay would bring in a good return; while an artistic talent, banned to these Northern parts, would not lack all light."[5] In this educational work in the cause of higher art, Goethe's genius showed itself at its lamest. It is not surprising that the wind of artistic inspiration listed to blow in quite another direction from that which Goethe recommended. But it was inevitable that Goethe should attach immense importance to this attempt to found a true tradition of art in Germany. He believed that his failure

---

[1] WA. 48, pp. 65 foll.
[3] *Ibid.* p. 20: "Grundschatz aller Kunst."
[4] *Ibid.* p. 60.

[2] *Ibid.* p. 4; cf. p. 223.

[5] *Ibid.* pp. 21-2.

to re-create Greece in his own poetry was due not only to the meaner forms of German life, but also to the lack of any tradition which could help the man of genius like himself quickly and easily over the first stages of artistic production to the fulfilment of the highest tasks that his genius might set him. Raphael was an example of the genius who was born already on the pinnacle of a great tradition. All the preparatory work had been done for him by the artists of the quattrocento, so that he could devote all his energies to the production of the highest art. So too the masterpieces of Phidias and Lysippus were possible only because earlier artists had made the way straight. With some bitterness Goethe felt that he had been left to blaze his own trail, to make his own mistakes and learn from them, and so had wasted half his life and the best part of his energies in fruitless or mistaken labours.[1] He was determined to do his part at least to start German art in the right way, so that the period of experiment might be as short as possible.

The same desire to educate the public in Greek standards of taste was shown by Goethe in certain aspects of his conduct of the Weimar theatre during these years. The tone was set in *Paläophron und Neoterpe*, an allegorical improvisation, hastily composed in October 1800, to celebrate the advent of the new century. Here for the first time the German trimeter was heard upon the stage; while simultaneously Goethe introduced the use of masks, not indeed for the chief characters but for mute subsidiary figures. Both these experiments were repeated in the following years. In January 1802, in Wilhelm Schlegel's *Ion* two characters appeared in masks;[2] and in June masks were used, half in jest, for allegorical figures in Goethe's *Was wir bringen*, and Goethe announced his intention of returning soon to the full technique of the Attic stage with mask and cothurnus, and begged his audience to accustom themselves to the practice.[3] Between 1801 and 1807 several comedies of Plautus and Terence were performed in masks.[4] The trimeter was used by Goethe

---

[1] *Antik und Modern*, WA. 49, 1, pp. 149–56. Cf. also WA. 13, p. 72, line 29; WA. IV, 15, p. 213; Eckermann, 3 May 1827.
[2] WA. 40, p. 77.
[3] *Was wir bringen*, Scene 19: WA. 13, 1, p. 83; cf. WA. 40, p. 75.
[4] JA. IX, p. 419. Cf. WA. 35, pp. 145, 147; WA. IV, 16, p. 447.

in *Was wir bringen*, and was brought on the stage on two other occasions in 1802 by the production of A. W. Schlegel's *Ion* and Friederich Schlegel's *Alarkos*. Only the last speech in the *Ion* is in trimeters, but they are worthy echoes of their Greek models. The trimeters in *Alarkos*, on the other hand, are a curious bastard creation. Metrically they are true trimeters, but they are rhymed; yet not truly rhymed, for only the vowel sound, not the consonants, of the last syllable of each line corresponds with that of the lines preceding and following. Goethe apparently admired them, for his chief reason for performing *Alarkos* was that "these extremely important metres" could be spoken and heard.[1] In such efforts to re-introduce Greek ways it seemed indeed that Helen had left only her empty garment in Faust's hands. Yet the use of masks was not entirely an empty imitation of Greek forms.

> Doch dieses lässt vom Höheren und Schönen
> Den allgemeinen ernsten Abglanz ahnen.
> Persönlichkeit der wohlbekannten Künstler
> Ist aufgehoben; schnell erscheinet eine Schar
> Von fremden Männern, wie dem Dichter nur beliebt,
> Zu mannigfaltigem Ergötzen, eurem Blick.[2]

Goethe's object was to eliminate the individual element from stage representations, and stress the ideal significance of the characters.[3] The Greeks, with their instinct for ideal characters, had discovered the simplest means for accomplishing this.

What Goethe achieved in stage technique with his masks, he attempted also to produce in his one great poetic work of this period, *Die Natürliche Tochter*. In its form this play is not Greek at all. The subject too is a modern one, in so far as it has any position in time. But the characters are formed on what Goethe believed to be Greek principles. They are stripped utterly of all individuality, even of such as mythological names could give. They bear labels—king, duke, secretary, governor—not names; and they are treated as representatives of the type

---

[1] Letter to Schiller, 9 May 1802 (WA. IV, 16, p. 83).

[2] *Was wir bringen*, Scene 19 (WA. 13, 1, p. 83): "By these means a solemn reflexion of the lofty and beautiful is suggested. The personality of well-known actors is obliterated. At once appears, for you to look at, a multitude of strangers, as the poet wills, to give you varied delight."

[3] Cf. WA. 40, p. 74.

whose label they bear. It was a new technique for Goethe.[1] Never before, certainly not in *Hermann und Dorothea*, where the subsidiary characters also have no names, had he withdrawn so completely into a world of abstractions. He probably thought that he was doing as the Greek tragedians had done. Schiller at least regarded the characters of Greek tragedy as "ideal masks": Odysseus in the *Ajax* and *Philoctetes* was the "ideal of deceitful shrewdness"; Creon in the *Oedipus* and *Antigone* was "simply cold regal dignity"; and Schiller added: "Such characters are obviously a great advantage in tragedy. They expound themselves more quickly, and their features are firmer and more permanent. Truth does not suffer through this type of character, since they are no more mere logical beings than they are mere individuals."[2] It is hard for us to recognise even a reflexion of the vigorous figures of Greek tragedy in the bloodless shadows of the *Natürliche Tochter*. The influence of Greek art is almost more obvious. The second, third and fourth scenes of the third act[3] contain an ideal representation of paternal grief, constructed and executed in accordance with the principles which Goethe saw embodied in the Laocoön group. Like Laocoön the duke is stripped of all unessential attributes such as nationality or rank; he is the man, the father, suddenly bereft of a beloved child. This "profound-*naiv*" idea is composed of a number of aspects, all of which are given expression in such a way as to illustrate and emphasise the basic idea. This was the manner of conception and execution which Goethe admired in Greek works of art such as the Laocoön and the frescoes of Polygnotus,[4] and which he recommended so urgently and with so little success to the artists of his day. Goethe's picture of the father's grief cannot move us emotionally, since we can feel no sympathy for so unreal a character as the duke; but it is undoubtedly a powerful manifestation of poetic art.

The *Natürliche Tochter*, which was finished in March 1803, marks a stage in Goethe's retreat from pure Hellenism.[5] After the *Achilleis* and the *Helena* fragment, he never again attempted

---

[1] Cf. Gräf, *Drama*, III, p. 550.
[2] Letter to Goethe, 4 April 1797 (Jonas, v, p. 168).
[3] WA. 10, pp. 307-25.   [4] See above, pp. 218 foll.
[5] Cf. WA. 40, pp. 79-80.

to reproduce the form of Greek epic and drama (except in his continuation of the *Helena* in 1825). In the *Natürliche Tochter* form and material are modern; only the idealising technique is borrowed from the Greeks. In *Hermann und Dorothea* too Goethe had cleansed the modern world of its insignificance and raised it out of its meanness by contact with the Greek spirit. But there the purifying agent had been a vision, a spiritual experience of the greatest intensity, an ideal of life. The idealisation of the material in the *Natürliche Tochter* sprang only from an intellectual belief in the efficacy of a certain artistic technique which Goethe held the Greeks had evolved. Hellenism had ceased to be a vital urge from below; it was in danger of becoming a barren intellectual ideal.

In February 1804, Goethe turned seriously to the publication of a work, which he had long planned as a worthy monument to the great founder of German classicism, Winckelmann.[1] The composite essay, which contained hitherto unpublished letters of Winckelmann and contributions from Meyer and Wolf, was published in the summer of 1805 under the title *Winckelmann und sein Jahrhundert*.[2] Goethe's contribution was written between December 1804 and April 1805. In it he stressed Winckelmann's personality, insisting that its greatness was based on its affinity to the Greek nature. In this way Goethe gave himself the opportunity of making full confession of his Hellenic faith. The Greeks achieved the perfection of humanity by balanced co-ordination of all human faculties and by contentment to live and work and suffer within the world. By achieving this ideal they fulfilled the last and highest objective of the created world. "For to what purpose is all this array of suns and planets and moons, of stars and Milky Ways, of comets and nebulas, of created and creating worlds, if at the last a happy man does not rejoice unwitting in his existence?"[3] Out of this perfection of vigorous life grew the flower art, which gives permanence to the necessarily transient condition of earthly perfection, and reveals in ideal reality the man as god, the god as man.[4] The Phidian Zeus was the highest manifestation of this highest function of spirit.

[1] Cf. WA. 46, p. 391.
[2] *Ibid.* pp. 1–101.
[3] *Ibid.* p. 22.
[4] *Ibid.* p. 28.

At the same time as Goethe thus depicted the absolute beauty and value of the Greek existence, he contrasted the modern world with it. No modern could ever achieve that balanced co-ordination of all faculties by which the Greeks had produced their unique achievements.[1] The modern man attempts to know and to achieve the infinite and, failing, must resign himself to a limited field of activity.[2] He is hopelessly divided within himself,[3] the result of his divorce from Nature in his social and religious life. In the matter of knowledge and science the Greek may have been at some disadvantage, since the firm unity of his character made it hard for him to divide his attention sufficiently to advance far in any one branch of technical knowledge; but his case was not as hopeless as that of the modern, who loses himself in an infinity of unconnected sciences and lacks the formative element in his character that might make a whole out of these disjointed parts.[4] The pagan characteristics and beliefs that gave the Greek his "indestructible soundness",[5] alike in good fortune and bad, Goethe held to be fundamentally opposed to the Christian view of life.[6]

So in a last eloquent outburst of admiration and longing Goethe said farewell to his Greek endeavour. The note of resignation runs strongly through the whole essay. He had ceased to struggle. He had failed to make Greece live again; he must be content to look on antiquity as something eternally distant, as something past and gone.[7] In those dark late-winter months of 1805, with the ideal that had supported him for twenty years no longer valid, with no new goal to take its place, Goethe's vitality was at its lowest ebb. He was sick himself, and he was racked by fears for Schiller's health. "In doloribus pinxit", he wrote to Schiller, should be the motto for his *Winckelmann*.[8] The sun of Greece had set, and no new dawn yet glimmered to lighten his darkness. All that he could do was to rear this monument to a dead ideal, and wait till the germs of life began to stir once more in his spirit.

---

[1] *Ibid.* p. 21.
[2] *Ibid.* p. 22.
[3] *Ibid.* p. 23.
[4] *Ibid.* p. 24.
[5] "Eine unverwüstliche Gesundheit."
[6] *Ibid.* pp. 25–6.
[7] *Ibid.* p. 38.
[8] 20 April 1805 (WA. IV, 17, p. 273).

He had at last fully accepted his fate. He was a modern and a northerner; there was no escape. In May 1805 he wrote:[1] "The Greeks, and some Romans too, practise a very tasteful segregation and purification of the different categories of poetry; but it is not possible to recommend only those models to us Northerners. We have other forebears to boast of, and have many another model in view. If the romantic tendency of uncultured centuries had not brought the vast into contact with the grotesque, how should we have got *Hamlet, Lear, La Devoción de la Cruz, El Principe Constante?* Since we shall never reach the favoured position of the ancients, it is our duty to maintain ourselves courageously on the eminence of our barbaric advantages." His resignation was still touched with bitterness, as the delicate sarcasm of the last sentence shows.

Greece had been, he saw it now, merely one more experience. But it was an experience of such a depth, such a fullness, such intensity, that he could be excused for having taken it for the end and purpose of his life. No other experience that he had had, not Shakespeare, nor Ossian, not the changes that Lotte Buff or Lili or Frau von Stein had wrought in him, none of these had held him so long, had exercised his vast powers so imperiously, had changed and deepened his perception of things, as Greece had done. Nor can any experience of his later years compare in importance with that of Greece. All were transitory and shallow in comparison.

To estimate what his experience of Greece had given him, it will be well to look back twenty years, and consider Goethe as he was in 1785. He had been in Weimar ten years, and he was almost crazed with longing to get away over the Alps

---

[1] "Wohl findet sich bei den Griechen, sowie bei manchen Römern, eine sehr geschmackvolle Sonderung und Läuterung der verschiedenen Dicht-arten, aber uns Nordländer kann man auf jene Muster nicht ausschliesslich hinweisen. Wir haben uns andrer Voreltern zu rühmen und haben manch anderes Vorbild im Auge. Wäre nicht durch die romantische Wendung ungebildeter Jahrhunderte das Ungeheure mit dem Abgeschmackten in Berührung gekommen, woher hätten wir einen Hamlet, einen Lear, eine Anbetung des Kreuzes, einen standhaften Prinzen? Uns auf der Höhe dieser barbarischen Avantagen, da wir die antiken Vorteile wohl niemals erreichen werden, mit Mut zu erhalten, ist unsere Pflicht." (Notes to *Rameaus Neffe*. WA. 45, p. 176.)

to Italy. Two problems were torturing him: he lacked material on which to feed his creative impulse;[1] and he felt that the morality of self-denial, which Frau von Stein had taught him to pursue, had ceased to help him and was becoming sterile. The second problem was solved, as we have seen,[2] by his perception of the Greek man, who stood above the conflict of duty and inclination. For the first too he found the solution through Greece.

It may seem strange that in 1785 the German world was incapable of giving him material for his artistic urge, when a decade before it had provided all he needed. Why could he not have continued to create as he had done in *Götz*, in *Werther* or in *Faust*? It was not the *naiv* style that he was waiting to learn from the Greeks. *Werther* is, as Schiller said,[3] a *naiv* treatment of a "sentimental" subject; and the Gretchen tragedy in *Faust*[4] is as faithful a piece of objective presentation as any Greek achieved. Moreover Goethe's *Sturm und Drang* works are not merely *naiv*, they are not barrenly naturalistic; they have "significance", no less than the works of Goethe's Hellenism. The difference lies in the plane of significance which they symbolise. *Götz* is the picture of a strong spirit, conscious of its own integrity, struggling for the right in a chaotic world. *Werther* reveals the dangers that beset the genius's super-sensitive soul. The beauty and the cruelty of life are the hidden subject of the Gretchen tragedy. In the days of *Sturm und Drang* Goethe was primarily concerned with the regulation of his own relations with the outside world. The problems that were the material of his poetry, were therefore problems of conduct. In Weimar he grew out of this stage. *Iphigenie* and *Tasso* were the last subjects of this sort that interested him. Long before *Tasso* was finished, he had moved on to new problems. He had accepted the world as it was and its influence, for good or ill, on himself. He was now intent on probing the forces which created and maintained it. He longed to get behind the confusion of individual phenomena to the logic and beauty of the ideas that never change. Above all he wanted a vision of man as he should be, not as he was in

---

[1] See above, p. 122.
[3] *Werke*, xv, p. 53.

[2] See above, p. 195.
[4] 1775.

the world that Goethe knew. His scientific studies helped him a little towards his end, but far more was needed for the vision than a knowledge of the human skeleton. He must get where he could see humanity functioning as God intended, as a physical-spiritual unit. In Germany this was impossible. The forms that he saw were all in some way distorted and peculiar; they were stunted, quaint or monstrous; each one a law unto itself, a mockery of God's thought. In Germany there were too many veils between his eye and the eternal forms.

We have seen how he won the vision of man in Italy. The poetic works of the following years (except *Tasso*) were all re-expressions of this vision. Their "significance" is on a higher plane than that of *Götz* or the Gretchen tragedy. They are no longer concerned with isolated aspects of man's relations with the world. They reveal simply the existence and nature of man; and they do so with such an appearance of *naiv* truth to worldly reality, that we believe for a moment that human life really is as we see it here, beautiful, strong, sincere, in a word, godlike. Yet it is an ideal picture, that Goethe drew not from the world around him, but from the vision within him; and this vision he would never have won, if he had not wrung from the Greek statues and from Homer the secret of their ageless truth.

Many lovers of Goethe's poetry regret that he ever left the ways of his youth to pursue the barren ideal of Grecian form. They find the works of his Hellenistic period less vigorous, less full of human interest, less capable of stirring the heart than the great poems of *Sturm und Drang*. They believe that his poetic genius was made the unwilling slave of his intellect or of his instinct of self-preservation, which feared the unbridled power of a super-personal daimon, and took refuge from it in the well-prepared fortress of Greek forms.[1] In my opinion

---

[1] I hope I am not misinterpreting the words of other commentators of Goethe, when I suggest that J. G. Robertson and Miss Butler, with all their reverence for Goethe's poetic gifts, do regret his classicism, and do so essentially on the grounds I give here. Cf. Butler, *The Tyranny of Greece over Germany*, pp. 91 foll., 115, 123, 131; Robertson, *Life and Work of Goethe*, p. 138: "Rather might we say that the Goethe who believed that he had at last entered into the Holy of Holies of the artist's calling [in Italy], ceased from now on to be a creative artist at all"; also pp. 131, 137, 198 foll., 201. But cf. pp. 142-43.

Goethe's Hellenism was not the result of a conflict between his non-poetical self and his genius, nor is it in any way to be regretted by lovers of poetry. It came with the inevitable growth of his spirit, which passed beyond the stage of *Sturm und Drang* to seek the mystery of the forms of life. His poetic genius, which was an organic part of his whole existence and developed with it, could then be content only with material that reflected the new interest of his spirit. How freely and gladly, with what full use of all its vast powers, his genius worked in the service of the new ideal, is shown by the *Römische Elegien* and *Hermann und Dorothea*. They do not tear our hearts as *Werther* or the *Urfaust*; but by their moderate idealism, expressed in poetry of the highest order, they enrich man's spiritual heritage no less marvellously than the stormier poems of Goethe's youth. After *Hermann und Dorothea*, in the *Achilleis* and the *Natürliche Tochter*, it is true that an intellectual passion for Greek forms and practices led Goethe to harness his genius to ungrateful tasks. But by then Goethe's Hellenism was really over. Far below the range of vision of his conscious mind, his spirit was turning away from Greece, having drawn from it all that it could use. And it was his genius which first gave warning of the change. The strange insistence with which "Faust and company" forced themselves on his mind from the summer of 1797 onwards, and the undoubted excellence of the poetry that these unbidden guests brought with them, probably did more than anything to convince Goethe that Hellenism was not enough, and that the purpose of his life lay out and beyond it.

His spirit, as it unfolded one by one its hidden treasures, could not remain for ever in bondage to Greece. Goethe himself in later years admitted that his passion for Greece had blinded him to the genuine merits of other forms of life.[1] It is probable that he even regretted having spent so much of his time and of his best energies in a hopeless struggle. "The strangest error is that which affects ourselves and our abilities, when we dedicate ourselves to a worthy task, an honourable undertaking, for which we lack the necessary powers, when we strive after a goal that we can never reach. The resulting torment, that may be likened to those of Tantalus and Sisyphus,

[1] WA. 27, p. 278; WA. IV, 25, p. 82; Bied. II, p. 311.

is more keenly felt, the more earnestly one has striven. And yet often enough, when we see ourselves separated for ever from our goal, we find that we have discovered something else of value on the way, something that suits us, something with which we are by our nature intended to content ourselves."[1] These words, which appeared in *Kunst und Altertum* in 1820, do not refer explicitly to Goethe's Hellenism. But they fit the case so exactly, that one may assume Goethe had this experience in mind when he wrote them. In so far as he had tried to re-create Greek literature in his own poetry, he had certainly been attempting the impossible, and had only caused himself "Tantalisch-Sisyphische Qual". But he had won something permanent and infinitely valuable by all his striving: the vision of the Greek man, which never faded from his mind. Whatever stage of his development he might be in, whatever aspect of the world might for the moment have seized his attention, the form of life which the Greek had represented remained for Goethe alone valid and possible. "Jeder sei auf seine Art ein Grieche ! Aber er sei's."

[1] *Bedenkliches*, WA. 42, 2, p. 113. Cf. also WA. II, 3, p. 121: "Der wunderbarste Irrtum aber ist derjenige, der sich auf uns selbst und unsre Kräfte bezieht, dass wir uns einem würdigen Geschäft, einem ehrsamen Unternehmen widmen, dem wir nicht gewachsen sind, dass wir nach einem Ziel streben, das wir nie erreichen können. Die daraus entspringende Tantalisch-Sysiphische Qual empfindet jeder nur um desto bittrer, je redlicher er es meinte. Und doch sehr oft, wenn wir uns von dem Beabsichtigten für ewig getrennt sehen, haben wir schon auf unsrem Wege irgend ein andres Wünschenswertes gefunden, etwas uns Gemässes, mit dem uns zu begnügen wir eigentlich geboren sind."

CHAPTER VI

LAST YEARS: 1805–1832

Wir sind vielleicht zu antik gewesen;
Nun wollen wir es moderner lesen.

IN 1805, when he wrote his tribute to Winckelmann and said farewell to Hellenism, Goethe was fifty-five. Two-thirds of his life were gone, yet he had only just completed his "*Lehrjahre*". His struggle to master the Greek genius was the last great formative error of his life. When that stage was finished, his development too was done. Every potentiality of his nature had now unfolded itself and grown to its full stature. So long as he had still been developing, that aspect of his nature which was at any time growing most actively, tyrannised over his judgment and forced it to praise and condemn, accept and reject, in accordance with the needs of the active member. This was especially the case in his Hellenistic period. He measured all human achievement, and art above all, by Greek standards, and classed as worthless, or at best as of far inferior value, all art that was not founded on the Greek tradition. Now at last, his growing-pains over, he was ready to view the world without passion or predilection, and to find good in every creative influence. An extraordinary catholicity of interest is the most significant characteristic of the last twenty-five years of Goethe's life. Everything that lived and moved in the world around him attracted his attention, so that at times he was overwhelmed by the host of impressions, artistic, political, scientific, and religious, that poured in on him.

The broadening of his mind did not happen at a clap. The first unequivocal expressions of his new tolerance date in fact from the early months of 1808. To his old friend Jacobi he wrote, describing his interest in the character and in the dramatic works of Zacharias Werner: "I find it at times strange enough, old pagan that I am, to see the Cross set up on my own territory, and to hear Christ's blood and wounds preached in poetic

terms, without myself feeling any repugnance. We owe this
to the higher point of view to which philosophy has raised us.
We have learnt to value idealism, in whatever strange forms it
may appear."[1] Two months later he wrote to Jacobi again,
that he did not think so ill of the "so-called Dark Ages". "In
my father's house, I tell myself, are many mansions, and the
dark cellar down below is as much a part of the palace as the
sun-room on the roof....Even in those ages, that seem to us
dead and silent, there rang out a loud hymn from the chorus
of humanity to which the gods could well listen with pleasure."[2]
Twelve years before he had characterised the Middle Ages in
these words:

> Eingefroren sahen wir so Jahrhunderte starren,
> Menschengefühl und Vernunft schlich nur verborgen am Grund.[3]

Yet of Gothic architecture he had no love even in 1810.
When he first heard of Sulpiz Boissérée's efforts to restore,
at least on paper, the cathedral of Cologne, which had stood
unfinished since the Middle Ages, he declared the object of all
Boissérée's labour to be "valuable only in its place as a document
of a certain stage of human culture".[4] He regarded the pro-
posal to complete the cathedral according to the original plans
as a realisation of the tale of the Tower of Babel, and dismissed
the whole of medieval architecture as the "caterpillar and
cocoon stage" of taste. The enthusiasm of the younger genera-

---

[1] "Es kommt mir, einem alten Heiden, ganz wunderlich vor, das Kreuz
auf meinem eignen Grund und Boden aufgepflanzt zu sehen, und Christi
Blut und Wunden poetisch predigen zu hören, ohne das es mir gerade
zuwider ist. Wir sind dieses doch dem höheren Standpunkt schuldig, auf
den uns die Philosophie gehoben hat. Wir haben das Ideele schätzen gelernt,
es mag sich auch in den wunderlichsten Formen darstellen." 11 Jan. 1808
(WA. IV, 20, p. 5). Nevertheless Werner's comparison of the rising moon
to a holy wafer stuck in Goethe's throat (Bied. II, pp. 14, 15).

[2] 7 March 1808 (WA. IV, 20, p. 25). "In meines Vaters Hause, sage ich
mir, sind viel Appartementer, und der dunkle Keller unten gehört so gut
zum Pallast als der Altan auf dem Dache....Und da kommt mir denn doch
vor, dass immer noch in denen Zeiten, die uns stumm und dumm scheinen,
ein lauter Chorgesang der Menschheit erscholl, dem die Götter gern zuhören
durften."

[3] Vier Jahreszeiten, 86 (WA. I, p. 358): "Whole centuries we saw thus
stiff and frozen; humanity and reason crept unseen on the bottom."

[4] Letter to Reinhard, 22 July 1810 (WA. IV, 21, p. 360).

tion for such things he now recognised as inevitable; he had given up fighting against it.[1]

In May 1811, reluctantly enough,[2] he agreed to receive Boisserée in person and to listen to his explanation of the plans for the Cologne cathedral. For a week Boisserée, undaunted by a frigid reception, battered at the great man's prejudices. "On Tuesday (May 7th) when we were alone together with the drawings, he growled sometimes like a wounded bear; you could see what a struggle was going on inside him, and how he was taking himself to task for ever having misjudged such greatness." "After dinner (May 8th) we were sitting alone together. He praised my work with full warmth and emphasis. I had the exhilarating feeling, that a great and fair cause had triumphed over the prejudices of one of the greatest minds, with which in the last few days I had in very truth been wrestling."[3] Goethe made public confession to his conversion at different times during the last years of his life.[4] The most remarkable is perhaps that in which he speaks of the Cologne cathedral as "the most solid and splendid work, that has ever been begun on earth with a proper understanding of the necessities of art".[5] Without partisanship he contrasted the inner nature of ancient and medieval architecture in these words: "Ancient temples concentrate God in man; the churches of the Middle Ages strive towards God who dwells above."[6] He had given up judging all art by the standards of Greek achievement. He was content to recognise and to be grateful for the characteristic beauty of every genuine manner. Old German painting, Persian, Balkan or Chinese poetry, the *Nibelungenlied*, all these different expressions of man's artistic

[1] Letter to Reinhard, 14 May 1810 (*Ibid.* pp. 294, 296; also WA. IV, 20, p. 193).

[2] Cf. Bied. II, p. 115.

[3] Boisserée to his brother (*Ibid.* pp. 120, 125).

[4] *Herstellung des Strasburger Münsters* (1816), WA. 49, 2, pp. 168–78; *Cölner Domriss von Moller*, ibid. pp. 178–81; *Aussichten, Risse u. einzelne Teile des Doms zu Köln*, ibid. pp. 182–8; *Der Oppenheimer Dom*, ibid. p. 190; *Von deutscher Baukunst* (1823), ibid. pp. 159–67, especially p. 162.

[5] *Ibid.* p. 187: "Das tüchtigste, grossartigste Werk, das vielleicht je mit folgerechtem Kunstverstand auf Erden gegründet worden."

[6] *Maximen und Reflexionen*, WA. 48, p. 214: "Antike Tempel concentrieren den Gott im Menschen; des Mittelalters Kirchen streben nach dem Gott in der Höhe."

nature, and others besides, occupied him in the last two decades of his life, and won from him words of unfeigned delight. His view was broader; his judgment was freed from the tyranny of an absolute standard. But there was no reaction against the Greeks. His love for Greek things ran as an undercurrent to his intellectual activities through all the years up to his death. To some aspects of the Greek genius in fact he devoted more attention after 1805 than before. The pre-Socratic philosophers especially contributed many vital conceptions to his thought.[1] Their influence may be recognised not only in Goethe's ideas on the nature of light and other scientific subjects,[2] and in such poems as *Urworte Orphisch*,[3] but in subtler form in certain poems of the *Divan*[4] and in *Pandora*.[5]

At times the old passion for Greece welled up and occupied the main channel of his thoughts. So in 1817 and for some years after, he spent long hours of study on the Elgin Marbles, the Aeginetan sculptures and the frieze from Bassae,[6] all of which had become generally known at about the same time. Dissatisfied with the small-scale reproductions in published works, he arranged for life-size drawings of two groups from the pediment figures of the Parthenon to be sent from England. They arrived in January 1819; in June a cast of the horse head from the east pediment arrived for Goethe's order.[7] These new discoveries[8] brought about no change in Goethe's views on Greek art; they were rather the confirmation of those conclusions that he had drawn from the Apollo Belvedere, the Zeus of Otricoli, the

---

[1] Cf. C. Bapp, *Aus Goethes griechischer Gedankenwelt*, Leipzig, 1921.

[2] WA. II, 3, pp. 1–4, 108–13; 7, pp. 37, 203; and *Klassische Walpurgisnacht*, WA. 15, 1, pp. 146–76. Cf. JA. xiv, p. 348.

[3] WA. 3, 95. Cf. Letters to Knebel, 9 Oct. 1817 (WA. iv, 28, p. 272), and to Boissérée, 16 July 1818 (*Ibid.* 29, p. 240).

[4] Cf. JA. v, pp. xlviii, 335, 383.

[5] Cf. Morris, *Goethestudien*, I, p. 279.

[6] Elgins: WA. iv, 28, pp. 96, 140, 282, 292, 304, 389 foll.; WA. 36, pp. 105, 124, 145. Bassae: WA. iv, 29, pp. 45, 105 foll.; WA. 49, 2, p. 16. Cf. G-J. xix, 11. Aeginetans: WA. iv, 22, p. 320; 28, pp. 282, 390; 29, p. 105; WA. 49, 2, p. 20; 36, pp. 76, 124.

[7] WA. iv, 31, p. 180; Letter to August v. Goethe, 14 June 1819.

[8] Goethe had previously seen drawings of some of the Parthenon sculptures in Rome in 1787 (see above, p. 169), and in Darmstadt in 1814 (WA. iv, 25, p. 57) he had seen casts of part of the frieze. Cf. also G-J. xix, p. 9.

Ludovisi Juno and all the other remains of ancient art that he had found in Italy. For this very reason the Elgin Marbles were for him of supreme value. He had no desire to go again to Italy; but he would not be surprised to find himself one day on the road to the British Museum. "You would have to share my conception of what these remains mean, in order to see how utterly reasonable the absurdity of such a journey would be....For after all here alone [in the Elgin Marbles] are law and evangel side by side. Everything else one could, if need were, do without."[1] He advised every German sculptor to go to England and live there for as long as possible for the purpose of studying the Elgin Marbles.[2] It seems he realised that they were worth more than all the statues in Rome together.[3]

The Elgin Marbles brought about a renaissance in Goethe's active interest in Greek things. Between 1817 and 1823 he not only finished and published two essays on ancient art, *Myrons Kuh* and *Philostrats Gemälde*,[4] which he had begun some years before; he also followed closely the controversy between Hermann and Creuzer on Greek mythology;[5] and in 1820 and 1821 he revised and published the digest of the *Iliad* which he had made for his own use in 1798.[6] In connexion with this work he returned with delight to Homer's world, and revived his long-dormant interest in the Homeric question.[7] With obvious relief he came back to a belief in a personal Homer, an arch-editor of genius, and greeted the work of the younger critics who opposed the Wolfian heresy, in these lines:

> Scharfsinnig habt ihr, wie ihr seid,
> Von aller Verehrung uns befreit,
> Und wir bekannten überfrei,
> Dass Ilias nur ein Flickwerk sei.

[1] Letter to Sartorius, 20 July 1817 (WA. IV, 28, pp. 189, 412).
[2] WA. 49, 2, p. 60.
[3] Cf. WA. IV, 28, p. 390; 36, p. 254; Bied. III, p. 302.
[4] WA. 49, 2, p. 3 and 49, 1, p. 61.
[5] WA. IV, 28, pp. 266, 272; 31, p. 276; 33, p. 242; Bied. III, p. 266; WA. 36, p. 173.
[6] WA. 41, 1, pp. 266–327. Cf. WA. IV, 34, pp. 39, 41, 95, 133, 233, 254.
[7] Cf. WA. IV, 34, pp. 41, 96; 35, pp. 147, 170; 36, p. 191; 38, p. 122. Cf. Bied. II, p. 433.

Mög unser Abfall niemand kränken;
Denn Jugend weiss was zu entzünden,
Dass wir ihn lieber als Ganzes denken,
Als Ganzes freudig ihn empfinden.[1]

In 1821 he began a new study of Euripides, which continued at intervals up to the last weeks of his life, and produced his reconstruction of the lost *Phaethon* from the extant fragments,[2] his translation of the last scene of the *Bacchae*,[3] and his uncompleted essay on the *Cyclops*.[4] Euripides became towards the end his favourite Greek author. In the last November of his life he resolved to read "this priceless Greek poet" steadily through the coming winter, in the Greek text, with help from translations.[5] Only three weeks before his death he defended Euripides in vigorous terms against the criticisms of the scholars, and dwelt with especial emphasis on the terrible beauty of the *Bacchae*.[6] A year before he had characterised as "arme Heringe" those who could not appreciate Euripides's greatness.[7] From the spring of 1825 until the summer of 1830 he lived with especial intensity in the Greek world, for he was engaged in finishing the *Helena* and in writing the fantastic introduction to it, the *Klassische Walpurgisnacht*.[8]

Certainly Greece remained to the end his foremost, in a sense his only, love. She no longer ruled the aesthetic world as despot and lawgiver; she sat enthroned in a heaven apart, above the rest. Goethe was insistent now that the products of other civilisations should not be compared with what the Greeks had produced. So the Persian Ferdusi, and the old German *Nibelungenlied*, should never be compared with Homer.

---

[1] *Homer wieder Homer*, WA. 3, p. 159: "You have in your clever way freed us from all reverence; and we asserted too glibly that the *Iliad* was only a patchwork. Let no one take offence if we change our mind, for young men have been able to fire us to think of him rather as a whole, to feel him joyfully as a whole."

[2] WA. 41, 2, pp. 32, 63, 243.   [3] *Ibid.* p. 237.

[4] *Ibid.* p. 467. Cf. WA. 36, p. 433; WA. IV, 42, p. 220; *Ibid.* 38, p. 172.

[5] *Ibid.* 49, p. 146.   [6] Bied. IV, p. 435.

[7] *Ibid.* p. 325.

[8] *Helena*: begun mid-March 1825, finished June 1826. *Klassische Walpurgisnacht*: begun April 1826 (cf. Gräf, *Drama*, II, pp. 329, 331), finished July 1830 (cf. Gräf, p. 555). For the intermediary stages see Gräf, pp. 353, 366 foll., 378, 515, 533 foll., 544, 550, 555.

The result would only be disappointment and a failure to appreciate their characteristic beauties.[1]

On the other hand any attempt to set Greek things down on a level with the achievements of other cultures was abhorrent to him. When F. Creuzer attempted to prove a common origin for the myths of all Indo-Germanic peoples,[2] Goethe did not conceal his displeasure. "When the attempt is made to leave the Hellenic circle of god-in-man and to point to every region of the earth and indicate similarities in word and form, here the frost-giants, there the fire-brahmas, it causes us really too much pain, and we take flight again to Ionia, where loving spring-daemons mate, and bring forth Homer."[3]

> Auf ewig hab' ich sie vertrieben,
> Vielköpfige Götter trifft mein Bann,
> So Wischnu, Cama, Brama, Schiven,
> Sogar den Affen Hannemann.
> Nun soll am Nil ich mich gefallen,
> Hundsköpfige Götter heissen gross.
> O, wär' ich doch aus meinen Hallen
> Auch Isis und Osiris los.[4]

This was Goethe's opinion of the gods of other races. To suggest that Zeus, and Apollo and Pallas, were even distant cousins of these monsters, seemed to him no better than wanton sacrilege.

The Greeks were different from all other races. "One has to make allowances for all other arts, to Greek art alone one

---

[1] *Noten und Abhandlungen zum Divan. Warnung*, WA. 7, p. 108.

[2] In *Briefe über Homer und Hesiodus, vorzüglich über die Theogonie*, Heidelberg, 1818, pp. 38, 55, 93 onwards.

[3] WA. IV, 28, p. 267: cf. WA. IV, 31, p. 276; 33, pp. 242–3: "Geht's nun aber gar noch weiter, und deutet man uns aus dem hellenischen Gott-Menschenkreise nach allen Regionen der Erde, um das Ähnliche dort aufzuweisen, in Worten und Bildern, hier die Frost-Riesen, dort die Feuer-Brahmen, so wird es uns gar zu weh, und wir flüchten wieder nach Ionien, wo dämonische liebende Quellgötter sich begatten und den Homer erzeugen."

[4] WA. IV, 35, p. 237; cf. WA. IV, 25, p. 274: "I have banned them for ever; I am done with many-headed gods—Vishnu, Cama, Brahma, Shiva, even the monkey Hanneman. Now they want me to feel at home on the Nile and call dog-headed gods great. Oh! would that I were rid of Isis and Osiris from my halls."

is eternally in debt."[1] So in 1827, while talking with Eckermann about the age of "*Weltliteratur*" which was dawning,
he said: "However much we value foreign literatures, we must
not cling to one in particular and try to take that one as our
model. We must not think the Chinese, or the Serbian, or
Calderon, or the Nibelungen can be that. If we are in need of a
model, we must always go back to the ancient Greeks, in whose
works the object of representation is always beautiful humanity
(der schöne Mensch). Everything else we must look at from a
purely historical standpoint, and take in what is good in it as
far as may be."[2]

Goethe's reasons for setting Greek culture in this unique
position were the same now as they had been at the height of
his Hellenism. In their art and literature the Greeks had expressed Nature's intentions more perfectly than was commonly
the case in the world of phenomena. He cited two horse heads
from the Parthenon: "The English, the best judges of horses
in the world, are forced to admit that two antique horse heads
are more perfect in form than those of any breed extant to-day.
These heads date from the best period of Greek art. Our
wonder and admiration is not to be explained on the assumption
that those artists were working from more perfect individuals
than those which exist to-day. The reason is rather that they
had, with the progress of time and art, themselves become
something, so that they brought an inner greatness of spirit to
their observation of Nature."[3] A French visitor in 1828 re-
ported him as having said: "Celui qui veut faire quelque chose
d'idéale, doit avoir amené son développement intérieur à un
point tel que, comme les Grecs, il puisse élever la réalité
mesquine de la nature à la hauteur de son esprit. Le rôle de
l'artiste est de transformer en une réalité sans lacunes ce que
dans la nature, par suite d'une faiblesse intime, ou de quelque
obstacle extérieur, est resté à l'état d'intention."[4]

The other chief reason for the unique value of Greek culture
was that for the Greek the object of art and the centre of all
spiritual activity had been "der schöne Mensch".[5] This was

---

[1] WA. 48, p. 183.
[2] Eckermann, 31 Jan. 1827. Cf. WA. 41, 2, p. 233.
[3] Eckermann, 20 Oct. 1828.   [4] Bied. IV, p. 166; cf. III, p. 24.
[5] Bied. III, p. 339; cf. WA. 41, 2, p. 233.

what gave the Greek tradition its eternal value. Man in any age had only to look back at what the Greeks had been and had created, to see himself as he was in intention and as he might be in fact, with labour and the grace of God. The form of European man especially was akin to the Greek.[1] In Goethe's view European culture could advance only when it based itself on the Greek tradition. This is what he meant when he said: "We should still be living in barbarism, if the remains of the ancient world in its different forms were not extant."[2] After the Roman Empire, which had continued in the Greek tradition, had been destroyed by barbarians and Christianity,[3] there had come a vast break in the tradition; and European culture had resumed its advance only when the achievements of the ancient world had once again become known and its standards, in part at least, accepted.

Just as, after 1805, Goethe's interests widened to include all the known civilisations of the globe, so his style of composition became more catholic. It is only necessary to study the multiplicity of metres in the *Divan* and their origins, to see how gladly Goethe's genius, free at last of the elegiac distich, sprang around among the rhythms of the earth and danced with this or that as the whim seized it.[4] In his dramatic style too Goethe gave up the orthodox iambics of *Iphigenie*, *Tasso* and the *Natürliche Tochter*, as well as the strictly Greek form of his early *Helena* fragment, and developed a form of extraordinary rhythmic and stylistic diversity. The Second Part of *Faust* shows this style at its fullest development. Yet in his dramatic writing Goethe never cut himself loose entirely from the Greek tradition. In *Pandora* (1807–1808), in the *Löwenstuhl* (1813–1814), in *Epimenides* (1814) and in the Helena act of *Faust* Greek themes and forms appear, mixed with modern thoughts and modern metres.

In *Pandora* Goethe turned once again to the ancient legend of Prometheus, which twice before had stirred his poetic phantasy. The story of Pandora's box and the traditional contrast between the characters of Prometheus and Epimetheus form the basis of the action; but the myth is adapted and extended to fit

[1] This idea already in 1799. Cf. WA. 47, p. 292.
[2] Bied. IV, p. 288.
[3] Cf. *Ibid.* p. 308.   [4] Cf. JA. v, p. xxvi foll.

Goethe's needs, with a freedom that he hardly employed even in the days of *Sturm und Drang*. The action of the play was to represent (it too is unfinished) a second coming of Pandora with a second and more marvellous box and at the end the rejuvenation and assumption of Epimetheus.[1] Around this central theme, itself an invention, Goethe grouped other *motivs*, all more or less freely found: two daughters of Pandora by Epimetheus; a secret love between one of these and a son of Prometheus; a violent quarrel between the lovers; the suicide and the miraculous resurrection of the youth; his Bacchic triumph; the reconciliation of the lovers, and their dedication as priest and priestess of the temple which is revealed when Pandora's second box is opened; the conflict of opinions over this box between the different types of men; and the strange contents of the box: seated daemons of art and knowledge half hidden by a curtain.[2] The content of the play is partly "sentimental": a dream of more than earthly bliss, as Morris suggests;[3] partly allegorical: a representation of the nature and value of culture to man. Nothing in the play is in any sense *naiv*. Frankly and fully Goethe admitted his modernity, and used the figures of Greek mythology to give living shape to his modern thoughts.

The outer form of *Pandora* is also a marvellous blend of old and new. The basic metre is the trimeter, and some of the lyric metres are much simplified forms of those employed in the Greek tragic choruses. But many of the lyrics are rhymed; and in general the style, despite a few Graecisms,[4] has little in common with the truly Greek accents of the *Helena* fragment. As Harnack points out,[5] the form of *Pandora* is a development of the Greek tragic form towards that of opera. Already in 1800 Goethe had conceived his *Danaiden* as suitable for treatment as a kind of opera or "ernsthaftes Singstück",[6] while at the same time approaching in form the earliest Aeschylean tragedies. The unfinished opera text, *der Löwenstuhl*, with its Greek metres[7] and highly romantic material was an attempt

---

[1] Cf. Goethe's plan for the unwritten second part: WA. 50, pp. 457–60.
[2] Cf. Morris, *Goethestudien*, I, p. 277.   [3] *Ibid.* pp. 273 foll.
[4] Cf. Wilamowitz-Moellendorf, *Reden und Vorträge*, 1913, p. 393.
[5] *Essais und Studien*, 1899, p. 117.
[6] WA. IV, 15, p. 232.   [7] WA. 12, p. 425.

to carry the process a step further. In *Epimenides Erwachen* there are no Greek metres, but the form is the same: a structure of iambic dialogue, enlivened and adorned by lyric interludes. In the Second Part of *Faust* the same form is there in all the acts, but so freely abused by the careless assurance of the master, that we hardly realise its presence. If it were not there, the strict Greek form of the opening of the third act would strike our aesthetic sense as something incongruous, as too sudden a change of key. Instead we greet it with relief, for we feel that this is the basic form, the tonic, from which all that has gone before and all that follows are modulations, organically related, however distant they may be.

How strange that from the "noble simplicity and quiet greatness" of Greek art Goethe should have developed a poetic style of such extravagant richness and diversity! Nothing could better prove his deep understanding of the vitality of the Greek genius. Yet it is not so strange, for it is the road that modern art has often followed, when it has been deeply imbued with the spirit of Greece. The romantic, the sentimental, the complex in the modern soul meets the Greek instinct for living form, and there results something like Palladio's Rotonda, St Peter's, the Judgment Day, or *Prometheus Unbound*, something "ein wenig toll",[1] something in fact "*Barock*", as the Germans understand the term. Goethe at least never lost touch with the Greek element from which his "*Barock*" sprang. When in 1825 he turned in earnest to finish the Second Part of *Faust*, it cost him no more effort to write the trimeters and tetrameters that were needed to finish the Greek section of the *Helena*, than it did to compose in the diverse forms which the romantic sections demanded. Harnack has pointed out how far more varied and expressive the trimeters of the final *Helena* are, than those of the *Helena* fragment of 1800. His labour on the ancient metres in *Pandora* (1807 and 1808) had given Goethe this technical mastery of his medium.[2]

The *Helena* and the *Klassische Walpurgisnacht* were the fruit, now plucked at leisure, with the passionless ease of his old age, of Goethe's life-long love of Greece. Every impression of

[1] See above, p. 129.
[2] Otto Harnack, *Ueber den Gebrauch des Trimeters bei Goethe. Vierteljahrschrift für Literaturgeschichte*, v, pp. 114-19.

Greece that his eighty years had brought him, the "rasende Erzzauberin Medea" on the Frankfurt puppet stage no less than the revelation of Homer in Sicily, or the Elgin Marbles, contributed something to this strange complex of Hellenic, half Hellenic and modern phantasies. Here, in the purest poetic symbolism, Goethe summed up his relations with the Greek spirit and his belief in its vital importance to modern man. But the symbolism is of a kind that makes interpretation hard. The pictures which Goethe presents in the Second Part of *Faust* may satisfy our poetical perception and may seem to it to be full of meaning. But if we attempt to catch this meaning and define it in intellectual terms, it flees our grasp and we are left with a confusion of pictures and but little meaning. This is true in some degree of all the Second Part and especially of that series of scenes which portray Faust's relations with the Greek tradition. The fundamental symbolism is not in doubt: Faust's mating with Helen represents Goethe's own victory in the struggle to know the nature of beauty; the choice of a Greek figure to symbolise ideal beauty was inevitable, since Goethe had won his knowledge of beauty through study of Greek art, and believed that, of all men, the Greeks had had the deepest insight into the laws of life that create beauty. So much is clear and may be re-expressed in intellectual terms without difficulty. But when we examine the separate themes of the Helena episode—Faust's journey to the Mothers, the first apparition of Helen, his dream of Leda, Chiron and Manto, his descent to Hades, Phorkyas, Lynceus, Euphorion, and many more—and try to relate them to the basic symbol in such a way as to give them all organic significance, then we must say good-bye to certainty and all pretence to a provable thesis, and frankly admit that any interpretation we may suggest is only conjecture. Even when we have Goethe's word for some point of interpretation, as for instance that Euphorion is the personification of poetry,[1] we must be careful not to apply this definition too rigidly. Euphorion is an elastic creature, who can expand and contract so as to suggest now all the audacious energy of youth, now merely the "well-known features" of Lord Byron.

Every scheme of interpretation breaks down when logically

[1] Eckermann, 20 Dec. 1829.

applied. The autobiographical principle for instance, though it helps us to understand why Goethe included some of the episodes in the Helena series,[1] is not the only key that we need. We cannot say that all the stages of the Helena episode correspond to events or stages in Goethe's approach to Greece; nor can we say that every stage in his approach to Greece is represented by some episode in Faust's search for Helen. There is, for instance, nothing in *Faust, Part II*, which represents Goethe's attitude to Greece in the days of *Sturm und Drang*, when he felt above all close kinship with the heroes and demigods; and by no stretch of ingenuity can Faust's approach to Helen through the monsters of the *Klassische Walpurgisnacht* be equated with any stage in Goethe's own approach to Greece.

The world in which Faust is seen in the first act of Part II is a sordid one. It moves in obedience to the elemental forces of greed, fear, jealousy, anger, laziness; no higher ideal, no conscious purpose, save such as these dictate, is present in the minds of any of the characters. Faust himself shows no higher striving; and the Carnival which he provides for the Kaiser's entertainment, is itself a reflexion of this sordid world. It is intended to be a "cheerful festival",[2] and it begins brightly enough with choruses of Italian gardeners and flower-girls. But very soon it has deteriorated into a shouting-match between different types of poets, amongst whom only the "night- and grave-poets" can make themselves heard; and they only to announce that they are in communication with a "lately resurrected vampyre". In an attempt to restore cheerfulness to the scene, the Herald calls on figures of Greek mythology. The Graces appear, but only for a moment, and are followed by the Fates, who do not let the onlookers forget their sinister role in human life. With the Furies, then, fair of form indeed, but bringers of strife and destruction, the note of anxiety returns strongly, and reaches another climax when the loathsome figure of Zoilo-Thersites, struck by the Herald for his mocking speech, turns first into an egg and then into an otter and a bat, which in their exit brush the feet and heads of the onlookers and nearly cause a panic. The figures of Greek legend have done nothing to restore cheerfulness or even

[1] Cf. Fairley, *Goethe as revealed in his poetry*, 1932, p. 80.
[2] Line 5067.

dignity to the Carnival; and so it continues. Neither Plutus in his dragon-car nor the Great Pan himself can keep the proceedings from falling at frequent intervals into a world of magical tricks, which terrify the onlookers and quite destroy their holiday mood.

This first entry of the Greek tradition into *Faust* was meant by Goethe to show it as it is misused by the sophisticated world for the superficial purpose of light entertainment. Of course the Greek figures in the Carnival have no power to raise the world out of its sordid elements, for they are part and parcel of that shallow world; not the powers themselves, as the Greeks knew them, but their empty forms, turned by the misuse of time into ciphers, pretty conventions, allegories. It is not Pan who enters at the end in triumphal rout, but the Emperor dressed as Pan; and his beard which burns in the magic mock-fire, is seen to be a false one.

Faust's only interest at the Emperor's court is to use his and Mephisto's magic powers for the entertainment of the shallow-minded Emperor. He appears himself hardly less shallow. By chance then, through over-confidence in his own magic, he is brought back on to the road of striving. He promises the Kaiser to produce for him the shades of Paris and Helen. Mephistopheles can help but little, and he disapproves the scheme, feeling instinctively that it will lead Faust into a different world, where he, Mephisto, will have little to say:

> Du wähnst, es füge sich sogleich;
> Hier stehen wir vor steilern Stufen,
> Greifst in ein fremdestes Bereich,
> Machst frevelhaft am Ende neue Schulden,
> Denkst Helenen so leicht hervorzurufen
> Wie das Papiergespenst der Gulden.—
> Mit Hexen-Fexen, mit Gespenst-Gespinsten,
> Kielkröpfigen Zwergen steh' ich gleich zu Diensten;
> Doch Teufels-Liebchen, wenn auch nicht zu schelten,
> Sie können nicht für Heroinen gelten.[1]

[1] Lines 6193–202: "You think, it can be done at once; these are steeper heights to climb. You stretch your hand out into another realm entirely, and at the end make new debts with unforgivable audacity. You think you can conjure up Helen as easily as the sham paper guilders. With witch-nonsense, ghost-weavings, pot-bellied dwarfs, I am always at your service; but devil's darlings, though not bad in their way, will never pass for heroines."

And so Faust is forced to undertake himself the perilous journey to the Mothers, from whom alone he can win the shade of Helen. Already from afar the spirit of Greece is helping him to free himself from magic and stand before Nature "a man alone".[1] The journey to the Mothers is the first step on the upward road for Faust, the road that will lead him, through knowledge of Beauty and the satisfaction of work, to the full realisation of his personality. It is no chance that the objective of this first step is Helen, the Greek way of life, the Greek ideal of beauty.

The whole episode of the journey to the Mothers, and the first appearance of Helen on the magic stage at the Emperor's court, is one of the most poetically effective in *Faust*. For that very reason it would be unwise to dogmatise on its significance. At the end Faust, beside himself at sight of Helen's beauty, tries to seize her; there is an explosion; Helen vanishes, and Faust falls senseless to the ground, and remains unconscious until he sets foot on Greek soil at the beginning of the *Klassische Walpurgisnacht*. Here perhaps the biographical principle of interpretation may be applied, and we may suggest that this first vision of Helen represents Goethe's first awareness of Greek beauty as an ideal, during his early years in Weimar;[2] that he assumed too soon a full understanding of the nature of Beauty, was presently disappointed and rebuffed, and was able to continue his search and finally win to perfect knowledge only on the classical soil of Italy and in constant contact with the remnants of the Greek tradition. Be that as it may, it is at least clear that Goethe meant to teach that knowledge of the Greek ideal was not a prize to be had for the taking, but must be won by single-minded and courageous diligence.

Faust cannot recover from his swoon until he sets foot on classic soil. But when he does so, what a strange un-Hellenic world he sees around him! Against a background of ghostly glimmering watchfires of the Pompeian and Caesarian hosts, sphinxes, bird-clawed sirens, griffons, ants and Arimaspians[3] are congregated to celebrate the Classical Walpurgisnight on the field of Pharsalia. Why should Goethe have chosen to

---

[1] Line 11,406.   [2] See above, pp. 90–2.
[3] Goethe planned at times to introduce yet other monsters of antiquity. Cf. Paralipomena 123, 99, WA. 15, 2, pp. 204, 189.

introduce Faust to Greece through such a world of monsters? Why should he, who had often condemned the civilisations of Egypt and India for their monster-gods, and had extolled Greek legend for its pure anthropomorphism, now choose to emphasise the monster-tradition in classical mythology? Almost he seems to capitulate to Creuzer's comparative view of mythology,[1] and to grant that the Greek world of legend is not essentially different from that of barbarian peoples.

Certainly we cannot conceive Goethe at the height of his Hellenism, in 1800, when he began the *Helena*, writing the *Klassische Walpurgisnacht* as it now stands. But the delight which the old Goethe took in the hideous forms of Greek fable does not indicate any change in his conception of the basic value of the Greek achievement. It is only a symptom of that broadening of view which had taken place after 1805, of a readiness to admit that all human civilisations have their roots in the same elemental forces,[2] which are not themselves beautiful and are only sometimes shaped to beautiful ends by the higher instincts in man. All those parts of the *Klassische Walpurgisnacht* in which Faust takes little or no part, the opening scene with Mephistopheles and the Sphinxes and Sirens, and the later scenes in which are shown Pygmies and Lamias, Dryads and Oreads, Empuse, Seismos[3] and the Graiae, Nereus, Proteus, Galatea and all the lesser powers of the deep, depict these elemental forces. Fittingly the act ends with a paean to Eros and the four Elements. Neither the Olympian gods, who are power expressed in form, nor the heroes, human representatives of these highest forms, have any place in the *Klassische Walpurgisnacht*, which shows us Greece on its lowest plane. But these elemental forces, so Goethe will tell us, are as essential to the greatness of Greece, as are its unseen roots to a forest tree. Without them Helen would not be great as well as perfect; and it is indispensable for Faust to realise their existence and their nature, before he can proceed on his quest of Helen.[4]

---

[1] See above, p. 269.
[2] Gundolf, *Goethe*, p. 679: "Dumpfe Mächte und Kräfte."
[3] Paralipomenon 123: WA. 15, 2, p. 206, Enceladus.
[4] In his diary Goethe referred to the *Klassische Walpurgisnacht* as "Helenas Antecedenzien": WA. III, 10, pp. 283 foll.

Faust is only superficially interested in the monsters. Because he feels that they represent the first stage on his road to Helen, he is ready to see what good he can in them. At sight of the Sphinxes and the Sirens he exclaims:

> Wie Wunderbar! das Anschaun tut mir Gnüge,
> Im Widerwärtigen grosse, tüchtige Züge.
> Ich ahne schon ein günstiges Geschick.[1]

And they rouse in him memories of the heroes who had dealings with them.[2] After this one brief contact with the monsters, Faust leaves them to Mephistopheles, and sets out to learn tidings of Helen. At once he moves into a higher world. He seems to see the mating of Zeus and Leda. It is a vision of double significance: the bathing maidens, not heroic forms indeed but beautiful human forms, mark the first step upwards, away from the monster-forms of sphinx and siren; and his being present at the moment of Helen's begetting, shows that he has learnt the lesson of his disastrous attempt to seize her prematurely, and is ready to begin at the beginning and learn her nature thoroughly, before he dares to possess her. Once before, in the troubled swoon that followed his first sight of Helen, he dreamt of Leda and the Swan.[3] Now he sees the same scene enacted before his bodily eyes.

Faust next meets Chiron. As a centaur Chiron is of course a monster; but he is also the "ideal tutor",[4] who educated all the heroes of the Herculean age, and so he is part of the higher world. Through him Faust moves on towards knowledge of beautiful humanity. In Chiron's description of the Argonauts Faust is given a picture of the manly ideal, expressed in its many aspects by the different heroes and in something near perfection by Hercules.[5] Already he is far removed from the splendid ugliness of the sphinxes. His mind is ready for fresh news of Helen; and so he learns that she once sat where he now sits, on Chiron's back. In Chiron's description he sees her as she then was, a girl on the threshold of womanhood, her full majesty still undeveloped, but of irresistible charm.[6] After

---

[1] "How marvellous! their aspect pleases me. Though repellent, they show great, sturdy features. They give me promise of a happy lot": lines 7181–3.
[2] Lines 7185–6.   [3] Lines 6903–20.
[4] "Urhofmeister": WA. 15, 2, p. 208.
[5] Lines 7365–94.   [6] Lines 7400–33.

the vision of her begetting, this picture of her is the next stage of preparatory knowledge.

The realisation that he is speaking to one who once carried Helen on his back makes Faust break out in passionate longing:

> So sei auch sie durch keine Zeit gebunden!
> Hat doch Achill auf Pherä sie gefunden,
> Selbst ausser aller Zeit. Welch seltnes Glück:
> Errungen Liebe gegen das Geschick!
> Und sollt *ich* nicht, sehnsüchtigster Gewalt,
> Ins Leben ziehn die einzigste Gestalt?
> Das ewige Wesen, Göttern ebenbürtig,
> So gross als zart, so hehr als liebenswürdig?
> Du sahst sie einst; *heut* hab' ich sie gesehn,
> So schön wie reizend, so ersehnt wie schön.
> Nun ist mein Sinn, mein Wesen streng umfangen;
> Ich lebe nicht, kann ich sie nicht erlangen.[1]

Chiron suggests he should seek to be healed of his mad purpose by the Sibyll, Manto; to which Faust replies:

> Geheilt will ich nicht sein, mein Sinn ist mächtig;
> Da wär' ich ja wie andere niederträchtig.[2]

To make Greece live again "gegen das Geschick" must seem a crazy project to the common sense of common minds. For Goethe that more than human task had been the breath of life for twenty years. Desire and accomplishment had both been vast; his failures no less heroic.

Goethe intended that the *Klassische Walpurgisnacht* should end, or Act III should begin, with Faust's descent to Hades in Manto's company, to win Helen's release from Proserpina. The scene was planned as early as the rest of Act II, but it was

---

[1] "So let her too be unbound by time! Achilles found her on Pherae, outside all time. Rare happiness: to win love even against the doom of Fate! And shall I not, by the power of my longing, draw that uniquest form over into life? that eternal being, co-equal of the gods, no less great than tender, no less austere than kind? Thou sawest her once; to-day I saw her, as fair as she was charming, as much desired as fair. Now my mind, my very being is in strictest thrall; I will not live if I cannot attain her": lines 7434-45.
[2] "Healed I will not be. My purpose is mighty. I should be mean-minded as others [if I were willing to be healed]": lines 7459-60. Cf. line 7488.

never carried out.[1] In all the sketches which Goethe made for
it,[2] the same basic idea is present: the precedent established by
Helen's meeting with Achilles on the island of Pherae is to be
followed; Helen may return to life on condition that she does
not leave Spartan soil, and that Faust shall win her favour on
his own merits, without help from gods or magic. The latter
condition continues the lesson which Faust has already learnt,
that Helen can be won only through hard work inspired by
passionate desire. So too Goethe had not spared himself in his
pursuit of Greece; the fruitful knowledge of the Greek tradition,
which in the end did so much for the development of Goethe's
spirit and of his poetry, was won by enormous labour. The
other condition—that Helen must remain on Spartan soil—
was not always part of Goethe's plan. The earliest fragmentary
sketch of the *Helena* (Paralipomenon 84),[3] which dates probably from 1798, and the detailed sketch of the Second Part
(1816), which purports to give the original plan as Goethe
conceived it in 1775,[4] both show Faust finding and winning
Helen in Germany. It is possible that the change of plan was
brought about simply by Goethe's desire to re-create Greek
tragedy, for which purpose it was necessary that Helen should
appear against a Greek background; and that the condition
was then introduced by Goethe in 1826 to explain the change
of scene from Germany to Greece. More probably, however,
this condition expresses a conviction to which Goethe had come
in the course of his long struggle with the Greek genius: that
Greek beauty cannot be transplanted bodily and made to live
again in the modern world, separated from the conditions of
time and place upon which it grew up. The modern who
would know Greece must make pilgrimage thither, must
dwell there, breathe the air of Greece and experience what
Greek beauty was; but in the end he must return to his own
world and go on in it alone. This was the lesson which Goethe
had learnt from the *Achilleis*.[5]

---

[1] Cf. Eckermann, 15 Jan. 1827.
[2] Paralipomena 99, 123, 157: WA. 15, 2, pp. 190, 210, 224. Dates
respectively: Nov. 1826; 17 Dec. 1826; 18 June 1830.
[3] WA. 15, 2, p. 184. See above, p. 242.
[4] *Ibid.* p. 176. See above, p. 240.   [5] See above, pp. 227–232.

The *Helena* fragment of 1800, essentially unchanged,[1] opens the third act of the Second Part. Goethe's first task, when he returned to work on *Faust* in 1825, was to complete this antique section of the *Helena*.[2] This he did with the addition of some three hundred lines—trimeters, choruses, and trochaic tetrameters. The object of the antique section of the *Helena*, thus completed, was to portray objectively the Greek world which Faust was to experience in his mating with Helen. In these first six hundred lines of Act III we have then the expression in poetical terms of Goethe's valuation of Greece. Nowhere else, neither in his poetry nor in his essays, did he define so succinctly what Greece meant to him. But the definition is in poetical terms, and must be translated and re-expressed before it can be grasped by the intellect. We are given a picture, from which we must abstract the meaning.

We see a central figure, Helen, heroic in stature and in spirit, of in-born dignity and poise, firm in the face of danger, a mistress accustomed to rule and be obeyed. She moves against a background of elemental forces no less sordid than that of the Emperor's court, or that in which Mephisto found himself so much at home in the *Klassische Walpurgisnacht*. The chorus belong to this elemental world, as Phorkyas is not tired of emphasising. They are vampires,[3] all-devouring locusts;[4] they sway from one emotion to another, having no higher purpose, no will but what the moment dictates. They rail at Phorkyas like fish-wives; then flatter her when she seems their only salvation.[5] They are haunted throughout by a feeling of their unreality; and at the end they are shown to have no personality; they return to the elements of which they are made.

Goethe knew that life in Greece had been as cruel, as petty, as senseless, as much a disordered conflict of warring elements, as at any other time or place in the world.[6] There were barbarians even among the heroes before Troy.[7] But the Greeks had learned to shape the elemental forces. They had given them

---

[1] The trimeters were given more variety (cf. Harnack, *Ueber den Gebrauch des Trimeters bei Goethe*, in *Vierteljahrschrift für Literaturgeschichte*, v, pp. 114–19), and Helen's long opening speech was broken up by choric interjections.
[2] Cf. Gräf, *Drama*, II, p. 305.
[3] Line 8821.   [4] Line 8779.   [5] Line 8957.
[6] Cf. Bied. II, p. 205 (No. 1522).   [7] Line 9015.

form and purpose, had made beauty out of confusion. Helen is the symbol not of all Greek life but of this highest achievement of the Greeks, this principle of form, of ordered purpose, of self-control and mastery. Wherever in *Faust, Part II* Helen's influence is absent, there the elemental forces, selfish, aimless, weak, ephemeral, hold sway. In the first act everything is sordid except Faust's journey to the Mothers and the apparition of Helen. All those parts of the *Klassische Walpurgisnacht* which have nothing to do with Helen, show us the ugly elemental world; in which indeed Homunculus preserves a higher purpose. But who is to say what Goethe "meant" by that riddling sprite? In the first scene of the third act we are shown the contrast between the elemental world and the higher principle, between the chorus and Helen. Then in Faust's castle, where Helen is acknowledged supreme mistress and queen, the elemental world is for the first time banished quite; all is noble, dignified, purposeful. But with Helen's return to Hades, the elements sweep in and obliterate every trace of the nobler existence that has gone before. The act ends with a wild Bacchic orgy:

Und nun gellt ins Ohr der Cymbeln mit der Becken Erzgetöne,
Denn es hat sich Dionysos aus Mysterien enthüllt;
Kommt hervor mit Ziegenfüsslern, schwenkend Ziegenfüsslerinnen,
Und dazwischen schreit unbändig grell Silenus öhrig Tier.
Nichts geschont! Gespaltne Klauen treten alle Sitte nieder,
Alle Sinne wirbeln taumlich, grässlich übertäubt das Ohr.[1]

But though Helen is gone, her spirit lives on in Faust. Nothing now will satisfy him but unceasing toil to win a measure of order from the aimless elements, of which the ocean is now the symbol:

Sie schleicht heran, an abertausend Enden,
Unfruchtbar selbst, Unfruchtbarkeit zu spenden;
Nun schwillt's und wächst und rollt und überzieht
Der wüsten Strecke widerlich Gebiet.

[1] "And now the brassy din of cymbals and of pots splits the ear, for Dionysus has revealed himself in mysteries. Forth he comes with the whirling goat-foots, male and female, the while Silenus's long-eared beast cries shrill, unchecked. No restraint! Pronged claws tread all propriety to the ground. The senses reel and spin; the ear is stunned with loathsome din": line 10,030–35.

Da herrschet Well' auf Welle kraftbegeistet,
Zieht sich zurück, und es ist nichts geleistet,
Was zur Verzweiflung mich beängstigen könnte.
Zwecklose Kraft unbändiger Elemente!
Da wagt mein Geist sich selbst zu überfliegen
Hier möcht' ich kämpfen, dies möcht' ich besiegen.[1]

Through Helen Faust is set on the upward road; from the moment of her leaving him, he never ceases to "strive towards the highest existence". Mephistopheles still plays his magic tricks; but whenever Faust is in the forefront, there the action of the play is powerful, its meaning profound; his presence bans the triviality of the elemental powers.

The significance of Helen's figure is clearly seen when we consider the play as a whole in this way, and observe what effect she has upon the tone and subject-matter of the action. Before she appears all is shallow and unreal, the characters are without a purpose, the sport of Mephisto's petty magic. She brings with her purpose, dignity, form, which she imparts to Faust and through him to the world in which he moves. And this was what the Greeks had done for man. They had taught him to give form to raw vitality, to control and shape his life in accordance with an inner vision of beauty; to be pure man not half beast; in short to be civilised. For Goethe in his old age the only valid distinction between man and man, or nation and nation, lay in the degree of civilisation which they had attained, or of barbarism in which they still dwelt. In so far as modern man was civilised, he owed this merit to the Greeks. This, in prosaic terms, is the meaning of the Helena episode in *Faust*.

[1] "It creeps up at every point, unfruitful itself, spreading unfruitfulness. Now it swells and grows and rolls and covers the horrid stretch of desert land. There wave succeeds to wave, rejoicing in its strength, and then withdraws—and nothing is accomplished! It fills me with despair and apprehension—the aimless force of unbridled elements. There my spirit shall dare to surpass itself. Here I will fight, this I will conquer": lines 10, 212-21.

CONCLUSION

SINCE the Germanic lands of Europe became civilised, two contrasting tendencies have revealed themselves in European culture. The art of the northern peoples has been great for its content; that of the Mediterranean lands for its form. This crude generalisation, too often lightly used, now hackneyed by the shallow minded, now discredited by the intellectual, who ask: What is content? what is form? remains yet in essence true. Its truth is obscured by closer definition, but is revealed by illustration: the North produced a Riemenschneider; the South, Michelangelo. Shakespeare repels the French by his formless power; Racine to most of us is a frigid formalist. Wagner would express the universe; in the birthpains of his mighty message, he grunts and whines and whistles; but the listener is no wiser, unless he knows by intuition or previous study what these sounds are meant to mean. Verdi clothes a trivial theme in melody; he has said nothing, but he has made something.

A German singer, trained in Italy, will often render Italian opera more perfectly than an Italian. So a northern genius, if he submits the unruly impulses of his deep-feeling soul to the discipline of southern form, may achieve something which is both of the North and of the South, which is fully European. Bach did this deliberately; the Viennese tradition, at the blending point of northern and southern Europe, enabled Mozart and Beethoven to rise above the limitations of their race, and to become complete representatives of Western man. In literature such perfect blending can hardly be achieved, for the language binds the poet, for good and ill, within the bounds of his nationality. Yet many poets have made the attempt; and none have fought so hard to break their bonds, and in the struggle have won so much, as Goethe. Born with the searching soul of the northerner, he found he could not express what was within him, until he had found the secret of southern form. Already in the earliest years of his genius, the clear-seen images of Mediterranean culture helped him as symbols to find poetic form for his thoughts. But that was not enough. Step by step, over more than twenty years, he was driven on by the creative force within him, to approach more closely to the outward forms of expression which southern Europe has evolved. The slowness of the process and the "deutscher Ernst" with which he pursued his purpose, ensured that the mingling in him of North and South should be a real fusion, so that he not only assimilated the technique of the southern artist, but in effect re-created the forms out of the same mentality as had at first produced them. So, when the fusion was complete, he spoke with a clear voice, in accents as majestic as the themes he treated were profound. He had become more than a German poet; he was the voice of Europe.

Goethe is, before all else and in an intense degree, a European. Not merely that in his poetry he borrowed ideas or forms from almost every European literature, and knew the art of Europe, in its many national forms, as thoroughly as any man of his day. He stands as a symbol of Europeanism in his whole attitude to life: in his worldliness. He was worldly in a practical sense, in his relations with his publishers for instance; and he was worldly in a spiritual sense, in that he demanded of art and of poetry that it should express itself in forms which could be apprehended by the senses. In his approach to the secrets of Nature through scientific investigation he was worldly, and he was European. The important part which he allowed his intellect to play in his art and in his life, marks him also as a European man. Kayserling said of him that of all the great spirits who have been in close touch with the supersensual essence of life, Goethe lived most constantly and with most pleasure on the surface, among the phenomena. This was the European.

Goethe was born in an age in which the European way of life, which the Renaissance had established, was losing itself in empty forms, barren intellectualism, or sentimentality. His task from the first was not to destroy this form of life, but to make it real again, so that the best spirits of the coming generations could feel that it was worthy to continue and to develop. But first he must be sure what was the essence of Europeanism. Here too the example of the southern, and above all of the Greek, way of life was indispensible to him. For the Greeks had first lived the European life. They had defined its form, and had done so with a clarity and perfection not achieved by the

Romans or by the babel of tongues and styles that we call the Renaissance. Whether or not he realised it with his conscious mind, this, even more than the need for mastery of southern form in poetry, was the reason and the justification for the years of ceaseless labour and struggle which Goethe devoted to the Hellenising of his mind and spirit. Before he could make modern Europeanism a word of power, he must establish and make real the basic form of Europeanism, the Greek form of life.

Goethe himself indeed looked on the Greek as the ideal type of all mankind, not merely of European man. To him, at the time of his Hellenism, European culture was the only culture that mattered, and it was inevitable that he should regard the Greek, the perfect European, as being identical with the perfect man. He rarely considered other civilisations, except in so far as they might have bearing on the historical development of European culture. Since Goethe's day the greatness of the eastern civilisations has become so well known in Europe, that an attitude such as Goethe's is no longer possible. We realise that European civilisation is only one, not necessarily the first, among equals. So we can estimate Goethe's Hellenism at its real worth. It was an effort to establish the basis of values upon which European civilisation has been built, to purge our culture of the impurities and extravagances which it has acquired in the course of two thousand years, and so to give it a second youth, in which it might conquer new worlds for the human spirit. Many, since Nietzsche threw the first stone, have denied that Goethe understood the nature of the Greek genius or had any conception of the Greek's attitude to life. Even if this were true, it would not detract from the value of Goethe's vision of Hellenic man. This vision is not to be judged by its historical truth but by its vital force. It has worked as an entelechy, or formative power, first on Goethe himself, then through his poetry and his life on men in many lands to hold them true to the best in our common culture. To live again, an ancient ideal must pass through the living medium of a modern mind. Goethe was this living medium; this is for us the significance and the value of his Hellenism.

APPENDIX A

DATE CHART

(This chart was not finished before war broke out. I have therefore not been able to make the final revision which should have been made, or to fill in certain serious gaps. Nevertheless I feel it is of value as it stands and have preferred to include it, though incomplete, rather than to leave it out altogether. Most items are given with page references to the text of this book. Those not mentioned in the text are given source references, so that the student can pursue them for himself.)

1749	Aug. 28	Johann Wolfgang Goethe born in Frankfurt am Main.
1755		Puppet play of Medea, **16**. Winckelmann's *Gedanken* published, **12**.
1756		Cur-Bayrisch troupe play classical tragedies, **16**. Goethe started Latin, **17** n.
1757		Ackermann troupe play Voltaire and Racine, **16**.
	Summer	*Metamorphoses*. Pomey, and Loën's mythology; *Iliad* and *Télémaque* read, **17**.
1758	Summer	Started Greek, **18**.
1759		French theatre in Frankfurt, **20**.
1760		His *Schäferspiel*, **20**. Corneille and Racine read, and Corneille's essays on the Unities, **20**. *Roman in mehreren Sprachen*, **23**.
1761		
1762		Ackermann troupe again, **22**.
1763		
1764		Greek philosophy in Brucker, **24**.
1765		Morhof, **26**.
	Oct.	Arrival in Leipzig, **28**. Attempt to learn Greek from modern Greeks, **29**.
	Dec.	Enters Oeser's academy. First acquaintance with Greek art, **35**.
1766	Jan.	Mythological wedding-ode, **40**. Winckelmann's *Gedanken* and Lessing's *Laokoon* read, **42-46**.
	Winter	Arranges Breitkopf's gem collection, **35**.
1767	May	*Ode an Prof. Zachariae*, **41**.
	Summer	*Phaedo* read (?), **30**.

1768	Mar.	Visit to Dresden, **36**.
	May	*An Venus*, **41**.
	June 8	Winckelmann murdered, **42** and n.
	July	*Musarion* read, **48**.
	Aug.	Exchanges German books for Greek texts, **33**.
	Sept.	Return to Frankfurt.
		Pygmalion, **41**.
1769	Nov.	Visit to Mannheim antiques, **37**.
	Winter	The lost essay on Laocoön, **39** and **47**.
1770	Feb.	*Ephemerides*. Remarks on Greek art, **47**.
	Apr.	In Strassburg.
		Phaedo read, **33**.
	Sept.	Herder arrives in Strassburg, **50**; Goethe's genius breaks through, **51** fol.
	Winter to	Begins to read Homer in Greek, **51**.
1771	Spring	Herder talks to him of Greek tragedy, Orphic hymns, Pindar, **58, 63, 55**.
		Blackwell's *Life and Writings of Homer* read, **76**.
	Aug.	Second visit to Mannheim (?), **38** n.
		Return to Frankfurt. Translates Homer to Cornelia, **52**.
	Autumn	Work on Socrates-drama, **52**. Some Plato read.
		Theocritus read, **53**.
	Oct. 14	*Rede zum Shakespeares Tag*, **56**.
1772	Mar.	*Wandrers Sturmlied.*
	Spring and	Reading Pindar, **53**.
	Summer	*Ganymed* (?). (See *G-J.* xxix, p. 57.)
	Summer	Homer in Wetzlar, **64**.
		Reviews in *Frankfurter Gelehrte Anzeigen*.
1773		Translation of Fifth Olympian Ode, **54** n.
	Easter	Buys casts of antique heads, **66**.
	Aug.–Oct.	Drawings of heads of Apollo and Laocoön. Fragment of Laocoön essay, **66**.
	Christmas	*Künstlers Morgenlied.*
1774		*Ganymed* (?).
		Prometheus Ode, **62**.
1775	Nov.	Arrival in Weimar.
	Dec. 23	Homer in Waldeck, **84**.
1776	Spring	*Goethe und die jüngste Niobetochter*, **90**.
1777		*Proserpina*, **87** fol.
	Sept.–Dec.	*Triumph der Empfindsamkeit*, **85** fol.
	Winter	Reading Aristophanes, **91**.
1778		Earliest hexameters, **116**.
	July	Reading Mengs, **93**.
	Autumn	Reading Greek tragedy, **98**.

1779 Feb.–Apr.   *Iphigenie,* **95.**
     Sept.   Antiques in Cassel, **104.**
     Oct.   Homer in the Alps, **104.**
1780 June–July   *Die Vögel,* **91.**
     Sept.   Translation of *Golden Words,* **105.**
1781 May–Nov.   Tobler's translations of Greek tragedies read, **106.**
     Aug.   *Elpenor* begun, **107.**
     Summer   Orphic hymns, **113.** Anthology, **114** fol..
1782 Spring–Summer Epigrams, **115** fol.
     Mar.   Greek tragedians, **106** n.
1783 Mar.   *Elpenor* again, **107.**
                     Longing for Italy, **119** fol.
1784   Anthology, **114.** More epigrams, **115.**
1785
1786 Sept. 3   Journey to Italy begun.
     Sept. 12–Oct. 10 Re-writing *Iphigenie,* **131–134.**
     Sept. 15   Verona. Amphitheatre and stelae, **126.**
     Sept. 20–Oct. 14 Palladio's influence, **129.**
     Oct. 18   *Iphigenie auf Delphos,* **135.**
     Oct. 22   *Ulysses auf Phäa,* **163.**
     Oct. 29   Arrival in Rome.
     Nov. 10–Dec. 29 Final work on *Iphigenie,* **131.**
1787 Feb. 21   Departure for Naples and Sicily.
     Mar. 11   Pompeii, **151.**
     Mar. 23   Paestum, **152.**
     Apr. 2   Arrival in Palermo.
     Apr. 20   Segesta, **156.**
     Apr. 23–28   Girgenti, **157.**
                     Work on *Nausikaa,* **163.**
                     Homer, "*Urmensch*", "*Urpflanze*", "*Urlandschaft*", **159–162.**
     May 15   Back in Naples.
     May 16   Paestum again, **168.**
     June 6   Back in Rome.
     Aug. 22   Sketches of Parthenon frieze, **169.**
     Aug. 23 to   Secret of human form discovered, **169.**
1788   Apr.   Study of human form in nature and Greek sculpture, **170.**
     Apr.   Departure from Rome.
     June   Back in Weimar.
     Sept. 8   Ideal characters explained to Caroline Herder, **173** fol.
     Autumn   Essays on art in *Teutscher Merkur,* **178** and n., **215** n.
1789   *Römische Elegien,* **182** fol.
1790 Mar.–June   Journey to Venice.
                     Venezianische Epigramme, **181.**
1791

1792		*Reise der Söhne Megaprazons*, **187**.
1793	Jan.	Princess Gallitzin's gem-collection on loan, **188**.
	Feb.–May	*Reinecke Fuchs*, **188**.
	Nov. 18	Homer taken up again, **189**.
1794	May–June	Voss in Weimar, **190**.
	Summer,	New interest in Homer. Translations from Homer,
	Autumn	**190** fol.
	Summer	Friendship with Schiller, **192**.
1795	Apr.	*Die Befreiung des Prometheus*, **203**.
	May–June	The Homeric Question. Wolf in Weimar, **205**, **229** fol.
1796	May	*Hero und Leander*, **203**.
		Alexis und Dora, **204**.
	Sept. 11	*Hermann und Dorothea* begun, **205**.
1797	Mar.	*Hermann und Dorothea* nearly finished, **205**.
	Apr., May	Reading Homer, Aeschylus, **223**. *Poetics, Prolegomena*. Cf. *Tagebuch*.
	May 20	*Der neue Pausias* finished, **225**.
	May 21	Idea for sequel to *Supplices* (*Danaiden*), **225**.
	June	*Die Braut von Korinth*, **225**.
	June 22	Paralipomenen 1 (?), **241**.
	July	*Ueber Laokoon* begun, **219**.
	Sept.–Oct.	Other essays on art, **216**.
	Dec. 23	*Ueber epische und dramatische Dichtung*, and first idea for *Achilleis*, **226**.
		Euphrosyne, Amyntas, **225**.
1798	Late Mar.	Reading Euripides, **224**.
	Mar. 29–Apr. 9	Intensive study of *Iliad*, **224**.
		First detailed plan of *Achilleis*.
	May 16	*Achilleis* laid aside, **229**.
	May 24–27	*Einleitung in die Propyläen* begun.
	June	*Ueber Laokoon* finished, **219**.
1799	Mar. 9–Apr. 5	*Achilleis* fragment written, **232**.
	Mar. 31–Apr. 6	Reading Euripides, **224**.
	May	Sixth letter of *der Sammler und die Seinigen*, **220**.
	Nov.–Dec.	First work on *Natürliche Tochter*, **254**.
		Preisaufgabe: Aphrodite leads Helen to Paris, **252**.
1800	Summer	Preparations for *Helena*, **242**.
	Sept. 12–28	*Helena* fragment written, **243**.
	Oct.	*Paläophron und Neoterpe*, **253**.
1801	Oct.–Dec.	Work on *Natürliche Tochter*, **254**.
		Preisaufgabe: Achilles in Scyros and Achilles' struggle with the river.
1802	Jan. 2	Schlegel's *Ion* produced, **253** fol.
	May 15	*Iphigenie* produced.
	June	*Was wir bringen*, **253**.
		Preisaufgabe: Perseus and Andromeda.

1803 Apr. 2   *Natürliche Tochter* produced, **254**.
      Apr., May   Metres with Voss, *Helena* (?), **244**.
      Sept.–Dec.   Work on Polygnotus, p. 218.
                       Preisaufgabe: Ulysses and Cyclops.
1804 Feb.   First idea for *Winckelmann und sein Jahrhundert*, **256**·
                       Polygnotus.
      Aug., Oct.   Reading Greek tragedies with younger Voss, **251** n.
      Dec. 21   *Winckelmann* begun.
                       Preisaufgabe: Man in conflict with the elements.
1805 Spring   Note to *Rameaus Neffe*, **258**.
      Apr. 28   *Winckelmann* finished, **256**.
      May 9   Schiller's death.
1806   Considers Tell epic in hexameters. WA. 35, p. 247.
      July 27   First idea for *Pandora* (?). WA. III, 3, p. 147.
      Before Oct.   *Persae* read. WA. 35, p. 260.
1807   Schleiermacher's *Herakleitos* (cf. C. Bapp, *Aus
                       Goethes griechischer Gedankenwelt*, p. 5), and
      Sept., Oct.   Buhle's *Geschichte der Philosophie* (especially Hera-
                       clitus. Cf. Morris, *Goethestudien*, I, p. 279).
      Sept. 19   *Vorspiel zur Eröffnung des Weimarer Theaters* (Tri-
                       meters). WA, 13, 1, p. 25.
      Nov. 18   Reading Euripides. WA. IV, 19, p. 459.
      Nov. to
1808 June   *Pandora*, **271** fol.
      Jan. 11, Mar. 7 Letters to Jacobi on tolerance, **263** fol.
      Aug. 28   Comparison of antique and romantic tragedy.
                       Bied. 1, p. 534.
      Autumn   Mionettische Pastensammlung. WA. 36, p. 39.
                       Cf. *Schr. der G–G.* 7, p. 213.
1809 Jan. 30   *Antigone* (Rochlitz's adaptation) performed in
                       Weimar. WA. 36, p. 49, and IV, 20, p. 292.
      May   Hirt's *Die Baukunst nach den Grundsätzen der Alten*
                       received. WA. 36, 51, and IV, 20, pp. 346, 359.
      Aug. 28   On Aeschylus' use of the chorus. Bied. 2, p. 50.
1810
1811 May 3–8   Boisserée converts Goethe to Gothic architecture,
                       265.
1812 Apr.   First news of Aeginetan marbles. WA. 36, 76; IV,
                       22, pp. 320, 500.
                       Der Tänzerin Grab. WA. 48, p. 143. Cf. WA. IV,
                       22, pp. 359 fol., 500 fol.; WA. 49, 1, p. 193.
      November   *Myrons Kuh.* WA. 49, 2, p. 3. Cf. JA. 35, p. 356.
1813 Mar.   *Shakespeare und kein Ende* (contrast of ancient and
                       modern drama). WA. 41, 1, p. 52. Cf. JA. 37,
                       p. 302.
                       Greek sculpture. WA. 36, pp. 82, 83.
      Nov. 20   The Greeks as tyrants. Bied. 2, 205.

1814	May	*Epimenides*, **271**.
	Oct. 12	Parthenon reliefs in Darmstadt, **266**.
	Nov. 19	Admits his one-sided opinions on art at time of Italian journey. WA. IV, 25, p. 82.
1815	Jan. 2	Reading Homer and Hafiz. WA. IV, 25, p. 82. (Greek influence in *Divan*, see *G-J*. 33, p. 206).
	Feb. 4	*Proserpina* performed in Weimar. Cf. WA. 40, p. 106.
1816		Elgin Marbles, **266, 270**.
1817		*Anforderung an einen modernen Bildhauer*. WA. 49, 2, p. 53.
		Elgin Marbles and Bassae relief, **266**.
		Eleusinian remains studied. WA. 36, p. 125; WA. IV, 28, p. 293.
	Sept., Oct.	Interest in Hermann-Creuzer controversy on ancient mythology, **267, 269**.
1818		*Myrons Kuh* published. WA. 49, 2, p. 3.
	Feb.	*Relief von Phigalia* (Bassae). WA. 49, 2, p. 16.
		Antik und Modern. WA. 49, 1, p. 149.
		Philostrats Gemälde, **267**.
		Continued interest in Elgin and Aeginetan Marbles, **266**; and in Hermann-Creuzer controversy, **269**.
1819	Jan. 21	Drawings of Elgin Marbles arrived. WA. III, 7, p. 8.
		Warnung (in *Noten zum Divan*). WA. 7, p. 108.
	August	Reading Creuzer on mythology. WA. IV, 31, p. 276.
1820	Jan.	Antique painting. WA. IV, 32, p. 145; III, 7, p. 127; WA. 36, p. 170.
		Elgin Marbles and Bassae relief. WA. 36, p. 170.
	July–Sept.	Hermann-Creuzer controversy, **269**. WA. IV, 33, p. 242.
		Aristophanes' *Clouds*. WA. 36, p. 173.
	Dec.	*Iliasschema* revised, **267**.
1821	Apr.	*Prolog zu Eröffnung des Berliner Theaters*. WA. 13, 1, p. 115 (reference to Greek tragedy, p. 117).
	Oct., Nov., Dec.	Reconstruction of Euripides' *Phaethon* fragments, **268**. Cf. WA. IV, 35, pp. 133, 179, 192, and WA. 36, p. 191.
		Keen study of other plays of Euripides. WA. IV, 35, p. 193.
	Dec. 29	Translation from the *Bacchae* begun, **268**. WA. III, 8, p. 151.
1822	Apr. 16	*Philoctetes* read in Gersdorf's translation. WA. III, 8, p. 186; WA. IV, 36, p. 24.
1823	Feb. 2	The Greeks as touchstone of quality. WA. IV, 36, p. 296.
		Die tragischen Tetralogien der Griechen.

1823 July 27   Zauper's translation of the *Iliad*. WA. IV, 37,
                pp. 151, 154, 159.
     Oct. 7   Bust of Ludovisi Juno received. Bied. 3, p. 22;
                WA. IV, 38, p. 67, and III, 9, p. 126.
                Hermann's *Vorrede zu den Bacchae*. WA. IV, 37,
                pp. 244, 385; III, 9, pp. 139, 330.
     Oct. 28   *Gallitzinische Gemmensammlung*. WA. IV, 37, p. 246.
                Cf. WA. 49, 2, p. 104; G-J. 3, p. 319; JA. 35,
                p. 222.

1824 Feb. 11   New casts of antiques. WA. III, 9, p. 177; WA. IV,
                38, p. 46.
                Ueber die Parodien bei den Alten. Cf. WA. IV, 38,
                pp. 171, 229.

1825 Mar.   *Helena* continued, 268.
     May 1   Opinion of Euripides. Bied. 3, p. 201.
     May 12   Opinion of Menander. Bied. 3, p. 203.
     July 15   *Museum Worsleyanum* received. WA. IV, 39, p. 348
                and n.
     Dec.   Medusa Rondanini received. WA. IV, 40, pp. 194,
                196, 425. Cf. WA. IV, 39, p. 240; WA. 30, p. 238;
                WA. 32, pp. 39, 322; Bied. 3, pp. 267–8.

1826 Apr.   *Klassische Walpurgisnacht* begun, 268.
                Nachlese zu Aristoteles Poetik.
                Zwei Rätsel (altgriechisch). Cf. JA, 3, pp. 277, 382.
     May 20   *Phaethon* and Hermann's *Programm über den Philo-
                ctetes*. WA. IV, 41, p. 38. Cf. Bied. 3, p. 340.
     June   *Helena* finished, 268.
     Sept. 11   Terracottas in British Museum. WA. IV, 41, pp.
                148, 193, 226; WA. IV, 42, pp. 6, 9.

1827 Feb. 6   Pompeian murals. WA. IV, 42, p. 48.
     June 9   Reference to Euripides' *Cyclops*. WA. IV, 42, p. 220.

1828   Pompeian murals. WA. IV, 44, p. 57; WA. IV, 48,
                pp. 131, 151; WA. IV, 49, pp. 260, 267.

1829   Translations from Hippocrates in *Wanderjahre*
                (*Makariens Archiv*). Cf. Bapp, *op. cit.* p. 5.
     Aug. 9   Phigalean frieze. Bied. 4, p. 40.
                Newly discovered Niobid. Bied. 4, p. 154.
     Dec. 31   Letter to Zelter: *Samson Agonistes* and Greek
                tragedy. Cf. Eckermann, Jan. 31, 1830.

1830   *Die schönsten Ornamente und Gemälde aus Pompeii,
                Herkulanum und Stabiae*. WA. 49, 1, p. 161.

1831 June 19   Homer. WA. IV, 48, p. 248.
     Oct. 5   Plutarch read aloud by Ottilie. WA. IV, 49, p. 104.
     Nov.   Resolve to read Euripides, 268. WA. IV, 49, p. 146.

1832 Mar.   Greek tragedy, especially Euripides. Bied. 4, p. 435.
     Mar. 22   Death of Goethe.

APPENDIX B[1]

GOETHE'S THEORY AND PRACTICE IN WRITING GERMAN HEXAMETERS

(This Appendix is not an exhaustive study of Goethe's practice in adapting ancient metres to the German language. The problems with which he had to deal in writing German hexameters were the same as those which the trimeter and the choric metres presented to him. The general principles with which he attempted to solve the one set of problems may be assumed to be the same as those with which he approached the other.)

ANDREAS HEUSLER, in his invaluable essay, *Deutscher und Antiker Vers* (Strassburg, 1917), maintains that the experts on metre in Goethe's day, Moritz, Voss, and A. W. Schlegel, did not appreciate the difference between quantity and accent, and spoke of a "long" syllable when they meant an accented one.[2] This is certainly not true of Moritz, whose *Versuch einer deutschen Prosodie* Goethe had studied in Rome,[3] nor of Voss, to whom from 1793 onwards Goethe turned for guidance in writing German hexameters and elegiacs. In *Ueber den deutschen Hexameter* (reprinted 1831 from the preface to his edition of the *Georgics* of 1789), Voss makes it quite clear that a sense of time values was the basis of the ancient hexameter (p. 183); and in his *Zeitmessung der deutschen Sprache* (published together with *Ueber den deutschen Hexameter*) he ridicules (p. 8) those who think that "hoher Ton" (accent) is the same as "Länge" (quantitive length).[4] That fallacy produces such hexameters as:

Freund, komm heut | Nachmittag | her, sieh Herrn | Blanchard's
neu | Luftschiff hoch | aufziehn.

in which the dactyl is treated merely as a foot of three syllables with the first syllable accented. Equally, however, Voss condemned any attempt to write German hexameters according to the ancient rules of quantity. According to these rules the word "Menschenverstand" consists of four long syllables of equal value, and could therefore be scanned as two spondees in a hexameter. This is contrary to the genius of the German language; and in fact only a few pedant-poets of the sixteenth century have ever tried to write German hexameters

---

[1] See above, pp. 117, 213, 236.
[2] So also M. Bressem, *Der metrische Aufbau des Faust II*, Berlin, 1921, p. 121; and Fr. Vischer, *G-J.* IV, pp. 19 foll.
[3] *Versuch einer deutschen Prosodie*, pp. 11, 17.
[4] Also Bied. I, p. 225.

on these lines (cf. Heusler, *op. cit.* p. 3). Voss saw that in German a compromise must be made between the demands of accent and of quantity. He therefore produced his theory of "*Hauptbegriff*" and "*Nebenbegriff*". In the word "Menschenverstand" "Mensch-" and "-stand" are "*Hauptbegriff*" syllables, "-en" and "ver-" are "*Nebenbegriff*" syllables. The stem syllables of all verbs, nouns, adjectives and adverbs are "*Hauptbegriffe*"; prefixes and suffixes are "*Nebenbegriffe*". Voss's general rule was that "*Hauptbegriff*" syllables correspond to the long syllables of ancient metres, "*Nebenbegriff*" syllables to the short. The truth which Voss's theory embodied was the fact that in German even a syllable short by nature is somewhat lengthened when it receives an emphasis. Thus the adjective "érblich" and the past participle "erblíchen" both contain the syllable "blich" or "lich"; but "blich" in the past participle is appreciably longer than "lich" in the adjective "erblich". The reason for this is that "blich" in the participle is the important syllable, which determines the basic meaning or "*Hauptbegriff*" of the word; in "erblich" the "lich" is merely a suffix, which determines a subsidiary meaning or "*Nebenbegriff*". The theory established a reasonable compromise for use in German, in which there are so many gradations in the length of syllables that it is impossible to mark a clear line between "long" and "short" syllables. It was an adequate rationalisation of the practice which Klopstock had established by instinct in his *Messias*. The vast majority of the hexameters and pentameters which Goethe wrote "dem Gehöre nach" before 1793 (i.e. the epigrams of 1781–1786, the *Römische Elegien*, and the *Venezianische Epigramme*) comply with Voss's demands. The trouble with Voss's scheme was that it left innumerable words undefined.[1] Voss admitted that all pronouns, prepositions, conjunctions and such words as "nicht" and "sonst" were sometimes "*Hauptbegriffe*" and sometimes "*Nebenbegriffe*". This left too much latitude to the poet. He could, if he wished to, use "sonst", which is truly "long" owing to its accumulation of consonants, or "ihm", which can never be spoken as quickly as "es" or "-en", as the "short" syllables of a dactyl. So even in his *Achilleis*, which he had laboured to make metrically correct, Goethe could write:

Schūtz nĭcht | ĭst ĭhm dĕin | Hēlm.

"Ihm" and "dein" are long by nature, but not being specially emphasised in this case, could theoretically be treated as "*Neben-*

---

[1] Humboldt, who "corrected" Goethe's hexameters in *Hermann und Dorothea*, recognised this and tried to lay down rules to govern the doubtful cases (cf. introduction to his translation of the *Agamemnon*: *Gesammelte Werke*, III, pp. 20 foll.).

begriffe". The effect on the dactyl of these "long" words in the "short" syllables is to make it hopelessly heavy. It is the frequent recurrence of such overloaded dactyls which prevents Goethe's hexameters from giving full satisfaction.

The fact that Goethe could write such a dactyl as this, which is really a foot of three syllables of equal length with an accent on the first, suggests that he did not realise that the ancient hexameter is a duple-time meter; that is, that its foot is composed of two beats of equal length:

Arma vir | umque can | o.

$$\frac{4}{4}$$ 𝅗𝅥 ♩ ♪ | 𝅗𝅥 ♩ ♪ | 𝅗𝅥

When hexameters are read accentually, they tend to fall into triple time:

Árma vir | úmque can | ó.

$$\frac{3}{4}$$ ♪ ♪ ♪ | ♩ ♩ ♪ | 𝅗𝅥

It is much easier to read a dactyl such as "ist ihm dein" in triple time than in duple time. In the latter case "ihm" and "dein" must each be made half the length of "ist", which they are not by nature.

It is probable that Goethe scanned his own hexameters accentually and in triple time in the days of innocence before he began to go to school to Voss and the other experts on ancient prosody. The *Römische Elegien* and *Reinecke Fuchs* do not read easily in duple time owing to the frequency of overloaded dactyls of the "ist ihm dein" type. For instance in the distich:

Amor | bleibet ein | Schalk, und | wer ihm ver|traut, ist be|trogen.
Heuchelnd | kam er zu | mir|: Diesmal nur | traue mir | noch.

both lines have three dactyls in which one or both of the "short" syllables is really long: blēibĕt ēin|; wēr īhm vēr-| trāut īst bĕ-|; kām ēr zŭ|; Dīesmāl nūr | trāuĕ mīr|. Read in triple time the lines move along well enough. Any two lines of *Reinecke Fuchs* chosen at random show much the same proportion of overloaded dactyls, and, what is more important, an attempt to read these hexameters in duple time destroys at once the spontaneity, the impudent grace of the rhythm.

Goethe tried to grasp the essence of Voss's teaching before he wrote *Reinecke Fuchs*; but he failed because he had no personal contact with Voss.[1] In the summer of 1794 Voss was in Weimar, and in July Goethe and he corresponded on the subject of the prosody of *Reinecke Fuchs*.[2] These contacts came too late to affect

---

[1] WA. 33, p. 267.
[2] G-J. v, p. 38; cf. WA. 35, p. 35, and 33, p. 267.

the hexameters of *Reinecke Fuchs*, which was already published; but from now on Goethe realised the nature of the problem of adapting the ancient hexameter to the German language. He understood exactly the relative importance of quantity and accent, and he knew that the hexameter is a duple-time metre.[1]

The effect of this knowledge on his own hexameters is not easy to demonstrate. *Hermann und Dorothea* shows innumerable overloaded dactyls, and trochees too, which are equally destructive of a duple-time rhythm. But there is a higher proportion of true dactyls (bildete, richtige, etc.) and of spondees. There is no difficulty in reading such a line as

Lächelte | dann und | sprach zu | ihm mit | traulichen | Worten.

in duple time. Between *Reinecke Fuchs* and the *Achilleis* there is a whole world of difference. Despite occasional lapses, such as the dactyl "ist ihm dein",[2] the hexameters of the *Achilleis* move naturally in duple time. Only when read so, can their majestic beauty be felt. No more than the hexameters of *Hermann und Dorothea* are they composed entirely of true dactyls and spondees; but Goethe contrived to treat the overloaded dactyls and trochees, which cannot be entirely avoided in German, in such a way that they seldom disturb the even flow of the duple-time rhythm. Since he had known for nearly five years that the hexameter moves in duple time, and had spent a large part of those years in reading Homer, his ear was attuned to the true rhythm of the ancient hexameter.

Goethe's treatment of the trochee in the *Achilleis* deserves special attention. Many of the feet which Voss would have counted as trochees (i.e. consisting of one "*Hauptbegriff*" and one "*Nebenbegriff*") are quantitatively not trochees at all (strēbēnd- fērnēs schr|ēcklĭchĕs), and therefore support the duple-time rhythm. Most of the others comply in one way or another with the condition which Voss laid down[3] for the use of the trochee in German hexameters. Voss maintained that the first syllable of a trochee must be lengthened (or dotted, in musical language), so that the two syllables together should fill out the full two beats of the foot. He held that this lengthening could be used with great effect, as when the Cyclopes raise their arms

mit | grosser | Kraft.

| ♩. ♩ |

---

[1] Cf. Böttiger's report, Bied. I, p. 225; also WA. 35, p. 22, and Bied. I, p. 217. [2] Cf. also lines 133, 160.

[3] *Ueber den deutschen Hexameter*, p. 183.

The trochees in Goethe's *Reinecke Fuchs* cannot be read so without affectation:

Jede | Wiese | sprosste von | Blumen.

But in the *Achilleis* Goethe usually managed matters so that the first syllable of a trochee could reasonably occupy one-and-a-half beats. Thus in line 129:

Ārēs | schrēitēt | māchtĭg hĕr|ān, bĕ|hēndĕ, dĕr | Krīegĕr,

the pause after "heran" fills up the extra half beat. In other cases an accumulation of consonants makes the first syllable extra long:

...als hätte die Nacht ihr zur Ruhe
Nīcht gĕ|nūgĕt (line 134);

or the "*Pathos*" of the occasion permits of an unusual lengthening of the first syllable, as when Thetis swears by the banished Titans:

Spātĕ | Rāchĕr dĕr|ēinst (line 154);

or:

Jā, nōch | jētzt bĕ|trūbt dĭch dĕr | Fēhl (line 202).

It is extremely difficult to determine the principles which guided Goethe in his adaptation of the ancient hexameter to German. Even in 1798 and 1799 he was himself confused by the different counsels which his three expert advisers, Voss, Humboldt, and A. W. Schlegel, gave him.[1] Broadly speaking, however, his writing of hexameters falls into two periods: 1781–1793—early epigrams, *Römische Elegien*, *Venezianische Epigramme*, and *Reinecke Fuchs*; and 1794–1799—*Alexis und Dora* and the other elegies, *Hermann und Dorothea*, and *Achilleis*. In the first period he followed the practice which Klopstock had established in the *Messias*.[2] He scanned his hexameters accentually, taking only such regard for quantity as any poet does in the use of any modern, accented metre; and he scanned them in triple time. These hexameters had therefore very little resemblance to Latin or Greek hexameters, and cannot properly be judged by ancient standards. After meeting Voss in 1794, Goethe radically altered his approach to the German hexameter. He tried

[1] WA. 35, p. 184; and cf. *Schillers Briefe*, Jonas, VII, p. 41.
[2] WA. 35, p. 22; and 33, p. 267.

to treat it now as a duple-time metre, like the ancient hexameter, and for this purpose he paid far more attention to quantity. He never tried to write pure antique hexameters, in which the long syllables are often not the accented syllables; but he did in the *Achilleis* succeed in writing hexameters which suggest the ancient rhythm, since they move in duple time and usually avoid serious breaches of the ancient scheme of long and short.

INDEX

Made in the USA
Middletown, DE
11 August 2023